Scandalous Economics

Oxford Studies in Gender and International Relations

Series editors: J. Ann Tickner, University of Southern California, and Laura Sjoberg, University of Florida

Windows of Opportunity:
How Women Seize Peace Negotiations for Political Change
Miriam J. Anderson

Enlisting Masculinity:
The Construction of Gender in U.S. Military Recruiting Advertising during the All-Volunteer Force
Melissa T. Brown

The Politics of Gender Justice at the International Criminal Court:
Legacies and Legitimacy
Louise Chappell

Cosmopolitan Sex Workers:
Women and Migration in a Global City
Christine B. N. Chin

Intelligent Compassion:
Feminist Critical Methodology in the Women's International League for Peace and Freedom
Catia Cecilia Confortini

Gender and Private Security in Global Politics
Maya Eichler

Gender, Sex, and the Postnational Defense:
Militarism and Peacekeeping
Annica Kronsell

The Beauty Trade:
Youth, Gender, and Fashion Globalization
Angela B. V. McCracken

From Global to Grassroots:
The European Union, Transnational Advocacy, and Combating Violence against Women
Celeste Montoya

Who Is Worthy of Protection? Gender-Based Asylum and U.S. Immigration Politics
Meghana Nayak

A Feminist Voyage through International Relations
J. Ann Tickner

The Political Economy of Violence against Women
Jacqui True

Queer International Relations:
Sovereignty, Sexuality and the Will to Knowledge
Cynthia Weber

Bodies of Violence:
Theorizing Embodied Subjects in International Relations
Lauren B. Wilcox

CHAPTER 1

Making Feminist Sense of the Global Financial Crisis

AIDA A. HOZIĆ AND JACQUI TRUE

This volume is ambitious. It explores how scandals—and scandalous uses of and/or neglect of gender—have helped narrate the global financial crisis (GFC) into political oblivion.

The GFC has brought to light connections between domesticity and the macroeconomy, between distributional and identity-based inequalities, between private choices of seemingly gender-neutral investors and public regulation of the economy, between individual homeowners and abstract, global financial markets. Surprisingly, however—and despite fascinating work on the crisis done by feminist economists and critical political economists[1]—the bestselling books about the GFC have paid little or no attention to the gendered dimensions of the crisis. [2] We, instead, argue that critical feminist perspectives on the GFC can help us understand both the root causes of the crisis and the failure to significantly reform financial and macroeconomic models since the crisis.

Let us consider some of the major works analyzing the crisis and its aftermath. For instance, Mark Blyth's (2013) explanation of why flawed austerity policies were promoted by many governments after the GFC fundamentally overlooks how the gendered poor and the marginalized ended up as the disproportionate targets of austerity measures while the wealthy investors and financial institutions received massive bailouts. Similarly, Daniel Drezner's (2014) study applauds the global governance "system that worked" to stave off the crisis, but never mentions its origins in the securitization of housing mortgages *at the low end of the market*, which preyed upon groups with limited assets and access to credit, such as women and/or racial and ethnic minorities. James K. Galbraith's (2014) assessment of the post-GFC order argues that the GFC is a turning point, "a barometer of the rise of unstable economic conditions" (in contrast with the stability and growth in the postwar period) but does not recognize that this major structural change has coincided with women's rising employment globally and the marketization of caring work. Even Thomas Piketty's (2014) pathbreaking study of how capital compounds inequality (as income from assets grows at a faster rate than income from labor) never examines the relation between capitalism's systemic tendency toward crisis and the gendered structure of the economy—although he acknowledges (once!) that women are "significantly overrepresented in the bottom 50 percent of earners." Finally, in *The Global Minotaur* (2015) Yanis Varoufakis' deploys an obviously masculinist metaphor, that of the half man, half beast minotaur, to describe the functioning of the Wall Street-centred US capitalism, which had for decades financed American twin deficits (budget and trade) with the influx of surplus capital and goods from the rest of the world. The excesses of the Minotaur's reign created the crisis and led to his demise, leaving the global economy in disarray. Despite his astute critical eye, Varoufakis appears not to notice the gendered power at work in his own use of myth as resurgent banks assume financial dominance over households, governments and businesses. The "new normal" of gendered and racialized inequality and heightened sexualized and domestic violence after the GFC simply does not feature in any of these accounts. Indeed, as Zillah Eisenstein (2014) has remarked about Piketty, they all tend to look at capitalism, even if at times very critically, "as though labor has no actual body—no home that actually creates it. It remains abstract and therefore colorless as in white, and sexless as in male."

This volume, by contrast, is all but colorless and sexless.

Scandalous Economics has three main purposes. First, it surveys the landscape of the ongoing GFC and its consequences from the perspective of gender and feminist theory. It builds upon the work of feminist economists and their critically important recognition of those aspects of the economy that affect well-being but remain ignored by most macroeconomic analysis, such as unpaid care work. At the same time, the volume expands on the writings of our colleagues in cultural studies and feminist political economy who have long recognized the importance of representational practices for economic and political power.[3] Thus, we combine an analysis of the distributive effects of the crisis (*Feminist Economics* 2013) with *representations* of and *narratives* about the crisis and its causes, emphasizing the interplay between inequality and gender as well as class, race, ethnicity, and/or sexuality. We focus on the activities and the privileges of the advantaged—the "TED women" of the crisis (see True, Chapter 3 of this volume)—as much as on the victimization of the disadvantaged. In so doing, we challenge the dominant narrative of the crisis as a series of contagious events exogenous to the global capitalist system, which could or should be handled through the punitive containment of culprits (homeowners who cannot pay their mortgages, greedy public workers who have become accustomed to undeserved benefits, corrupt, overzealous traders and banks that have overextended their credit offerings, and states that cannot service their debt) (see Cameron, Nesvetailova, and Palan 2011; Brassett and Rethel 2015).

Second, the volume breaks new ground by arguing that normalization of the current economic order in the face of its obvious breakdown(s) has been facilitated precisely by co-optation of feminist and queer perspectives into the language of policy responses to the crisis. These strategies of co-optation, we suggest, are most visible if we look at the numerous scandals that the crisis has made apparent, as well as media narratives and popular culture that are *the* gendered *language* of the crisis. At the same time, the volume explores not just the multiple destructive manifestations of the financial crisis and its deleterious impacts on women and men, but also its productive potentialities for ethical and economic reordering of gendered social relations. *Scandalous Economics* embraces the Occupy movement and other critical analyses of the crisis—and, like these other critical traditions, considers alternative possibilities and modes of socioeconomic organization in the current system.

Last but not least, the third purpose of the volume is to show how feminist political economy analysis contributes important and distinctive insights to the critical enterprise in the fields of international political economy (IPE) and international relations more broadly. Just as feminist security studies emerged as a subfield in the international relations discipline after the events of 9/11, the GFC and its aftermath have given new impetus to the study of globalized political economic processes from a feminist perspective. Feminist scholarship, as exhibited in this volume, builds bridges between security studies and political economy: it is concerned with how masculinist modes of control pervade the practices of both financialization *and* militarization. The chapters in the volume highlight intersections between the security and finance sectors and reflect on the violent inequalities underpinning the contemporary global economy, linking escalating domestic violence with interstate conflicts and the surge in the numbers of refugees with the dispossessed. In short, this is a book about the continuum between Wall Street, the Pentagon, and

Fleet Street—and its resonances in households on Main Streets around the world.

In the remainder of this chapter we elaborate upon the way in which the three key concepts in this book—gender, scandal, and crisis—are theorized and employed. We then follow with an outline of the volume and its individual chapters, offering a glimpse of concrete and engaging applications of these concepts and their interrelation by our diverse group of colleagues and collaborators.

GENDER AND THE CRISIS

Feminist political economy conceives gender relations to be socially and historically constructed, rather than a mere characteristic of individuals and their behavior; that is, masculine, competitive, rational, and autonomous versus feminine, caring, emotional, and relational. Gender divisions and inequalities are present not only in the structure of the economy and its key sectors but also in the prior material division of the work of production from the work of social reproduction (that is, the social and affective provisioning of individuals and communities within households; see Bakker and Gill 2003). As a result, gender as a structure (see Harding 1986) both sustains and troubles the dominant paradigms of economic growth and sustainable development and their global governance. Gender is also a symbolic feature of economic institutions (think Davos man, Lehmann Brothers, bull market), including corporations and states and their style of doing business, especially the business of governing (Elias 2013). These myriad ways in which gender affects the governance of the global political economy are not always fully appreciated within the field of IPE. For instance, liberal commentators tout the gender makeup of individual decision-makers involved in governance as a key factor in achieving a more balanced approach to economic management and growth (Prügl 2012; True 2014). However, such commentators rarely mention the gender inequalities in the global economy or the gendered organizational logics of business corporations, which represent significant institutional barriers to that desired gender diversity in corporate governance or other forms of institutional economic decision-making (Prügl 2012; Elias 2013; Prügl and True 2014). In this volume, therefore, we analyze gender simultaneously as a feature of identity that shapes individual behavior, a structural division affecting the limits and possibilities of gender identities and roles, and as an integral part of our symbolic and normative order, which both constitutes and reinforces gender structures.

It is worth noting that the GFC, which has wiped out trillions of dollars and millions of jobs, initially appeared to be kinder to women than to men. The media, especially in the United States, promptly declared a "gender role reversal." The 2009 headlines were quite telling: "Will the Recession Change Gender Roles?" (*Business Week*); "Recession Prompts Gender Role Reversal" (*ABC News*); "The Gender-Bending Recession" (*The Nation*); and "They Call It the Reverse Gender Gap" (*The New York Times*). And yet, the GFC was triggered by the unsustainable securitization of mortgages—or of households, traditionally the feminized domain of everyday life. The veneer of equal treatment within an exploitative subprime market concealed the wider context of structural inequalities of race/ethnicity, gender, and age in housing and credit. Wyly and Ponder's (2011) analysis of the US Home Mortgage Disclosure Act (HMDA) data, for instance, confirms that gender inequalities compounded racial/ethnic inequalities in the segmentation of the high-cost subprime credit market (Dymski, Hernandez, and Mohanty 2013). The US National Mortgage Data Repository also provides circumstantial evidence of disproportionate representation of elderly African American women and some evidence of "bait-and-switch" tactics and persistently higher total fees among African American women. In other words, the crisis was anything but gender- or race-blind—either in its origins or in its consequences.

Thus, a few years after the initial shock, as the crisis continued to send tremors through the world economy, it became obvious that its gendered effects were not bringing about "Female Power" (*The Economist* 2009), as the media had predicted. While individual women did rise to power in key financial institutions (most notably Christine Lagarde at the IMF and Janet Yellen at the US Federal Reserve) to "clean up the crisis" (Prügl, Chapter 2 of this volume), data from Organisation for Economic Co-operation and Development (OECD) countries showed that, from 2009 onward, women continued to lose jobs, while male unemployment slowed down (OECD 2012).[4] In the United Kingdom, this was partly due to women losing 57.5 percent of the public sector jobs cut (Fawcett 2013). Even the initial gender reversal could only be attributed to increases in part-time work, and in some countries, such as Germany, to the establishment of women-owned businesses at higher rates than before as a survival strategy (*The Economist* 2009). Moreover, the post-GFC accounting clearly continued to privilege the measurable, "formal" economy over the household economies of developed and developing countries. Losses of immigrant (often female) labor and the effects of the crisis on countries dependent on migrants' remittances remained largely invisible.

But if the gendered effects of the GFC were at first ambiguous, prescriptions for the recovery from the crisis—especially in Europe, but also in Republican controlled state legislatures in the United States—were quite straightforward. Initial stimulus packages, mostly used to bail out the ailing banks and revive the stalled financial system, were quickly replaced by calls for budget cuts. The shift to austerity occurred in 2010, prompted by sovereign debt crises in Europe (Irwin 2013); excessive government spending was then retroactively linked—albeit with no reasonable evidence or logic—with the GFC itself. In the narration and re-narration of the crisis, the financial system was no longer to blame. Instead, the enduring crisis was the fault of governments' unsustainable support of welfare benefits. In the United States, healthcare reform—pejoratively called "Obamacare"—became the lightning rod of the Republican anti-state critique spread across social and traditional media platforms. In Europe, the blame game shifted to immigrants, refugees, and the lazy PIIGS (Portugal, Ireland, Italy, Greece, Spain), especially the Greeks. The ensuing cuts in public sector services in the heartlands of the crisis disproportionately affected women, since they made the majority of their workforce or made women's employment in other sectors feasible. As cultural theorist Stuart Hall wrote at the time, "women stand where many of these savage lines [of budget cuts] intersect" (Hall, cited in Sunderland 2009a).

And so, in some instances, the attack on budgets, the female-dominated public sector, and public services supporting women's employment and basic rights was overt. In the United States, the joining of neoliberal economics with religious fundamentalism led the Republican Party to link its budget proposals to the elimination of all federal and state funding for family planning and preventive health care for poor women (which activists coined a "war on women"). In the United Kingdom, driven by neoconservatism and austerity politics, David Cameron turned marriage into the centerpiece of his Big Society program. Cuts to the United Kingdom's public sector, as the Fawcett Society (2013; see also Rake 2009) showed in its gender impact assessment, affected many more women than men—as public sector employees, as unpaid caregivers, and as the group of citizens most likely to access public services for their own and their families' support. In Italy, and in the European Union neighborhood countries in Eastern Europe, the cornerstone of the government's austerity package became an increase in women's pension age under the guise of a "gender equality agenda."

In other instances, the consequences of the crisis may not have been immediately visible, but they were potentially harsher. They were concealed

in the quiet transformation of households hit by foreclosures, loss of benefits, youth unemployment and out-of-work men; a simultaneous decline
in marriage and divorce rates or, in short, more unhappy families staying
together and fewer people choosing to start new ones.[5] Not surprisingly,
after the GFC there was a notable increase in reported domestic violence,
including intimate partner economic violence and abuse, fueled by high
levels of economic stress and instability and associated risky behaviors,
such as excessive alcohol and drug taking (True 2012). In the United States,
men's violence against female intimate partners is correlated with the
length of unemployment; and the rate of perpetration of intimate partner
violence is 44 percent less for men with a female partner in employment
(Resko 2010). The gender-specific impacts of recession and austerity on
the loss of homes, unpayable debt, public sector job losses, and cuts to services have substantially increased the risk of violence for women, but especially for single mothers and refugee and ethnic minority women, while
diminishing the resources for police, community, and welfare services that
provide protection and enable the prevention of violence through various
access points supporting women in communities (McRobie 2013b).[6] This
is the case in a number of countries, which have downsized the services
for survivors of sexual and gender-based violence in the austerity budgets
that have followed the financial crisis. In many crisis-affected countries,
women's loss of income, right to housing, and mobility has had clear consequences for domestic violence, and the difficulties experienced in leaving
a violent partner.

Increases in male suicides are a further violent effect of austerity.
"Recessions can hurt, but austerity kills" (Henley 2013), David Stuckler
argues in his and Sanjay Basu's analysis, noting that there has been a
60 percent rise in male suicide in middle-age groups in Greece and up
to 10,000 more male suicides across Europe and the United States since
governments started introducing austerity programs in the aftermath
of the crisis (Stuckler and Basu 2013; also Allen 2014).[7] These increases
in suicide deaths, as well as increased reports of violence against women
exacerbated by economic insecurity, are not the inevitable effects of
financial downturns, but of political choices by governments. However,
the post-GFC intra-elite debate over macroeconomic policy, whether
to adopt austerity versus stimulus fiscal policies, has masked both the
post-crisis inequality and violence and their *political* causes. Moreover,
the lack of debate about these consequences of financial crisis and austerity has meant that the responses to escalating suicide and domestic
violence are limited to moral outrage and panic, which find their outlet
in media scandals.

Fictional and factual narratives have been historically entwined with financial crises and engaged in the (re)making of both economic structures and their meanings. The GFC is not an exception: it has been construed through media representations and academic analyses as much as through government and corporate policies. According to Bob Jessop (2012), competing narratives of the crisis have framed policy responses and, in doing so, some of them have become more equal than others. The dominant view that has emerged contends that this was the crisis *in* finance-led accumulation or, at most, *in* neoliberalism, and that, as such, it could be resolved with a set of other, different, neoliberal measures. In fact, argues Jessop, such was the emphasis on crisis *in* rather than *of* capitalism that "paraphrasing Baudrillard on the Gulf War, one could say that 'the Crisis' did not happen" (2012, 33). Alluding to the recurring tendency to link government spending and the crisis, despite all the evidence to the contrary, Paul Krugman (2015) says that the GFC and its aftermath have proven that "seriously bad ideas (. . .) have remarkable staying power." "No matter how much contrary evidence comes in, no matter how often and how badly predictions based on those ideas are proved wrong, the bad ideas just keep coming back," writes Krugman. "And they retain the power to warp policy." German philosopher Jürgen Habermas (2015) views the post-democratic "lulling to sleep of public opinion" as a symptom of the press transformed into "therapeutic journalism" and "marching arm in arm with the political class in caring for the well-being of customers, not citizens."

Financial narratives have, of course, also been traditionally gendered. As Marieke de Goede reminds us in the Afterword to this volume, her book *Virtue, Fortune, and Faith: A Genealogy of Finance* (2005) has convincingly shown that "gendered representation of financial crises as instances of madness, delusion, hysteria and irrationality has particular historical durability, which simultaneously constructs the sphere of financial normality or rationality." Gender stereotypes help to normalize high levels of financial risk-taking as appropriate and normal behavior. Similarly, Nancy Folbre (2009, xxiii) writes about the way in which one of the foundational concepts of neoclassical economics, self-interest, becomes morally complicated once its gendered construction is revealed. "Selfish women," says Folbre, "seem to pose a greater threat to society than selfish men." Tracing the location of this anxiety, she discovers that selfishness often included "two more colorful vices: greed and lust," both—unsurprisingly—privileging men (lust and greed were far more dangerous and "inappropriate" in women than in men) and equalizing capital accumulation with sexual prowess.

This volume focuses on a specific gendered narrative that has often accompanied financial crisis—scandal. Echoing the narratives that accompanied previous periods of financial exuberance—the seventeenth century financial bubbles and Victorian speculative ups and down—scandals tend to (re)combine lust and greed in a predictable manner, reminding us of the need to balance habitually masculine selfishness (generator of economic growth) with feminine altruism (protector of family) (see also Brassett and Rethel 2015). As "a public drama about the sins of private life" (Cohen 1996, 16), scandals literally bring to light indiscretions and iniquities that might concern the public yet have taken place in areas hidden from public eye and oversight. Like rumors and gossip, they both discipline and constitute communities. Scandals sanction disgraced individuals while binding those who have followed their development in an "imagined community of shared values" (White 2000, 65).

Scandals thrive in times of financial uncertainty because of their productive power. When the ground seems to be shifting, scandals can generate both new meanings and reassuring boundaries. They have four important aspects that make them so alluring during financial crises. First, through their revelations of secret, often intimate affairs, scandals actually reconstitute the divide between the public and the private sphere, and by doing so they reaffirm gender hierarchies. Second, scandals tend to personalize matters that cause public outrage, thus turning systemic problems into issues of individual failing. Third, and as a direct corollary, scandals always walk the thin line between visibility and invisibility. By calling attention to particular (usually) individual acts of visibly or patently inappropriate behavior, scandals' very public exposures can also blind the public to other issues at hand. Last but not least, scandals are dependent on—and beneficial to—media that promote them and the powers behind them; as John P. Thompson (2000, xi) has argued "scandal matters because, in our modern mediated world, it touches on real sources of power."

Thus, in the aftermath of the GFC, these conjoint dynamics of cover-up and scandal have recast and re-regulated the boundaries between public and private, morality and immorality, compounding economic and gender inequalities but also obscuring the suffering of those who do not find themselves in the media limelight. Paradoxically, and despite the fact that scandals are often made possible by violations of privacy, they rekindle the fantasy that there is a separate sphere of freedom, usually associated with women and domesticity, which is sheltered from the vagaries of markets and states. They put women back in their place by seemingly doing them a favor. And so the "spectre of gender" has been paradoxically visible in both scandals about the sexual exploits of men (such as Dominique

Strauss-Kahn, the former IMF head discussed in Chapter 9 by Celeste Montoya, and the indictment of Julian Assange, the founder of Wikileaks, for rape) and rational arguments about the returns from women's inclusion in the financial order.[8]

THE CRISIS AND CRISES

Along with Bob Jessop (2012), we argue that the GFC was not a crisis *in* capitalism but a crisis *of* capitalism. In fact, we echo the Occupy movement in starting from the assumption that _capitalism itself is crisis_.[9] In other words, in this volume we propose that crises are intrinsic to capitalism, rather than capitalism being in crisis today or yesterday or in the future. In addition, where most analysts see the crisis, we see multiples—seemingly disconnected, often forgotten, at times cascading. The global financial crisis may have been a unique historical "event," but like all events, it was also socially construed and, therefore, deserves to be richly examined in light of the key social, economic, and political relations that it congeals and creates (see March, Sproull, and Tamuz 1991).

Despite the fact that financial crises have become increasingly frequent, the notion of crisis has not been sufficiently theorized. Lingering Marxist thought continues to view crises not just as organic elements of capitalism, but rather as the preconditions of its revolutionary transformation. Resilient (neo)liberal thought portrays crises as random, unrelated blips on the surface of an otherwise sound market economy, which always brings itself back into equilibrium. In both cases, the crisis and its content seem subordinated to their outcomes or resolutions. The possibility, to invoke Jessop (2001) again, that both actors and structures may change from one crisis to another—or that crises may generate their own blind spots—is not usually addressed.

One of the rare thinkers who devoted considerable time to crisis as a concept was Czech philosopher Karel Kosík. Writing during the Prague Spring and its aftermath, in 1968–1969 (and we should ponder the similarities/differences between the crisis of communism at the time and the contemporary crisis of capitalism), Kosík (in Kosík and Satterwhite 1994) noted that the crisis of socialism was also the crisis of modernity. In a collection of essays, which also touched upon issues of representation of politics and of the crisis, he viewed modernity as "the system of universal manipulations (. . .), a developed and perfected system of commerce typical of the nineteenth century" (1994, 55). According to Kosík,

[c]haracteristic of the system of universal manipulability is not only the dominance of false consciousness in people's assumptions about themselves and the
world, but also—in particular and primarily—a diminishing and regressing ability to distinguish truth from falsehood and a massive lack of interest, or dulled
interest in distinguishing between truth and untruth, good and evil. (1994, 56)

The crises, therefore, thrive on delusions and self-delusions. The GFC—
and the global credit economy tied to it—may have exposed "social, political, moral, and philosophical conflicts and contradictions" (Kosik 1994,
145) but they have also generated veils of deception to hide them. We speak
of crises in spatial and temporal terms: we worry about diffusion, contagion, deadlines, and countdowns. We forget about their corporeal aspects,
the way in which they engulf and fracture bodies, the all-too-obvious metaphors of disease and emergency medicine used to describe crises and the
response to them. We should, perhaps, remember what Gramsci (1971,
276) argued, that in crisis "the old is dying and the new cannot be born; in
the interregnum a great variety of morbid symptoms appear." These morbid symptoms can be seen in the gendered spectrum of the GFC job losses,
austerity policies, suicides, and violence. At the same time, they hide in one
of the prevailing myths of the GFC: the familiar journalistic slogan that
"men made the crisis and it is up to women to clean it up," discussed by
Elisabeth Prügl in Chapter 2 (also O'Connor 2008; Prügl 2012). Thus, the
essays in this collection explore both spectral and "real" dimensions of the
relationship between gender and the financial crisis. As UK *Observer* journalist Ruth Sunderland (2009a) has argued, "we can't undo the crisis, but
we can change the terms of the analysis."

SCANDALS, SCANDALOUS, AND SCANDALIZING: OUTLINE OF THE BOOK

Reading the crisis through its realpolitik aspects as well as through its spectral manifestations in scandals and/or media representations, the chapters
in this volume address three sets of questions. They ask, "Who benefits
and who loses from the crisis?" from a distributive political economy perspective. But they also ask, "Who defines and narrates the crisis?" from a
constructivist political economy perspective. Most important, fully aware
of the fact that the crisis is ongoing (and despite assurances that the recession is over), the chapters address "Who is *becoming* through this crisis?"
The GFC has created an opportunity for contesting the normal, masculine
ways of governing the global economy. However, we argue that heightened

opportunity for rethinking the structures and processes of political economies has largely been concealed by populist scandals and the tendency to
focus on particular blameworthy individuals, corporations, and states.

Our questions about the financial crisis go beyond standard damage
assessments featuring women, such as, "Are women affected by the crisis
differently than men, and if so, how?" Is crisis the result of too much testosterone or male groupthink on Wall Street and in the city? Or, perhaps,
is it the rise of female whistleblowers sidelined for their nonconformist,
high moral ground that stands at the core of the crisis? (cf. Widmaier
2014). Rather, we treat the GFC as an event that is constitutive—not just
derivative—of both old and new identities, institutions, and practices in
the virtual, affective, and real economies (Peterson 2003). We ask what the
implications are of these reformed identities, institutions, and practices
for a so-called sustainable, equitable, and balanced global economy.

In working on this volume, we have consciously brought together an
international group of authors with diverse methodological orientations—
scholars whose work employs gender-informed conventional IPE analysis and authors influenced by cultural studies and critical theory. We
believe that feminist theorizing of the crisis provides us with an opening
to bridge interest- and identity-based scholarship, analyses of materially
based social relations and culture-driven gender studies, and exploration of economic inequalities and of their gendered cultural/media representations. Therefore, the volume is structured around four distinct
themes: *Scandalous Gendering*, *Scandalous Obfuscations*, *Scandalous Sex*, and
Scandalizing Reimaginings.

In Part I, *Scandalous Gendering*, we closely analyze the gendered ideologies that have shaped the GFC and the recovery from it. In Chapter 2,
Elisabeth Prügl highlights the simplistic gender myths about the GFC,
that it was a "man-made" crisis leading to the death of "macho" in financial institutions. She argues that despite the post-crisis media hype about
women as saviors with more prudent investment practices, symbolized
by the evocation of "Lehman Brothers and Sisters," the promise of a harmoniously gender-balanced financial sector has proven a chimera. In
Chapter 3, "The Global Financial Crisis's Silver Bullet: Women Leaders and
'Leaning In'," Jacqui True argues that the turn to women's leadership as a
crisis recovery response obscures the unequal social and economic effects
of the GFC for many women. Promoting (elite) women's leadership, she
argues, is the financial crisis's silver bullet. It enables states, corporations,
and the finance industry to redress perceptions of their risky and excessive behavior while avoiding major reform of the governance of markets.
In Chapter 4, "Finance, Financialization, and the Production of Gender,"

Adrienne Roberts critiques three overlapping narratives that have emerged in recent years regarding the supposed benefits of liberalized finance for gender equality. She argues that the GFC has given new impetus to calls for the necessity of investing in women in order to increase their participation in labor markets and to improve their ability to consume goods and services, including financial services, in the interest of economic growth globally.

Roberts!

In Part II of the book, *Scandalous Obfuscations,* we explore how policy responses to the crisis have re-narrated and thereby concealed systemic causes and effects of the GFC. In Chapter 5, Daniela Tepe-Belfrage and Johnna Montgomerie analyze the "Troubled Families" program, a part of the United Kingdom's post-crisis austerity package, which has attempted to rein in public spending and more effectively manage welfare provision. They show how poor and indebted families are being disciplined by public agencies into "morally" agreeable private lifestyles through a combination of educational and social services and community policing.

In Chapter 6, Ian Bruff and Stefanie Wöhl also reveal how public-private boundaries are re-regulated with the deployment of hard law by the European Union to discipline households in indebted Eurozone countries. They examine the Spanish and Irish cases and reveal the impact of the eponymous "six-pack" legislation, which in their view fosters the marketization of social relations *and* encourages the rise of a more authoritarian state.

In Chapter 7, Juanita Elias shifts our attention away from Europe and the heartlands of the crisis toward Asia. Given that the Asian region was less directly affected by the GFC, she considers how the prior 1997–1998 Asian financial crisis has affected economic governance and its gendered dimensions. The chapter explores how Asia's economic dynamism has come to be associated with an idea of Asian women as "shock-absorbers" during economic downturns and "drivers" of economic recovery, while other ongoing crises—impoverishment and precarity—simmer in the background. Guillermina Seri recounts similar obfuscations in her analysis in Chapter 8 of Latin America after the financial crisis. Despite the so-called "Pink Tide" (Turn to the Left) and the rise of female leaders in key Latin American economies, Seri demonstrates that the crisis has negatively affected women more than any other group. Her chapter exposes the degree of violent inequalities experienced by women in everyday life, and links the increasing rate of Latin American femicides to the social and economic instability wrought by the crisis.

Our next section, *Scandalous Sex,* turns to the visible manifestations of the crisis by focusing on its media representations and scandals. In Chapter 9, Celeste Montoya analyzes a scandal that may have come to symbolize the crisis: the sexual exploits of former IMF chief Dominique Strauss-Kahn, which played out while he was immersed in post-GFC recovery plans for the Eurozone countries. On a micro level, argues Montoya, the "DSK Affair," as it has come to be known, represents a re-enactment of a classic rape script: a powerful rich white man is accused of sexually assaulting a black female domestic worker. On a macro level, the gendered, raced, and classed power dynamics take on a whole new dimension, given DSK's role at the helm of the International Monetary Fund and the complainant's status as a migrant hotel maid with asylum from Guinea, one of the poorest countries in the world, a former colony of France, and recipient of IMF funding. The chapter examines the parallels as well as the connections between these micro and macro level power politics of neoliberal exploitation.

In Chapter 10, Aida Hozić explores the institution of scandal by focusing on the phone-hacking affair in the United Kingdom, which seriously rattled Rupert Murdoch's media empire in 2011. The chapter addresses the conditions that make scandals propagate and examines the role that scandals play in societies in crisis, especially financial crisis. Drawing on Michel Foucault's analysis of sexuality and sexual scandals in the Victorian age, the chapter underscores the stabilizing effects of scandals on existing power relations and gender hierarchies.

In Chapter 11, "Gender, Finance, and Embodiments of Crisis," Penny Griffin examines how various scholarly approaches to and popular accounts of the crisis have represented, co-opted, and exploited human bodies. She asks how visual, oral, and written representations of the crisis reinscribe existing logics of capital mobility while circumventing valid social concerns and questions about the chain of responsibility for repackaged, "securitized" loans, for instance. The chapter argues that the GFC has engendered techniques of governance that fruitfully exploit gendered assumptions about bodies, human worth, and financial success, while further entrenching a masculinized, white, and elitist culture of financial privilege.

Finally, in Part IV, *Scandalizing Reimaginings*, we consider how the crisis is generating new subjectivities and new points of resistance, including, for instance, the resistance produced through queer economics, racialized struggles, the gendered dimensions of the Occupy protest movement, and feminist science fiction. While it is difficult to assess the political and gender effects of contemporary movements that are contesting the power of financial capitalism and gross inequality, we take note of the ambivalent messages that they send.

Anna Aganthangelou proposes in Chapter 12 that a racial bodily matrix shapes global political economy and the dynamics of the European Union.

Yet most analyses of the GFC ignore these relations. She interrogates the recent meltdowns of peripheral economies such as Greece to rethink the significance of this matrix. The chapter examines the discourses surrounding interventions made via two memoranda signed by Greek political leaders, the European Union, the International Monetary Fund, and EBank, a key EU report on the definition of over-indebtedness, and two documentary films. Agathangelou argues that debt is a technology of governance, with death at its forefront, and shows how legal regimes are transformed, with banks and the state becoming key instigators of direct violence.

Nicola Smith considers what it might mean to queer "the" economic crisis in Chapter 13. She argues that—given that same-sex and other nonnormative sexualities are routinely erased in debates about "the economy"—it is clearly important to explore the material effects of crisis on queer lives. But she also contends that it is not enough simply to "add queer and stir" to discussions of economic crisis—particularly given that a central thrust of queer theory has been to critique notions of sexual identity as coherent and stable and for them to be organized and policed as such. Rather, a queer political economy of crisis should also interrogate how "crisis" itself is constituted through heteronormative gender logics and power relations, for "the economic, tied to the productive, is necessarily linked to the reproduction of heterosexuality" (Butler 1997, 274). In order to illuminate these themes, Smith explores how neoliberal policy responses to the crisis in the United Kingdom are serving to disadvantage lesbian, gay, bisexual, transgender, and queer (LGBT/Q)[10] communities and others who fall outside heterosexist, married monogamy (such as single parents), and how heteronormative imaginaries of "the family" are themselves playing an important role in reproducing the neoliberal economic order.

In Chapter 14, Wanda Vrasti starts from an observation that the ongoing financial crisis is simultaneously a crisis of imagination (an inability to envision alternatives) and a crisis of reproduction (which has now spread beyond the sphere of feminized domesticity). In her exploration of possible lessons of this double crisis, she turns to materialist feminism developed in Italy, Germany, and the United States in the 1970s, as well as to feminist art and science fiction. Her aim is to resurrect the "utopian impulse" of feminism, which would not only lament and critique contemporary capitalism but also creatively push back against it. Her reimagining of the provocative lessons of the crisis finds inspiration in Silvia Federici's concept of "self-reproducing" movements and views the Occupy movement, with its emphasis on reproduction over disruption, as its embodiment. Alternatives to capitalism, Vrasti argues, can now only be sought in the revolution of daily life or, as she puts it: "a politics of resistance today is also a politics of reconstitution of reproduction."

Tying together these chapters envisioning political and economic alternatives to the status quo in the Afterword to this volume, Marieke de Goede analyzes novel ways in which gender and finance were interwoven in political practices of representing the GFC and in the political search for new stabilities after the GFC. Her chapter provides a historically informed theoretical reflection by a major scholar of discursive political economy and crisis. In her analysis of sexualized imaginations of the GFC, de Goede turns to immensely popular films—*The Wolf of Wall Street*, and *The Inside Job*—and combines them with the focus on obscure financial instruments such as ABACUS. She finds, along with many other authors in this volume, that in the aftermath of the GFC, gender is back—and with a vengeance. But, in her conclusion, de Goede also warns against easy refoundations of gender and values that scandals might have encouraged. Instead, she proposes that we stay attuned to complex politics of responsibility in the crisis and to the critical voices both within and outside the financial industry—as a way of seeing beyond the impoverished field of policy options and thinking ethically about the global political economy.

CONCLUSION

Critical feminist perspectives are highly attuned to power and marginalization in productive and reproductive economies. They do not just combine class and gender analyses and evacuate race, sexuality, nationality status, and so forth; they embody a self-critical reflexive stance toward *all* social relations and the politics of knowledge and media invested in the reproduction of current political-economic orders. Crucially, the critical feminist perspectives on global political economy in this volume must be distinguished from the "spectre of gender" now ever present among transnational business, neoliberal governments, and elite women leaders. Adrienne Roberts (2012) refers to the latter as the emergence of "transnational business feminism." This limited form of feminism is actively engaged in changing gender norms to empower individual women and to remove institutional and social barriers to help markets function more effectively and legitimately in the aftermath of the GFC. It does not address the structural roots of violence, inequality, exclusion, and thus oppression. Moreover—and it is a deep paradox—transnational business feminism contributes to the devaluation of the economic activity of many people the world over, but it renders even more invisible the productive and reproductive power of women's labor in times of crisis and of apparent stability.

The GFC and the scandals linked to it have created an opportunity for contesting masculinized ways of governing the global economy. However, this opportunity is surrendered when we focus our attention on blame-worthy individuals, groups, and nations and reduce gender analysis to stereotypes of masculine and feminine behavior. Instead of wonder-women saviors, diligent household savers, and governments that cut public provisioning, collective agency and political will are needed to shine the light on unequal economic governance and outcomes and their effects on local and global societal cohesion

Scandalous Economics, as we have coined this volume, exposes the morbid symptoms and the scandalous narratives of the global financial crisis, allowing us to interrogate the very metaphor of crisis and its gendered logics, and importantly, how it has been deployed as a call to order to restore anew our liberal capitalist conventions. By invoking *scandals* as the language in which the GFC has played out and has been represented, we intend to ignite a broader conversation about what is "truly scandalous" about this contemporary crisis and the responses to it. In so doing, we restate one of the key purposes of a feminist perspective on the global political economy: to expose the material and ideological forces underpinning particular projects of global governance of the world financial order. The chapters in this volume reclaim the power of feminist theorizing to reveal the intersecting forms of power and marginalization in the global political economy and to interrogate the conditions and possibilities for an alternative imagining of financial order.

NOTES

1. Some scholarship and research has highlighted the gendered dimensions of the crisis and the centrality of the household in capitalist booms and busts, however. See the special issues of Pearson and Sweetman's Oxfam Working in Gender and Development Series (2011), *Feminist Economics* (2013), Pearson (2012); Rubery (2011); Montgomerie and Young (2010); Enloe (2014). See also Schwartz (2009); Schwartz and Seabrooke (2009); and Rai, Hoskyns, and Thomas (2014) on the effects of crises on the depletion of household economies and women's social reproductive labor in particular.
2. For example, Brill (2009); Geithner (2014); Greenspan (2013); McLean and Nocera (2010); Suskind (2011); Bernanke (2015); Paulson (2010); Irwin (2013); and Ahamed (2009). Recently biographies have been published by women who have sought to regulate women in the finance industry; see Bair (2012) and Warren (2015).

3. See in particular V. Spike Peterson (2003); Marchand and Sisson Runyan (2010); Zalewski (2013); Shepherd (2013); Griffin (2015a).

4. Female unemployment rose to a 25-year high in the United Kingdom in 2012, with over one million women unemployed (OECD 2012).

5. For data on these demographic changes as a result of the financial crisis in the United States, see Chowdhury (2011); Wilcox (2011).

6. The United Kingdom abolished the Social Fund, which was used as an emergency payment from benefit offices to support those in "dire need," such as domestic violence survivors.

7. Researching the causes of men's suicides in the United Kingdom, the Samaritans (2014) found that male suicide increased during the recession for two reasons: "men in mid life and from disadvantaged backgrounds compare themselves against a gold standard which prizes power, control and invincibility;" and with "the decline of traditional male industries these men have lost not only their jobs but also a source of masculine pride and identity." The study also noted the emotional dependence of men on a female partner.

8. For instance, statistical evidence demonstrating the paucity of women on corporate boards and management executives across countries has linked this paucity to suboptimal decision-making against the backdrop of the GFC (McKinsey and Company 2007; Joy et al. 2007; Gladman and Lamb 2013; True 2013).

9. The expression is borrowed from the Occupy movement's banner in front of St. Paul's Cathedral in London, on display in October 2011. See also the documentary *Capitalism is the Crisis*, available on YouTube at http://www.youtube.com/watch?v=fYFw3O--2R0, which features interviews with Leo Panitch, Chris Hedges, and Derrick Jensen.

10. The "Q" in LGBTQ is sometimes used to denote "questioning."

CHAPTER 2

"Lehman Brothers and Sisters"

Revisiting Gender and Myth after the Financial Crisis

ELISABETH PRÜGL

"If Lehman Brothers had been Lehman Sisters, run by women instead of men, would the credit crunch have happened?" (Sunderland 2009a). This question animated discussions at the World Economic Forum in February 2009 and swept through the international press subsequently. It kicked off a frenzied engagement in the international media with the gender question in international finance. Articles adduced masculinity as a variable that may have caused the crisis, speculated about the more prudent investment styles of women, and predicted the fall of "the macho men's club called finance capitalism" (Salam 2009). By the summer of 2010, Hanna Rosin (2010) in *The Atlantic* magazine confidently predicted "the end of men" and the dawn of matriarchy.

Perhaps it should not have been surprising that feminism finally had caught up with misogyny on Wall Street and financial centers around the world, long known for their sexism—from treating women as sex objects to cutting them off from the most lucrative opportunities. But why did these critiques emerge then? What role did they play in the context of the financial crisis? Is it really plausible that women running the financial sector could have avoided the crisis?

The discourse around gender in the aftermath of the financial crisis amounted to an exercise in meaning making via the construction of man. This construction involved a redefinition of woman as a new Other of man, which, when transferred to the financial crisis, explained man's failure. To man, the doer, woman, the inessential, became a signal of the alternative and a remedy. Inserting gender into discussions of the crisis enabled a narrative of fall, rise, and redemption through which finance capitalism was reborn, apparently chastened and reformed.

The financial sector is one of the few bastions of virtually uncontested masculine privilege remaining in the aftermath of feminism. Various strands of literature have documented how thoroughly the sector is gendered in its discourses, institutional practices, and organization. Marieke de Goede has shown how gendered discourses historically have helped legitimize and give meaning to various financial practices. For example, reflecting the ambiguity toward "paper money" in the eighteenth century, Daniel Defoe introduced the image of "Lady Credit" as "a virtuous virgin or a gentlewoman on the one hand and a spoiled flirt, a demanding mistress, and a prostitute on the other," which in any case needed to be controlled (de Goede 2005, 29; de Goede 2000). Contemporary associations of financial crises as resulting from irrational exuberance continue to echo this theme. Gendered images also have served to legitimize gentlemanly financial speculation by counterposing it to promiscuous gambling, an unstable boundary even today. Focusing on the 2008 financial crisis, Penny Griffin (2013a) finds similarly gendered imagery in the debates around responsibility for the crisis. She identifies a culture of privilege, competitive success, and masculine prowess that contributed to the crisis, but remains hidden.

Linda McDowell (1997) finds such gendered imagery extensively reflected in the institutional and organizational realms of the financial industry. She explores the culture of the industry in the City of London, the way in which people "do gender" in their various workplaces in banks and investment companies, and shows how gender, class, and race are activated through exclusionary recruitment practices, the segregation of women and men into different branches, and sexist language and promotion practices. She also remarks on the morality plays of movies about the financial sector, which typically stage young men challenging patriarchal authority only to come to a fall and to be made whole through the restoration of the old order. Focusing more narrowly on compensation practices in securities firms on Wall Street, Louise Marie Roth's (2006) research confirms some of McDowell's findings. She questions in particular the supposed neutrality of performance evaluations and the bonus system and argues that gender stereotypes powerfully influence organizational practices, enabling vast inequalities in compensation.

Feminist economists have traced gender in macro-economic structures and policies in addition, suggesting that gender inequality both contributed to the financial crisis and was accentuated in its effects. Helene Schuberth and Brigitte Young (2011) have proposed that the virtual male monopoly on financial policymaking produced gender-biased policies, including groupthink, which facilitated the crisis. Others have argued that various forms of social inequality—including gender inequality—helped bring about the crisis by reducing demand and by redistributing wealth to a class of rentiers (Fukuda-Parr et al. 2013). Feminist economists also have documented the gendered effects of the crisis in the areas of employment and work and have urged interventions to counteract these (Antonopoulos 2009a; Elson 2010; Seguino 2010).

The literature thus shows gender at work in the discursive constructions of finance, in the social meanings and unequal outcomes produced through organizational practices, and in the economic effects generated through gendered policies—including in times of crisis. Given the persuasive evidence of gender as deeply entrenched in the discourses and practices of finance, it is interesting that the topic gained publicity in the aftermath of the crisis. Why then and not before? Here I take a critical look at this debate and in particular at the rhetoric of responsible woman that fueled it. I build on de Goede's insight that talk about financial crises historically has drawn on gendered imagery. I add to de Goede's methodological instruments, which draw from Foucault and Butler, a focus on myth.

Roland Barthes (1957) has suggested that myth is a type of speech chosen by history. It does not emerge from the nature of things, but lives and dies in historical context. In this sense, the myth of the financially prudent woman cannot be thought as separate from the financial crisis of 2008 and the subsequent economic downturn. Like myths in general, it helped make sense of a situation that was unfamiliar. Barthes suggests that myths are second-order semiological systems: A first-order system produces a sign, the associative total of signifier and signified. Unlike a signifier, which is empty, a sign is full of meaning. Yet, in the second-order system of the myth, the sign of the first system again becomes an empty signifier, to be filled with meaning that belongs to a different category. In other words, in a first-order system the sign "woman"—depending on context—may signify a human being of the female sex. Emptied of meaning and displaced into a myth, "woman" may come to stand for a variety of ideas from the fickleness of Fortuna in Machiavelli to the passivity of Nature in Bacon, from the betrayal of Eve in the Old Testament to the succor of the good mother in the New.

Simone de Beauvoir (1989) has suggested that there is an existential structure to the location of woman in myths. Woman in myth appears as the absolute Other who enables male transcendence: "A myth always implies a subject who projects his hopes and his fears toward a sky of transcendence" (de Beauvoir 1989, 142). For de Beauvoir, man is this subject. In seeking to assert himself, he encounters obstacles—nature, dearth—that produce a need for struggle, for enterprise, for taking possession. His endeavors set him up against other men and leave him alone striving in the world. But he dreams of quiet, contentment, and plenitude, and he finds it in woman. She is the intermediary between man and nature, a fellow human being though not one that competes, a stranger yet the same. Most important, she is inessential: Characterized by immanence, she accepts man's sovereignty and can be trusted not to revolt or make him into an object. She is the absolute Other, an empty signifier to be filled with multiple meaning, a cipher onto which man can project all his "dreams, fears, and idols" (de Beauvoir 1989, 139).

Within myth, "woman" operates as a metaphor that helps make sense of something new and unknown. As Eve Kittay (1988) has pointed out, metaphors connect two unrelated fields to each other. In doing so, they allow us to better understand something that we do not know well by semantically relating it to a field that is familiar. As both an empty signifier and as something intimately familiar, "woman" offers itself as the raw material of metaphor and myth par excellence.

Gaining understanding through myth has political effects (Barthes 1957, 229–233). Myth transforms history into nature, empties a political situation of reality, and establishes what is deeply contradictory and power-laden as self-evident and blissfully clear. In other words, myth depoliticizes. It does not deny the existence of things, but "it purifies them, it makes them innocent, it gives them a clarity which is not that of an explanation but that of a statement of fact" (Barthes 1957, 230, trans.). Myth always has an intention, a motivation. It produces an alibi that hides the historicity of things, fixes human beings in their places, immobilizes them, and produces facts as eternal.

This chapter approaches the discourse on women and the financial crisis as the production of a myth. Dichotomies of gender are reconstructed by recalling a presumably categorical difference between man and woman. Woman is then lifted into a story that associates her with financial caution and risk aversion and calls forth her civilizing and moderating influences, which are available to mediate between male aspirations for profit and unpredictable economic vagaries. The distinction between reckless man and responsible woman provides a new meaning structure that offers insight into the unfamiliar of the crisis, provides a correcting mechanism, and reassembles the bourgeois worldview of social and economic harmony.

The myth of the prudent woman in finance has been constructed in the international English-language press since the fall of Lehman Brothers, and reports in this press constitute my data. I have accessed articles dealing with gender and the financial crisis through the Lexis/Nexis database of international English-language newspapers and in a close reading have identified major themes.[1] The database includes print media of the Anglophone world, but also of non-English-speaking countries that seek to address an international audience, such as the *Japanese Business Digest*, *Agence France Press*, and *Deutsche Presse Agentur*. Written in the hegemonic idiom of the contemporary world order, the papers are consumed by an international ruling class. All of the articles identified stem from news media produced in the global North, reflecting the disorientation generated by the crisis in the hegemonic ideologies of postindustrial capitalism. I also followed source references to academic and policy studies identified in the articles, in particular if I found them cited more than once. Finally, I eclectically have adduced materials from English-language media not included in the Lexis/Nexis database as I became aware of them. By tracing the production of the myth of woman in finance in these various texts, I identify the outlines of a morality play that begins with a story of fall and rise, continues with a re-signification of woman and man on the basis of academic research, and triumphs in a coda of redemption.

ACT I: THE FALL OF WALL STREET MACHISMO AND THE RISE OF WOMAN

The images of disgraced bankers testifying before Congress, Bernie Madoff going off to jail followed by a coterie of accomplices and insider traders, and the public outrage over outsized pay packages of people who ruined the economy for some sounded the death knell of Wall Street machismo. That is, these images were interpreted as the fall of a particular form of masculinity that had gained ascendance in the 1980s in parallel with what Susan Strange (1997) has called "casino capitalism." She conjured up the image of "rooms full of chain-smoking young men" sitting "in the towering office blocks that dominate all the great cities of the world" and playing games "that involve sums of money so large that they cannot be imagined" (Strange 1986, 1). These men could be found equally in New York, the City of London, and banking centers around the world. They proved their masculinity by making huge amounts of money and spending it conspicuously.

They benefited disproportionately from neoliberalism, an economic ideology radiating from the United States that proposed market deregulation and envisioned a disembodied economic subject taking advantage of the opportunities thus provided. They celebrated extreme gambles and risk-taking and operated through relatively closed male networks. They measured their success in exclusively monetary terms and signified this value through the possession of goods, including women. This is what we have learned from the press since the fall.

The financial sector has long been disproportionately male, and this became something to be remarked on after the collapse of Lehman Brothers (Kay and Shipman 2009; see also Schuberth and Young 2011). Newspapers and policy papers reported data provided by Catalyst, a US nonprofit research and advisory organization working to advance women in business, and by the British Equality and Human Rights Commission, all highlighting this fact. According to Catalyst, in the United States women accounted for only about 18 percent of corporate officers in the finance and insurance industries in 2008, and for 7.3 percent of chief financial officers in Fortune 500 companies (Catalyst, n.d.). In the United Kingdom the Equality and Human Rights Commission found considerable occupational segregation in the financial sector, with more than twice as many male as female managers and professionals (Equality and Human Rights Commission 2009, 27). Beyond sex ratios, the culture of Wall Street and the City became an object of scrutiny. In the United Kingdom, the Parliament's Treasury Select Committee went after "sexism in the City," and the press reported the testimony of women who had worked in finance speaking of harassment and a macho culture. Apparently visits to strip clubs and lap dancing clubs after work were standard (Allen 2009). And equally scandalizing, the study by the Equality and Human Rights Commission found massive pay inequities. In some of the United Kingdom's top finance companies, women received around 80 percent less performance-related pay than their male colleagues. Overall the pay gap in the industry was 39 percent, rising to 47 percent when bonuses and performance-related pay were factored in (*Birmingham Post*, September 8, 2008). Parliament expressly linked machismo to the financial debacle.

In the United States, in the meantime, announcements of Wall Street machismo's fall took the form of stories of successful challenges to sex discrimination. The three major Wall Street firms—Citigroup's Smith Barney, Merrill Lynch, and Morgan Stanley—all had paid out more than $100 million each between 1990 and 2006 to resolve sex discrimination suits (Roth 2006, 1). In early 2008 Morgan Stanley reportedly paid another $54 million to settle a class action lawsuit charging sex discrimination, and Citigroup another $33 million (*Evening Standard*, April 4, 2008). In 2009—according to a front-page story in *Forbes Magazine*—five female executives charged Citi with "recession discrimination." Apparently women accounted only for 12 percent of executives in their department, but they made up 45 percent of those laid off (Raghavan 2009).

Long a curse of the industry, sex discrimination lawsuits now became part of a larger narrative of the decrepitude of Wall Street, with machismo on the Street woven into the story of decline (National Council for Research on Women 2009, 29). The logic was spelled out most clearly in Iceland, where the crisis had bankrupted the country, leading to a collapse of the government. Halla Tomasdottir, co-head of a women-run financial and investment company that fared well during the crisis, became a favorite source for the international press. In the English-language edition of *Der Spiegel*, she explained, "The crisis is man-made. It's always the same guys. Ninety-nine percent went to the same school, they drive the same cars, they wear the same suits and they have the same attitudes. They got us into this situation—and they had a lot of fun doing it. . . . It's typical male behavior" (Ertel 2009). Einar Mar Gudmundsson, an influential Icelandic writer, seemed to agree with this assessment. The *Washington Post* quoted him as follows: "These financial vikings who made the country bankrupt were in a way like little boys playing with toys" (Sullivan and Jordan 2009). Macho masculinity and male irresponsibility were identified as causes of the financial crisis.

Not surprisingly, predictions of "the end of macho" and "the end of men" proliferated in the aftermath of the financial crisis, casting the follies of Wall Street masculinity as accelerating what was identified as a long-standing and now inexorable trend. Reports of disproportionate job losses for men fueled these speculations. In the words of Reihan Salam in *Foreign Policy* magazine (2009), "For years, the world has been witnessing a quiet but monumental shift of power from men to women. Today, the Great Recession has turned what was an evolutionary shift into a revolutionary one." Or in Hanna Rosin's (2010) words, "Man has been the dominant sex since, well, the dawn of mankind. But for the first time in human history, that is changing—and with shocking speed." Implicitly recognizing its enmeshment with patriarchy, these articles linked the crisis of finance capitalism to a crisis of masculine domination. They predicted the end of an era of male dominance, prefiguring the rise of woman and joining a parade of articles adducing evidence for the new march of history.

In Iceland, Jóhanna Sigurdardóttir was appointed prime minister in January 2009, forming an interim government with 5 of 11 ministers in her cabinet female. Soon after, debt-ridden Lithuania elected its first woman president, in Salam's words, "an experienced economist with a black belt in karate named Dalia Grybauskaite." On the day she won, Vilnius's leading newspaper reportedly bannered this headline: "Lithuania has decided: The country is to be saved by a woman" (Salam 2009). In the meantime, in Iceland, two women, Elin Sigfusdottir and Birna Einarsdottir, took the reins of two failed, nationalized banks, Glitner and Landesbanki, and the international press introduced to its readers a line-up of female investors actively seeking to shape the financial sector there, among them pop singer Björk, who created an investment fund in her own name to back sustainable environmental projects and local cultural enterprises.

Women apparently also took over the reins of finance in the United States, according to *Time* magazine becoming the "new sheriffs of Wall Street" (Scherer 2010). President Obama named Mary Schapiro to head the hapless Securities and Exchange Commission. Elizabeth Warren chaired the panel that developed the TARP[2] bailout and led the charge in advocating for new consumer-finance regulations. The press discovered Sheila Bair, chair of the Federal Deposit Insurance Corporation, who early on had sounded a public alarm over practices on Wall Street, and it rediscovered Brooksley Born, former head of the Commodity Futures Trading Commission, who blew the whistle on derivatives years ago, only to be silenced by the "boys club of US economic leaders," including Alan Greenspan, Robert Rubin, the lobbyists of Enron and the financial companies (Zacchion and Scheer 2009).[3] According to a May 2010 story in *Time* magazine, "three of the five SEC commissioners are women; the head of the White House Council of Economic Advisors is a mother of three; and in the Senate women have been leading the charge for tougher regulations." Where women did not seem to manage a similar rise, as in the United Kingdom, the press bemoaned the matter: ". . . with the exception of Ann Godbehre, who took a senior post at Northern Rock, there is little sign of women taking seats vacated by disgraced male bankers in the UK because for most women sex discrimination exists at the very top of corporate Britain" (Sunderland 2009a). The United Kingdom seemed to fall behind, as Iceland, Lithuania, and the United States showed the way into a new world of finance led by women.

The story of the fall of Wall Street macho and the rise of financially savvy woman introduced an entirely new narrative of the financial crisis. No longer were AAA-rated collateralized debt obligations, the unrealistic capital requirements of banks, and the dearth of regulation the culprits of the crisis. Instead, the story of the crisis became a drama of the sexes: macho Wall Street bankers brought to their knees and a feminine phoenix rising from the ashes of casino capitalism. As in any myth, two domains not logically connected were brought to bear upon each other, with one helping make sense of the other. The myth of reckless man and prudent woman enacted a feminist happy ending and created meaning in the face of a failure incomprehensible both in its complexity and enormity. If the story did seem somewhat unlikely—Salam found it necessary to add an emphatic "seriously" after announcing the end of the era of male dominance—journalists and policy analysts managed to make it credible by drawing on academic studies that have reinterpreted woman as the more prudent financial manager.

ACT II: THE NEW SIGN OF WOMAN

The story of the fall of Wall Street machismo and of woman rising was buttressed with research evidence attesting to women's superior financial skills. A number of studies in behavioral finance were now widely quoted to show that women tend to take less risk than men, and that this does not affect their financial performance. The press offered these studies as evidence that the crisis might have been avoided had there been more women in the financial sector and that women's aptitudes might be crucial to overcoming the crisis. While studies suggested that there was a difference in degree between women and men in financial behavior, the press frequently turned this suggestion into an assertion of categorical difference. Woman emerged as the Other of man, all that he was not, but also that allowed him to reconnect to his economic endeavors after failure.

The oldest cited study, by Brad Barber and Terrance Odean, was published in 2001 and explores the behavior of clients of a brokerage company. The researchers found that men traded 45 percent more than women, and that the higher frequency of trading reduced men's net returns by 2.65 percent compared with 1.72 percent for women (Barber and Odean 2001).[4] The article is often interpreted to suggest a connection between gender and overconfidence, but the authors do not test this relationship. Instead, they are interested in the relationship between overconfidence and returns and—drawing on studies that show women lack confidence in areas that are defined as masculine, such as finance—use gender as a proxy for overconfidence. Thus the conclusion that "boys will be boys" (the title of the article) is problematic because presumably men's level of overconfidence in their own abilities would fall if they were less familiar with finance. Vice versa, one might predict that if women were to become more familiar with finance, they also would become overconfident in their skills and prone to excessive trading.

In a 2008 study, Daniela Beckmann and Lukas Menkhoff (2008) probe precisely this case. Instead of studying the trading behavior of individual investors, they explore the behavior of fund managers. They reason that female and male fund managers are similarly educated and thus, unlike individual traders, would be similarly familiar with finance and thus similarly confident in their abilities. Beckmann and Menkhoff indeed debunk the association between gender and overconfidence, but—like a number of other studies they cite—still find a correlation between gender and risk-taking. Female fund managers tended to be more risk averse and tended to shy away from competition, though to a lesser degree than in Barber and Odean. Beckmann and Menkhoff find the importance of gender differences to be relatively small compared to competing influences, but relevant nonetheless. While their evidence for greater female risk aversion is thus at best mixed, the authors' conclusion is that "women will indeed be women" and, not surprisingly, this is what the press picked up.[5]

In her critique of the literature on women and risk, Julie Nelson (2012) cites this study as an example of "digging for difference." Like other studies of its genre, its interpretations seem to be driven by gender stereotypes and a bias toward reporting difference while ignoring the size of difference and the considerable similarity in the financial behaviors of women and men. Reviewing data from 24 published articles on gender and risk and applying a measure of similarity, Nelson concludes, "Instead of difference, similarity seems to be the more prominent pattern, with well over half of men and women 'matching up' on risk-related behaviors in every study" (2012, 23). She identifies societal pressures to conform to gender expectations and locations in the social hierarchy of power as confounding, third variables.

In the business literature, the Barber and Odean article has received a steady stream of citations, with a significant one-year jump in 2008.[6] Apparently the theme of the prudent woman also influenced academic writings that year. The studies for the most part affirm a tendency toward risk aversion for women but yield contradictory findings on whether women are more or less skilled financial managers, analysts, or accountants than men (e.g., Niederle and Vesterlund 2007; He et al. 2008; Barua et al. 2010; Kumar 2010; Nordén 2010).

A set of interdisciplinary studies cited in the press draws on neuroscience to further suggest a gender difference in financial behavior. These studies establish a relationship between levels of testosterone, risk-taking, and profits. In an experiment with female and male MBA students, researchers at the University of Chicago found that students who measured higher levels of testosterone (both in their saliva and in prenatal exposure) were less risk-averse (Sapienza et al. 2009). The researchers do not argue an essential gender difference, recognizing instead that both women and men have testosterone—although men on average tend to have more. And they find that testosterone matters most in those individuals (both women and men) with lower levels. In other words, at the low end of the scale (mostly for women), levels of testosterone were a better predictor of risk aversion than at the high end of the scale (mostly for men). Gender differences disappeared for those individuals with similar levels of testosterone. The researchers also found that levels of testosterone influenced career choice: those with high testosterone and low risk aversion were more likely to choose careers in finance.

In a similar study, researchers at Cambridge University in addition connected testosterone and risk-taking to trading profits. And they did find that testosterone mattered for men. They measured testosterone levels among 17 male city traders twice a day and found that their morning testosterone was higher on days when they made more than their average profit (Coates and Herbert 2008).[7] In other words, morning testosterone predicted earnings. But these researchers also shied away from making an argument about gender—indeed they did not have the data. Instead, John Coates, one of the researchers, interpreted the relevance of the findings for the press as follows: "If testosterone reaches physiological limits, as it might during a market bubble, it can turn risk-taking into a form of addiction. . . . At times like these, economics has to consider the physiology of investors, not just their rationality" (cited in Sunderland 2009a). What would have been considered an asset in times of casino capitalism—risk-taking—now was redefined as a danger.

It is clear that these studies probe complex connections. The research on financial behavior finds that gender has no effect on overconfidence, but has an effect on risk aversion, even if this effect may be small. The research on testosterone suggests that gender is not the key variable to explaining risk-taking or profits; instead, hormones matter, and the studies contradict each other as to whether hormones matter in males.[8] Yet, these studies were easily reduced to interpretations that men will be men and women will be women. Thus, Katty Kay and Claire Shipman claimed in the *Washington Post* (2009) that "new research says a healthy dose of estrogen may be the key not only to our fiscal recovery, but also to economic strength worldwide." They continued to assert that women "seem to be wired for collaboration, caution and long-term results." And Ken Hunt (2009) nervously asked in the *Mail and Guardian*: "Is it possible that men just aren't genetically cut out to be prudent investors? Has Darwinian programming—which has traditionally favored aggression and risk-taking—undermined the ability of males to make rational decisions when it comes to playing the market?"

None of the studies actually is about estrogen, nor have researchers connected testosterone to economic recovery. Furthermore, none of the studies makes an argument about "hardwiring" or genes. And to the extent that there are studies about evolution and risk behavior, they focus on men's status positions in groups and not on aggression (e.g., Ermer et al. 2008). But distinctions between risk-taking and risk aversion, more or less testosterone, though continuous and influenced by a range of variables in the human environment, easily map onto the fixed binary of man and woman, empty signifiers a priori, which through these associations are filled with new meaning. Interestingly, these new meanings constitute a reversal of previous associations. Where feminine risk aversion previously was interpreted as a potential drawback for a financial career, it was now celebrated as due caution. And where masculine risk-taking previously was interpreted as an asset, it became a liability in the context of the crisis.

Though seemingly new because of the reversal of values, the constructions of gender produced here evoked familiar associations of woman with succor, householding, and mending, supporting man, a doer who had erred. In associating the crisis with the presumed nature of woman and man—both their timeless difference in inclinations to risk-taking and their biological makeup—academic research contributed to creating a myth that emptied both gender and the financial crisis of history. Boys would be boys and girls would be girls eternally. Accordingly, the men in charge of finance were predestined to failure by their natures; woman, the Other, flexibly filled out her new role and by her opposing nature showed the way forward.

CODA: REDEMPTION—SAVING FINANCE CAPITALISM TOGETHER

The new construction of woman may have made her available to build a bridge to the unknown future of finance capitalism. But in a post-feminist North, woman also seemed to challenge her alterity, not content to establish a new connection to the uncertain for man and then withdraw from the stage. Instead, as announced in the story of her rise, she seemed intent to become a player in history. Woman strove to become a One, a maker and doer, a challenger to man. The myth resolved this challenge by introducing the trope of mutuality through which man finds redemption while answering to the aspirations of woman. A series of future- and policy-oriented studies completed the narrative, turning the spectre of the rise of woman into a happy end of togetherness. They demonstrated that including women was good for business, the bottom line, and thus the future of capitalism.

One often-quoted study of this type was by Roy P. Adler and Ron Conlin of Pepperdine University, who for several years starting in 2001 traced the business performance of Fortune 500 firms (Adler and Conlin 2009). They found that those firms with the best record for promoting women into management were 18 to 69 percent more profitable than the industry median, depending on whether the measure was revenue (18 percent), profit (34 percent), or equity (69 percent). A second study, conducted in 2004 study by Catalyst, similarly found that companies in the top quartile with regard to women on their management teams had financial returns 34 to 35 percent higher than companies in the lowest quartile (*The Bottom Line* 2004). McKinsey, the management consulting firm, did a similar study in Europe in 2007 and found that companies with three or more women in senior management functions scored higher on measures of organizational excellence, including, among others, leadership, accountability, motivation, and innovation. Moreover, companies with the highest level of gender diversity outperformed the average of their sector in terms of return on equity, operating result, and stock price growth (McKinsey & Company 2007).

Most researchers involved in these types of studies were cautious not to assert that women in management caused economic success, recognizing that correlation is not causation. Adler and Conlin (2009) suggest that there could be at least three explanations for the correlation between diversity and performance: First, promoting women could indeed lead to higher profitability. Second, it could be the case that firms with higher profitability feel freer to promote women. Finally, it is possible that there are third factors explaining the correlation. The authors submit that executives of successful companies may simply make smarter choices, which includes picking the best brains regardless of gender. But in making women's difference productive for the solution of the crisis, these cautions seem like pesky footnotes. The larger message of all these studies is to argue—implicitly and explicitly—the desirability of having women in business for reasons including, but not limited to, profitability.[9]

Policy-oriented studies published after the crisis explicitly added the experience of the crisis as a reason for promoting women. At the height of the crisis, Michel Ferrary, a professor at the CERAM business school, concluded from his study of French companies that those with the greatest percentage of women in management performed the best during the crisis. The fewer female managers a company had, the more its share price dropped during the crisis. For example, BNP Paribas bank, whose management team was nearly 39 percent female, weathered the crisis far better than Credit Agricole, where management was just 16 percent female (cited in Sullivan and Jordan 2009; Allen 2009).[10] The New York–based National Council for Research on Women, in a study on women in fund management, reviewed a range of research discussed earlier in this chapter and suggested, "With crisis comes opportunity," and ". . . the crisis itself compels us to ask whether we can afford NOT to tap the differing experiences, perspectives and investment styles that women bring to fund management." Specifically, "the tendency of many women investment managers to be more patient and consistent, as well as their tendency to examine more conflicting data when making investment decisions, adds a moderating effect to highly turbulent markets and may be especially significant during market downturns." Thus, the study concluded, "we must seize those opportunities and create a more stable, sustainable system—one that includes women as well as men" (National Council for Research on Women [NCRW] 2009, 12).

Ernst and Young, the accounting firm, seemed to agree. It sponsored and released a report at the 2009 World Economic Forum on "Using the Strength of Women to Rebuild the World Economy," which argued for a more equitable inclusion of women into economies worldwide, including international business. The authors suggest that "there may be no quick fix to the current financial crisis, but a sure-fire, long-term resolution [sic] is to advance more women into leadership positions and provide the right environment for new perspectives to be heard. The evidence is clear that doing this improves corporate performance—and the numbers prove it" (Ernst and Young 2009, 20). They approvingly quote Klaus Schwab, founder and executive chairman of the WEF: "Greater representation of women in senior leadership positions within governments and financial institutions is vital not only to find solutions to the current economic turmoil, but to stave off such crises in future" (Ernst and Young 2009, 2).

The NCRW and Ernst and Young reports were released with much fanfare—the latter also was introduced at "a Washington power lunch with female law makers" (Kay and Shipman 2009)—and they were eagerly picked up by the press. So was the Ferrary study, which according to the CERAM website was cited in virtually every major French newspaper and was picked up in the international media as well. The studies constituted an appeal to ring in a new era of business, including a new culture of responsibility in which women and men work together harmoniously. Nicholas Kristof (2009) explained in the *New York Times* the new consensus, as reflected in discussions at the World Economic Forum: Lehman Brothers should not have been Lehman Sisters, but it should have been Lehman Brothers and Sisters.

In their new togetherness, woman and man thus were envisioned to create more stable, more sustainable, less crisis-prone businesses. Man would no longer see woman as an object to be possessed, but as a partner who makes a needed contribution. She would moderate where he went for extremes, inject reason where he was driven by animal spirits, restrain where he was prone to excess. Valorized by the markets, by her ability to contribute to profit, she became an upgraded helpmate, entering first class to bring to it civility, no longer as a stewardess toward his destination but as a competent associate in a common endeavor. A new harmony of gender foreshadowed his redemption.

Lehman Brothers and Sisters, Years after the Crisis

morality play

We seemed to arrive at a happy ending. As finance capitalism had caused global disaster, only to be bailed out just in time, the international English-language press helped make sense of what happened by staging a morality play of fall, rise, and redemption. It found one explanation for the crisis in male predominance and arrogance in the financial sector, identified an antidote (i.e., womanly virtues), and found a happy ending in the gender diversification of the financial sector. Wall Street machismo was shamed and fell. Threatened by the rise of woman, it purportedly embraced feminine values, re-emerging chastened and perhaps reformed in a way that would lead it to consider woman more favorably.

The play enacted the seemingly constant need to match men and women in time of crisis, recreating the couple in finance in a new, but invariably heterosexual, way.[11] It differed significantly from the plot lines characteristic of Wall Street movies in the 1980s discussed by McDowell, which typically ended with the triumphal restoration of banking patriarchy. It also differed from the historical themes that de Goede identified, which employed femininity to signal temptation and wantonness. Instead, the play presented here picked up on feminist themes that apparently had begun to inform both journalists and academics and that allowed for the possibility of women's superior financial skills. Does the myth of the financially prudent woman thus augur a future of women's equality? Has patriarchal banking power been replaced with a new ideal of women's empowerment?

Barthes (1957, 213) points out that the meanings of myths are always slippery because their images are impoverished and incomplete. Thus woman reduced to prudence is no more than a caricature. It is precisely this truncated depiction that makes the myth mobile and mythical figures ready for re-signification. In the case of the financially prudent woman, one possibility would be a rewriting that maintained the gender characteristics identified and use them to justify woman's secondary status. In a commentary in *The Daily Telegraph*, Tracy Corrigan offered just such a re-signification, warning "that women's supposed gift for avoiding risk will ultimately work against them." This is what she said:

> There is something about the whole notion that I find faintly troubling— particularly, . . . the claim that there is some "essential nature" that makes women intrinsically suited to the downturn. Does that mean we're less good at managing in boom times? Or that we should be confined to certain departments at big companies—human resources, corporate communications and now risk management—but still miss out on the top jobs? And what if our failure rates turn out to be higher then [sic] the men's, simply because we've been put in charge of all the duds, like Icelandic banks?

Ally Fogg's angry intervention in *The Guardian* echoed Corrigan's assessment. In Fogg's opinion, the Lehman Sisters "nonsense" "reflects a kind of lazy, sugar-and-spice gender essentialism" that works only in the context of a patriarchal system and its social expectations toward women (Fogg 2013). Both journalists anticipated a reinterpretation of the myth, one that did not contradict its binary form but shifted its meaning.

Their skepticism was justified. On the one hand, the myth of the financially prudent woman solidified after the crisis. New findings by John Coates affirmed the link between financial behavior and hormones, including not only testosterone but also cortisol and oxytocin. Cortisol, the stress hormone, promotes feelings of anxiety that may rise during a crash. It is dampened by oxytocin, which women produce in larger quantities than men. In a crisis men thus tend toward the "fight or flight," while women tend toward each other. Coates concludes that women running trading floors would reduce the extremes of market booms and busts. The evidence helped make the issue of women's financial caution a matter of quasi-religious conviction for at least one journalist reporting the findings: "I believe promoting more women on Wall Street and in the City of London is part of the solution to the world's financial ills, helping to ensure that banks and other institutions resist the urge to pursue suicidal strategies" (Hindle 2010). Indeed, institutions outside finance and business also were being lectured now on the feminine antidote for financial loss, from the Sydney diocese of the Anglican Church to the Vatican (Jensen 2010). And Janet Yellen's appointment to head the US Federal Reserve was celebrated as a "catalyst for change" as she joined other women likely to oversee the next "Committee to Save the World": Angela Merkel, the German chancellor, and Christine Lagarde, the managing director of the International Monetary Fund (Casey 2013; Wade 2013). Margaret Thatcher could be added to this league of economic housekeepers who, like Angela Merkel, have justified austerity with the need to balance the checkbook and the household budget, fueling the persistence of the myth of the responsible woman.[12]

On the other hand, the myth of the financially prudent woman has received competition, and re-significations of woman multiplied as the crisis receded. One figure that made a comeback was woman the temptress. Thus in a reported study by Brian Knutson at Stanford, male students were shown pictures of partially clothed women and men kissing in order to activate the nucleus accumbens, the part of the brain stimulated when one eats delicious food or looks at an attractive person. In financial tests administered subsequently, the men became more likely to make high-risk gambles (Sommer 2010). Michael Lewis, celebrated author of *Liar's Poker* on the culture of Wall Street, spelled out the implications in a presentation at the London School of Economics a year earlier, arguing that the increased presence of women on Wall Street distorted the judgment of male bond traders: "They may have compelled the male risk-takers to 'show off for the ladies,' ... or perhaps they merely asked annoying questions and undermined the risk-takers' confidence" (reported in Adams 2011).

Another figure resuscitated was woman the witch. She took the form most pronouncedly of Blythe Masters, a JPMorgan Chase banker, who was vilified as the creator of credit default swaps (CDS). Described as both brilliant and duplicitous, Masters apparently convinced American International Group (AIG) to acquire a large position of CDS contracts, leading the insurer to the brink of collapse during the crisis. Bloggers called her a "wicked witch" and *Bloomberg Businessweek* "one of the destroyers of the world" (Barrett 2013). In the *Washington Post*, she joined a line-up of other women playing a role in the financial crisis, including Anastasia D. Kelly of AIG, who oversaw the company's failed risk management and control systems, and Erin Callan, chief financial officer of Lehman Brothers, who in March 2008 still assured the world that, unlike Bear Stearns, the company was not about to collapse (Weiner 2013). The witch and the temptress joined the figure of the prudent woman in a discursive contest over the meaning of femininity in the financial sector.

Myths are thus slippery, and given the status of woman as the Other par excellence, gender myths may be particularly unstable. But myths are not random; they are not just ideology. Barthes (1957, 215) proposes that we read myths as something that is, like history, both true and at the same time unreal. The myth of the financially prudent woman made visible pervasive gender discrimination in the financial sector. It put a spotlight on women who took on responsibility to improve financial governance in the aftermath of the crisis. And it questioned extreme risk-taking as the default behavior in financial dealings. What makes the myth of the financially prudent woman unreal is the deliberate assembly of selected characteristics—in this case, gender and risk aversion—to weave a seemingly coherent narrative of a new femininity related to finance. It thus narrowed the view to a miniscule slice of historical truth, which it then reworked and transported outside history. As de Beauvoir reminds us, the purpose of such myths is not to give agency to women, but to facilitate a transition, to build a bridge across the gap between man's financial aspirations and the contingency of financial realities. In the myth, woman continues to enshrine an "Eternal Feminine, unique and changeless" against the "dispersed, contingent, and multiple existences of actual women" (de Beauvoir 1989, 253).

The myth of the financially prudent woman thus both revealed and hid. It recognized the profound failure of a particular form of financial dealing and thus the need for change. It also revealed pervasive sexism and provided legitimacy to a feminist challenge. Indeed, the myth of the financially prudent woman offered justification for her aspiration to leave behind the role of the Other and become a doer. At the same time, the myth obscured. It hid "the pressures that are built into the structures of the capitalist system to produce maximum returns in the shortest possible time" (Fogg 2013). It hid the sexism in hiring and promotion practices, the predatory forms of lending that particularly hurt poor women, and the privileging of financial interests, which continues to benefit men disproportionately in regulatory practices. It hid the way in which businesses continued to be run to fit male experiences and preferences, generating pervasive inequalities. And it hid the sexism intrinsic in the micro-practices of Wall Street that amount to the creation and enactment of international financial markets in all their frenzy and ruthlessness (see Ho 2009; Fisher 2012).

Indeed, there is little evidence of chastened behavior on the part of financial institutions. The leaders of financial investment companies showed remarkably little repentance when called to testify on executive pay or their fraudulent double-dealings with collateralized debt obligations. And women are no more visible in finance than they were before the crisis. On the contrary, *Forbes* magazine reported in February 2009 that 72 percent of the 260,000 crisis-related layoffs in the financial and insurance sector were women, although women made up only 64 percent of the sector before the crash (Raghavan 2009). Women have been severely underrepresented in regulatory reform initiatives (Schuberth and Young 2011),[13] and reforms have been disappointing in their reach and ambition.

Thus, in the new world order of patriarchal finance capitalism that emerged after the crisis, women indeed may have risen, perhaps as regulators, perhaps as traders or analysts on the Street or in the City, doing their work as regulators and traders always have. The myth of prudent woman in its fickleness may have either boosted or failed these women in their endeavors. But in its tenuous relationship to truth, it provided meager guidance for their ways of being. Instead, it has proliferated an abundance of meanings fed by the notion of woman's Otherness, a new ground of contestation for these women over a truth of their own against the projections on them of man's dreams of moderation, fears of excess, and idols of profit.

NOTES

1. For the paper published in *International Political Sociology* I searched articles from November 6, 2007, to November 6, 2009. For this update I extended the search to November 6, 2013.
2. TARP stands for Trouble Asset Relief Program and was put in place in October 2008 with the purpose of buying mortgage-backed securities that had rapidly lost their value from US financial institutions.
3. The story was reported in the *Washington Post* in May 2009 and made it onto PBS's *Frontline* news magazine in fall.
4. Cited, among others, in Morrall (2008); Hunt (2009); Basch (2009).
5. Their findings were confirmed in a 2009 study of fund managers in the United States that found female managers to be more risk averse, following "less extreme and more consistent" investment styles and trading less than male managers. But the purpose of this study was not to find out whether gender explained investment styles and risk-taking; it thus did not control for other influences (such as, for example, the number of hours worked or the types of funds women and men managed). Instead, the purpose of the study was to measure fund performance by gender. Like Barber and Odean, this study found that more cautious behavior of women did not affect their performance. See Niessen and Ruenzi (2009).
6. This is the result of a search in the Business Source Premier database, using various combinations of search terms and regardless of whether the search is limited to academic articles only.
7. Also cited in Allen (2009), 2.
8. How exactly hormones matter remains an open question. Coates (2009) found that they mattered much less once he took into consideration social variables, such as experience.
9. And they rarely quote evidence that contradicts their findings, which does exist as well. For example, Adams and Ferreira (2009) found that women have an impact on the attendance record on boards and find more equity in compensation in companies with diverse boards. But they also find a negative effect of diversity on performance, suggesting that diverse boards have fewer defenses against takeovers.

More recently, Bansak et al. (2011) found that financial institutions with more women in senior management were less likely to have to accept money from the Troubled Asset Relief Program (TARP), the US government's effort to rescue faltering banks after the crisis. However, the number of women executives had no impact on the volatility of a company's stock returns.

10. The results of the study apparently did not undergo academic review and appeared only on the CERAM website.
11. Compare Wexman (1993). Thanks to Aida Hozic for alerting me to this book.
12. Thanks to Aida Hozic for pointing out the complicity of Merkel and Thatcher in reproducing the myth of the financially responsible woman.
13. Also reported in *Daily News*, February 26, 2009.

CHAPTER 3

The Global Financial Crisis's Silver Bullet

Women Leaders and "Leaning In"

JACQUI TRUE

INTRODUCTION

The aftermath of the global financial crisis (GFC) has made it pervasively clear that few women were in the drivers' seats of the global economy and that men dominated the lending institutions that contributed to the crisis. The world over, financial and economic governance institutions have drawn their leadership from one narrow demographic: white, well-educated, elite men. Senate and Select committee hearings on the GFC in the United States and the United Kingdom have revealed male domination not only at the top of the private banks and financial institutions, but also in the leadership of central banks and national regulatory and global governance organizations, and among the ranks of financial journalists and politicians scrutinizing economic decision-making (Rake 2009; Young 2013). Whether or not we take seriously the headlines that linked the crisis to male groupthink and excessive testosterone-filled trading floors (as Elisabeth Prugl discusses in, Chapter 2, this volume), the association between the financial sector's male dominance and near-system collapse demanded a response. The light shone on the finance industry's skewed leadership by gender called into question the credibility of the industry's governance and decision-making. That reversal of fortune has made women leaders the silver bullet for the global financial sector, enabling corporations and states to redress perceptions of their risky and excessive behavior while avoiding major reform of the governance of markets.

Since women's leadership was identified as a major "gap" contributing to the 2008 financial crisis, the space has opened for women leaders to lead the charge in the makeover of post-GFC capitalist institutions. Well positioned to fill the perceived leadership "gap," elite women have given the liberal capitalist makeover a personal touch—showcasing their individual success and hardships, both representing and rallying women's aspirations in capitalist political economies. These personal narratives of self-disclosure, however, are thoroughly disempowering because they reduce individual women's situations to the product of their self-denying choices. Gender power relations, not least of all the gendered structural inequalities that are built into the competitive capitalist system, are obfuscated in these accounts. The personal is emphatically *not political*; it is an economic opportunity.

Developing this argument further, this chapter examines three influential texts on women's leadership that have gained significant attention since the GFC—and thus can be seen as addressing the crisis of leadership and governance that led to the crisis.[1] These texts are the following: *The Atlantic Monthly* essay "Why Women Still Can't Have It All" (2012), by former Princeton professor cum State Department policy advisor Anne-Marie Slaughter; *Lean In: Women, Work and the Will to Lead* (2013), by Facebook chief operating officer (COO) Sheryl Sandberg; and *Wonder Women: Sex, Power, and the Quest for Perfection* (2013), by Deborah Spar, Barnard College president and former Harvard Business School professor.

One implication of the narratives in these texts is that had women been more involved in the economy and the leadership of the economy, the GFC might not have happened. Thus, women are just as blameworthy as men— and the upshot is, our political and economic institutions are off the hook.

THE WOMEN'S LEADERSHIP TURN

The turn to women's leadership as a curative is evidence of the politics of gender after the GFC. Rational arguments supported by powerful evidence link the participation of women in markets to the economic competitiveness of nations and the degree of gender balance on boards to higher investment returns (World Economic Forum 2011a; McKinsey and Company 2007; True 2013). Research has also linked the paucity of women on boards and executives (Joy et al. 2007; Deloitte 2011; Gladman and Lamb 2013) to suboptimal decision-making against the backdrop of the financial crisis.

Credit Suisse Research Institute (2012) found that firms dominated by men have recovered more slowly after the 2008 financial downturn than firms with a more balanced, male-female decision-making ratio. Expanding women's leadership, then, is the GFC's silver bullet. However, only women's leadership that is all embracing of markets is promoted—not that leadership which seeks to tether market forces. For instance, Wesley Widmaier (2015) documents how women lawyers in key US regulatory positions challenged the utilitarian positions of their male economist colleagues, but, lacking the same "transactional career sponsors" as men, they failed to secure reform of financial markets after the GFC.[2]

In the post-GFC climate, women leaders who admit to having spent most of their personal and professional lives "steering explicitly clear of any feminist agenda" (Spar 2013, 4; also Sandberg 2013) finally found an enlightened version of liberal feminism. As Judith Warner (2013) described the changed climate, "while public opinion stands firmly behind family-friendly change, politics stand in the way. With the women's leadership gap glaring before us, something has to give." Paradoxically, however, the new female "role models" for leadership, economic growth, entrepreneurship, and reform have served to diminish the focus on the new hierarchies generated by the crisis: where class inequality intersects with gendered inequality and is compounded by endemic racialized and ethnic oppression.

The abundance of a post-crisis literature on women's leadership is US-centric—emanating from the centers of financial and state power. The debates within this genre are few and far between, amounting to minor quibbles over whether "women still can or can't have it all." Stunningly clear in the slew of books on women's leadership is the remarkable consensus on the importance of women's economic activity as a major solution to both women's and societal, even global, problems (see also Chapter 7 by Juanita Elias in this volume). Ensuring global growth after the GFC is the capitalist conundrum of our time. Thus, the narratives about personal struggles and quests to bring more women into leadership shape core perceptions of and responses to the GFC. They scandalously conceal the financial institutions actually responsible for the GFC and the effects of the crisis on women *outside* the leadership class. The new genre of women's leadership above all illustrates the productive power of global capitalism to co-opt the dynamism of social movements—in this case feminism—in order to shore up the survival of the liberal capitalist system.

As we have seen in other eras, financial capitalism reinvents itself precisely by incorporating its critics. Thomas Frank (1997) argues in *The Conquest of Cool* that capitalism went through a cultural revolution in the 1960s, co-opting the rebellion of the counterculture youth movement by grafting their slogans onto consumer advertising.[3] The current penchant for women in the boardroom is indicative of a similar cultural revolution inside capitalism. With the women's leadership genre, the telling question directed at financial markets, "where are the women?" has become the basis for the creation of a new common sense about inclusive markets and women taking the reins. Feminism and capitalism share the promotion of individuality, difference, and transformation—although the accumulation and profit-generating purpose of capitalist transformation cannot be compared with the emancipatory purposes of gender transformation. However, critical feminist ideas about women's autonomy and power to bring about a social change mirror women's struggles in the corporate world amidst constant economic change.

With the turn to women's leadership interrogated in this chapter, economic power can be seen to both produce and circumscribe feminist alternatives to masculinist ways of governing. Promoting more women leaders easily fits within the ambit of increasing the pool of talent and the efficiency of labor markets, which includes the market in leaders who can govern institutions effectively. Violence against women can be addressed as a cost to business, government, and the economy, but not in terms of the conditions of gendered social and economic inequality that may cause or exacerbate this violence. Dominant masculine modes of leadership, including the drive for competitiveness, the willingness to take risks at significant costs, and the high levels of remuneration within grossly unequal pay structures are patently not up for discussion by advocates of women's leadership (see Knights and Tulberg 2014).

The movement to grow women's leadership is one response to the post-GFC crisis of legitimacy. The normalization of the global economic order in the face of its near breakdown and substantial disparities is facilitated by bringing women in and normalizing gender roles under the ambit of the heteronormative family and market (see Chapter 2 by Elisabeth Prugl and Chapter 13 by Nicola Smith in this volume). Reducing social and economic inequalities to a homogenizing gender line ("we need more women in leadership," "to close gender gaps," etc.), however, obfuscates them. Capitalism is driven to bring everyone with purchasing power into the fold, while erasing the political salience of the unequal gendered relations that position women working double days for love and for money.

Analyzing three high-impact texts on women's leadership after the financial crisis, I seek to reveal the structures and processes that these narratives cover over. First, I show how the focus on women's leadership in these texts shapes perceptions and responses to the economic crisis. In particular, that focus distracts us from addressing the structural inequalities in the political economy that position the majority of women—especially women from racial and ethnic minority and recent immigrant groups, who are disproportionately engaged in unremunerated care work—as sources of flexible and cheaper labor relative to men. Second, I illustrate how the discussion of deficits in women's leadership in these three texts reinforces a masculine approach to governing political economies associated with the financial crisis and the politics of austerity. This mode of governance rewards masculine qualities of risk-taking, competitiveness, rationality, and a work ethic in the public sphere outside the home, while devaluing feminine qualities of caring, emotion, cooperation, and a work ethic in the private, household sphere (see Wöhl 2014).

Overall, this analysis illustrates the role of economic power in enabling and constraining cultural discourses of women's leadership; and conversely, examines how women's leadership discourses shape economic power after the GFC in a productive way.

ANALYZING THE WOMEN'S LEADERSHIP MANIFESTO(S)

Since 2008 some of those lauding the potential and continued expansion of global markets have been "TED-Talks" women in the first world. They include Anne-Marie Slaughter, who points out that we need more women in positions of power but that women can't have it all and power may not be for all women; Sheryl Sandberg, who encourages women to "lean in" and corporations to bring more women into their boardrooms; and Deborah L. Spar, who exhorts women to put aside the quest for perfection and fear of failing to take on leadership roles that will improve our collective institutions. Not surprisingly, all three "TED women" are connected by less than one degree of separation.[4] Both Anne-Marie Slaughter and Deborah Spar refer in their article and book, respectively, to Sheryl Sandberg's call to women and girls to "lean in," citing her commencement address at Barnard College, at the invitation of Spar, who is Barnard's president. Sandberg claims that this address was the first time she had openly discussed the "women's leadership ambition gap." Though Sandberg does not explicitly invoke Slaughter's *Atlantic Monthly* essay, the title of chapter 9 in her book, "The Myth of Doing It All," echoes Slaughter's assertion that "women still can't have it all." Mindful of their "intertextuality" (Hansen 2006), I consider each of the women's leadership texts in turn.

Doing It All for the Walmart Women

Anne-Marie Slaughter's essay, published in *The Atlantic Monthly* in July–August 2012, "Why Women Still Can't Have It All," is the most read article in 100-plus years of the *Atlantic*. Previously an international relations/international law academic and dean of the Woodrow Wilson School at Princeton, in her essay Slaughter shares her personal discovery that women can't have it all—a demanding career and a satisfying family life—at least not at the same time. Work/family balance is a myth, in Slaughter's view, and top leadership positions come at a severe cost for family life and particularly for mothers.

Slaughter did not come to this realization until she had climbed the commanding heights to deputy-secretary level in the US State Department. Once she found that playing an active role supporting her teenage son's development was at odds with her capacity to sustain the leadership role, for the first time in her life at the age of 50, she understood what structural gender discrimination is. This is unsurprising since those in positions of privilege, women and men, are the least likely to notice structural inequality and marginalization, and the most likely to reinforce them. "When you're left out of the club, you know it. When you're in the club, you don't see what the problem is" (Shannon 2010). Given this, however, it is hard to see how women's leadership alone will improve the lot of women further down the ranks of the labor market. Yet Slaughter states that "we are the women who could be leading, and who should be equally represented in the leadership ranks."

Like Sheryl Sandberg and Deborah Spar, Slaughter believes that it is "top women" who must create the policies to benefit women, specifically policies that address the barriers and limits that women face in the workplace and in their careers. Sounding like a pitch for Hilary Clinton's US presidential campaign, she asserts, "We may need to put a woman in the White House before we are able to change the conditions of the women working in Walmart." Her key argument is thus remarkably close to her fellow women's leadership advocates. She writes further,

> The best hope for improving the lot of all women, and for closing ... a "new gender gap"—measured by well-being rather than wages—is to close the leadership gap: to elect a woman president and 50 women senators; to ensure that women are equally represented in the ranks of corporate executives and judicial leaders. Only when women wield power in sufficient numbers will we create a society that genuinely works for all women. That will be a society that works for everyone. (2012)

In her essay, Slaughter mentions the important of valuing the work of parenting and other unpaid roles, typically done by women on their own terms. She connects the absence of women in leadership positions to their work in the home: "Advanced economies don't value the work women have traditionally done, and we are stuck with the statistics on women's participation and leadership that we've had since the 1990s" (Fox 2014). This recognition of the public-private gender division of labor structuring the economy goes beyond Sandberg's dictum that men and women should equally share household and parenting roles. Slaughter (2012) recounts the speech by Lisa Jackson, the director of the US Environmental Protection Agency, at Princeton University, in which she asserted that "empowering yourself doesn't have to mean rejecting motherhood, or eliminating the nurturing or feminine aspects of who you are." She challenges masculine norms, stating that if women are ever to achieve real equality as leaders, "then we have to stop accepting male behavior and male choices as the default" and "insist on changing social policies and bending career tracks to accommodate *our* choices, too."

There is no mention of changing economic policies, so what does that "bending" mean in practice? Slaughter refers to the need for women to accept a nonlinear career "with periodic plateaus" to remain in jobs that work for their families and the need for men to recognize that "supporting families means more than earning money." In the end, her policy prescriptions only tinker with existing institutions. Though Slaughter is convinced that it is structural policy issues—rather than women's lack of commitment or not dreaming big enough (à la Sandberg)—that explain why there are so few women in leadership roles, she does not explore alternative ways of ordering political economies. She lists masculine norms—such as the notion that work should take place primarily in the office, that work should be put first over family, the fact that school schedules do not fit work schedules, and so on, but she does not fundamentally question public-private boundaries. However, her choice of a case study in women's leadership is insightful. It stands in contrast to the individuals from the finance sector discussed in Sandberg and Spar's books. Slaughter points to US Democratic senator Elizabeth Warren, a key player in the regulation of finance after the GFC, as an exemplary woman leader who has redefined the arc of a career and of success. Elizabeth Warren is most famous for her efforts to hold the federal government accountable for prosecuting the banks whose risky, self-serving behavior caused the GFC. Following the 2008 crisis, Warren served as chair of the Congressional Oversight Panel created to oversee the Troubled Asset Relief Program (TARP), and her advocacy on behalf of consumers led to the creation of the US Consumer Financial Protection Bureau.

In November 2014, Anne-Marie Slaughter told the audience at a G20-international women and leadership conference that "nothing could have prepared her for the tsunami of reaction to the article." My whole frame has changed pretty dramatically," she said. "I don't think women on their own will be able to make it unless we make broader social changes and involve men." At the many talks she has given since the article was published, Slaughter says she is aware that for every woman in the room, there are about four others who are not there. "They haven't made it and we need to concentrate on them and not the ones who have." With this concern for the excluded women, Slaughter contradicts her earlier premise in the *Atlantic* essay that prioritizing getting women into leadership roles ("the White House") will deliver the most benefits for women ("in Walmart"). Yet her understanding of the structural barriers that women confront seems only to penetrate the surface of the problem; with the fix on women's leadership, only the symptoms, not the structures, of gendered inequalities in capitalist economies are made visible.

Leading by Leaning In

In her May 2011 Barnard commencement address and the last chapter of her 2013 book, Sheryl Sandberg urges young women to put their "foot on the gas pedal" and get into the competitive game of rising to the top echelons of leadership. She signals a challenge to young women: "Lean in to your career and run the world. Because the world needs you to change it. Women all around the world are counting on you" (2013, 26). Sandberg doesn't say why the world needs to change or why women in particular are counting on that change. The context matters, however. The commencement address took place in New York City, just two and half years after the United States' US $700 billion bailout of the financial system headquartered there during the global financial crisis. Sandberg was at the time the Chief Operating Officer (COO) of Facebook, whose first public offering in 2012 of over US$100 billion was underwritten by the major investment banks that were the beneficiaries of the 2008 Emergency Economic Stabilization Act bailout.

Recounting a myriad of statistics, including the stark figure that just 4 percent of Fortune 500 CEOs are women, Sandberg is up front in *Lean In* that her focus is on the highly personal, rather than the structural forces, that hold women back. She believes they go hand in hand, but that "the personal is something that women can more readily control" (quoted in

Warner 2013)—how ironic, given the feminist adage that "the personal is political," itself a product of political and economic structures. For Sandberg, rather, the personal is emphatically "not political." Indeed, it is intentionally depoliticized. She writes, "We hear a lot about inequalities in the workplace"; however, "internal obstacles deserve a lot more attention" (2013, 9). Sandberg focuses on bending women and gender norms to fit the prerogatives of economic progress, rather than bending institutional frameworks to fit women's lives: "Conditions for all women will improve," she argues, "when there are more women in leadership roles giving strong and powerful voice to their needs and concerns" (2013, 8).

In turning to women's leadership as a solution to women's struggles, Sandberg argues that there is not just a gender gap in leadership, but a major leadership ambition gap, with women falling short. Drawing on her own experience, she observes that when a girl tries to lead, she is labeled as bossy. She acknowledges that we need to "understand the external pressures" and the gender stereotypes "that force women to play it safe and stay put," but she keeps firmly focused on the prize: "employed women reap rewards including greater financial security, more stable marriages, better health and in general increased life satisfaction" (2013, 24).

Sandberg's message is pitched at "any woman who wants to increase her chances of making it to the top of her field or pursue any goal vigorously" (2013, 10). Each chapter of *Lean In* hones in on an adjustment that women could make to improve their chances of success. These range from saying yes to career opportunities to sit at the table, not curtailing your ambition in anticipation of starting a family or holding yourself to unattainable standards, to choosing a true equal as a partner, finding a good mentor, and substituting "we" for "I" when negotiating. Sandberg doesn't claim that women are better than men at leadership. In her book she positively endorses the leadership of Goldman Sachs men in the 1990s on at least four occasions. Partner Bob Steel's breakfast or lunch only (rather than dinner, where alcohol and sexual innuendos may be involved) policy with employees is highlighted for its fairness. He apparently adopted the policy because he did not want to be perceived as taking advantage of female employees by having dinner with them (Sandberg 2013, 73). She also recalls Robert Rubin's enlightened effort to ask her, the junior woman in the room who had not spoken up, what she thought of the proposal being discussed (2013, 80–81). At no point does Sandberg mention the few women partners at Goldman Sachs. In 2013 just two of the 13 partners were female (Tyre 2013). She praises the Goldman Sachs woman who invented derivatives for the firm in the 1990s then left the firm in 2000, but skirts the role played by Goldman Sachs in the GFC (2013, 50). Yet the

US Senate Permanent Sub-Committee on Investigations inquiry into the GFC found that Goldman Sachs directly contributed to the crisis by deliberately misleading investors and setting out to depress the US mortgage market, making huge profits as it began to crash in 2007 and mid-crisis (*The Guardian* 2011). We can only surmise whether the presence of women leaders would have made any difference to the masculine mode of governing financial risk.

Rather, Sandberg cites nontraditional conceptions of leadership expressed by top women: that "the ability to learn is the most important quality a leader can have" (2013, 35) and that "leadership is about making others better as a result of your presence and making sure that impact lasts in your absence" (2013, 158). If more women in positions of power are the solution that Sandberg is championing, then one is left wondering, what is the problem? Is it that the system needs shoring up? Much is promised from the current wave of female leadership: the more of them, the more they will do for other women, presumably including those who have lost their homes and jobs as a result of the GFC. These other women that women leaders might help could also include domestic workers who lobbied for a bill of rights in California where Sandberg resides and "employs staff to keep her house, raise her children and throw her women's leadership dinners," vetoed by the governor of the state in 2012 (Grant 2013). According to Sandberg, with increased numbers of women in leadership roles in corporations and politics, there will be less pressure to conform, better work-life policies, smaller gender gaps in executive compensation, and more women in mid-level management (2013, 172). As Melissa Gira Grant (2013) wrote in the *Washington Post*, "Sandberg's understanding of leadership so perfectly internalizes the power structures of institutions created and dominated by men that it cannot conceive of women's leadership outside of those narrow spaces."

In the final chapter of *Lean In*, Sandberg quotes a male CEO friend who says "off the record," that "it's easier to talk about your sex life in public than to talk about gender [read: power]" (2013, 149–150). I would submit that it's easier to talk about individual gender issues and women leaders than it is to talk about the gendered institutions and the system of power that made the financial crisis.

Wonder Women Are Not Perfect

By contrast with Anne-Marie Slaughter and Sheryl Sandberg, the GFC is the explicit point of departure for Deborah L. Spar's book, *Wonder*

Women: Sex, Power, and the Quest for Perfection (2013). Spar is firmly on the side of bringing women leaders in to help with the post-GFC cleanup. Like Sandberg, her feminist enlightenment is recent (2013, 27). Ironically, it was the financial crisis that has opened the space for Spar and others to air their personal struggles and market their versions of female leadership. She notes that, "during the economic downturn [her words] of 2008–09, six percent of senior level women lost their jobs compared with only one percent of senior level men. Below the executive level, job losses were equal" (2013, 8). Bolstering women's leadership and empowering women are logical responses to the crisis in this telling.

In a 2009 opinion piece for the *Washington Post*, Spar observes that the "Y chromosome was particularly overrepresented at the highest levels of power and in those sectors most deeply implicated in the current crisis" (Spar 2009). In her book, she quotes Christine La Garde's maxim that "gender-dominated environments are not good . . . I honestly think that there should never be too much testosterone in one room" (Faiola and Mufson 2011, cited in Spar 2013, 191). For Spar (2009; also 2013, 193ff) the financial crisis exposed the need for women in leadership positions:

> [N]ot only because they can manage as well as men but because they manage differently than men; because they tend—over time and in the aggregate—to make different kinds of decisions and to accept and avoid different kinds of risk. We need women who will say no to bad decisions based on male-dominated rivalries and clubby golf course confidences. We need women to blow the whistle when risks explode and to challenge the presumptions that too many men, clustered too closely together and sharing a common worldview, can easily indulge. As the constant wail from Wall Street should remind us, diversity isn't just nice in theory. It makes for better business. (Spar 2009)

Spar argues that gender differences are a resource for organizations and societies and, citing behavioral psychology,[5] asserts that women leaders may be more effective than men in governing to avoid crises and their devastating consequences. She writes,

> Groups of men tend to cluster around risky behaviors and organizations run by women avoid them. . . . We see evidence of these patterns across the financial sector and other areas where the bets are large and the risks tangible. There are very few women, still, in hedge funds and venture capital and yet a disproportionately large number of women who have acted in recent years as whistleblowers calling attention to dangerous behaviors that others chose either to participate in or ignore (2013, 195).

As further testimony to this view, Spar affirms the "small but mighty group of women" who were dubbed the new sheriffs of Wall Street: Sheila Bair, Mary Schapiro and Elizabeth Warren (2013, 190) as the United States was in the midst of the financial crisis (Scherer 2010). This group might also include the disproportionately female "whistle-blowers," such as those to whom Marieke de Goede alludes in the Afterword to this volume.

At the same time, Spar is at pains to never blame men—or the economic system—for poor governance and decision-making: "None of these stories suggest that anything particularly egregious is going on. It's not as if evil men are sitting in the corner offices plotting ways to keep women from gaining more ground" (2013, 8). She gives as an example Lehmann Brothers and their 30 executives devoted solely to running inclusion and diversity programs in the firm. However, Spar argues that these programs do not work because they don't address women's gender-specific needs and issues in contemporary, highly competitive workplaces. Workplace structures need to accommodate women's differences from men for the greater benefits of the organization and to value their different perspectives, priorities, and channels (2013, 195). Whereas Anne-Marie Slaughter (2012) acknowledges that you can't have it all "with the way America's economy and society are currently structured," Deborah Spar states that "having control over your schedule is the only way women who want to have a career and a family can make it work" (2013, 198). This leads to the question of who in today's workplaces has control of their schedule. Very few women and very few countries, including the United States, have taken up or legislated the right to request flexible work.

Ultimately, Spar sees women's struggles with having both a career and a family as part of the existential condition of being female, rather than anything structural or socially constructed about "who cares for the kids" (Folbre 1994). Not dissimilarly to *Lean In, Wonder Women* is focused on self-help, and Spar strongly endorses Sandberg's "lean in" approach to women's leadership (e.g., 2013, 190). She urges women to shed their unrealistic "feminist" expectations and, instead of seeking perfection in all things, to become savvy about the inherent trade-offs in life: "Rather than trying to change the world, women are obsessed too often with perfecting themselves" (2013, 171). This personal predilection of women is apparently the root of gendered inequality, rather than masculinist institutions that thrive on risk, greed, and corruption! Women are stuck with being only 16 percent of the leaders "because so many of them are choosing to stop" (2013, 181).

And so we come full circle. Men made the crisis, but women are also blameworthy because they "leaned back." Women have unique biological attributes for leadership, but they must stop being selfish and "lean in"; if they don't, they have only themselves to blame (and definitely not men). Spar's assumption that "women's difference" is biologically rooted neutralizes her argument, expunging from it the key ingredient—the structural power of gender—which could explain why women do not lead and which has the power to transform institutions.

SCANDALOUS OBFUSCATIONS?

The narratives of Slaughter, Sandberg, and Spar hardly challenge masculinist power in organizations or structural inequalities in the global economy that represent significant institutional barriers to the desired gender diversity in corporate governance or other decision-making forums. Their rallying cries to women do not address their material situations and that of their households—or indeed the situations of vulnerability to gendered violence in which many women find themselves after the crisis and in the context of austerity budget cuts in many countries, including the United States (*Feminist Review* 2015). That is because they are largely silent on actual structural solutions to gender inequalities, such as redistributive economic policies and representative gender quotas. As critical feminist theorist Nancy Fraser (2013a, 223) argues, "[c]apitalism would much prefer to confront claims for recognition" of women's identity and difference "over claims for redistribution" of resources to the work of social reproduction. That is because capitalism's regime of accumulation on a world scale is fundamentally based on the expansion of women's waged labor and the dis-embedding of markets from democratic political regulation.

It is not just that redistributive remedies are needed, but that state responses to the GFC have further undermined that possibility, as the chapters in this book show (Chapter 5 by Daniela Tepe-Belfrage and Johnna Montgomerie for the United Kingdom, Chapter 6 by Ian Bruff and Stefanie Wöhl for Spain and Ireland, Chapter 7 by Juanita Elias for Southeast Asia, Chapter 8 by Guillermina Seri for Argentina, and Chapter 12 by Anna Agathangelou for Greece). The impact of the financial recession and austerity measures has disproportionately affected women with respect to loss of homes, unpayable debt, public sector job losses, and cuts to services. In the United Kingdom, research shows that these economic impacts have increased the risk factors for women's vulnerability to violence (unemployment, precarious work, stress, debt), especially for single mothers and refugee and ethnic minority women in the United Kingdom, while diminishing the resources for services that provided protection and enabled the prevention of gender-based domestic and sexual violence through various access points supporting women in communities (McRobie 2012).[6]

Sheryl Sandberg's book and the movement it has spurned have far-reaching implications for the restoration of capitalism and the justification of inequality after financial crisis. Sandberg has kick-started a "Lean-in" women's empowerment foundation using her dot.com start-up skills. She launched a "Ban bossy" campaign that aims to create awareness of how gender stereotyping from birth hampers women and girls' aspirations to top careers and leadership positions. In partnership with Getty, her foundation is collecting a library of images devoted to the powerful depiction of women, girls, and the people who support them that can be purchased and deployed in advertising and marketing.[7] Currently the collection features over 2,500 images of female leadership in contemporary work and life. Sandberg has also spearheaded "Lean-in" circles in business organizations, on university campuses, and in communities—a sort of twenty-first-century version of 1960s feminist consciousness-raising groups. However, this time around, "the personal is not political" so much as economic. A new neoliberal set of gender identities has been generated through GFC, as Adrienne Roberts discusses in Chapter 4 of this volume. Gender stereotypes are chided by this "lean-in" feminism as institutional barriers to efficient markets that relegate women to nurturing rather than leadership roles. Only Slaughter discusses the devaluing of feminized care work in the global economy. But she does not examine this devaluation and depletion of care and care workers in any systematic way (cf. Rai, Hoskyns, and Thomas 2014) or suggest ways of redressing the misrecognition of this work as "love's labor" or of redistributing resources to it.

In the quest to build a movement that changes the meaning of femininities in popular, work, and organizational cultures, Sandberg is promoting a form of gender consciousness that conceives gender to be a mere characteristic of individuals and individual behavior (masculine, competitive, rational, and autonomous versus feminine, caring, emotional, and relational), rather than a historically and socially constructed, structural relation. Her book, TED talk, and web platforms hardly refer to contemporary gender divisions of labor in the market and household or to masculine styles of doing business wherein human beings are conceived of inputs and costs that can be cut or trimmed. By encouraging more women to "lean in," Sandberg is effectively bringing more people into capitalism. "I believe that if more women lean in, we can change the power structure of our world and expand opportunities. . . . More female leadership will lead to fairer treatment for all women" (2013, 171). This idealistic vision distracts us from scrutinizing finance capitalist practices and institutions after the GFC and at the same time restores their integrity with an injection of female aspirations and energy.

As with Spar's book, the implicit argument of *Lean In* is that if the rewards of capitalism don't accrue to most women, this is in part their own fault, as they fail to put themselves forward. In not stepping up for the leadership challenge, women are, moreover, a brake on the economy. It's not the fault of men, the economy, or the government, stupid—it's women and our internalized gender norms that are holding back progress! Yet as Rosa Brooks (2014) points out, "in a world in which 'leaning in' at work has come to mean doing more work, more often, for longer hours, women will disproportionately drop out or be eased out." That is because most women are already laboring in the household and the community as well as in the labor market, and most don't have the financial resources of Sandberg, Slaughter, and Spar to "lean on" immigrant women, women of color, and poor women to pick up the slack (Eddo-Lodge, Hills, Penny, and Tobia 2015). None of the contributions to the women's leadership genre tells us how *these* women can "lean in." In the future, Sheryl Sandberg (2013) tells us, "there will be no female leaders. There will just be leaders" (172). One wonders, where will that leave us?

CONCLUSION

Since the global financial crisis (GFC) we have witnessed the intensification of gendered inequalities and the co-optation of feminist discourses. While capitalist crises have multiple causes and multiple deleterious consequences for many groups, the perceptions and responses to the GFC have been shaped by the turn to women's leadership. Financial crises and scandals create opportunities for contesting the normal ways of governing the global economy. However, these opportunities have been foreclosed. By the narratives of successful women leaders deflect our attention away from the need for collective institutional responses to reform the financial system and toward blameworthy individuals, most often men, but also "wonder women" leaders who, it is claimed, will restore the stability and profitability of institutions.

Popular attention to women's leadership is generating new gendered subjectivities that are empowering for some and in some ways, and that facilitate the expansion of markets. The choice to "lean in" or "lean out," however, is not an unencumbered one in capitalist societies where individuals, largely women, are responsible for the social provisioning and care of families and communities. Indeed, the choice is shaped by even greater constraints as a result of post-crisis austerity policies that have reduced further the state's responsibility for that social provisioning. Structural inequalities embedded in capitalist states, moreover, cannot be overcome with the addition of women leaders, if all they do is tinker with work-life balance policies and not with how value and power are distributed. Feminist leadership must address redistribution and recognition remedies for the gender injustice that affects women workers, their families, and entire societies. Such leadership must go beyond career advice for the promising elite. Indeed, we should be ruthlessly critical of all campaigns that call themselves "feminist," such as the books and essay discussed in this chapter, lest feminism become the handmaiden for the restoration of pre-crisis, unfettered capitalism.

NOTES

1. Similar to the scrutiny of these texts on female leadership, Prugl and True (2014) evaluate four international public-private partnership programs aimed at addressing women's economic leadership using feminist ethical criteria: Goldman Sachs's 10,000 women's entrepreneurship program, the World Economic Forum's Gender Parity program, the European Union's gender-balance in economic decision-making program, and the United Nations' women's empowerment principles program.
2. These women regulators included Bethany Born, who led the Commodity Futures Trading Commission, which held key responsibility for regulating derivatives; Sheila Bair, who led the Federal Deposit Insurance Corporation, which had significant financial resources and responsibility for closing down insolvent banks; and Elizabeth Warren, who provided the blueprint for a new agency in the Consumer Financial Protection Bureau as well as leadership in the early crisis as chair of the Troubled Asset Relief Program Congressional Oversight Panel.
3. For example, the "think young" 1960s Pepsi campaign and the 1980s "dare to be different," "think differently" Apple computer marketing campaigns (see Frank 1997).
4. The list of TED women, of TED-talk fame (or the 0.1% of women), could be added to—think of Hilary Clinton berating Wall Street in her pitch to the American working people in the race for the US presidency; of Mme. Christine Lagarde, IMF chief, and her retort to Greece as full of tax evaders; Arianna Huffington of *Huffington Post* and her book *Thrive* (2014) in the same genre, and so on—retaining the same one degree of separation.
5. Spar cites Deborah Tannen's research on women and men's communication styles; Groysberg on the differences in women and men's networks; Coates and Herbert on the association between risk-taking and higher levels of testosterone; and Niederle and Westerlund's game theoretic study of gender differences in risk-taking.
6. In many crisis-affected countries, women's loss of economic and social status, mobility, and rights to housing—are major risk factors for sexual and gender-based violence (see True 2012, chapter 7).
7. For the library of images, see http://www.gettyimages.com.au/collections/leanin.

CHAPTER 4

Finance, Financialization, and the Production of Gender

ADRIENNE ROBERTS

INTRODUCTION

This chapter seeks to document, unpack, and critique three overlapping narratives that have emerged in recent years regarding the supposed benefits of liberalized finance for gender equality. These distinct but interrelated narratives are (1) that the global financial crisis (GFC) has laid bare the reality that women's economic activity is key to saving national economies; (2) that the extension and deepening of financial markets will have the effect of eliminating gender inequality; and (3) that investing in women is profitable for a range of private companies, including banks and investment firms. While the "business case" for gender underpinning these three narratives is not new in itself, the GFC has given new impetus to calls for the necessity of investing in women in order to increase their participation in labor markets and to improve their ability to consume goods and services, including financial services, in the interest of economic growth globally.

These three narratives have been perpetuated by a number of different actors, including some of largest regional and international development institutions (such as the World Bank), certain state agencies (especially development agencies), a number of transnational corporations (including several large banks and investment and accounting firms—many of which were implicated in bringing about the GFC), intergovernmental bodies (including the United Nations and the OECD), and several nongovernmental organizations. While I have more fully documented this growing coalition of what I have called "transnational business feminism" (TBF) elsewhere (Roberts 2012, 2014), in this chapter, my aim is to draw attention to three distinct yet overlapping narratives that appear in a range of their documents, policy initiatives, and programs. The purpose of doing so is not to suggest that there is a coherent, pervasive, and top-down set of discourses and practices, but rather to document, unpack, and critique some of the dominant common themes that have emerged regarding the commensurability of gender equality and "financialization" post-GFC. Though I will more fully explain what is meant by "financialization" at a later point, it essentially refers to a set of processes that have created the conditions under which financial relations have become (1) increasingly important as means of accumulation for financial and more traditional firms, and (2) increasingly central to people's daily existence.

The *first* narrative, which will be referred to here as the "women as saviors" narrative, asserts that the greater integration of women, particularly women from the Global South and so-called emerging market economies, into formal financial and labor markets will help to alleviate poverty, to sustain communities, and to stimulate stagnating national economies in the wake of the GFC. Building on arguments developed by a number of contributors to this volume (e.g., Prügl 2012; Elias 2013; Griffin 2013a; Prügl and True 2014), I outline the ways in which this narrative engages in *scandalous gendering* by positioning women *qua* women as uniquely qualified to assess and manage financial risk, while systematically ignoring the extent to which the extension and deepening of global finance have perpetuated inequalities at the intersections of gender, class, race, and nationality. Gender is also deployed here as a means of saving, rather than challenging, neoliberal finance-led capitalism.

The *second* "technocratic equality" narrative argues that new financial technologies have helped to eliminate gender-based discrimination in financial and credit markets by standardizing risk assessment models and ultimately removing the physical markers of gender, race, and class that may cause discrimination. I argue that in so doing, this narrative performs a *scandalous obfuscation*, which erases gendered and racialized bodies as constitutive of the social relations of finance. That is, the treatment of finance as an objective tool that is used to allocate assets and liabilities across time and space erases the embodied and socially embedded relations that undergird finance. This removes from view various forms of discrimination based on the social organization of difference, that is, sexism, racism, and a host of other "isms" that mainstream discourses understand to be separate from and ultimately antithetical to the rational operation of markets.

The *third* overlapping narrative is the "womenomics" narrative, which emphasizes the profits, or "gender dividend," that can be made by promoting women to the highest ranks of banks and investment firms. I argue that one of the problems with this narrative is that it *scandalizes reimaginings* of approaches to gender equality that do not conform to the dominant model that has been formulated by corporations and which privileges economic empowerment through labor and financial market integration. Before moving on to elaborate on each of these narratives, this chapter begins with an explanation of the feminist historical materialist perspective that underlies this work.

THEORIZING GENDER, FINANCE, AND FINANCIALIZATION
The Inseparability of Power, Production, and Social Reproduction

One problem with the three narratives noted in the previous section is their framing of the extension and deepening of finance as a natural and inevitable outcome of technological progress that is largely de-linked from broader relations of power and production. They also rely on a modernizationist approach to development whereby it is assumed that the extension and deepening of finance will ultimately integrate the "excluded" into a more sophisticated sphere of political and economic development. A third limitation of these approaches is that they tend to see structures of gender as operating alongside markets, rather than being an integral part of these historically specific social relations.

In contrast, the feminist historical materialist perspective underlying this chapter understands the extension and deepening of finance, the interlinked discourses/practices of development, and gender relations to be firmly located within historically constituted social relations of power, production, and social reproduction (Bakker and Gill 2003). That is, rather than seeing the growth and deepening of finance as a natural and inevitable outcome of human "progress," from a historical materialist perspective, different forms of production emerge as dominant in different historical moments. These forms of production do not emerge naturally, or even as the inevitable result of technological change, but rather are connected to historically specific configurations of power relations (2003, 26). Thus, for instance, the dominant form of production, or what we might think of as power–production, in any particular historical period is deeply shaped by the form of the state, by the structures of ownership and control that are in place (i.e., legal regulations protecting private property), and relations between labor and capital.

As Bakker and Gill explain, a feminist historical materialist analysis draws attention to the ways in which forms of power–production are also fundamentally mediated by structures of gender inequality, along with structures of racialization and sexuality (2003, 26). To put it differently, rather than seeing relations of production and gender relations as separate, from a feminist historical materialist perspective, power-production relations operate *through* structural hierarchies of class, gender, race, sexuality, and so on. In terms of finance-based relations of production and accumulation, the crucial point to stress is that finance is not a gender-neutral technical or pseudo-scientific tool or technique that is used in the allocation of assets and liabilities across time and space. Rather, finance is deeply bound up with structures of gender. These intersections include the gendered underpinnings of financial modelling (i.e., the privileging of the "rational" and "utility-maximizing" individual, who is implicitly male [England 1993; Benería 2003]), gender-based inequalities in wealth and asset ownership (which may be reproduced by regressive tax systems [Deere and Doss 2006; Deere, Alvarado, and Twyman 2010; Montgomerie and Young 2010; Roberts 2013]), the rewarding of certain masculinized forms of behavior (such as aggressiveness and risk-taking) in the field of finance (McDowell 1997; De Goede 2005), and the positioning of men in the majority of top positions in the institutions of global financial governance (Schuberth and Young 2011).

In addition to understanding power–production as intersecting with structures of gender, feminist historical materialism understands power–production to be inseparable from relations of social reproduction. In one oft-cited definition, Cindi Katz describes social reproduction as "the fleshy, messy, and indeterminate stuff of everyday life" (2001, 711). In her important work on the topic, Isabella Bakker has explained that markets cannot function without the underlying work of social reproduction, which includes the work associated with (a) biological reproduction (including social constructions of motherhood); (b) the reproduction, socialization, and education of the labor force; and (c) the reproduction and provisioning of care (Bakker 2007, 541; see also Katz 2001; Bakker 2003; Bezanson and Luxton 2006).

Gender and "Financialization"

Recent critical scholarship within the field of international political economy (IPE) has further sought to locate the growing importance of finance within the broader power relations that constitute "financialization." Though this term is heavily debated in the literature (Epstein 2005; Krippner 2011; Lapavitsas 2013), it is generally meant to capture a social transformation over the past several decades whereby more and more profits have been accrued through financial channels than through the sorts of activities that are traditionally associated with production (i.e., manufacturing). While some writers emphasize the *dominance* of finance over other forms of industry, historical materialists tend to warn against overemphasizing the separation between finance and industry, not least because finance (or interest-bearing capital) extends *across* a range of institutional structures (including firms, governments, and households) (Fine 2010). A further dimension of financialization has entailed the greater integration of individuals and households into financial markets, as banks have sought new means of generating profits, which have been lost, in part, as firms have been able to move away from their reliance on banks by raising capital directly on the open market (Dos Santos 2009; Lapavitsas 2011). This then leads to a form of "financial expropriation" as greater proportions of workers' earnings are dedicated to paying interest (Bryan, Martin, and Rafferty 2009; see also Lapavitsas 2014).

From a feminist historical materialist perspective, therefore, the interconnected discourses and practices that seek to link financial deepening—by which I mean the extension of finance and its penetration into more and more spaces of daily life—to gender equality have not emerged naturally, but rather are part of a broader set of social transformations that have strengthened the power of finance over labor. This does not affect all workers equally, but rather, as the following examples will show, women, along with the global poor (a majority of whom *are* women) and certain racialized minorities, have increasingly been identified as potentially lucrative consumers, borrowers, and users of financial services. This is partly because of women's greater integration in the paid labor force and their growing consumer power, but also because of shifts taking place in social reproduction that have linked these relations to finance as well. Housing, for instance, has been linked to finance through the privatization and securitization of mortgages, while forms of consumption have been linked to financial markets as more and more people use credit cards to pay for food and other basic necessities. Education, which is also a key component of social reproduction, has been financialized through the student loan industry, while security in old age is now increasingly met through pension plans that invest heavily in financial markets. These examples all point to an important transformation in the sphere of social reproduction, which has been structurally linked to the broader processes of financialization noted earlier.

The perspective of feminist historical materialism, then, allows us to locate the emerging discourses and practices seeking to integrate greater numbers of women into financial relations within broader structural transformations taking place in the power–production–social reproduction nexus. Women are key to the expansion and deepening of finance, not simply because of their potential as a new (so-called untapped) workforce or consumer force, but also because of their location at the intersection of production and social reproduction.

THREE SCANDALOUS NARRATIVES OF GENDER EQUALITY AND FINANCE

Scandalous Gendering

The first narrative that has become increasingly salient in recent years is based on the idea that women *qua women* constitute good investments. Extending women access to finance, it is argued, will help integrate them into the economy as consumers and workers, particularly as entrepreneurs. This will ultimately have the effect not just of empowering women, but also of stimulating stagnating national economies in the wake of the financial crisis, especially in the Global South, where women's labor remains a vast "untapped resource."[1] This view is exemplified by World Bank president Robert Zoellick, who argued in 2010 that a "host of studies suggest that putting earning in women's hands is the intelligent thing to do to aid recovery and long-term development."[2]

Echoing this sentiment at an Asia-Pacific Economic Cooperation (APEC) High-Level Policy Dialogue on Women and the Economy, then Secretary of State Hillary Clinton suggested that "[t]o achieve the economic expansion we all seek—we need to unlock a vital source of growth that can power our economies in the decades to come. That vital source of growth is women" (Clinton 2011, 2). Applauding the noble cause of advancing rights for women and women's equality, Clinton claimed that the goal of the summit was much bolder: "to grow our economies and ensure shared prosperity for all nations and all people" (2011, 2).[3] This view supports a longer interest within APEC in promoting gender issues and gender equality in the name of economic development (for a more detailed history, see True 2008a, 2008b). This interest culminated in 2011 with the creation of the APEC Policy Partnership on Women and the Economy (PPWE), a public-private entity dedicated to streamlining gender within the organization. At their

2012 annual meeting, the four policy areas identified as key to improving women's economic participation were (1) access to capital; (2) access to markets; (3) capacity and skills building; and (4) women's leadership.

As Juantia Elias (2013) has further documented, the World Economic Forum (WEF) has been important in advancing the "women as saviors" agenda through their Global Gender Gap Reports and other means. The WEF (which is a private, business-led international organization) claims to have found a "strong correlation between a country's gender gap and its national competitiveness," meaning that those countries with the smallest gender gaps (in the areas of political and economic participation, health, and education) are also the most competitive countries globally.[4] Drawing extensively on literature published by private banking, investment, and accounting firms, the WEF maintains, therefore, that women will be key to economic recovery, particularly in Brazil, Russia, India, and China, otherwise known as the BRIC economies (2013, 162).

In some respects, the growing attention given to gender equality at the level of global economic governance reflects the success of decades of feminist scholarship and activism emphasizing the contributions of women to economic development and the well-being of people and communities. Further, the policy areas identified by APEC, the WEF, and others do correctly identify some of the major barriers to women's economic empowerment. However, the "women as saviors" discourse and the policies that this underpins are also based on a "scandalous gendering" that deploys gender in essentialist ways and fails to account for the intersections of gender with hierarchies based on class, race, sexuality, nationality, and so on. Gender is also deployed here as a means of *saving*, rather than *challenging*, neoliberal finance-led capitalism.

In contrast to the "technocratic equality" narrative that will be outlined in the following section, which erases the body from the social relations of finance, the "women as saviors" narrative draws on women's biological and socially and historically constructed positions as mothers and nurturers, which is precisely what makes them ideal workers and consumers (Chant and Sweetman 2012). This latter line of argument is mainly used in reference to women in the Global South and emerging markets, producing them as what Himani Banerji has called "people of the body" (cited in McNally 2001, 4). Just as Marx and subsequent Marxists have emphasized capitalism's tendencies toward equalization and differentiation, so too might we point to the simultaneous operation of equalization and differentiation of gender that has taken place through financialization and has been naturalized in the narratives outlined here. In terms of the former, financialization has drawn more and more women (and certain aspects of social reproduction) into global markets and therefore into its tendencies toward abstraction. Yet, at the same time, the processes of *differentiation* work to produce women as distinct financial subjects from men and to differentiate women in different parts of the world through the contradictory erasure and reinscription of the body.

It is important to note that the focus on gender "gaps," which refers to differences *between men and women* (as imagined homogenous groups), has come about at a time when, in many places, these gaps are narrowing compared to gaps *among women* (i.e., along class, racial, and other lines) and *among men.* The WEF's Global Gender Gap Index offers the most obvious example of this trend. The purpose of the index is to identify the gap between men and women in the areas of (1) economic participation and opportunity, (2) educational attainment, (3) health and survival, and (4) political empowerment. These gaps are then mapped onto the WEF's Global Competitiveness Report and various measurements of gross domestic product (GDP). According to the WEF, this method supports the finding that

[a] country's competitiveness depends on its human talent—the skills, education and productivity of its workforce. Because women account for one-half of a country's potential talent base, a nation's competitiveness in the long term depends significantly on whether and how it educates and utilizes its women. (WEF 2013, 36)

The index is explicitly directed at measuring gender *gaps* rather than *women's empowerment,* which is presumably more difficult to measure and would require the WEF to move beyond its exclusive focus on "outputs" (WEF 2013, 3).[5]

The WEF does not offer a clear explanation of this move. Rather, it simply asserts that "[o]ur aim is to focus on whether the gap between women and men in the chosen indicators has declined, rather than whether women are 'winning' the 'battle of the sexes'" (WEF 2013, 4). While there is much in this statement that begs further explanation, within the context of the report, the point is to suggest that the focus is exclusively on *gaps,* and that once these gaps have been closed, the index does not go on to measure those areas where women have achieved more than men. As such, the index does not capture the closing of gaps as the result of falls in the political, economic, and social attainments of men and boys. Nor does it capture the extent to which gaps are growing between rich and poor women, between rich and poor men, between rural and urban areas, and between high- and low-income countries. This omission is important, as there is considerable evidence to suggest that these dynamics are indeed at work and that they complicate the gender gap narrative.

For instance, while the gap between male and female participation in the labor force has been declining globally since 1990, this has largely been due to a worldwide fall in male labor force participation rates (Elborgh-Woytek et al. 2013, 6).[6] At the same time, according to the Organisation for Economic Co-operation and Development (OECD), between 1985 and 2005, earnings inequalities in high-income countries increased *among* women (by 11 percent) and *among* men (by 10 percent), while the gender pay has marginally declined overall. In other words, the gender pay gap has declined slightly (though it remains significant) because class inequalities have widened (Perrons 2012, 214). In many of the advanced capitalist countries, the gender pay gap is the widest in high-income professions, which includes many jobs in banking and finance, while the smallest gap is in the lower paid professions.[7]

At the same time, in the wake of the GFC, the "women as saviors" narrative is helping to legitimize, albeit in historically specific ways, the argument long held by neoliberal approaches to development that the liberalization of trade and finance will ultimately bring the "excluded" into a more sophisticated sphere of political and economic development. This does not imply the retreat of the state, but rather (and in contrast to earlier articulations of the neoliberal Washington Consensus) the state is seen as playing a key role in supporting transnational public-private partnerships for gender equality and development (Prügl and True 2014), not to mention in sustaining processes of financialization through the injection of huge amounts of public money into the financial and banking sector from 2008 onward.[8] However, the focus on "inclusion" fails to account for the ways in which neoliberal-led development has at best perpetuated and at worst increased levels of informal employment globally (Jütting and de Laiglesia 2009; ILO 2013). While it is notoriously difficult to measure informal employment, recent attempts by the ILO to capture these trends show that the number of people employed in domestic work worldwide, much of which is informal (and 83 percent of which is performed by women), has grown from 33.2 million in 1995 to 52.6 million in 2010. These are very conservative estimates and do not count the estimated 7.4 million children under the age of 15 employed in domestic work (ILO 2013, 42). The global economic crisis was also projected to increase informal labor among women in the short term as they moved into the informal sector in order to try to protect household income (Braunstein and Heintz 2008; ILO 2011), as well as women's reliance on credit (both formal and informal) in order to finance consumption, buy food, and otherwise meet the costs of social reproduction (Elson 2010).

Scandalous Obfuscations

The second narrative that reappears in a significant amount of the literature produced by private banks, investors, and financiers (as well as some of the business press), assumes that the deepening of liberalized finance will automatically eliminate gender inequality through technological developments that will ultimately erase the human body, and with it, the possibilities of discrimination. As Alec Morley, senior vice president of small business banking at one of Canada's "Big Five" banks explains, the decision about whether or not to extend a loan is no longer made on the basis of personal opinion. "What has happened," he said, "is that we have moved to a very standardized risk model, like a grid, where you look at a standard set of factors like credit rating, debt service coverage, and the value of any security a borrower is providing." This means that ultimately, "the human element has been removed and, along with that, the risk for gender bias has been removed" (Johne 2011). Or, as Jacoline Loewen, a Toronto-based financier, writer, and business school lecturer has put it, "[m]ost finance people see numbers, not gender, and if you have a fundamentally good business and you know how to make money for an investor, then you will get money (quoted in Johne 2011)." From a feminist historical materialist perspective, what this means is that the structural dimensions of gender that shape the economy have effectively been removed from view.

Anna Nikolayevsky, the founder and chief investment officer of Axel Capital (a New York–based hedge fund), makes a similar argument to financiers in a report published by the National Council for Research on Women (NCRW) advocating an increase of women in hedge fund management. Nikolayevsky explains that while women may currently be underrepresented in this field, this gender difference will naturally decrease over time as capital, which is implicitly disassociated from power and gender relations, will automatically be directed toward those (abstract) investors who generate the highest returns: "over the long term, capital is gender blind and will be allocated according to merit" (NCRW 2009, 24). The NCRW report also cites a statement made by Gena Lovett (partner and director of operations of Alexandra Investment Management) at an event aimed at improving the status of minority groups in finance: "The only color we're interested in is the color green" (2009, 24).

In a recent article analyzing books (published in the United States between 2002 and 2011) that offer investment advice for women, Micky Lee (2014) identifies a similar appeal to the neutrality of markets:

"gender is not a factor on any level in mastering the nuts and bolts of smart financial management" (Orman 2007, 1); "the basic principles of investing are the same, no matter what your gender or station in life" (Morris and Morris 2003, 6); "whether stocks, bonds, or real estate, investments do not care if it is a man or a woman" (Kiyosaki 2006, 7); "money is gender-neutral" (Bodnar 2006, 1); "discrimination in financial matters is not the barrier it once was. 'Green is green'" (Bridgforth and Perry-Mason 2003, xxv). (2014, 6–7)

These books offer contradictory advice, encouraging women to use their supposedly unique talents as sensible investors, well trained in the basics of home economics. Yet, of particular interest here is the appeal to a neoclassical vision of the market as objective and neutral, no longer constrained by the "irrational" barrier of gender discrimination.

While these are only a select few examples, the logic underpinning them will be familiar to many. The argument is that the financial subject, as an embodied gendered individual, has been erased as the result of new technologies, and has been replaced with an abstract financial subject. The growth of credit-rating agencies and risk-assessment models, along with the development of securitization processes (which have helped to establish a globally agreed-upon threshold of risk and therefore reduced subjective assessments based on non-market factors), are key to these developments, helping to develop supposedly more efficient, accurate, and non-discriminatory means of assessing one's credit worthiness (Leyshon and Thrift 1999, 441–444; Dymski 2009, 160). Implicit in the examples detailed by Lee, the new tools available to individual investors, which allow them to bypass banks and financial advisors, linking them directly to financial markets, also ostensibly feed into the broader elimination of gender difference.

Proponents of these new technological developments—which include governments and nongovernmental agencies—point to the benefits of the replacement of potentially biased individual assessments with supposedly objective mathematical formulas. This also makes sense from a neoclassical economic perspective since biases represent "non-economically motivated" choices that may not be in the best interest of lenders (Becker 1957)— though this says little about the interests of particular groups to profit from structures of inequality. While this argument reflects technological innovations that are used much more readily in the advanced industrialized counties, it also underpins arguments made by the World Bank and others in favor of the need to further liberalize finance in the Global South and to open up banking sectors to greater competition, which will render the costs of discrimination unbearable (Muravyev, Talavera, and Schäfer 2009).

However, the technocratic equality narrative produces what the editors of this collection label "a scandalous obfuscation" in the sense that it masks the historical roots, systemic causes, and the bifurcated effects of financial deepening. In terms of the former, the extension and deepening of finance are naturalized and depoliticized, and the integration of women into financial markets is presented as the natural and inevitable outcome of technological development. This ignores, among other things, the history of social struggles that have taken place over access to finance and credit, which, prior to the late 1980s, saw this as a social good that needed to be addressed through community action and state intervention in markets, rather than as something best assured through liberalized financial markets (Austin 2004; Rankin 2013). Rather, efforts to address these problems through the extension and deepening of finance, which are crucially supported by states (Soederberg 2014), need to be understood within the broader context of financialization outlined earlier.

At the same time, the technocratic equality trope obfuscates the extent to which financial markets, as with other markets, are not abstract and technical coordinating mechanisms but rather are relations of power that are constituted in and operate through the social relations of gender. While certain interests have profited immensely from the proliferation of finance, others have experienced particularly appalling forms of financial expropriation. Subprime mortgage lending in the United States offers a vivid example in this regard, as the large profits made by lenders (who had generated an estimated $100 billion in annual revenues by the mid-2000s) and investors (i.e., in mortgage-backed securities) were based on the dispossession of women, racialized minorities, and the lower classes more generally.[9] Women are overrepresented among those who lost their homes to foreclosure, as well as among those who lost home equity in the collapse of housing prices (Ginty 2010; Roberts 2013). More broadly, it has been found that women are targeted for some of the most aggressive debt collection practices, as they are perceived to be more likely to submit to aggressive tactics than men, not least because they have less savings, fear losing assets in a drawn-out legal battle, and tend to be less geographically mobile due to their roles as carers (Stringer 2000, 8; Goldberg 2006, 737).

From a feminist economics perspective, as Irene van Staveren explains, gender may also be factored into what economists call "transaction costs," reproducing gender-based "distortions" in financial markets (see Table 4.1). These, combined with gender-based inequalities in production and social

Table 4.1. GENDER-BASED DISTORTIONS IN FINANCIAL MARKETS

Type of Gender-Based Distortion	Transaction Costs for Credit Institution	Transaction Costs for Female Borrowers
Information constraint	Women are perceived as risky, not creditworthy enough; information gathering might go though an intermediary (husband).	Women have lower literacy rates and are less mobile, which results in low access to financial market information.
Negotiation constraint	Women have less experience in taking formal credit, which requires more time from bank personnel.	Women may need husband's permission; have higher opportunity costs to travel to a bank; women may face discriminatory attitude by bank personnel.
Monitoring constraint	Women's economic activities may be more difficult to monitor since they are often in different and smaller scale sectors than men's activities that are financed through credit.	Women may find it difficult to control their loans in the household when other family members (particularly men) find it in their right to exercise control over this money.
Enforcement constraint	Women often lack formal property rights, which makes it difficult for creditors to claim a collateral when a loan is not repaid.	Women may be more susceptible to pressure, intimidation, or violence from creditors of their agents; women may lose control over their loans in the household while still being responsible for repayment.

Source: van Staveren (2011, 27, adapted from S. Baden 1996).

reproduction that condition women's lower levels of earnings and savings compared to men, have important and ongoing implications for women's integration into financial markets.

As these examples suggest, financial markets are far from neutral spheres of activity where bodies marked by gender and race cease to matter. It is only by retaining a neoclassical view of markets, which separates the supposed automatic functioning of markets from gender and other social relations, that one can maintain that gender inequality will automatically be eliminated through the spread of new computing and informational technologies. In contrast, a critical feminist approach reveals a much more complex picture, as financial deepening has drawn upon and rearticulated gender difference and inequality in new ways, while this difference has been obfuscated through a discourse of technocratic equality.

The third overlapping narrative of "womenomics" has been perpetuated by a growing number of financial and accounting firms in recent years. One of the first uses of the term "womenomics" was in an investment report that Kathy Matsui produced for Goldman Sachs in 1999. Matsui and her team, who were looking at the prospects for growth in Japan, argued that the women who were entering the workforce in growing numbers (out of both necessity and choice) were also becoming an important source of income and consumption growth. In the context of Japan's demographic problems, it was believed that women were key to offsetting the negative impact of a shrinking labor pool on income and demand growth over the long term (Goldman Sachs 2005, 1). Womenomics, then, was about figuring out the economic implications of this shift and identifying those companies that were most likely to benefit from this trend. Goldman Sachs has subsequently published a series of additional forecasts based on the womenomics approach and has used it as the basis of a philanthropic initiative, *10,000 Women*, which is linked to a number of global initiatives that include participation from the likes of the World Bank, a number of OECD governments, various NGOs, and others (Goldman Sachs 2009, 2010; cf. Roberts and Soederberg 2012).

A related line of argument has been popularized by the financial consulting firm Deloitte, which released a report entitled *The Gender Dividend: Making the Business Case for Investing in Women* in 2011. The "gender dividend" emphasizes the "steady benefit that is earned by making wise, balanced investments in developing women as workers and potential leaders as well as understanding women as consumers and their impact on the economy and the bottom line" (Pellegrino, D'Amato, and Weisberg 2011, 4). As Anne Weisberg, Deloitte's own "director of talent" explains, companies must be driven by "talent," and under-utilizing or ignoring women decreases a firm's potential competitive advantage. This has some resonance with the "technocratic equality narrative," as the focus is not on women per se, but rather on non-discrimination and diversity in decision-making. At the same time, female employees are key to better understanding the growing power of women as consumers. "The bottom line—and that is what this is all about—is that there is a Gender Dividend to be reaped by any company or country that invests in women" (Weisberg 2011).

While the focus of firms like Goldman Sachs and Deloitte on the private profit to be reaped from gender equality may seem unsurprising, in 2011 the newly formed UN Women released its own report entitled *The Gender Dividend*, which argues that countries fundamentally operate like businesses and that the economic, legal, and cultural barriers to women's participation in the economic and political spheres ultimately harm national competitiveness. The report cites the same handful of sources as many of the private sector reports, though it does diverge from the latter in emphasizing gender equality as an important goal in itself. Yet, in stressing the need to "liberate the world's greatest untapped development resource" (UN Women 2011, 5), the report also essentializes and commodifies women.

Overlapping with womenomics and the gender dividend is a third emerging framework of "gender lens investing," which claims to bring the thesis about the moral imperative to support women together with the thesis that investment in these types of companies realizes good returns. Among the leaders of this self-proclaimed new "movement" is the Women Effect Investment team at the Criterion Institute, which is trying to build the field of gender lens investing in order to create "durable and systemic change for women worldwide—both as investors and beneficiaries of invested capital."[10] For this team of investors, the "gender lens" is meant to identify three types of investments: those that increase access to capital for women entrepreneurs and have women in leading positions; those that promote gender equity in the workplace and across the supply chain; and those that increase the number of products and services that benefit women and girls (i.e., socially responsible businesses).[11]

While "womenomics," "gender dividend," and "gender lens investing" ostensibly sound like feminist concepts, they differ sharply from those forms of critical feminism that go beyond an "add-women-and-stir" approach to question the various power relations that constitute contemporary world order and to problematize the ways in which the reproduction of a liberalized financial regime privileges white, male, elite interests. It is not unimportant that some of the firms most vociferously advocating the new gender agenda are also among those implicated in bringing about the GFC, which has been well documented to have led to a number of setbacks for gender equality. Nor is it unimportant that these firms have come to take on roles as "expert" producers of knowledge about gender, which is firmly rooted in strategies of profit maximization.

The danger is that as financial and consulting firms increasingly come to set the terms of the gender equality agenda, they will also serve to "scandalize reimaginings" of alternative means of improving gender equality outside liberalized financial markets, in addition to performing some of the scandalous obfuscations and genderings noted earlier. As Dauvergne and LeBaron argue, "[t]aking a business approach to philanthropy allows capitalists to invest in societal development without foregoing profits" (2014, 42) and creates a platform from which they can continue to resist forms of regulation on the basis that they are already engaged in "giving back" to the global community. The fact that these initiatives are voluntary, do nothing to challenge the dominance of corporate power, and often end up reproducing power imbalances—including those between large financial firms and local communities and grassroots organizations, between the Global North and South, between the rich and the poor, and between women and men—are largely overlooked.

The preceding analysis begs the questions of what an alternative approach to gender equality might look like. Without trying to offer a 10-step prescription about how to change the world, one might begin with suggesting the need to create a global framework, underpinned by strong enforcement mechanisms, to mandate that *all* corporations promote gender equality in the workplace and across the supply chain. This should be a concern not only of individual or institutional investors, but also for the global community more broadly. At the same time, there should be a global financial transaction tax that directly transfers money from wealthy investors and financiers to those most negatively affected by short-term financial flows. Projects aimed at increasing women's individual access to credit should be supplemented with projects aimed at supporting forms of women's collective action to promote access and rights to resources, even where this may be difficult to measure.

Rather than working within a framework that focuses on bringing about change within a capitalist system that remains more or less unchanged, which fails to challenge many of the power relations that intersect and overlap with those of gender, a much more effective approach would involve some consideration of alternatives that already exist, as well as those that can be brought about through future collective action. In one recent book on alternatives to capitalism, Chris Rogers (2014) explains that alternatives can take three different forms:

1. *Alternative capitalisms* that involve the re-regulation of forms of capitalism in favor of producing optimal social and economic outcomes (and which may capture some of the projects noted earlier).
2. *Alternatives to capitalism* that place social and civil goods *above* the goal of pecuniary gain and that emphasize collective or community property rights rather than private property rights.
3. *Anti-capitalism*, which involves various forms of resistance, including resistance via attempts to influence the state, to take control away from the state or to act independently outside the state.

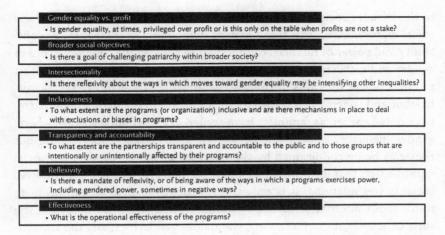

Gender equality vs. profit
• Is gender equality, at times, privileged over profit or is this only on the table when profits are not a stake?

Broader social objectives
• Is there a goal of challenging patriarchy within broader society?

Intersectionality
• Is there reflexivity about the ways in which moves toward gender equality may be intensifying other inequalities?

Inclusiveness
• To what extent are the programs (or organization) inclusive and are there mechanisms in place to deal with exclusions or biases in programs?

Transparency and accountability
• To what extent are the partnerships transparent and accountable to the public and to those groups that are intentionally or unintentionally affected by their programs?

Reflexivity
• Is there a mandate of reflexivity, or of being aware of the ways in which a programs exercises power, including gendered power, sometimes in negative ways?

Effectiveness
• What is the operational effectiveness of the programs?

Figure 4.1 Feminist criteria for evaluating alternatives to capitalism and anti-capitalism.

While alternatives to capitalism and anti-capitalism are best poised to address the critiques noted earlier, they should be understood as processes rather as pre-set ideals and pre-defined struggles toward some clearly defined utopia. At the same time, it is important to identify and articulate the feminist criteria upon which we might evaluate alternatives to capitalism and anti-capitalism, as well as a criteria that can be applied to those public-private partnerships (PPPs) (and individual investment funds) that claim to be working toward eliminating gender inequality.

Lisa Prügl and Jacqui True (2014) have made an important intervention here, developing a criteria for PPPs based on (1) inclusiveness and mechanisms to deal with exclusions or biases in programs; (2) public transparency and accountability; (3) reflexivity; and (4) operational effectiveness.[12] The criteria that feminists have developed for evaluating the gender-responsiveness of civil society organizations and the partners with whom they engage are also useful here (Motta et al. 2011). Taken together, useful criteria might include those noted in Figure 4.1.

CONCLUSION

The purpose of this chapter has been to suggest that recent years have witnessed a growing preoccupation on the part of a number of public and private institutions with the promotion of greater access to credit and financial services as a means of addressing global gender inequality. However, when viewed from a critical feminist perspective and in relation to the broader social processes of the financialization (of production *and* social reproduction), this trend may be doing more to increase the profitability and power of financial capital than to address the complex issues of gender and racialized inequality, which must be seen in relation to a host of other power relations, including the growing power of capital relative to labor and widening class disparities. Contrary to the mainstream narratives noted earlier, as feminists have argued in this volume and elsewhere, gender inequality should not be viewed as a market imperfection, but rather as being conditioned by the relations of power–production–social reproduction that also constitute financial markets, which are themselves social power relations. It is only through doing so that we can begin to think about alternative forms of feminist praxis that move beyond the sorts of scandalous obfuscations, scandalous genderings, and the scandalizing of reimaginings outlined here.

NOTES

1. Women have been described as the "world's most underutilized resource" by a number of institutions, ranging from the United Nations (UN Women 2011) to Goldman Sachs (2009).
2. "World Bank Group Private Sector Leaders Forum Announces New Measures to Improve Women's Economic Opportunities." Press Release No: 2010/084/PREM.
3. Key steps in achieving this goal include addressing inheritance regimes that discriminate against women, facilitating the transfer of citizenship status onto their children, eliminating gender bias in taxation, and improving access to credit and bank accounts.
4. See http://www.weforum.org/issues/global-gender-gap (accessed December 5, 2011).
5. Decades of work in the field of gender and development has tried to elucidate the conditions necessary for translating access to credit and financial services into women's empowerment, which include a broad range of social, cultural, and economic factors (Pankhurst 2002; Marlow and Patton 2005; Murthy, Sagayam, and Nair 2008; Kabeer, Mahmud, and Tasneem 2011; Baden 2013).
6. There are strong regional variations in this gap, with the largest gap (51 percentage points) occurring in the Middle East and North Africa, with the second largest gap identified in South Asia and Central America (35 percentage points or more), and the lowest gap found in the OECD countries and Eastern and Middle Africa (approximately 12 percentage points) (Elborgh-Woytek et al. 2013, 6). However, these numbers also conceal important trends associated with the gender-based division of labor, as women are highly overrepresented in sectors characterized by low status and pay (ILO 2010). Even in the OECD countries, where greater proportions of women are employed in the so-called formal sector, they are highly concentrated in the service sector, which employs around 80 percent of women (Elborough-Woytek et al. 2013, 6).
7. In the United States, for instance, the gender wage gap is highest for "financial managers," where women earn 66 percent of men's median earnings, than in any

of the other 20 most common female occupations (IWPR 2012, 1). In the United Kingdom, among all major industrial categories, the full-time gender pay gap is widest for financial and insurance activities, standing at 38.6 percent for both mean and median earnings. It was narrowest in the transportation and storage sector (Perfect 2011, 3). Statistics compiled by Eurostat also indicate that for almost all EU Member States, the gender pay gap in the financial and insurance activities sector is "sizably higher" than in the business economy as a whole, where the gaps in Estonia and the Czech Republic reached 44.9 and 44.8 percent, respectively (data available at http://epp.eurostat.ec.europa.eu/statistics_explained/index.php/Gender_pay_gap_statistics#By_economic_activity).

8. According to one account, the total cost of constructing sewers and water systems throughout the world's cities and providing household connections to water and sewage to three-quarters of the urban population in developing countries amounts to a mere 5 percent of what was guaranteed to banks by the American and European governments at the outset of the GFC (€280 billion) (Hall 2008, 6).

9. According to one study, Hispanic households experienced the largest drop in wealth, as their average net worth fell by 66 percent between 2005 and 2009 (from $18,359 to $6,325). The net worth of black households dropped 53 percent (from $12,124 to $5,677) while white households lost 16 percent of their net worth (from $134,992 to $113,149) (Taylor, Kochhar, and Fry 2011, 5). Class inequalities also increased within each group, with the richest 10 percent of Hispanic, black, and white households increasing their share of the group's wealth overall.

10. http://catalystatlarge.com/2014/07/01/women-effect-investments/ (accessed December 21, 2015).

11. http://www.alliancemagazine.org/feature/the-women-effect/ (accessed December 21, 2015).

12. Prügl and True applied this criteria to *10,000 Women* (led by Goldman Sachs), the World Economic Forum's Women Leaders and Gender Parity Program, the EU's Programme on Gender Balance in Decision-Making Positions and the Women's Empowerment Principles for Business (initiated by the UN Global Compact-UNIFEM). While their findings were somewhat mixed, they went a long way in highlighting a number of important shortcomings from a feminist perspective.

PART II

Scandalous Obfuscations

CHAPTER 5

Broken Britain

Post-Crisis Austerity and the Trouble with the Troubled Families Programme

DANIELA TEPE-BELFRAGE AND JOHNNA MONTGOMERIE

INTRODUCTION

The 2008 financial crisis exposed the major flaws in contemporary financial markets; the continued public policy response is an unprecedented commitment to open-ended corporate welfare to the financial services sector, in particular, to banks. In the United Kingdom, at last count, the costs of the initial bailout and subsequent rounds of quantitative easing are conservatively estimated at £1.3 trillion (National Audit Office 2013a), with other much higher figures measuring ultimate "costs" of the financial crisis. Importantly, there is a blank check attached to existing public expenditure commitments to the financial services sector because "the Treasury retains the unquantifiable ultimate risk of supporting banks should they threaten the stability of the overall financial system again" (National Audit Office 2013a). "Too Big to Fail" is now the norm because the financial services sector—referred to as the City—is given a blank check by government to protect against losses, all in the name of economic stability and competitiveness. Why this policy is not a scandal perplexed even then governor of the Bank of England, Mervyn King, in his testimony before Parliament in 2011:

> The price of this financial crisis is being borne by people who absolutely did not cause it. . . . Now is the period when the cost is being paid, I'm surprised

that the degree of public anger has not been greater than it has. (King, cited in Inman 2011)

The non-scandal of corporate welfare to the City is the "strategic silence" in the political economy of welfare reform brought in after the 2008 financial crisis. Britain's "Age of Austerity" describes a wide range of post-financial crisis policies designed and justified using the discourse of scandal; it was "Labour's Debt Crisis" that created high public debt levels (in large part to bail out the City) and unsustainable costs to taxpayers (Bramall 2013; NEF 2013; JRF 2014). This phrasing deliberately evokes "Austerity Britain," which was the period directly following World War II, when wartime rationing continued to rebuild the war-torn nation; this period is burned into the national memory as a painful but manageable time because "we are all in it together." Evoking historical memories of austerity as "difficult but necessary" in order to rebuild silences the deeply unequal process through which austerity is made possible—in particular, how the "household" sector (more so than the "private" sector) has borne the majority of tax costs for the bailout, as well as the most spending cuts to public services. This chapter looks at how poor women with children were made targets of scandal in post-crisis Britain, depicted as burdens to the public finances, and how in doing so they became the objects and subjects of reform to fix "Broken Britain." More specifically, this chapter analyzes the Troubled Families Programme (TFP). The TFP is one of the flagship programs of the coalition government to change the lives of Britain's "problem" families, aimed at disciplining the lifestyles of families facing multiple problems, including children truanting or being involved in antisocial behavior due to the costs for the "public purse." We highlight how the focus on "families" as subject/objects of reform is pivotal to gendering the process of welfare reform. We demonstrate the significance of the TFP in revealing a fundamental shift in the role of social policy from addressing the causes of poverty to managing (or governing) the effects of poverty. We draw on the work of Loic Wacquant and his lens of the *social panopticum* to make sense of these public policy developments. Finally, we conclude by reconsidering the non-scandal of corporate welfare in the wake of the financial crisis and ask what our collective (lack of) engagement with welfare families might tell us about the prospects for critical political economy to inform meaningful social change.

Feminist political economy is most apt for explaining how public welfare for corporations is justified while public welfare to households is vilified—principally because it can conceptualize inequality as more than a function of income (Piketty 2014). Indeed, inequality is socioculturally enacted through power relations, the effects of which can be clearly observed in income inequality but are not limited to it. Evaluating sociocultural inequality within capitalism is made possible by a rich understanding of "the household" as the site where paid and unpaid labor coalesce to provide the necessary conditions for production, consumption, and social reproduction. More important, feminist political economy explicitly recognizes that not all "households" are created equal, using intersectionality as a frame; therefore, race, gender, and class oppressions are interrelated and compound one another, affecting the vulnerabilities of particular groups. In this analysis we see how poor urban women and children living with "multiple disadvantages" become targets of/for reform in the wake of financial crisis and protracted economic stagnation.

Of course many critical theories offer their own concepts to frame "why" corporations, or the private sector, are favored over citizens, the household sector. For example, different variants of Marxism explain the relative power of factions of capital or conceptualize power simply in terms of the general abstraction of the labor-capital conflict (Poulantzas 1973; Gill and Law 1993). Poststructuralists offer an altogether different account of power, in which the governmentality of finance is created and made through the conjuring of different neoliberal subjectivities (De Goede 2005; Langley 2007). However, both approaches are fundamentally weak in conceptualizing the household and therefore offer only a generalized theory of the "power" of finance, albeit very different theories of power. By contrast, feminist political economy is able to make visible "how" financial power dominates because intersectionality provides a conceptual and methodological framework to evaluate what differences and inequalities matter: the "welfare mother" or single woman with children, collecting state benefits and living in publicly funding housing (in this case also struggling with addiction or mental illness), is made an object of opprobrium while "the banker" or the wealthy urban male elite, close to political power, is tolerated as a necessary evil to ensure global economic competiveness. These differences are not simply functions of sets of identifiable social variables (gender, race, class); rather, they are sets of power relations that are made to matter through structure, discourse, and everyday practice (Bedford and Rai 2010; LeBaron 2010).

The case study of the TFP demonstrates how public policy mobilizes morality to make women and children the objects of government reform in post-crisis Britain. "Troubled Families" became a scandal because it justified welfare spending cuts (Levitas 2012; Wintour 2014). Using a feminist political economy perspective reveals the gender and class dynamics that make this scandal significant. The "Troubled Families" discourse, for example, mobilizes long-standing narratives of poor women with children as a "threat" to the general public. Right up until the Beveridgean welfare state, unmarried women with children (generally referred to as "whores") were conceived of as a threat to public decency, while married poor women were a threat to public stability because they "bred" countless children to fill the legions of the underclass. Today, "troubled families" are similarly a threat to the public finances and stability. As Prime Minister David Cameron stated in a speech on "Troubled Families" at the Sandwell Christian Center in December 2011 shortly after the riots in London and other English cities in August 2011,

> I want to talk about troubled families. Let me be clear what I mean by this phrase. Officialdom might call them "families with multiple disadvantages." Some in the press might call them "neighbours from hell." Whatever you call them, we've known for years that a relatively small number of families are a source of a large proportion of the problems in society. Drug addiction. Alcohol abuse. Crime. A culture of disruption and irresponsibility that cascades through generations. We've always known that these families cost an extraordinary amount of money. . . . (Cameron, 2011c)

As of August 2014, the cost of "troubled families" is estimated, this time very generously, at £30 billion, which includes the direct cost of benefits and estimated indirect cost of services to these families (Hellen 2014). To put this in some perspective, this is equivalent to a mere 2.3% of the (conservative) estimate of "direct" costs of £1,300 billion of taxpayer money already spent supporting the City. In this context, it is clear that the "costs to taxpayers" are marginal when compared to any other line budget of expenditure. What is more relevant is the powerful imaginary of the threat that "troubled families" pose to the rest of society. In short, a troubled family constitutes a threat not simply because it has problems, but because it supposedly causes problems that must be dealt with using public money and services. Poverty becomes the problem, not the result of the wider problems of inequality. The eradication of poverty is perceived as being in the victims' own hands; existing power relations and their potential role in the reproduction of poverty are not questioned.

One the one hand, this chapter does not offer a traditional policy analysis that focuses on the process of design, assessing actionable variables and determining whether key objectives were met. On the other hand, it does analyze the TFP to highlight how scandal is inscribed on the bodies of poor women by making them visible in highly stylized ways to garner public support for welfare cuts. This is firmly embedded in feminist theory that consistently aims at making visible the perspective of those neglected. We strategically juxtapose the politically enforced silence on the endless flow of public money into financial markets, which supports men's assets and capital power more than women's given the large gender gaps in wealth, as the non-scandal to lay bare the blatant misogyny behind political agenda for welfare reform in contemporary Britain. By doing so, we seek to engage with other critical approaches to political economy that are capable of identifying the asymmetrical power between welfare-dependent families and welfare-dependent bankers but are still unable to discern or articulate how this process is deeply gendered in regard to material structures and symbolic meaning. Therefore, there is agreement on "why" this is happening: the state is downloading costs or individualizing responsibility; however, the process of downloading and/or individualizing is highly uneven. It is women and children who are being vilified and services to poor families that are being cut; the sharp end of the neoliberal stick is not wielded uniformly, and too much abstraction, rather than concrete relational analysis, can unwittingly make it seem that way.

GOVERNING POVERTY

The necessity to govern poverty and social insecurity is at the very core of the functioning of the capitalist state. Especially in times of economic crisis—as poverty rates are scandalously increasing and the potential disagreement and protests of those affected by crisis need to be silenced—the question of how to govern poverty becomes crucial to policymakers.

In this context, the particular neoliberal face that the governance of social insecurities and poverty takes under the current coalition government and ongoing austerity cannot be seen as something entirely new. Rather, it builds on a liberal tradition to structure poor relief in punitive ways oriented toward getting the poor to work, independent of scandalous pay or working conditions. Indeed, the underpinning ideology to posit individuals as rational and freely choosing individuals who choose poverty that should best be governed by markets has a long tradition, especially prominent in the Anglo-American world (Trattner 1994; Ashcraft 1996). Similarly, educational and social services in the United Kingdom build on a tradition that has historically seen the governing of criminality and poverty being closely intertwined. The Poor Laws of the nineteenth century are just the most prominent example of instilling morally and ideologically derived conceptions of discipline into the poor, while providing some form of assistance to the poor to protect them from the very extreme expressions of the market (Polanyi 1944).

And for more recent times, as Rodger highlights, "the normal face of the welfare state is to manage the incentives of the population to work, and pay taxes and social insurance, and to discipline those who refuse to participate in the form of institutionalized solidarity that the welfare state represents" (2008, xi).

Looking at the ways in which poverty and social insecurity are governed highlights the entanglement of welfare and crime control, disciplining practices, criminality, and criminalization that are at work in family intervention policy. Most work in political economy looking at austerity and social and economic responses to the financial crisis of 2008 has not paid attention to this. Exceptions include the work of Jacqui True (2012) on the political economy of violence against women, which looks at the criminalization of men under financial stress exacerbated by the globalization of competitive markets. Also, there is some work done on a "new constitutionalism," but this has not been really integrated into the core of gendered and (non-)gendered research on the topic (Gill and Cutler 2014). Therefore, we propose to take insights from critical criminology/critical sociology (Van Swaaningen 1997; Pantazis 2008; Rodger 2008; Wacquant 2009) seriously in order to achieve a deeper understanding of current scandalous political and economic developments.

This is particularly crucial at a time when "the relationship between welfare and discipline, and between social and economic policy and criminal justice, is changing from being an implicit feature of the welfare state development [to] becoming a more explicit and strategic characteristic" (Rodger 2008, 4). This change in the nature of welfare is driven by "a shift from a concern about structural causes of social problems to a preoccupation with 'choices, lifestyle and the culture of the poor themselves"' (Rodger 2008, 6). Here, it is no longer the actual factors of poverty, such as lack of income, poor housing, bad health, lack of access to health care, or lack of educational possibilities, but rather the lifestyles of the poor that are made responsible for societal shortcomings, and it is these lifestyles and life choices that are perceived in need of discipline (partly via criminalization).

"TROUBLED FAMILIES" AS A PUBLIC POLICY PROBLEM

As mentioned earlier, the TFP is one of the flagship programs of the UK coalition government to tackle "Broken Britain." Eric Pickles (MP), secretary of State for Communities and Local Government (the department that implements TFP), asserts that it seeks to reform the culture of avoiding taking responsibility for their [the Troubled Families] own lives:

> It's basically "dear Officer Krupke,[1] I've come from a single home, my mother's a drunk, it's not my fault," all that kind of thing. Sometimes when you meet some families, they have got the language, they are fluent in social work. (Pickles, quoted in Chorley 2012)

Much of the language of the TFP focuses on "turning around" the lives of these families through focused intervention and targeted support. Most of the staff implementing TFP are social workers or local authority workers with extensive experience. Interviews with key individuals in two locales, among those 10 councils which apparently have the most troubled families (Liverpool, Birmingham, Manchester, Essex, Lancashire, Kent, Bradford, Norfolk, Bristol, and Nottingham), who work with the implementation of TFP are presented here to demonstrate how government and social workers understand "troubled families" as subjects in need of reform. Per illustration, the initial process to define and categorize a "troubled family" was if they met five out of seven criteria: having a low income; no one in the family is working; poor housing; parents who have no qualifications; the mother has a mental health problem; one parent has a long-standing illness or disability; and the family is unable to afford basics, including food and clothes (National Audit Office 2013b, 16). Many of the seven are beyond the control of the families themselves, yet the political rhetoric to justify this program frames the problem as "cultural," not structural. Many are highly critical of the term "troubled families" (Welshman 2012), and here we use it to refer only to the government program; the families themselves are more aptly described as families faced with multiple problems and challenges (FPCs). The up-to-date criteria that stipulate a "troubled family" are "involved in youth crime or anti-social behavior, have children who are regularly truanting, have an adult on out-of-work benefits" (Department for Communities and Local Government 2014c).

TFP is designed to "turn around the lives" of what was claimed to be 120,000 Families in the United Kingdom by 2015 in order to relieve the costs that these families cause "the public purse" (Department for Communities and Local Government 2013). While the number of 120,000 families was dubious from the beginning (Levitas 2012), it emerged in August 2014 that new estimates suggest 500,000 families in Britain are now considered to fulfill the criteria (Watt 2014).

Phase one of TFP (until 2015) pays local authorities £2,000 for every family that signs up and an additional £4,000 on a payment-by-result basis for "turning around" the lives of participating families. Payment-by-result has been described as a neoliberal technology of governance that shifts extra costs that result, for example, from "lower efficiency" away from government and onto the "users" (Slavnic and Urban 2008). In the case of public services, such "low efficiency" could easily arise from the complexities that are involved in dealing with the complex needs of FPCs. At the same time, the instrument is creative and proactive rather than merely punitive in encouraging its users, in our case the councils, to find creative ways to "turn around" the lives of the families assigned to the program while, at the same time, doing so in financially efficient ways. The program encourages councils to appoint dedicated casework-ers to individual "failing" families to help them change their lives. A fam-ily is considered to be "officially" "turned around" when "each child in the family has had fewer than three fixed exclusions (from school) and unauthorized absences on no more than 15% of schooldays, in the last three terms; as well as a 60% reduction in anti-social behavior across the family in six months. In addition, the offending rate by all minors in the family must have fallen by at least a third in the same period" (Wintour 2013). Phase two of the TFP (begins late 2014) focuses on the 51 best performing areas, to be followed by a national five-year program from 2015. The new phase of the program aims to particularly focus on poor health as, according to government data, 71% of the troubled families have physical and 46% mental health concerns, while retaining its foci on, among other things, tackling antisocial behavior and getting parents into employment (Department for Communities and Local Government, 2014b).

Family Intervention Policy was first established under New Labour to tackle poverty, social exclusion, crime, and antisocial behavior, as well as poor health (Moran et al. 2004). This particularly focused on the tackling of poor parenting as a source of these "evils" (Parr 2011, 719). In this context, the courts were given more and more powers to clamp down on parental irresponsibility, for example the Parenting Order, introduced in 1998. Such orders require parents to attend parenting classes or counseling at threat of fines or even prison sentences issued to parents of children who offend (Parr 2011, 719). At the same time a moralizing discourse is employed that "emphasizes surveillance, classification, self-regulation, welfare condition-ality and community obligations" (Parr and Nixon 2008, 165). This points to an interesting paradox, in that unpaid parenting becomes "valued" by the state (i.e., "parentwork" when judged inadequate is penalized, rather than being renumerated and/or supported sufficiently when perceived as adequate).

To make sense of these developments, we believe Wacquant's work to be helpful. He is receptive to the historical specificity of different state approaches to the governing of social insecurity and poverty. His work focuses largely on the United States and France, but he provides some insights on other European states and their historically specific expressions of governing. In regard to the United Kingdom, he acknowledges the historical similarities with the other "liberal" prototype economy (US), yet he places the United Kingdom in a European context, where the punitive logic has extended more into the bureaucratic administrative apparatus, with less focus on imprisonment.[2]

Indeed, Wacquant identifies a particular European road to the governing of social marginality, where, in comparison to the United States, the agency of the police and the courts takes a much greater role than the prisons. While he is not sure for how much longer the "European way" will remain distinct from that of the United States, he identifies a panoptical logic at work throughout Europe, rather than a "segregative and retributive rationale" (Wacquant 2009, 24). Here, social services play a fundamental role in criminalization and disciplining "since they possess the administrative and human means to exercise a close-up supervision of so-called problem populations" (Wacquant 2009, 24). We believe this insight to be particularly fitting to analyse the United Kingdom's Family Intervention Policy.

Wacquant describes how social services and educational services are transformed into extensions of the penal apparatus, thereby institutionalizing a *social panopticum*, which, "under cover of promoting the well-being of deprived households, submits them to an ever-more precise and penetrating form of punitive surveillance" (Wacquant 2009, 24–25).

Yet, as argued by Wacquant,

the simultaneous deployment of the social and penal treatments of urban disorders' should not hide the fact that the former often functions as a bureaucratic fig-leaf for the latter, and that it is ever more directly subordinated to it in practice. Encouraging state social assistance, health, and education services to collaborate with the police and judicial system turns them into extensions of the penal apparatus, institutionalizing a *social panopticum*. (2009, 24–25)

This *social panopticum* then pretends to help and support the poor, but rather creates an ever better form of their control.

As Parr and Nixon's (2008) work shows, the bulk of family intervention projects in the United Kingdom are aimed at female-only households with a tendency "to blame female tenants for the 'inappropriate" behavior of their male partners or teenage sons. A similar finding is also seen in the use of Parenting Orders, which have been predominantly given to lone mothers" (Martin and Wilcox 2013, 157).

With the accuracy of statistics on Troubled Families being highly controversial in the first place, it is unclear how many of them actually are female-only households. Freedom of information (FOI) requests to central government and the 10 councils for data on the racial and gender composition of the most "Troubled Families," with over 50 percent reporting back to date, indicate that none, except Bradford, even collects data on the gender and basic composition of these families. It is alarming that basic demographic information is not collected, making it difficult to determine the extent to which single female-headed families with dependent children are, in fact, more likely to be considered "troubled." This is hardly surprising, given the strength of blame that is put on absent fathers (Tepe-Belfrage 2015). There seems to be a tendency, however, that single-mother households are overrepresented among Britain's "troubled families." An indication of troubled families being largely single-mother households is seen in the six case studies of troubled families compiled by the government, of which five are headed by single mothers (Department for Communities and Local Government 2014a). This suspicion was confirmed during interviews, with one interviewee suggesting the representation of single mother–headed households among the troubled families in that locale to be as high as 80 percent.

These tentative statistics reveal the strong gendered nature of the program, but it is not just the numbers that show this gender bias. Similarly, the discourses surrounding the program show a gendered perception of lifestyle choices and decisions made by the families. Importantly, TFP explicitly promotes a "heterosexual monogamous relationship with children" as the only norm to which families need to conform. This is significant because it shows how the state is regulating particular types of families and relationships in the private sphere, which is surprising heavy-handed for a government that derides "the Nanny State" at the same time as it implements a paternalistic state. One quote by a program manager of the TFP is particularly telling:

> I think there's an anomaly in [name of city removed by authors], in the sense of, going back culturally and in the government of the country, it was very much geared towards single-parents, and you're talking about women, aren't you? It was very much geared up towards women and women were given three-bedroom properties, for instance, and then felt the need potentially to fill those with children and in [name of city replaced by authors] that's happened, I think, astronomically, and the number of single families that we've got, single-parent families that we've got, is really high.

Indeed, interviews with program managers and social workers on the TFP reveal overall very strongly a distrust in the ability of the "troubled families" to make morally acceptable choices in relation to their lifestyles. The argument consistently presented was that choices in regard to parenting by the families that have signed up to the TFP are morally wrong and, more generally, that the poor and welfare dependent do not have an ability to evaluate the morality of their choices. One caseworker, for example, highlighted what she perceived as a morally problematic way of spending money: ". . . there is a culture in the poor areas to demonstrate and evidence your love for your children by buying them the latest things, so they might not have any money at all but they get in to a couple of years' debt to buy the latest X-Box or the latest mobile phone because that's cool." Similarly, a program director pointed to what he perceived as morally problematic relationships: "So there'll be three different surnames of those children who are siblings, so there will be males who come and go."

Bowman et al.'s (2014) discussion of "defective and disqualified consumers" who aim to own expensive and prestigious goods to "avoid the wrath, humiliation, spite and grudge aroused by not having them" is helpful here. As Bauman writes, social dignity is the most prized possession of all, and "non-shopping is the jarring and festering stigma of a life unfulfilled."

The lack of understanding of the social pressures of owning expensive goods and the moral condemnation of choices made by the families, including the very private choices regarding with whom and when to have children, is scandalous. Furthermore, in order to get the "morally wrong" poor to accept new frameworks of reference for parenting and to fulfill wider societal norms, disciplining and even criminalizing practices are widely accepted and perceived as right under the TFP.

Threatening families into participation in the TFP seems to be a widespread practice, with social workers and program managers acknowledging the problems in getting families to accept being "supervised" in the first place. As one program manager from Manchester acknowledged, "We do have a bit of a problem with engagement."

Similarly, a caseworker stated,

We have had quite a few [who did not want to cooperate, authors] and we're looking at kind of, how we get across to them the consequences of not engaging and what might happen in the future. And that's not to say it's a threat to them, it's a reality, really. If they carry on down this road, their children may end up in prison or whatever, so it's explaining the consequences to the family to try and encourage them to engage.

Indeed, while it is perfectly acceptable for everybody else in society to be wary of intervention from authorities, the same argument is questioned when brought forward by "troubled families" for their lack of engagement. The same caseworker stated,

> That they don't like authority; they think they'll deal with their own problems. They don't like being told what to do. They don't like being ... there's just so many problems in that particular family's life that they see a family intervention worker coming in as just an additional problem. . . .

Yet, while the TFP has not employed cash incentives for families to sign up, at least not yet, such incentives have been employed in other initiatives targeting particularly poor women's health in the United Kingdom. In Scotland, for example, women are provided "grocery vouchers worth £12.50 for each week if they abstain from tobacco up to a maximum of £650 for pregnant women, and currently in the Sheffield SOS Scheme, 490 women are being paid £140 to stop smoking during pregnancy" (ScHARR 2014). A similar scheme is currently trialed in Sheffield to encourage mothers among urban low-income groups to breastfeed by offering shopping vouchers (Boseley 2014).

This "infantilizing of adults" (Garrett 2007, 221–222) by questioning the moral integrity of the choices of adults is further highlighted by not telling the involved families that they are considered and called "troubled" when signing up for the program. Rather, as has been confirmed by our interviewees, the families are approached and offered extra help without disclosure of information as to why they are offered this help, or that they meet criteria that allow government and the wider public to call them "troubled families."

Thus, in summary, the discourses legitimizing the TFP overall reveal a strong tendency that the families targeted are in urgent need to be disciplined into "morally acceptable" lifestyles. The idea that welfare dependency has created a culture with too high costs for the public purse and lifestyles affecting the rest of society in a problematic way builds the questionable foundation of this discourse. Single mothers dependent on welfare are particularly and disproportionally affected. The feminist political economy approach at the core of our research has made us focus on these tendencies in the first place.

CONCLUSIONS

Austerity shapes the entire discourse of "troubled families"; that they are a burden on tight public finances is the only justification offered for this comprehensive policy initiative. TFP demonstrates how scandalous economics can be a classic bait and switch; it is the City of London and the failure of austerity-led growth that *cause* high public debt levels, but it is "troubled families" that require policy in order to get public finances in order. Policies like those in the TFP displace the causes of financial crisis and obfuscate structural inequalities in the remaking of "society" by casting economic problems, which could be addressed through economic policy, as social problems, which are therefore addressed through social (engineering) policy.

We see this most clearly in the moralizing about the welfare dependency problem as "getting something for nothing," which creates a scandal out of the urban poor. Meanwhile, this strategically ignores that bank bailouts and quantitative easing give banks copious amounts of public money for nothing! This chapter critically interrogates how scandal, morality, and economy intersect to create the objects and subjects of "reform": in this case, how poor, urban, largely female-headed families become a problem so that rich, urban, largely male-headed banks can continue to wreak havoc. Importantly, it is not simply about the divisions and inequalities between women and men, but how the rational, individualist, non-caring subject is promoted and privileged by public policy, even though it was precisely this subject that created the financial crisis in the first place.

NOTES

1. This refers to the musical West Side Story; lyrics to the song *Gee Officer Krupke* can be found here: http://www.metrolyrics.com/gee-officer-krupke-lyrics-westside-story.html.
2. Yet the number of prisoners in the United Kingdom has consistently increased as well, as new crimes are created with more severe punishments attached (Morris and Rothman 1997).

CHAPTER 6

Constitutionalizing Austerity, Disciplining the Household

Masculine Norms of Competitiveness and the Crisis of Social Reproduction in the Eurozone

IAN BRUFF AND STEFANIE WÖHL

INTRODUCTION

The global crisis that was sparked by the collapse of Lehman Brothers led many commentators to link the failure of neoliberal policy prescriptions to the dominance of men at the top of economic hierarchies, especially in the finance sector, as Elisabeth Prugl notes in Chapter 2 in this volume. We also concur with many in this volume that the post-2008 period of crisis management, attempted recoveries, and new forms of crisis has been characterized by the continuation of long-established structures of inequality, rather than their transformation toward a more equitable set of affairs. What distinguishes this chapter is our focus on the consequences of the intimate connection between increasingly authoritarian modes of governance and highly masculinized norms of competitiveness in the current period. This is producing growing entanglements between state-directed coercion and the household through (for example) enforced austerity measures, which have been leading to job losses in the public sector and more pressure on households through loss of income or even housing evictions.

For us, this focus is important because neoliberalism has much more to do with the reorganization of social relations and state formations along unequal and coercive lines than with the creation or development of "free" markets. As a result, our focus as critics of the current politico-economic order should shift to under-explored yet key sites that enable and perpetuate this order. Accordingly, this chapter argues that it is impossible to understand the post-2008 period without a central role being accorded to increasingly authoritarian state practices at a range of scales. Moreover, the coupling of greater capacities for state-directed coercion with highly masculinized norms of competitiveness—such as risk affinity, strong work ethics, liquidity, growth, and austerity—constitutes a strategy to displace the effects of crisis into another key site in the political economy, the household. An excellent illustration of these claims can be found in the trajectories of European political economies, especially in the Eurozone, after 2008.

After a critical discussion of neoliberalism and the state and how masculine norms are inscribed within (supra)national institutions and (re)produce gendered hierarchies, the chapter then considers the Eurozone crisis across two sections. The first focuses on the rise of more authoritarian forms of governance through the Fiscal Compact, the so-called Six-pack legislation, the Euro-Plus Pact, and the gendered nature of this crisis response. The second section concentrates on the variegated yet highly significant effects of these developments in two countries, discussing the intensified crisis of social reproduction and possible alternatives to the current politico-economic order. We focus on Spain and Ireland, because they show especially well the processes we seek to highlight. We conclude with reflections on the broader implications of our argument and suggestions for further research.

NEOLIBERALISM AND THE STATE

Neoliberalism's genesis in a period marked by the growing role of organized labor and welfare programs after the two world wars of the twentieth century had a significant impact on how its supporters sought to translate the strident rhetoric about "free markets" into policy and institutional change. As such, neoliberal ideas were "preoccupied with the necessary evils of governmental rule" and thus "framed by the distinctively post-laissez-faire question of appropriate forms and fields of state intervention in the socioeconomic sphere" (Peck 2008, 7). However, as argued by Martijn Konings (2010; see also Panitch and Konings 2009), there is an enduring tendency to pay lip service to neoliberalism's rhetorical and ideological valorisation of the "free market." One result is that it has become commonplace for a critique of neoliberalism to focus on the contradictions between "pure" neoliberal ideology and "messy" neoliberalizing practices. Of course, it is worth noting "how many present-day policy failures are still being tagged to intransigent unions, to invasive regulation, to inept bureaucrats, and to scaremongering advocacy groups" (Peck 2010, 7–8), despite the fact that many of the "appropriate" reforms demanded by neoliberals have been implemented across the world over the past four decades. However, this observation should be only the beginning, not the core of our critique.

To give one example, Friedrich Hayek, one of the key neoliberal intellectuals, argued in the 1970s that "the political institutions prevailing in the Western world necessarily produce a drift [towards the destruction of the market] which can be halted or prevented only by changing these institutions" (1973, 9). This quote appears to conform to common views of neoliberal ideology: the demand that those parts of society which are restricting the space for market forces be reformed in order to move society toward the ideal state of affairs. But Hayek is actually going much further, in our view: in the quote, he states that political institutions *necessarily* produce an anti-market drift. Hayek claims that he is defending a conception of democracy and is only attacking those conceptions that are incompatible with capitalism (9), yet many forms of democratic participation and governance would fall foul of this categorization. Hence, antidemocratic tendencies are at the forefront of his conception of democracy. His subsequent argument implies that there is a need to restrict strongly the power of elected parliaments in favor of the creation of institutional safeguards, which makes it possible for the executive branch of the state coercively to enforce obedience to general rules that are applicable to all:

> The root of the evil is thus the unlimited power of the legislature in modern democracies, a power which the majority will be constantly forced to use in a manner that most of its members may not desire. What we call the will of the majority is thus really an artifact of the existing institutions, and particularly of the omnipotence of the sovereign legislature, which by the mechanics of the political process will be driven to do things that most of its members do not really want, simply because there are no formal limits to its powers. (1973, 11; see also Hayek 1944, 1960)

As we shall see in our analysis of new supranational governance mechanisms in the European Union and the case studies in this chapter, in the current period this manifests itself in (supra-)national constitutional and quasi-constitutional changes that restrict significantly the scope for future generations to overturn a permanent emphasis on austerity and on undemocratic decision-making. Restricting the rights of parliaments to decide on national budget consolidation independent of the supranational level is only one of many examples in the European Union underpinning this emphasis, as we will explain further.

In other words, the conditions for neoliberal order are *not* realized through the unleashing of market forces alone, as per neoliberal rhetoric; nor is the state significant only in periods of transition toward the utopia of a market order, as per "pragmatic" interpretations of this ideology. Instead, we should see the state as a *permanent* and *necessary* part of neoliberal ideology, institutionalization, and practice. For it is state-directed coercion insulated from democratic pressures that is central to the creation and maintenance of a politico-economic order that actively defends itself against impulses toward greater equality and democratization (see also Klein 2007). Moreover, and as the next section on masculinity and gendered hierarchies discusses, state-directed coercion is central to neoliberalism in highly gendered ways. Next to our analysis of EU hard law in the successive section, our case studies in the final section of this chapter will illustrate the decline of social rights through changing forms of governance at the national level, enforced by the supranational level, toward executive forces. This affects gendered norms, relations, policies, and social reproduction in more restrictive and limiting ways since the onset of the crisis.

MASCULINITY AND GENDERED HIERARCHIES

As already noted, the state and its specific institutions are central to neoliberalism's worldview. However, there is more to the argument than this initial observation, not least because the state, as a relation of social forces and its institutionalized form (Poulantzas 1978), is gendered in ways that extend beyond the fact that men tend to occupy higher positions within state institutions (and elsewhere, in global firms and finance). The state and the market economy are highly gendered, class distinct, and racialized because the public/private divide has historically shaped this division of labor and institutionalized gendered practices of the state: historically, binding women legally to the private household; nowadays, keeping mostly women of lower class status still in low paid, precarious employment, and migrant women of lower class status "doing the dirty work" (Anderson 2000) of caring and cleaning in global care and commodity chains. As noted in other chapters in this volume, the media narrative of women cleaning up the financial mess left by men is therefore profoundly misleading in the way it obscures the deeply gendered nature of state formations, capitalist economies, the crisis, and responses to the crisis. The media narrative only highlights one side of the problem, namely essentializing "women" as a group, seemingly better able to clean up the messy world of bankers' permissive investments. This observation can be related to the state and its institutions: they are not merely the instrument or representation of men as a group creating policies in their own favor. Men neither have uniform interests as a group, nor do they adjust legislation over and against women as a uniform group, as is apparent in the possibility for well-educated women to enter state institutions and to climb institutional hierarchies. Therefore, the observation that the state's centrality to neoliberalism's worldview cannot be expressed in gender-neutral terms goes well beyond a discussion of male dominance at the top of institutional hierarchies. While it is important to note this from a liberal gender equality perspective, as with our critical view of the consensus on neoliberalism, it should be our starting point and not the core of our critique of the contemporary politico-economic order.

Accordingly, we conceptualize the state and its institutions not as a set of objective, universal "things" separate from the societies they are part of: rather, they are the materialization of unequal relations of power in the form of laws, procedures, institutions, and conventions that have significant effects on how these societies evolve (Bruff 2011; Wöhl 2014). By recasting the state and its institutions in this way, we can appreciate how they are key sites in the politico-economic order for the playing out of social struggles and the ideas embodied in and promoted by them. Hence, in gendered state theory, the state can appear not only as an institution of repression and coercion, but also as a relation of forces, where gendered hierarchies, identities, and subject positions are continuously (re)produced across multiple sites (Brown 1995).

Examples of the gendered ideas embodied in and promoted by social struggles include norms and capabilities that are historically associated with men, such as rationality, strength, power, strong will, competitiveness, and working outside the home. These all shape our cultural understanding of recognition in society and accordingly of how to act in social contexts and within institutions. This gendered cultural order has significant consequences for how another key site in the politico-economic order, the private household, is viewed, for a full understanding of this order is impossible without an appreciation of "a whole host of [concealed] social relations and forms of work that are essential to the reproduction of people and communities" (Roberts 2012, 96; Fraser 2014). Social reproduction within this politico-economic order encompasses affective labor, such as personal caring for dependents including the very young, the infirm, and the elderly, and social provisioning of the essentials of life for the household to function. The artificial distinction between public labor ("productive") and household labor ("domestic") generates a continual devaluation of this work in both financial and symbolic terms, with much of it remaining unpaid and feminized. Hence the private household is constructed as a site that is "naturally" more appropriate for women to dominate, for the norms and capabilities associated with women—such as care, emotions, passivity, and sharing qualities—are also present in this construction.

Having this gendered politico-economic order in mind, we trace in the following section how masculine norms are still central to neoliberal policies, gender regimes, and thus capitalist (re)production in economic crisis. Masculinized norms have proved to be integral to the gendered nature of the responses to crisis, which have reinforced gendered hierarchies across a number of sites. In particular, they have provided for a tight coupling of increasingly authoritarian state practices and an enhanced affirmation of the "benefits" of competitiveness for society as a whole. Moreover, as we discuss with regard to the Eurozone, this strategy to displace the effects of the crisis from the "public" to the "private" has intensified the crisis of social reproduction experienced by households across Europe.

THE EUROZONE CRISIS

Since the onset of the financial and economic crisis in the European Union, crisis narratives on state debt and financialization have often focused on specific demands in the name of "necessity" (Jessop et al. 2015). Neoliberal ideas, such as the freedom of the market, combining a discourse of personal responsibility, competitiveness, individualism, and market-oriented rationality with the withdrawal of the state from providing or ensuring the delivery of welfare policies, have become even more dominant than prior to 2008 (Young et al. 2011). Regaining international competitiveness and restoring growth are the main line of argumentation used to promote and defend the new modes of economic governance designed to implement this crisis response. Moreover, these new modes are considerably more authoritarian and coercive than their predecessors, leading to the reinforcement (sometimes in new ways) of gendered hierarchies, norms, and segregation in paid and unpaid work.

The Rise and Enforcement of Authoritarian Governance

The rise of authoritarian forms of neoliberalism is centered on the increasing frequency with which constitutional and legal changes, in the name of economic necessity, are seeking to reshape state and institutional power. This is taking place in three key ways:

1. The more immediate appeal to material circumstances as a reason for the state being unable, despite "the best will in the world," to reverse processes such as greater socioeconomic inequality and dislocation;
2. The deeper and longer-term recalibration of the kinds of activity that are feasible and appropriate for non-market institutions to engage in, diminishing expectations in the process; and
3. The reconceptualization of the state as increasingly non-democratic through its subordination to constitutional and legal rules that are deemed necessary for prosperity to be achieved (Bruff 2014, 115–116).

While such developments can be observed across the world, the most compelling example of this shift can be found in the European Union's response to the financial and especially the Eurozone crises. While some of the new arrangements had a previous life prior to 2008—such as the Stability and Growth Pact from 1996 on budget deficits—there has been a qualitative change since then. Put simply, the response challenges representative democracies by moving powers from parliamentary to executive branches of the state at the national and supranational level (Habermas 2011; Bieling 2012).

One of these new economic governance processes is the so-called "Six-pack" legislation from 2011. Noteworthy alone in this context is the gendered symbolic meaning of the term "six-pack," referring not only to a six-pack of beer but also to a highly trained man's abdomen. With this legally binding legislation of five ordinances and one directive, the Stability and Growth Pact is strengthened through the enhanced emphasis on competitive restructuring. The Six-pack legislation has fostered masculinized social, political, and economic orders during economic crisis through changes in the polity and in policymaking. This legislation highlights the self-binding, prospective nature of the reforms for all EU member states, whether they are in bail-out mode or not.

The "Six-pack" has installed a procedure geared toward the avoidance and correction of macroeconomic imbalances through binding sanctions against member states. This legislation has been pursued by heads of state and national finance ministers within the European Council and the

Council of the European Union, and also by national governments of member states (Klatzer and Schlager 2011). Moreover, with the subsequent introduction of the "Two-pack" regulations designed to increase the surveillance of member states in these matters by the European Commission, the executive judgment of the Commission, in particular the imposition of sanctions against member states, can act through "Reverse Majority Rule" (Oberndorfer 2011). This procedure enables the Commission's proposals to be accepted as valid if they are not prevented within 10 days by the European Council's veto with a simple majority, thus enforcing the already authoritarian "Six-pack" in undemocratic ways.

The Fiscal Compact, signed in 2012, sought to supplement these provisions with the installation of a so-called "debt brake" mechanism, meaning that austerity measures can now be required from all member states that lie above the state deficit of 3 percent of GDP or trespass the 60 percent state debt threshold, without having to consult national parliaments beforehand. If this is not respected by the member states that signed the Compact (almost all of them), the Commission can now install independent bodies at the member state level to monitor the implementation of the rules imposed (Bieling 2012). Member states are also expected to respond to suggestions made by the Commission for budget consolidation, which are often driven by a focus on austerity measures, before their respective national parliament is consulted (Fischer-Lescano and Oberndorfer 2013). In the case of Eurozone countries, governments can additionally be fined if they do not respect the limit (Wöhl 2014). It is not yet clear how much time will be given to make the "necessary" adjustments, but the underlying principle is that member states could be forced via even more financial sanctions to implement austerity measures, against the will of their citizens.

The political rationality behind and the argument in favor of this procedure is that it provides *quick* and *effective* capabilities for *action* during the current (and possible future) crises by enhancing *competitiveness*. This procedure limits the scope for processes of democratic decision-making, since the 10-day time span for examination, deliberative consideration, and possible veto by the European Council is very short and thus unrealistic. Moreover, the European Parliament is not involved in the process, despite its oversight function ("co-decision") in EU institutional architecture. Only the Council can veto Commission propositions within the 10-day timeframe. Besides these procedures, the European Court of Justice (ECJ) can be called upon by other member states to guarantee that all member states align with their agreed-upon measures. Even though the ECJ is supposed to uphold legislation in the European Union, it was not designed to intervene in member states' disagreements. Now, the ECJ can impose fines of 0.1 percent of GDP if signatory states do not respect the treaty.

It is therefore of no surprise that legal scholars view many of these new economic governance mechanisms—for example, the reverse majority rule, the deliberate side-lining of the only democratically elected institution, the European Parliament—as in contravention of EU law (Oberndorfer 2015). Existing legal provisions and procedures have been cast aside in favor of measures that have an overwhelming focus on austerity in the name of competitiveness; moreover, these measures have been designed in a manner that seeks to prevent different, more socially inclined visions of how to respond to the crisis from becoming law, now and in the future.

Gendering the Crisis and the Crisis Response

A key consequence of the economic governance measures discussed in the preceding section is that a form of masculinized economic knowledge, with its norm of competitiveness for growth, is privileged over alternative economic solutions and historical gendered knowledges of crisis management (Ferber and Nelson 2003; Walby 2009). The symbolic realm of ideas has played a key role, because culturally constructed assumptions of competitiveness, risk affinity, liquidity, quick decision-making, expertise, growth, and austerity—to name but a few—are highly gendered, masculinized codes and imaginations (de Goede 2004; Griffin 2013a). Hence, a specific neoliberal form of economic knowledge and gendered symbolic order supports the discourse around the implemented austerity policies and their economic decisions. The focus on competitiveness and growth also neglects gender-equality policies, such as gender budgeting and gender mainstreaming, within the austerity measures (Karamessini and Rubery 2014), even though all member states have agreed to implement gender mainstreaming at all levels of policymaking. As Shirin Rai and Georgina Waylen remark, "in times of crisis, the focus on restoring growth continues to displace the debates on gender justice. Feminist work continues to inhabit the margins of mainstream economics, development studies, and political economy as well as policymaking at the national and international levels" (2013, 14–15). Gendered economic knowledge and alternative forms of economy are not even discussed in this context (Young and Scherrer 2010).

More broadly, a knowledge/power complex led by (among others) the International Monetary Fund (IMF), the ECB, the European Commission, and Europe's ministers of finance have drawn a line from structural adjustment programs already imposed from the 1980s onward in Latin America,

Africa, and East Asia to the austerity measures now being enforced across Europe, especially in the states receiving bailouts (Greece, Ireland, Portugal, Cyprus) (Rodrigues and Reis 2012). As can be seen from our earlier discussion, the focus of the new economic governance measures is clearly on expenditure, which was already attested to by the "Europlus Pact" signed in March 2011 and which called for sustainability in public finances by lowering pensions, health care, and social expenditures.

Hence, from a gender perspective, we see the harsh results of these structural adjustment programs and austerity policies discursively reinforced by the aforementioned masculinized symbolic order and masculinized norms of competitiveness in different member states: for example, the unemployment rate of women is similar to that of men across the continent, but women are more likely to be in part-time, low-wage, temporary and/or precarious employment. Moreover, since questions of social reproduction, public health and welfare services are not even considered within the new deficit and debt thresholds, women are disproportionately affected in private households as well as on the labor market.

As a result, the crisis of social reproduction—already badly affected by the onset of crisis in 2008—is becoming more intense. Indeed, during times of capitalist crisis, the public/private divide and accompanying unpaid labor in the social reproduction of private households is often reinforced in order to secure the capitalist mode of production. Juanita Elias in Chapter 7 of this volume examines the feminist economic and political economy scholarship that revealed these same dynamics in the aftermath of the East Asian crisis in the late 1990s and numerous crises in Latin America (Benería 1992; Ferber and Nelson 2003; Young 2003; Elson 2010; Waring and Sumeo 2010).

Nevertheless, the nature of the Eurozone crisis response also indicates the qualitatively different nature of these mechanisms from those embodied in "traditional" structural adjustment programs. Contemporary European surveillance is characterized by a permanent, continent-wide conditionality regime that is aimed at all states, regardless of their economic performance. In other words, structural adjustment in the European Union is now preemptively self-imposed in the name of a universal goal, as opposed to being reactively imposed on specific crisis-hit countries. This conditionality regime not only takes us back to the earlier discussion of Hayek's view of democracy, and the "need" for capitalism to be defended against democracy with coercive measures like imposing austerity with binding legislation, such as the Six-pack or the Fiscal Compact, and with the strengthening of executive authority. It also shows that economic governance regimes consider interests particularly affecting women only insofar as they are compatible with masculinized neoliberal forms of knowledge and norms: competitiveness, growth, risk affinity, and individual responsibility. One key consequence is that the household is increasingly the target for a permanent displacement of the effects of crisis away from (supra) national states, which are reconfiguring into less democratic entities. In consequence, at the same time that the public/private divide is reinforced, there is a growing imbrication of the household with the legal injunctions and measures being imposed by austerity. This increasing entanglement is no irony or paradox; it is the inevitable outcome of a crisis response that is both deeply authoritarian and gendered, as we will show in the following case studies.

EFFECTS OF THE GENDERED, AUTHORITARIAN RESPONSE TO CRISIS

There are a number of reasons that a focus on Spain and Ireland is especially interesting for considering the effects of the gendered, authoritarian response to the financial and economic crisis. This is because both countries share some similarities, while also exhibiting significant differences. On the former, prior to 2008, Spain and Ireland, especially the latter, were considered "model" economies for others to follow should they wish to move closer to income per capita levels in richer European countries such as France and Germany. Rapid economic growth and consistently falling unemployment characterized both countries from the mid-1990s to 2008. However, the effects of economic success were just as likely to have material benefits for the population as they were to encourage a huge growth in speculative investments in housing by both private individuals and banks—which had momentous consequences after 2008. In addition, the strong rise in the number of immigrants living in these countries, combined with the continuation of a strong norm of the male breadwinner, led to the growth in paid household work for immigrant women and precarious employment for Spanish and Irish women on the labor market. Insofar as women profited by entering the labor market, even in precarious employment, and by taking up mortgages, the neoliberal ideology of individual success supported the discourse around the "Celtic tiger" and the Spanish boom in the years prior to 2008.

On differences, Ireland was forced to seek a bailout from the Troika in November 2010 and was placed under a punitive structural adjustment program, whereas Spain has (to date) successfully resisted this eventuality. Furthermore, in the eyes of many observers, Irish society has accepted the "need" for punishing and long-lasting austerity to a much greater extent than in Spain: the latter has been rocked by the emergence of the *Indignados* movement and the more recent creation of the *Podemos* political party, while Ireland has had lower levels of public protest as well as a muted response by Irish trade unions to drastic welfare cuts. Nevertheless, and in keeping with the earlier discussion, what is interesting in these two cases is how the gendered, authoritarian response to the crisis has had similar impacts on the household, intensifying the crises of social reproduction that the immediate post-2008 period had already generated. Moreover, this was the case even in early 2015, when media and political discussion of a recent return to economic growth in both countries was masking the highly unequal distribution of this growth and the continued harsh effects of austerity. In other words, although it is always possible to observe diversity across Europe in the effects of the crisis and the responses to it, particularly in the Eurozone we can observe a broad range of developments that are taking place across borders. As discussed earlier, fostering a competitive regime focused on growth and employment, but ignoring the quality of precarious employment and the absence of employment, affects both women and men of different age groups and social backgrounds.

In the labor market, both countries witnessed a large increase in unemployment: Spain with more than 25 percent total unemployment for those aged 20–64 in 2013, in comparison to 5.9 percent for men and 10.3 percent for women aged 20–64 in 2007. Ireland reached almost 15 percent in 2013 compared to 4.6 percent in 2007. Notably, Irish women were less likely to be unemployed than their male counterparts—11 percent compared to 17 percent in 2013—but men were still significantly more likely to be in employment (Barry and Conroy 2014, 190–193). In Spain, men and women had similar unemployment rates in 2013, and the same was the case for the proportion of contracts that were fixed-term (approximately 25 percent each, twice the EU average). However, the proportion of part-time work stood at 13.3 percent: 23.4 percent for women compared to 5.3 percent for men (Castellanos Serrano and Gonzáles Gago 2013, 208). In the period prior to the crisis, from 1995 to 2007, women's employment rose from 34.8 percent in 1995 to 58.0 percent in 2007 for those aged 20–64 in Spain. Nevertheless, this apparent improvement of labor market prospects masked the fact that, in 2007, part-time work for 15–64-year-olds was at 3.9 percent for men and 22.7 percent for women (Gonzáles Gago and Kirzner 2014, 230). In Ireland, employment stood at 60.7 percent for women aged 15–64 in 2007 compared to 54.9 percent in the first quarter of 2012 (Barry and Conroy 2014, 189), while men's employment was at 77.6 percent in 2007 and fell to 62.4 percent in the first quarter of

2012 (Barry and Conroy 2014, 189). Again, an apparently more equal situation masked other, gendered effects of the crisis (see later discussion on emigration).

On austerity policies, cuts in welfare services hit hardest for those with the lowest incomes. In Ireland, healthcare expenditure has fallen and charges (for example, to see a doctor) have increased. Low-income households were also adversely affected by the cuts to social transfers and by changes to taxation. On the former, examples include the retirement age being raised from 65 to 70, and pension entitlements, care allowances, disability payments, one-parent family payments, and child benefits have been reduced. On the latter, there has been the introduction of the Universal Social Charge, the widening of tax bands, and the reduction in tax credits (Barry and Conroy 2014, 196). In Spain, there has been a similar pattern. The largest of the cuts in public spending have affected education and social and health services, but there have been other significant changes, such as the raising of the retirement age from 65 to 68 (and the need for individuals to pay more for their pension) and the abandonment of the planned increase in parental leave for fathers from 13 to 28 days. Moreover, the one-off payment of €2,500 for the birth of a child, introduced in 2008, was canceled in 2010, and the minimum wage was not adjusted for inflation (Castellanos Serrano and Gonzáles Gago 2013). As a result of these policies, the risk of falling into poverty rose to above 20 percent, especially significant when one considers the fact that, by 2012, 3 million people without a job were not entitled to unemployment benefits. The dissolution of the equality ministry in Spain also had the effect that no efforts were made to implement gender budgeting in consolidation packages.

Earlier, we argued that a discussion of women's position in society ought to be the start rather than the core of our critique. Accordingly, we can say at this point that it is clear that women in particular have suffered in a second phase of the crisis after 2010, which hit public sector employment and retail, compared to men's job losses in the first phase of the crisis in the construction sector in Spain and Ireland (González Gago and Kirzner 2014; Barry and Conroy 2014, 191). As women are concentrated in lower income groups, they are affected more strongly by deteriorations in the labor market and by cuts in the provision of social transfers (Oxfam 2014). However, even though more women entered low-paid employment after 2008 in order to support the household, this has not led to a change in gendered norms (i.e., even if men are unemployed or in involuntary part-time work, women do not take over the breadwinner position). Hence, men still spend most of their time in paid employment and/or leisure, while women are more likely to be employed in short-term and part-time occupations *and* to take over or continue with work in the household. As Antonopoulos already predicted in (2009a, 23), "income poor households will also witness a rise in women's time poverty" since the combination of precarious, low-wage employment and unpaid household work leaves women with more constraints and therefore less leisure time. This trend has grown in importance as many European countries have diluted or removed worker protections. The goal of gender equality should therefore not be an alignment of deprived positions in different employment sectors for both women and men—that is, equality through a race to the bottom—but rather to change the intrinsic features of capitalist reproduction in the symbolic and material fields in favor of a more equitable state of affairs in a broader sense.

One coping mechanism for the household is migration, but in different ways. In better economic times, Spanish and Irish households may have employed immigrants—such as Ecuadorians in Spain and Poles in Ireland—to take over social reproductive work. The crisis and the growing entanglements between the household and state-imposed austerity have led to a partial return to older forms of social reproduction in that fewer households now employ immigrants for such work, taking on the unpaid responsibilities once again. These changes in household work mean that even *within* households there is another displacement of the crisis, from the state to the household and then to migrant households, which has led to emigration from both Spain and Ireland. A further displacement has been the emigration of often highly educated Spanish and Irish men and women to other countries (inside and outside the EU) in the search for jobs. For example, Germany and Spain signed a bilateral agreement on youth vocational training because over 55 percent of Spaniards between 16 and 24 years of age are unemployed and have little prospect of finding employment in Spain. Furthermore, the emigration of over 300,000 Irish citizens abroad, of which four out of 10 were under 24 years of age, shows how much the crisis has affected the lives of young people in particular (Oxfam 2014, 2). This process is also gendered to the extent that men are more likely to emigrate, further sharpening the public/private divide in the sense that the "productive" work is now undertaken in a different country from the "domestic" work in the household.

Of course, it may prove to be the case that the household is unable to absorb the punishment imposed by economic crisis and austerity policies, even with the aforementioned displacement strategies in operation. Hence both countries, and especially Spain, are well known for evictions. In Spain's case, hundreds of thousands of families have been evicted since the onset of the crisis, a situation made worse by a 1909 mortgage law that permits banks to demand repayment even *after* foreclosure of the property.

Ireland's figures are much lower, partly due to a smaller population but also because a loophole created as part of the immediate response to the financial crisis made it difficult for lenders to demand repayment on mortgages taken out before 2009—only post-2009 loans and mortgages could be pursued. The recent removal of this loophole, combined with fast-rising house and rental prices in the Greater Dublin area (which contains 40 percent of Ireland's population), make it inevitable that a new, more intense, wave of repossessions, foreclosures, and homelessness will emerge.

All in all, it is clear that the similarities between Spain and Ireland paint a depressing picture of the lived experiences of austerity and the growing entanglements between the household and state-directed coercion. Next to the developments described here, gender equality–related institutions have been shut down, have had drastic budget cuts, or have been enclosed in other bodies of government since 2008 in both countries. This shows that questions of gender equality are subsumed into the discourse and policies of competitiveness, austerity, and masculine restructuring of economies by neoliberalized states.

Nevertheless, we must always keep in mind that authoritarian responses to capitalist crises are "partially responsible for new forms of popular struggle" that seek to create and live in a different kind of world to the one being imposed on them (Poulantzas 1978, 246). In Spain, alternative forms of economy, such as community kitchens, have been established. This was augmented by broader developments, such as the national *Indignados* movement, which began on May 15, 2011, and the *Plataforma de Afectados por la Hipoteca* (Platform of Those Affected by Mortgage Debt, PAH), the latter of which gained strong momentum and eventually forced the Spanish parliament to reconsider a law on housing evictions (Wöhl 2013). Effective strategies to prevent evictions were also supported by the populace, especially those responsible for executing them, such as local firefighters. Most recently, the wave of localized acts of resistance and self-organized community activities has manifested in the rapid rise to prominence of the *Podemos* party, a Syriza-type rejection of both austerity and the established political parties, which will be one of the largest parties after the December 2015 national election. It was noted earlier that Ireland has appeared to be more muted and restrained, yet there was also a prominent Occupy movement, which has since 2012 diffused into local activities, supplementing those that were already taking place across the country. Examples include the weekly Sunday demonstrations in Ballyhea, the growth of a squatters' movement, and larger-scale protests in major cities and towns. These disruptive acts of resistance have led to the gradual delegitimization of large parts of the political establishment, which for

Ireland—a country dominated for almost a century by the Civil War parties, *Fianna Fail* and *Fine Gael*—is a potentially seismic shift. The rise of *Sinn Fein* and of a large number of independent members of Parliament are indicative of the still-growing scale of dissatisfaction. Moreover, the explosion of protest from late 2014 against the imposition of water charges indicates that, if anything, discontent with austerity is higher than ever, with possibly significant consequences for the Spring 2016 national election.

CONCLUSION

The discussion of Spain and Ireland links our argument to the conceptual passages earlier in this chapter. Therefore, it is worth reiterating that a feminist critique of the crisis and of crisis responses is most effective when it demonstrates clearly that so-called "public" and "private" sites within the politico-economic order need to be considered together, rather than as separate domains. This fact may seem obvious, but as we have noted, it is easy to slip into a position that implicitly accepts that neoliberalism is about the creation and promotion of free markets and/or that focuses too strongly on the impact of the crisis on women per se. Our discussion of the state's necessary and permanent role in the reorganization of social relations in more unequal and authoritarian ways, and of the centrality of masculinized notions of competitiveness to both the constitution of and the responses to crisis (i.e., the "necessity" of austerity and the priority given to "productive" work) has shown why this is the case (see also Kofman 2014).

In addition, this approach is of benefit when considering the concrete aspects of the last several years of crisis in the Eurozone. It enables us to highlight the growing imbrications of legal injunctions and measures which constitutionalize drastic austerity policies with households that increasingly find themselves the target of strategies to displace the effects of crisis away from authoritarian governance practices. It also helps us to understand two things: that discourses about crisis are important in and of themselves and also in how they materialize into and across (supra) national institutions (Jessop et al. 2015); and that such practices help produce new forms of contradiction, crisis, and potentially emancipatory change through the way in which they are entangled with households (see Harcourt 2014). Women in affected European communities, for example, are searching for alternatives to neoliberalism by organizing alternative forms of community kitchens and centers to create public rooms for discussion and support, such as "Solidary Space for Women," organized by a feminist group in Greece.

Inevitably, this chapter has not been able cover everything fully. For example, we have not discussed one notable outcome of the greater pressure on households, namely the increased violence that permeates them. This includes violence against other people, such as violence against women, perpetuated by males who are suffering a profound symbolic as well as material crisis because they are unable to be the provider for the household. It also covers violence against the self, with suicide rates—especially for males—now significantly higher in many European countries, particularly those in Southern Europe. Furthermore, this chapter has not discussed in depth the cracks within the neoliberal camp (cf. Kannankulam and Georgi 2014): "capital" is fractionated, with some elements much more in favor of further neoliberalization than others. The state is never simply the instrument of capitalist rule, despite attempts to institute an "authoritarian fix" (Bruff 2014). Further research on these and other areas will contribute to a fuller understanding of the contemporary period.

Nevertheless, and in the context of the formation of a new European Commission seemingly determined to continue further down the path outlined in this chapter (Oberndorfer 2014), our view is that a satisfactory analysis can only be achieved with the expanded conception of capitalism that a feminist critique of the current politico-economic order can provide (Fraser 2014). Accordingly, we conclude with the observation that feminists need to continue asking how gendered norms, laws, and policies are stabilized by and are stabilizing of capitalist crisis, while also potentially productive of new, more equitable modes of living.

CHAPTER 7

Whose Crisis? Whose Recovery? Lessons Learned (and Not) from the Asian crisis

JUANITA ELIAS

There is no doubt that the impact of the 2008 global financial crisis (GFC) was felt across much of Asia. For example, in China falls in industrial productivity led to significant increases in unemployment, triggering migratory flows back to rural areas (Chan 2010). In Southeast Asia, economic slowdowns in the world's major market economies led to falls in industrial demand and associated falls in productivity in key sectors. But in other areas, such as employment growth, the picture was decidedly mixed, with many Southeast Asian states not registering significant rises in unemployment (Lee and Ofreneo 2014). Indeed, unlike the Asian financial crisis of 1997, Asian states appeared "resilient" in the face of crisis, their "recovery" assured. Thus this chapter stands in contrast to many of the other chapters in this book that focus on the gendered origins and impacts of the current "global" economic crisis of 2008 onward (see Chapters 5, 6, and 8).

Asia is, of course, a huge region of the world, and a region of considerable economic, political, and cultural diversity. It is certainly not my intention in this brief chapter to provide a comprehensive and detailed account of the experience and aftermath of financial and economic crises in Asia. Rather, I focus on the *gender politics* of crises in Asia via the development of two lines of argument: first, an argument about gender and the governance of crisis. I focus on one of the ways through which the Asian crisis set the scene for the GFC—specifically, the way in which the construction of the crisis as a uniquely *Asian* crisis played a role in the failure of calls for a new international financial architecture. Although feminists (as well as other critical scholars and practitioners) had sought to influence debates around the new international financial architecture, their voices were lost as reform agendas were abandoned. In the contemporary era, I point to how gender has, nonetheless, increasingly come to the fore of global governance agendas. Within the context of the current economic crisis, I examine the way in which certain key global governance actors engaged in gender work have come to associate Asia's economic dynamism with an idea of Asian women as "drivers" of economic recovery. These governance narratives that reify the Asian woman in such a manner are problematic, not simply because they rest on essentialist assumptions, but also because they fail to recognize the mechanisms through which gender inequalities are sustained within capitalism. Thus, in the second part of this chapter, I develop an argument regarding the material experience of crisis on women. I seek to challenge the ways through which the language of "crisis" obscures the extent to which ongoing forms of crisis, impoverishment, and precarity are experienced in the everyday lives of Asian women and their households. Earlier feminist writings on the impacts of the Asian crisis (as well as earlier writings on the 1980s debt crisis and current analyses of the impact of the GFC and austerity on women) point to how women's unpaid labor served as a significant "shock absorber" during economic downturns. But by drawing upon evidence from "resilient"/"booming" Asia, it is shown to be just as important to examine the gendered everyday forms of crisis and crisis management that the poor experience in their daily lives, and not only during recessions.

In developing both of these lines of argument, I constantly refer back to earlier feminist writings on the Asian crisis, identifying the points of commonality and difference between feminists writings on both events. Indeed, it is worth noting that in the context of both the Asian crisis and the GFC, gendered narratives were deployed that presented the crises as stemming from forms of hyper-masculine excess. DeGoede's essay "Mastering Lady Credit," for example, took the Asian crisis as a starting point for developing arguments concerning the construction of the "risky" and "dangerous" behaviors of financial managers (DeGoede, 2000) (an early echo of the stories of testosterone-fueled derivatives traders that emerged after the 2008 Lehman Brothers collapse (Prügl 2012; Brassett and Rethel 2015). The trope of rational economic actors (men) "losing their heads" during the Asian crisis did, however, compete with a more dominant understanding of this crisis that placed the blame on Asia's "crony capitalism." Thus, the 1997 crisis was presented in deeply orientalist language as a financial "tsunami," a "hurricane," a "tropical storm" (Chernow 1997; Davies 1997; Hirsh 1998) created by the economic irrationalities of Asian elites. This was an understanding of the Asian crisis that fundamentally obscured the extent to which it had emerged as a crisis within contemporary capitalism— "essentially a product of the globalization of financial markets" (Bello 1998). The accusation of "crony capitalism" also reflected some deeply gendered assumptions. Thus Ling (2004) observed the mimicry of the Asian "tiger" developmental states in the years prior to the crisis—their adoption of a form of capitalist development that had many of the trappings of Western capitalism, but also served to challenge it in important ways (see also Han and Ling 1998). Moreover, this was a particularly gendered form of mimicry, or "hypermasculinity" (Nandy 1983). Thus

> Liberal elites in the West saw their chance and seized it. Smarting from almost two decades of hypermasculine taunts from Asia, they lambasted the region for its crony capitalism. Not only were the Asians wrong about the fundamentals for a healthy modern economy, but they were also morally unfit to lead the global economy. (Ling 2004, 125)

As will be argued in this chapter, the formulation of the crisis as an *Asian* crisis meant that even though some liberals in the West realized that the International Monetary Fund (IMF) had "gotten it wrong" (Ling 2004, 131), the idea of crony capitalism persisted and undermined agendas that sought out significant, progressive, and emancipatory changes to systems of global economic governance. Although the fallout of the Asian crisis did lead to calls among both academic and civil society commentators for the forging of a new, more gender-sensitive, international financial architecture, the global economic governance of gender has increasingly been captured by corporate actors (for example via UN partnerships with key corporations and corporate-linked foundations, and business-led organizations such as the World Economic Forum). Interestingly, post-GFC, the World Bank—one of the pioneers of instrumentalist "business case" or "smart economics" arguments for more gender equality—has begun to display a more cautious and sensitive approach to gender equality issues (World Bank 2012). And yet, the corporatization of gender equality initiatives continues apace, leaving little room for alternative visions that seek to challenge the capitalist economic structures through which gender inequality is maintained.

This chapter is structured as follows. In the first section of the chapter I am primarily concerned with exploring the representation of Asian women within post-GFC global economic governance regimes. This discussion is contextualized within an understanding of how and why demands for a more gender-sensitive and equitable international financial architecture in the post–Asian crisis period came to be effectively captured by corporate and neoliberal interests. The representation of Asian women as economically resilient subjects, efficient workers, and "good" investments and consumers in post-GFC discourse is thus shown to stem directly from the way in which gender issues came to be incorporated into global governance mechanisms during the course of the 2000s. The second part of this chapter returns to feminist writings on the Asian crisis, noting how these writings provide a comprehensive account of the multiple ways in which external economic shocks impact on women and their households. But what is perhaps more important is how they draw attention to the perpetuation of precarious gendered lives and, furthermore, how these precarities are sustained within the current capitalist global gender order.

FROM ASIAN CRISIS TO "WOMEN AT THE WHEEL"

In this section, I focus my attention on how key international organizations and corporate actors engaged in the global governance of gender equality issues have reproduced deeply essentializing notions of women's role in economic growth and development. The mobilization of the idea of Asian "women at the wheel" (WEF 2011) of the post-GFC recovery invariably reflects Asia's economic dynamism and the rise of female middle-class spending power in the region. And yet, the continual reproduction of deeply gendered inequalities in Asia (witnessed in terms of things like India's declining female labor force participation rate, regional levels of violence against women, and the effective exclusion of married women with children from full-time work in states such as Japan) has meant that Asian women's empowerment is often seen as providing a "solution," enabling states to become more competitive, to escape the dreaded "middle-income trap," and, in the case of Japan, to lift the economy out of recession.

I suggest that the development of this idealized view of the Asian woman as driving the region's economic growth reflects significant shifts in the global governance of gender issues both in terms of (a) ongoing commitments to highly economistic "business case" approaches to mainstreaming gender into policy making processes across a range of international organizations, and (b) the rise of global governance arrangements that increasingly position corporate "partnerships" and corporate actors as key players in gender equality projects (Bexell 2012; Elias 2013; Prügl and True 2014; Roberts 2014). In the discussion that follows, I locate the emergence of these corporatized gender agendas within broader debates about the need to transform and to "gender" global economic governance that emerged out of the crises of the 1990s (including the Asian crisis), before turning to examine in more detail the representation of Asian women within current global governance discourse.

What Happened to Agendas for Reform? The Disappearance of the Debate on the New International Financial Architecture

Many of the feminist analyses that emerged in the years following 1997 sought to link their analysis to debates concerning the need to develop a new, more socially just, international financial architecture, or to other proposals for the reform of global economic governance. I briefly overview some of these claims before turning to examine the ways in which a concern with gender *has* emerged in areas of global economic governance—albeit in ways that are thoroughly compatible with practices of neoliberalism. Indeed, what can be witnessed is the co-optation of gender equality and women's leadership claims in ways that serve to paper over the egregious gaps and inequalities generating in and through capitalist crisis.

To provide some examples, Aslanbeigui and Summerfield (2000) wrote of the "important opportunity for women to help reshape the global financial architecture" (2000, 82). Singh and Zammit (2000) argued that "[i]t is vital that women should formulate and articulate their own ideas on what best serves their interests in order to make a significant input into the discussions on the so called global financial architecture" (33). More concretely, Thanh Dan Truong (2000, 160) argued that the financial architecture needed to recognize "a gender equal social-policy" in which states took on more of the socially reproductive burdens associated with women's labor and provided effective social protection regimes (see also Elson 2002). Feminist economist Lourdes Benería (1999, 77) displayed slightly more caution. Linking her analysis to a critique of masculinized and mobile financial capitalism, she stated that "[a]fter two triumphant decades, crises in global capitalism may finally have brought Davos Man to a turning point, as an increasing number of people decry his excesses. The Asian crisis led to a break in the Washington Consensus; and the notion that 'there is no alternative' to the neoliberal model seems increasingly less acceptable"; Benería went on to suggest that "[t]he present danger is that proposals for global governance might be introduced in a top-down fashion and without a real world-wide democratic debate." Invoking a Polanyian notion of double-movement, Benería suggested that feminists could play a significant role in challenging the gendered assumptions upon which global economic governance operated. And yet it is Benería's warning that change would be introduced in ways that privileged the interests of elites that is the far more prescient aspect of her analysis.

The aftermath of the 1997 crisis did indeed lead to a sense that the space for including gender issues in development thinking was expanding. While global financial architectures might not have been completely rebuilt, the post-1997 period saw international financial institutions (IFIs) embrace notions of poverty reduction and socially inclusive development (Carroll 2012). The active incorporation of some more critical voices into institutions such as the World Bank (less so, the IMF) gave a rising prominence to gender issues in international development. And yet, this process of reform was limited by the extent to which gender equality claims had to be made to fit an existing neoliberal "business case" logic (Bergeron 2004; Griffin 2009). In the following discussion, I turn to examine how and why gendered issues are mobilized in current discussions of Asia's relationship to the "global" financial crisis, an analysis that reveals the deep limitations of business-case approaches to gender equality. Fundamentally, the post–Washington Consensus did not lead to a rethinking of neoliberal macroeconomic policy frameworks, with gender simply being "added on" to existing ways of "doing" development and "gender" (Griffin 2009). The emergence of the post–Washington Consensus out of the Asian crisis is significant here. Although there were concerns about the manner in which the IFIs had undertaken structural reforms in Asian states in terms of the impact of policies on levels of poverty and the top-down imposition of reforms, what was not up for question was an overall development model based on market-led economic growth.

Furthermore, while organizations such as the World Bank have since the 1990s had a long-standing interest in gender issues, True (2013) highlights the rather more "informal" nature of the global governance of gender—a process that takes shape largely outside formal institutions. This consists of "transgovernmental elite policy and advocacy networks and the policy coordination, diffusion and learning that they make possible" (2013, 333) and is, increasingly, a form of governance in which corporate voices and actors have come to prevail. In such a context, feminist agendas have come to be co-opted into a range of powerful business initiatives and partnerships that position women as those best able to deliver competitive and equitable economic growth and as those least susceptible to corruption and the excesses of corporate/financialized capitalism (Bexell 2012; Prügl and True 2014; Roberts 2014). As I have discussed elsewhere (Elias 2013), this is a distinctly post-feminist, celebratory gender discourse in which women's empowerment is equated with women's increased involvement in the market economy, whether through engagement in microenterprise schemes or through the increased representation of women on corporate boards.

In a recent analysis of how the World Economic Forum has developed a concern with gender issues (Elias 2013), I suggested that two particular feminized economic subjectivities are emphasized: "Davos woman" (the elite business woman pursuing socially minded philanthropic projects) and what Rankin (2001) terms "rational economic woman" (the microentrepreneur able to provide both income and care for her household). Both perspectives position women as those best able to deliver sustainable pro-poor economic growth—essentially providing the "human face" of globalization in ways that do not alter the underlying structures of capital accumulation in any meaningful sense. Furthermore, the articulation of deeply essentialized and heteronormative understandings of female economic subjectivities emerged with particular force in the aftermath of the GFC and the subsequent European sovereign debt crisis. Thus Prügl (2012) notes the rise of the popular myth that women could play a role in "cleaning up" the morally dubious practices of global financial firms, while Brassett and Rethel (2015) point to the "discursive move to domesticate reasoning about finance" (e.g., in terms of equating sovereign debt with household debt) in ways that enhanced the legitimacy of key female economic leaders such as Christine Lagarde and Angela Merkel.[1] Underpinning all of these competing conceptualizations of post-crisis womanhood is a consistent undervaluing of women's engagements in the socially reproductive economy—women's qualities in "cleaning up" and managing household budgets are naturalized and are not recognized as stemming from women's subordinate position within the household. This problem is especially apparent when we examine representations of ordinary Asian women within the current gender and global governance discourse.

Asian Women to the Rescue of Global Capitalism?

As this now more corporatized gender and development discourse that celebrates women's contributions to economic development and growth has emerged, we see that certain groups of Asian women come to be positioned as those that can play an important role in the post-2008 economy. Asia's economic strength, it seems, is increasingly related to discussions and debates about the role and position of women in Asian societies. Two narratives emerge: first, that of the enterprising, socially responsible, and hard-working Asian woman (the microentrepreneur, remittance sender, and socially minded consumer); and, second, arguments concerning how backward social practices in Asian societies are retarding economic growth. As will be shown, this second set of narratives is especially prevalent in relation to discussions of the Japanese economy (an economy frequently characterized as being in a situation of permanent economic crisis) but it is not exclusively confined to that one state.

These two narratives are neatly combined in the following statement from the United Nations Economic and Social Commission for Asia and the Pacific:

> Asia has been and remains the anchor of the global economic recovery, but to sustain this growth requires the creation of greater regional economic resilience— and one of the best ways to achieve this is through the empowerment of women.... Investment in women and girls is essential for poverty reduction and development. It is a low-risk strategy for growth. (UNESCAP 2012)

While it is no doubt the case that such statements reflect the way in which gender policy advocates have had to couch their demands in terms of the business case for investing in women, the language used in this statement is certainly interesting. For example, we should note the use of "resilience speak" that has coincided with the rise of post-GFC austerity measures and state cutbacks—a discursive turn that reflects a growing policy consensus concerning the capacity of systems to tolerate and to adapt to external shocks. And yet, resilience narratives operate to obscure (or, at worse, to celebrate) the increased economic burdens that poor women (usually in the West) face. As Joseph (2013) notes, policy framings of the concept of "resilience," for all their talk of the adaptability of *systems*, tend to emphasize a deeply individualizing (and neoliberal compatible) account of human activity in which agents are to take personal responsibility for their own adaptability in times of crisis. Thus the need for regional economic resilience described in the UNESCAP quotation is rooted in individual women taking responsibility for and managing investments in their human capital. We can see, furthermore, how a particular set of ideas developed in post-GFC austerity-afflicted North America and Europe are increasingly being applied to discussions of women in the Global South, in particular to women in emerging economies. Indeed, the rational economic woman identified in Rankin's work on female microentrepreneurs in Nepal (Rankin 2001) appears to be the embodiment of the resilient economic subject— providing essential income and socially reproductive labor for their households (with the role of microenterprise in reproducing the conditions of poverty in the first place conveniently missing from this discourse).

Another notable linguistic marker in the UNESCAP quotation concerns the use of the language of risk—reflecting, yet again, the way in which key management/business terms have been imported into discussions of gender and development. The discussion of risk is now commonplace in discussions of gender issues within both international organizations and private-sector organizations/groupings that are engaged in the development of global governance agendas. For example, in World Economic Forum (WEF) commentaries, blogs, and events, the "risks" posed by the high levels of gender inequality found in many Asian countries are emphasized (Ishikura 2014; Sneader 2014)—a view that fits with the overall tendency within the WEF to present gender inequality and other pressing social and environmental concerns as business risk issues that astute business people need to manage effectively (WEF 2014). Thus not including women on corporate boards in countries such as India or Indonesia is a "business risk" issue because of the need for business to respond to the growing demands from an expanding middle-class female customer base (Bagati and Carter 2010; Manpower Group 2011).

The language of risk also reflects assumptions about women's presumed risk-averse economic behaviors—characteristics that were also emphasized following the events of 2008 (contrasting women's essentialized "nature" with risk-taking by men on trading floors). In WEF publications we see that women are characterized as having a "natural prudence" (Hausman et al. 2010, 31) that is discussed in relation to the role as managers of household finances (and which also makes for more benevolent forms of public spending when women have greater control of public finances). Reference is made in these publications to a Goldman Sachs report entitled "The Power of the Purse" in which claims are made regarding the role that an expanding global female middle class can play in economic recovery, especially in the BRIC (Brazil, Russia, India, and China) economies (Hausman et al. 2009, 24–25; WEF 2009; Hausman et al. 2010, 31). This emphasis on women within the BRICs invariably reflects the way in which the search for "signs of 'hope'" post-GFC meant that "the pre-existing story of the BRICs was reworked to include a consumption dimension" (Sum 2013, 553). Thus increased consumer-led demand among the middle classes in the world's new and rising powers would bolster the economic recovery, and more fundamentally, increases in middle-class *women's* spending power had the potential to guarantee a more socially just recovery—because women's spending decisions reflect household, rather than individual, priorities (Goldman Sachs 2009, 12–13). Thus, women are "at the wheel" (WEF 2011) of the post-financial-crisis economic recovery centered on both the BRICs and Asia through their retail power, but also engaging in acts of consumption that enable them to break with traditional gender stereotypes in favor of an empowered gender identity as consumer.

Moreover, the political and economic empowerment of women in Asia is conceptualized as contributing to the region's long-term economic growth (WEF 2012). The significant gender gaps that exist in India, for example, are frequently presented as holding back the country's economic development. Hence, in a statement released to coincide with the 2009 WEF India Economic Summit, it was argued that "[e]qual rights for women is [sic] a business and economic imperative. It is fundamentally important to ensure their talent is not wasted" (my emphasis). Furthermore, "[s]uccess within companies should be determined by merit, not gender. To this end, companies should be made more accountable; they need to measure their progress on gender parity and report on it" (WEF 2009, 9). Not only is equality presented as serving business interests, but statements such as this present the market itself as a gender-neutral institution—that better functioning, more accountable, business systems are those best able to deliver equitable gender outcomes.

Most recently, low levels of female labor force participation have been presented as a key risk to Japan's long-term economic prospects. Japan is one of the states in Asia that has experienced ongoing economic crises and recessions going back to the 1990s, and government rhetoric has long focused on the need to increase women's labor force participation in order to raise economic competitiveness (Takeda 2008; Dales 2013). This rhetoric was more recently picked up by the IMF in comments from Christine Lagarde. At the IMF 2012 annual meeting in Tokyo, Lagarde pointed to the low levels of female labor force participation and suggested

> [b]ecause there is this ageing problem . . . we believe that women could actually help very much. . . . It's critically important the world over but it's particularly important in Japan . . . [research] indicates that women could actually save Japan . . . [if there were] better kindergartens and better assistance and cultural acceptance that women can actually do the job, it would be excellent for the Japanese economy. (Lagarde cited by Agence France-Presse 2012)

Lagarde's comments certainly display an understanding of the more overt discriminatory barriers that women face in the Japanese labor market and also the barriers to their participation in terms of child care. While there is some recognition of (some of the) socially reproductive work that women are engaged in (it is interesting that Lagarde makes no mention of deficiencies in Japan's system of elderly care), a look at the IMF policy note *Women, Work and the Economy: Macroeconomic Gains from Gender*

Equality (Elborgh-Woytek et al. 2013) presents the "solution" to increasing Japanese women's low labor force participation in terms of widening and deepening the reach of the market into the socially reproductive sphere. Thus the report recommends that Japan further liberalize the market for childcare provision, encouraging the growth of private sector providers, and eliminate tax deductions for dependent spouses that are seen to perpetuate the male salaryman–stay at home housewife patriarchal ideal. Certainly the Japanese state has played an important role in shoring up these deeply patriarchal gender norms, but looking to the market economy to provide a solution to women's subordination demonstrates the IMF's overwhelming conceptualization of the market as a gender-neutral space providing the kinds of progressive opportunities that serve to undermine backward and patriarchal local gender norms. Lacking in this perspective is any acknowledgment that markets might function in ways that support gender inequality—privatization and IMF-sanctioned fiscal reform are simply seen as an easy way of achieving gender equality.

GENDER AND CRISIS: BACK TO THE FUTURE?

This section of the chapter seeks to critically assess the extent to which Asian women can be conceptualized as a "locomotive" for global economic recovery and a more just global economic order. This is, of course, a narrative that is highly individualizing and fails to consider the ways through which structures of gender equality are maintained and reproduced within capitalism. Most notably, the lack of value ascribed to women's socially reproductive roles means that the discussions of "resilience" (women's role in shoring up economic systems in time of economic crisis/downturn) and "risk" (women as both risk-averse economic subjects and as low-risk "investments") are incomplete—they fail to identify where these positive feminine economic virtues come from, and significantly overstate their importance. Indeed, it is easy to unpack such claims by looking back to feminist literature on the Asian crisis. This section thus examines this earlier literature, before turning to explore the extent to which forms of crisis continue to be experienced in the everyday lives of Asian women, particularly among the poor.

Evaluations of the impacts of the Asian crisis on women and their households pointed to the gendered impacts of the crisis in terms of increases in poverty and unemployment among women, growing gender wage gaps, gendered health impacts, increases in women working in the sex industry, as well as increased levels of child labor (Aslanbeigui and Summerfield

2000).[2] It is worth focusing on these analyses because they provide a useful indication of the way in which women's economic "resilience" is performed via the exploitation of the socially reproductive economy—but also because they point to an alternative feminist understanding of "risk" that places the socially reproductive economy at its center, demonstrating the way in which the existence of the socially reproductive economy *enables* the kinds of risky financial behaviors that trigger crises in the first place.

The fallout of the Asian financial crisis resulted in the IMF imposing austerity regimes across a range of East and Southeast Asian states (specifically Indonesia, South Korea, and Thailand). The imposition of cuts in public expenditure in the aftermath of 1997 was widely criticized because the underlying problem in the Asian crisis was not a budget deficit (most crisis-affected states had been running healthy surpluses). Although the real economies in many afflicted states were relatively strong, the IMF plowed ahead with policies of liberalization and corporate governance reform, which, in many ways, served to further panic investors now wary of the spectre of Asian "crony capitalism." The impact on women was striking, as across crisis-affected states women's engagement in the informal economy increased, while their engagement in unpaid domestic work (including things like growing vegetables or meal preparation) increased. Poor households ate less, and spent significantly less on education and health care, with women household members especially affected by these altered consumption practices (for example, women were most likely to forgo meals) (Knowles et al. 1999, cited in Elson 2014; Thomas et al. 1999). In the Philippines, women's working hours increased dramatically as women took on extra work outside the home as a crucial household survival strategy (Lim 2000). The extent to which households bore the brunt of economic recession is starkly revealed in research from Indonesia by Thomas et al. (1999) in which household size was shown to actually increase following the crisis as households joined together—especially in terms of urban households migrating to join extended families in rural areas where the cost of living was lower, a shift that invariably reflected increases in urban unemployment (Thomas et al. 1999, 532) as well as government policies that sought to encourage this reverse-migration trend as a means to curtail rising social and political tensions in the cities (Silvey and Elmhirst 2003, 865).

Thus Diane Elson writes that it is through critical feminist analyses of the 1997 financial crisis that we are able to see how "the financial system had developed so that risk was off-loaded from those who took risks (mainly high income men) to women, especially low income women, who had to adsorb the risks, because they could not liquidate their responsibility for their children" (Elson 2014, 193). Hence, the Asian financial crisis "is a good example of downloading risks to the kitchen" (Elson 2002, 3). Elson's argument is important not simply because it draws attention to the impacts of financial crisis on women, but because it contains a much more significant critique—pointing to the way in which gendered processes, assumptions, and biases are central to the operation of financial markets themselves. The financial system is thus understood as operating within the context of a gendered political economy that enables risk-taking or acts of extreme financial mismanagement to take place (see also Peterson 2003, 153). For scholars such as Truong, this gendered political economy was sustained by state policies in many "miracle" economies—in particular, their role in upholding an anti-welfarist gender order that served to adversely incorporate women into the region's industrial development and left them especially vulnerable during the crisis (Truong 1999, 2000). Within this gender order, a politics of nationalism, which constructed "good" women as, first and foremost, homemakers, served an important ideological purpose (Silvey 2000; Truong 2000; Pettman 2003).

This is not, however, to assume a static gender order. For example, economic development in Asia prior to the 1997 crisis led to shifts in popular perceptions regarding women's role and position both within and outside the household. Silvey's work from Indonesia demonstrates how these shifting cultural norms fed into wider discourses concerning the gendered nature of Indonesia's crisis and the need for a reassertion of traditional (rural) values (Silvey 2000). The growth of the sex industry after the crisis and the pressure for women internal migrants to return to rural areas meant that women who migrated to find work were easily stigmatized. Thus "the morality of young women's autonomous mobility, and the prostitute as a symbol of the threatened social order, have emerged as defining local tropes of the post-1997 period of political and economic upheaval" (156). Indeed, it is useful at this point to cite Jan Jindy Pettman's argument that in understanding economic shifts in Asia "[s]peaking the language of globalization, or Asian miracle or crisis, functions to disguise the gendered nature of these transformations and the unevenness, the inequalities, and the costs of transformation" (Pettman 2003, 176).

Pettman's argument that we need to recognize how gendered transformations are racked with "inequalities" and "costs" also provides an important entry point into thinking about the ongoing experience of economic crisis in the lives of Asian women. Despite the imaginary of booming Asia and the rhetoric of the "Asian century," the non- or even anti-welfarist orientation of Asian states continues to shape poor women's lived experiences. Japan is very significant in terms of the discussion of "crisis" so central to this volume, given its ongoing characterization as a nation in economic and political crisis following decades of economic growth and prosperity. Economic changes have led to the dismantling of the state's corporate-oriented semi-welfare state. But writers such as Broadbent (2013) point out that the restructured Japanese welfare system has become increasingly dependent on low-paid and precarious female employment—in other words, we can see little evidence of how a more privatized welfare system is opening up greater opportunities for female empowerment in the manner discussed in the IMF concept note mentioned earlier. Broadbent takes the example of the home-care industry (the provision of caring services for the elderly in their homes), which, since 2000, has been outsourced to the private sector. The industry has benefited from the ability to recruit working-class women who lack access to employment in other sectors because of discriminatory employment practices that construct women as mere "part-time" workers. The liberalization of the welfare state in Japan is thus shown to be mediated via gendered inequalities, while the real costs of Japan's economic stagnation is disproportionately borne by "women, workers, and their families" (140).

Broadbent's analysis gives an indication of how "crisis" is experienced within the sphere of everyday life—in terms of women's increased engagement in highly precarious and low-paid forms of work centered on households. Vij (2013) also takes up the theme of gendered precarity in Japan, but points not to a sudden increase in feminized forms of precarity, but to the centrality of precarious, feminized affective labor to Japanese capitalism. The current economic crisis in Japan has triggered growing concerns around the rising precarity of male full-time work, while ignoring the extent to which women's work (both paid and unpaid) offers little in the way of security (see also Dales 2013). Indeed, numerous recent studies from Asia point to varied ways in which multiple forms of economic crisis are borne by women and their households, be it in terms of the rise of poor women's migration for marriage and domestic work within the region (Lee 2012; Elias 2013), the impact of pension reforms on poor working women in Sri Lanka (Ruwanpura 2013), or the daily struggles faced by middle-class women to balance work and caring responsibilities in states such as India and Malaysia (Elias 2011; Hill 2013). Perhaps the most significant issue that authors such as Broadbent and Vij raise, however, is the discussion of precarity and precarious lives, and how this is a deeply gendered phenomenon. Lee and Ofreneo's work, for example, while not engaging a gendered approach, does make the argument that the lack of significant unemployment impacts of the GFC in Southeast Asia belies the extent to which the region has witnessed a rise in precarious forms of work. Spitzer and Piper (2014) have looked at the impact of the GFC on migrant workers in the

Philippines, focusing in particular on the case of the Philippines. Their findings complement those of Lee and Ofreneo (2014) in that they suggest that although the current economic crisis did result in the return home of many Filipino migrants, "the response to this most recent crisis could not be extracted from the ongoing series of economic crises that Philippine workers and their families have faced at home and abroad for decades" (1008) (see also Bélanger and Giang 2013 on the relationship between precarity and gendered migrants in Vietnam). Of particular relevance to this chapter is Spitzer and Piper's conclusion that

> . . . we hope to complicate the current notion of global economic crisis that is often both western-centric and ahistorical, in favor of a conceptualization that attends to the historically situated, interpenetrating, and multiple crises affecting the Global South in general and many migrant workers in particular. (1019)

Much of Asia may not have experienced the GFC in quite the same manner as the rest of the world, but the daily struggles and forms of impoverishment faced by women and their households in Asia cannot be side-lined from any discussion of crisis. Crises are not one-off "traumatic events" (Brassett and Clarke 2012), or ("tropical storms"); rather, via a focus on women's working lives both within and outside the household, we can observe the way in which economic and social crises associated with state restructuring and the increased strains on the socially reproductive sphere are continually reproduced and sustained. As this chapter has illustrated, feminists writings on the "crises" of the 1990s (the Asian crisis) and the early 2000s (the "global" financial crisis) have consistently pointed to the way in which women experienced impoverishment in the fallout of these crises and the way in which households, and women's labor within households in particular, are rendered, to use Elson's term, "infinitely elastic" (Elson 1989b, 58). That is, they are viewed as able to easily cope with and support policies of welfare retrenchment, liberalization, and privatization. Indeed it is the continuities in these literature that provide us with important insights into the ongoing forms of crisis that accompany the widening and deepening of the market economy into all spheres of social life—including the household (Gunawardana and Elias 2013).

CONCLUSIONS

The 2008 "global" crisis, while invariably having some gendered impacts on Asian economies (for example, in terms of layoffs in the highly feminized

Cambodian garment sector), was largely focused on parts of the world outside the region, specifically in Europe and North America. Thus, though this chapter has largely focused on contemporary Asia through the lens of feminist writings on the 1997 crisis, future research on the theme of gender and crisis in Asia needs to further explore the extent to which the apparent economic "resilience" of many Asian economies belies the extent to which other, deeply gendered, forms of economic "crisis" underpin the experience of late capitalism in the region (a research agenda that also has lessons for how we understand the gendered impacts of "crisis" in other parts of the world). How, for example, do states across Asia continue to face significant difficulties and dilemmas with regard to gender equality—difficulties and dilemmas that are shown to stem from forms of crisis in the socially reproductive economy? Rai, Hoskyns, and Thomas (2014) employ the term "depletion through social reproduction" in order to encapsulate the extent to which sustained attempts to progressively increase women's contribution to the productive economy have not been matched by any significant declines in women's engagement in the socially reproductive economy. Such pressures are experienced in women's everyday lives in relation to the persistence of gendered forms of inequality within and outside the household, as well as specific pressures such as rising costs of living and levels of household indebtedness, and increased burdens being placed on informal family support networks, including older family members, in order to support women's work outside the household (including employment overseas).

Looking back to feminist writings on the Asian crisis clearly triggers a certain level of disappointment—when feminist economists in particular saw the crisis as some kind of turning point that would lead the way for a Polanyian-style reform, reining in unfettered financial capitalism (Benería 1999; Aslanbeigui and Summerfield 2000; Singh and Zammit 2000; Elson 2002). Talk of a new international financial architecture in the late 1990s and early 2000s was largely empty, and the idea that this created some kind of opening for a more gender-just international order was somewhat naïve. And yet, the critical insights underpinning this literature remain important—not least work by Elson (2002, 2014) and Truong (1999, 2000) that focused on how the financial economy is sustained by the material practices of households—who are forced to adsorb the shocks of financial crisis because of the need to sustain the lives of those who are raised within them. The Asian financial crisis did not in any sense prove to be the tipping point that ushered in a more socially just and gender-equitable global order. But, at the same time (without wanting, myself, to sound spectacularly naïve), there is a need to consider how certain contradictions in the current global capitalist gender order might create opportunities for resistance and change. One avenue might be to challenge existing gender narratives in global governance—narratives that rest upon a deeply individualized notion of the resilient and risk-adverse Asian woman who bears some responsibility for global financial recovery. A focus on social relations of reproduction and gendered modes of precarity do, of course, challenge this individualization narrative. But the challenge lies in finding ways of mobilizing these critical counter-narratives and finding ways of bringing them to bear on discussions of the global governance of gender.

NOTES

1. Interestingly, the role of ideas of gender and sexuality in legitimating responses to crisis has parallels in the Asian crisis. In the aftermath of the crisis, Asian states as elites formulated "a self-righteous hypermasculine front" (see Ling 2004) for domestic political purposes. This included attacks on the power of trade unions in South Korea, as well as the Malaysian prime minister's turn against his (perceived as Western-leaning) deputy Anwar Ibrahim—leading to Anwar's arrest on trumped-up charges of sodomy.
2. The feminist literature on the Asian crisis has considerable similarities with literatures on the impact of structural adjustment programs in the 1980s and early 1990s. These studies demonstrated the many burdens that women took on as the state's role in the economy was increasingly pushed back. Thus women were increasingly involved in managing already overstretched household incomes in order to pay for privatized services and disproportionately took on social welfare functions that had previously been provided by the state (Elson 1989a; Benería and Feldman 1992; Çagatay, Elson, and Grown 1996).

CHAPTER 8

"To Double Oppression, Double Rebellion"

Women, Capital, and Crisis in "Post-Neoliberal" Latin America

GUILLERMINA SERI

We are Latin American women and our identity was forged in the Resistance to the colonial conquest of our territories and the sacking of the commons in our land. Five centuries later, we continue confronting patriarchy and colonialism in new forms, now with the action of transnational corporations in the region, which with the support of governments pollute the commons while the silent genocide of our peoples continues.

—Manifiesto feminista contra la megaminería y el modelo patriarcal colonial extractivista

Smiling and waving to the crowd, three female Latin American presidents—Brazil's Dilma Rousseff, Argentina's Cristina Fernández, and Chile's Michele Bachelet—celebrated the latter's return to office on March 11, 2014. The image established an iconic milestone for the progress that women and democracy have made in the region, marking a stark contrast to the memories of the patriarchal military dictators from the past. The gains seem even more significant as these three female leaders form part of the "Pink Tide," the moderate turn to the left of several Latin American governments that, since the early 2000s, have proclaimed their commitment to progressive reforms (Friedman 2007). Claiming to have moved toward a "post-neoliberal" order, in contrast to the shock therapy, privatizations, and budget cuts of the 1990s, the policies endorsed by left-of-center governments somewhat tempered the effects of the crisis since 2008. For as the 2008 recession expanded out of Wall Street, Latin America experienced a boom thanks to the high international prices of oil and agricultural products. Additional fiscal resources from higher exports allowed governments to avoid cuts in social spending while implementing conditional cash transfer programs (Espino, Esquivel, and Enríquez 2012). The region remained afloat, and politicians got themselves re-elected.

Yet the impact of such programs on women was a different story. Neither regional economic gains nor the consolidation of female political leadership, laws, or social policies seemed sufficient to advance the conditions of most women or to prevent violence against them. If anything, they made contrasts clearer by exposing Latin America's economic status quo and its ultimate reliance on the exploitation of women and on forms of violence against them. Women, as Jacqui True notes, are disproportionally affected during financial crises, which increase the chances for gender violence (2012, 102, 301).

By exposing what True identifies as the "political economy roots of violence against women," this chapter contends that femicide has emerged as the main scandal resulting from the crisis in the region (2012, ix). Femicide, the murder of a woman simply for being a woman, has gained visibility across Latin America in recent years as the crisis unfolded (Famá 2012). As we learn about the extent of such crimes, the Mexican "maquiladora city" of Ciudad Juárez stands out as a perverse paradigmatic scenario where labor exploitation and violence against women conflate. Ciudad Juárez became known for hundreds of femicides committed against girls and women since the 1990s. A similar pattern manifested in other Central American locations, where many of the victims were workers in the maquiladora assembly plants that expanded with NAFTA and the neoliberal deregulation of production and trade (Lagarde y de los Rios 2009, xi; Robertua 2012, 27, 45; Ballinas 2013). With 306 femicides recorded in 2010 alone, the highest number in two decades, Ciudad Juárez has shown signs of a worsening violence against women in the aftermath of the 2008 great recession (La Jornada 2011). The violence exhibited by the Mexican city is just the tip of a broader pattern extending throughout the region. As True shows, increased domestic violence accompanied the recession around the world (2012, 105).

Femicides stand at the top of a violent structure securing the expropriation of women's labor. This exploitation is double: while paid consistently lower wages than men, women also find themselves forced to perform unpaid labor, making it possible for wages to be kept low and for production costs to be "externalized." Thus, women have to fix the environmental and health damages caused by economic activities through their own efforts. The double exploitation of women as both low-paid workers and unpaid laborers sustains extraordinary profits. It also places women, as Silvia Federici (2012, 108) explains, in a position to serve as "shock absorbers" for bumps in the global economy. In turn, the perpetuation of these terms owes much to the persistent, deep-seated complicities between patriarchal structures, the gendered division of labor, and violence against women.

In what follows, I reconstruct key economic and extra-economic layers of women's inequality and exploitation with a focus on the aftermath of the 2008 crisis and its current comeback. Crises intensify the demands placed on women and bring about extra pressure in all forms of female work—formal, informal, and unpaid (ECLAC 2013, 11). The voices of women and feminist accounts illuminate different aspects of women's double exploitation and help to understand the pervasive violence against women and the scandal of femicides brought to light by the crisis in present-day Latin America.

THE SCANDAL: AT THE JUNCTURE OF LABOR EXPLOITATION, TRAFFICKING, AND FEMICIDES

"Stop femicide," "stop women from disappearing in democracy"—the 2012 Encuentro Nacional de Mujeres ended in a massive march, with protestors carrying banners calling for "equal job, equal pay," for treating the trafficking of women as a crime against humanity, and for the Argentine government to declare a Gender Violence National Emergency (*Télam* 2012; *Redaccion* 3 2012). Approximately 35,000 participants from Argentina, Paraguay, Colombia, Honduras, México, and other Latin American nations gathered in 2012 in Posadas, and more than 20,000 Argentines met again in 2013 in San Juan (*Territoriodigital* 2012). Held annually since 1986, the Encuentros have become a robust forum and a showcase for the region's women's movement (Bellotti 2002). Gender-specific forms of poverty and exploitation, corporate pollution, the decriminalization of abortion (legal only in Cuba, Guyana, and Uruguay), the plight of the indigenous peoples, femicide, and other forms of violence against women fill the agenda of the Encuentros as much as they haunt women's lives in Latin America. Moreover, crises increase the chances for gender violence, as True notes (2012, 102, 301).

Just how prevalent are the abuse, violence, and exploitation of women in the region? In Mexico, 46 percent of participants in a 2011 study described suffering themselves from violence that ranged from battery to sexual abuse, while more than one-third of female survey respondents from 18 Latin American countries expressed knowing at least one other female victim of domestic violence (Latinobarometro 2006; Cruz Vargas 2012; Gherardi 2012, 32).

Femicide is the most vicious form of violence against women. Although precise data are often lacking amidst an "information deficit," more than 1,100 femicides were officially documented across 10 Latin American countries in 2011. Two years later, 295 women were murdered in Argentina alone (*La Nación* 2013a). Femicide rates have reached 13.9 per 100,000—the world's highest rate—in El Salvador, 9.8 in Guatemala, and 11.1 in Mexican states such as Chihuahua, Baja California, and Guerrero. Most cases remain unresolved. Despite the ratification of the Inter-American Convention to Prevent, Punish and Eradicate Violence against Women by 32 Latin American countries, and even when appropriate laws are passed, as in 2008 in Guatemala, judges have shown reluctance to acknowledge femicides.

Femicide and other forms of violence against women seem to find free reign in zones where neoliberal globalization manifests "in the most extreme manner," as Weissman put it (2009, 239). Jacqui True agreed, noting how violence against women has prevailed in "free trade zones" in developing countries (True 2012, 117). Maquiladoras, the Mexican and Central American industrial assembly plants in special tax zones, epitomize neoliberal forms of labor exploitation. Specializing in electronics and clothing, maquiladoras spread from Mexico and Central America since the 1960s, gaining new impulse under NAFTA's deregulation. Like industrial assembly plants elsewhere, maquiladoras became known for hiring mostly young, single women, selected based on stereotypical assumptions of females' obedience, discipline, flexibility, and attention to detail (Dominguez et al. 2010). These women are at times also represented as irresponsible and unreliable, see their rights denied and find themselves treated as "easily expendable" as Weissman noted (2009, 226).

Most maquiladora workers live close to the factories in shacks lacking in infrastructure and services. Despite taking second jobs, they survive in conditions of indigence. Deprived of legal protections and geographically isolated, women working in maquiladoras are subjected to long, exacting hours and are paid extremely meager salaries while enduring grueling labor and sexual abuse by male managers during work shifts, as well as facing the risk of sexual attacks after leaving work (True 2012, 83).

As in the maquiladora enclaves throughout Mexico, Guatemala, and other Central American countries, wild capitalism, unemployment, poverty, a weak to nonexistent rule of law, and economic and social exclusion expose the lawless faces of the state and capital at a scandalous proportion in the bodies of women (Weissman 2009, 226). In light of this situation, femicide appears to be the tip of a structure of violence that naturalizes discrimination against women and deprives them of resources, power, life opportunities, and access to money, education, and rights. Behind the cruelty of femicide lie ways in which the world market turns women into the ultimate link of exploitation and even into commodities (Dunaway 2001).

"Girls go missing like hens," noted Irene Cari in Salta, Argentina (Benitez and MacKenzie 2011). As many as five million Latin American girls and women are estimated to have been pulled into trafficking networks, a clandestine global business generating $32 billion in annual profits. Women account for more than half of individuals subjected to forced labor and for 98 percent of those forced to sexual exploitation (International Labor Organization 2008, 3; Godoy 2010; International Labor Organization 2012, 13–15). In Mexico, 24,000 migrant women from Central America disappeared after falling prey to "coyotes" and other criminals under the presidency of Felipe Calderón alone (*Emeequis* 2013). In Brazil, between 2005 and 2011, trafficking rings forced hundreds of women into prostitution in Spain, Switzerland, Italy, Holland, Portugal, and France (Leroy Cerqueira 2013).

Trafficked women are often mistreated and criminalized by the very institutions that should help them, as evident in the police's reluctance to take families' reports of kidnappings or in their treatment of victims as criminals. In turn, the UN Special Rapporteur on the human rights of migrants, Gabriela Rodríguez Pizarro, explains that corruption is the main reason why governments do not investigate or take responsibility and why the trafficking of women continues to thrive (Ruiz 2013). Testimonies have further confirmed this claim. For example, one Argentine survivor, after being held captive with others in the basement of a farm in the country's northwest region, recalled seeing provincial government minibuses arrive to pick up girls and take them over the Bolivian border. She noted that none of these official buses was ever checked, which highlights the various layers of governmental complicity involved in the trafficking of women (Benitez and MacKenzie 2011).

Legislation is being passed, but this is just one step. A speaker at the 28th Encuentro Nacional de Mujeres conference in Argentina summarized this situation: "We got the law of sexual education but it is not being implemented, the law of violence [against women] but it has not been assigned a budget, the law of trafficking of women, but it has not been regulated; the proposal for legal, safe, and free access to abortion is not being discussed" (Ripol, 2013). Trafficking markets are difficult to dismantle. Public budgets tend to be insufficient for supporting the necessary policing and oversight. In many districts, shelters for battered women are "collapsed" (*Tiempo Argentino* 2013). Local "caudillo" governments often resist federal laws protecting women. Widespread state complicity and ineffectiveness in addressing the violence against women led the Inter-American Court of Human Rights, in 2010, to declare the state of Mexico guilty of violating "the right to life, integrity, and personal liberty" for three cases of femicide committed in Ciudad Juárez in 2001.

WOMEN'S DOUBLE EXPLOITATION AND CRISES IN LATIN AMERICA

Barbara Sutton reconstructed women's experiences of the 2001 crisis in Argentina as "an all-encompassing, even violent, force affecting body, emotions, relationships, and intimate aspects of their lives" that turned women's bodies into territories of global restructuring (2011, 58). Women are disproportionally affected during financial crises. Behind the personal consequences brought by a crisis lie persistent economic, social, and political structural inequalities.

Gender inequality is apparent in Latin America. Constituting 41 percent of the region's urban labor force of 277 million, in 2012 one-third of women (33.7 percent) did not earn an income of their own, and those who did worked mostly informally in shops and housekeeping (58 percent), making significantly less than men—as little as almost half the income of males in Mexico (Seligson, Smith, and Zechmeister 2012, 40; Bárcena et al. 2013, 38–39; ECLAC 2013b, 71). Despite having similar and even higher qualifications than men—equal access to primary education was reached in the 1990s in most Latin American countries, with females gaining a greater presence in secondary and post-secondary education—women in the region have little access to well-paying jobs (ECLAC 2005, 108; Bárcena et al. 2013, 36). Gender income gaps captured in femininity indexes show regional averages of 119.76 percent for urban poverty and 129.47 percent for destitution, with the gap for poverty and destitution reaching 148.5 percent and 158 percent in Chile (ECLAC 2013b, 74) Thus, simply being a woman makes it more likely for an individual to be poor.

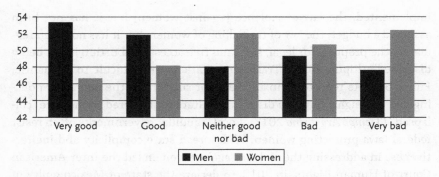

Figure 8.1 Economic situation, Latin America, 2012. "How would you characterize your economic situation?"
LAPOP 2012

Structurally deprived of income and resources, subjected to a double exploitation through both the labor market and household unpaid labor, women suffer from crises more intensely. First, as waged workers, women are paid consistently lower salaries than men for doing equal work. In addition, women have access to mostly temporary, unregulated jobs, such as those in the maquiladora sector described earlier.

In parallel to being more intensely exploited as waged workers, women contribute with their unpaid work. One of the main realms of women's unpaid labor is the household, a preeminent site of reproductive activities (ECLAC 2013a, 38). Care or reproductive labor comprises the tasks necessary to "maintain, continue and repair our world . . . our bodies, our being and our environment," as Fischer and Tronto explained (ECLAC 2013a, 110). Despite being indispensable to keeping individuals healthy and productive, this form of labor remains invisible and excluded from statistics. "Neither compensated nor socially valued," as LeBaron observes (2010, 893), not even recognized as work, the bulk of reproductive labor still falls on the shoulders of women (ECLAC 2013a, 37).

Historically, the separation of productive and reproductive activities that confined reproductive care labor to the household consolidated with the development of capitalism (LeBaron 2010, 898, 893). Capital expanded through successive waves by separating people from the means and resources needed for life and making these resources accessible only through the market. As goods and services available outside the market were transformed into commodities that could only be obtained with money, most individuals found themselves forced to sell their labor force and to work for a wage to meet basic needs. These instances of separation, also referred to as enclosures, were first identified by Karl Marx (1986 [1867]) as a single phase of "primitive" accumulation.

After high mortality rates accompanied enclosures and earlier phases of industrialization in Europe, industrial societies stabilized with the expansion of nuclear families among the working class. Thus, during the nineteenth century women were pushed back into households to take on the burden of reproductive work (Harman 1984; Poster 1988, 190–192, 194–195).

The household thus was consolidated as the main scenario of unpaid labor, reproducing labor power. Unpaid domestic reproductive labor compensates for wages lower than necessary to support workers and their families, thus subsidizing capital (Dunaway 2001, 6). As it is known, waged workers are paid not according to the value they produce, but to the cost of reproducing (or renewing) their labor power, including food, housing, clothing, and other necessities. A significant part of that cost is not reimbursed, however, but instead is shouldered by those providing for those goods through unpaid work, which in our societies are mostly women in charge of household chores (LeBaron 2010, 893). As the primary producers of "the labor–power commodity" within families, women—through their unpaid work—make up for wages much lower than they would have to be if workers had to reproduce their labor on the sole basis of their income (Federici 2012, 31).

Like industrialization, working-class nuclear families expanded in Latin America, radiating in the first half of the twentieth century from industrial centers in Mexico, Brazil, and Argentina. Still, semi-proletarian, networked households remained dominant among the Latin American poor and the rural populations.

Far from a one-time event, however, enclosures and the commodification of further dimensions of life continue to take place. Neoliberal restructuring brought a new wave of enclosures. First imposed through military rule in the mid-1970s in Chile and Argentina and then spreading in some cases with support of the popular vote, neoliberal policies dismantled legal and policy safety nets to subject individuals directly to the market. Turning basic public goods into commodities and leaving reproductive care work to individuals, neoliberal reforms also brought about massive job losses, thereby undermining working-class nuclear families. In the following years, Latin Americans witnessed a lower proportion—and duration—of marriages and a drastic increase of households headed by women, which in the decade prior to 2011 grew from 27.4 percent to 35.22 percent (ECLAC 2013b, 36).

The feminization of families overlapped with the expansion of networked semi-proletarian households. Prevalent among the Latin American poor, these households can survive on artificially low wages by compensating with other monetary and non-monetary resources, from growing food to producing items to be sold in the market to recycling trash. In turn, transnational commodity chains connect all agents, phases, and sites involved in the production of goods, reaching deep into semi-proletarian households and making even those outside the wage relation support extraordinary corporate profit through their household labor (Dunaway 2001, 6, 22).

The incorporation of women into the labor force has not altered the traditional division of labor in the household, however, which makes reproductive labor nearly an exclusively female burden (ECLAC 2013c, 32; ECLAC 2014, 30–32). Across Latin America, surveys have shown that women devote up to five times more time than men to household chores (ECLAC 2013a, 123). With a regional average of 9.5 weekly hours of additional domestic labor for women, the gender gap is quite evident: men devote 4 hours to domestic work versus women's 23 in Brazil, 13 versus 46 in Costa Rica, 7 versus 29 in Ecuador, 6 versus 29 in Honduras, 15 versus 43 in Mexico, and 15 versus 36 in Perú (Bárcena et al. 2013, 44–47). Gender differences in the time devoted to unpaid reproductive labor prevent women, especially those living in rural areas, from getting an education, earning a salary, and participating in communal or political activities (Antonopoulos 2009b; ECLAC 2011, 87; Seligson, Smith, and Zechmeister 2012, 77, 95; Bárcena et al. 2013, 44–47). Representations of the female body as what Barbara Sutton termed a "body-for-others" or as a natural, household resource freely available to provide for the needs of the family and too often disguised as affection naturalize and make invisible these forms of exploitation (Sutton 2011, 35; ECLAC 2013a, 114).

Available at lower wages, contributing unpaid domestic work to the reproduction of the labor force, and having to absorb environmental, health, safety, and production costs avoided by industries, women's labor is used to subsidize corporate profit. From their perspective, however, women charged with the care of family members are faced with the question of resisting the market's determination of "who should live and who should die," as Silvia Federici puts it, amidst the "privatized solutions" left to them, whether it be migrant labor or personal indebtment (Federici 2012, 132; see also LeBaron 2010, 902–903).

Economic forms of gendered inequality expose women to crises more intensely and "fuel the violence against women," as True observed (2012, 5). Overrepresented in unstable, informal posts, often lacking health services and unemployment benefits, in the context of a crisis women suffer job losses and budget cuts in education, health, and social programs more acutely than men (Espino, Esquivel, and Rodríguez Enríquez 2012, 342). This was clear in 2008. If attenuated by the commodity boom, the consequences of the crisis were felt across the region. The recession spread through commercial channels in the form of a decreasing demand for exports and rising fuel and food prices. Textiles, clothing, tourism, and agriculture—all sectors with a strong female worker presence—were rapidly affected, and thousands of jobs were lost. The open, deregulated Mexican economy, with its significant levels of poverty (37 percent) and high dependence on international trade (60 percent GDP), was the worst hit (Espino, Esquivel, and Enríquez 2012, 293–296, 327, 300). In 2009, unemployment affected men in industry and construction, and many women took precarious low-paying jobs, feeling forced to join a "highly gendered" labor market at their weakest to compensate for economic losses in their households (Roberts 2012, 94). Pushed to take precarious wages while burdened with unpaid reproductive labor, women's double oppression became manifest, thereby confirming the International Labor Organization's prediction that the crisis would affect Latin American women more adversely than their peers elsewhere. Indeed, in testimonies, surveys, and political slogans, women throughout the region reported being deeply affected by the downturn and expected it to last longer than men did (see Figures 8.2 and 8.3) (Bárcena et al. 2013, 41–54).

Women find themselves more intensely exposed to crises while being forced to compensate for the losses with unpaid work. Mirroring the sexist division of labor, Latin American women are overrepresented in the field of care work, where they hold 94.2 percent of the jobs, ranging from housekeeping to assisting the young, the elderly, and the ill (ECLAC 2013a, 132).

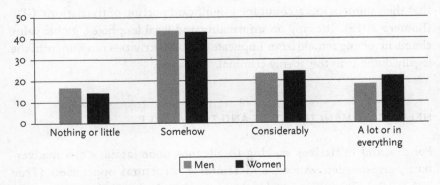

Figure 8.2 "How much is the crisis affecting you?" Latin America, 2009.
Latinobarometro 2009

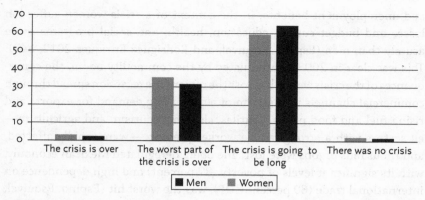

Figure 8.3 Opinion about the crisis, Latin America, 2009.
Latinobarometro 2009

Eighteen million women work as domestic laborers across Latin America and the Caribbean—a greater number than in most world regions—and two-thirds of them work without legal protection in Brazil and 80 percent in Argentina.

Embedded in "global care chains," female domestic labor has become a regional export product (ECLAC 2013a, 113). Even today, however, migrant domestic workers are still not recognized as workers by many unions or feminists (Enloe 1989, 29). Migration serves as a main market solution for poor Latin American women seeking jobs to assist workers in the Global North to take care of their families. Female migrant workers are often forced to leave their children with relatives and see their own mothering take the shape of remittances. If conducive to "crises of social reproduction" back home, the number of migrants from countries such as El Salvador, Ecuador, Haiti, Honduras, and Nicaragua becomes so large that their remittances account for a significant portion of the nations' GDP (Romero 2013). Thriving on informality and legal loopholes, global value chains involving female labor implicate them in activities ranging from the legally dubious to the openly criminal.

HELPING WOMEN: THE STATE AND THE MARKET

Policies and initiatives seeking to advance poor families can inadvertently overburden women and reinforce structural oppression (True 2012, 104). This seems to be the case of cash transfer programs and microfinance. Conditional cash transfer programs have been a central policy instrument in Latin America since the 2000s, used by governments to counter the crisis. By distributing modest cash allowances, these programs aim to help poor families meet their needs while improving the opportunities for their children to break out of the cycle of poverty. Families receive allowances for ensuring that their children attend school and have regular health controls and vaccinations (Bárcena et al. 2013, 59). With Brazil and Mexico as pioneers, Mexico's Oportunidades program provides 27 million people with cash, food, basic health services, and scholarships for children, while Brazil's Bolsa Familia covers over 12 million households, or 51 million people, with stipends delivered to female recipients (De Brauw et al. 2012, 5; Espino, Esquivel, and Enríquez 2012, 307–342). Following the same format, Argentina's Asignación Universal por Hijo (AUH) reached 3.5 million children under 18. By 2009, with 17 countries in the region implementing cash transfers, as the main social policy strategy in response to the crisis, these programs covered 113 million people, or 19 percent of the region's population (Bárcena et al. 2013, 54, 57).

Monetary allowances are claimed to have raised poor families' income by 10 percent and to have increased school attendance and health controls. When women are the designated recipients, the money tends to strengthen their autonomy in making decisions both within the household and in their personal lives. Enthusiasm for cash transfer programs grew stronger given their lower cost compared to traditional social policies. Even the largest of such programs in Brazil and Mexico cost less than 1 percent of these countries' GDPs (UNDP 2013, 84). Welcomed by experts and governments as tools for building more inclusive, democratic societies, cash transfer programs have shown, however, "modest" to negligible effectiveness in fighting poverty and reducing inequality. In particular, assessed through the lens of gender, the concept of conditionality behind cash transfers has proven troublesome.

The problem with cash transfer programs seems to be that rather than investing in improving public services, governments make women take on the burden of meeting children's health and educational standards amidst often overwhelmed hospitals and schools. These programs force women to devote still more time to traditional domestic chores, turn them away from earning their own money, and make them more dependent. Even in the best-case scenarios, when women are designated recipients of the stipends, it is only their status as mothers that counts, for it is the youth whom governments seek to protect. Built upon "social maternalist" assumptions, these programs' publicized success stories rely on women's unpaid labor (Espino, Esquivel and Enríquez 2012, 307, 309; Bárcena et al. 2013, 62–70).

Except for the small amounts of money they receive, families in need are left to meet health and educational standards by themselves. As Lena Lavinas aptly noted, "a flagrant contradiction" exists in governments demanding cash transfer beneficiaries to meet such standards, rather than taking responsibility for improving the provision of public health care and education. Thus, despite Latin American politicians' anti-neoliberal claims, Lavinas (2013, 38) concludes that, by making the poor individually responsible for public goods that should be provided by the state, cash transfers "pave the way for a retrenchment of welfare rather than its expansion." Especially when we consider the extra burden that these programs place on women, making them compensate with their own care for deficient or nonexistent public services, no progressive rhetoric can hide the complicity of these policies in further dismantling the democratic, inclusive aspects of the state (Marchand and Runyan 2010, 4). In the absence of comprehensive social programs, cash transfers might be indispensable, but they are also insufficient and onerous to women.

In parallel to social policies, others have seen the market as offering alternatives to women. Supported by the World Bank, scholars and practitioners whom Adrienne Roberts characterized as "pro-business feminists" advocate for helping women fully engage in market relationships by putting money in their hands to support their financial independence. "Gender" and "development" are pro-business feminists' key words.

Microfinance first entered Brazil in the 1970s. After booming in the 1980s and the 1990s, it gained a salient presence in Perú, Ecuador, and Colombia—countries where it offers returns as high as a 29 percent annual interest rate (Roberts 2012, 96–97). These initiatives are estimated to reach more than 10 million Latin Americans, mostly women, whose loans average $1,200 and who maintain a 95 percent repayment rate. The combined effort of the private sector, universities, governments, and NGOs to provide microcredit and microinsurance have been praised in this regard as tools for helping women gain financial independence by developing their "human capital" (Roberts 2012, 87). In 2010, the Inter-American Development Bank assessed the microloan portfolio to be $12.3 billion, with potential gains of $40 billion for microinsurance alone (Pedroza 2010). As bankers characterize women as "the world's most under-utilized resource," pro-business feminists treat "femininity" as a synonym with risk aversion and financial responsibility. These business-friendly feminists call for "feminizing" global finances to make them more "rational and sustainable"—virtues that they seem to believe that all women possess (Goldman Sachs as quoted in Roberts 2012, 90–91).

A number of feminist scholars and activists such as Chandra Mohanty object to these initiatives. With their neoliberal agendas, groups such as pro-business women attempt to co-opt feminism by claiming to embrace it while emptying its critical core (Mohanty 2013, 972). Despite their declared support for "gender justice," they ignore the mass of women taking micro-loans at abusively high interest rates. The latter seems more concerning, as many of those loans are used not as investments, but to meet basic needs, often forced upon women by their male partners. Under these conditions, rather than empowering women, as pro-business feminists claim they do, microloans often push them into debt and dispossession.

Nor has the gendering of the government necessarily helped thus far. Holding an average 26 percent of national legislative seats across the region, with the percentage of female legislators in Mexico, Costa Rica, Ecuador, and Argentina matching that in Germany and the Netherlands, women have made significant progress in taking office (Ballve 2011). Yet the situation of most has not clearly improved. The fact that Chile, Argentina, Costa Rica, Nicaragua, Guyana, Panama, and Brazil have all elected a woman president, for example, has not necessarily helped women's agendas—or so expressed the posters at the 2012 Encuentro Nacional de Mujeres, which depicted Argentine President Cristina Fernández de Kirchner as "not talking" (about femicide), "not seeing" (the trafficking of women), and "not listening" (to claims for decriminalizing abortion) (*Misiones Cuatro* 2012). If sustained efforts to fight inequality have placed a rising number of women in office, the mere "gendering" of institutions risks having a mystifying effect, as Federici warned, helping the status quo co-opt feminist struggles—not unlike the previously discussed gendering of finances (Federici 2012, 86). Furthermore, as Latin America's commodity boom wanes and policies leave gender disparities roughly unaltered, the recurrence and long-term effects of the crisis disproportionally fall on women's shoulders (Espino, Esquivel, and Enríquez 2012, 310).

CONCLUSION: AS THE CRISIS INTENSIFIES IN LATIN AMERICA

"We oppose Monsanto . . . because we know the health consequences that it brings. Every week in our neighborhoods people fall ill and types of cancer never seen before are diagnosed." María Godoy, from Córdoba, Argentina, used these words at the 2012 Encuentro Nacional de Mujeres to describe the death of her children from being poisoned by the fumigation of soy fields (*Télam* 2013). In countries such as Ecuador, Brazil, Bolivia, and Argentina, despite the "Pink Tide" leaders' anti-neoliberal claims, governments have continued to support the privatization of natural resources and the expansion of mega-mining and corporate farming. Politicians present corporate initiatives as promoting development and opportunities for the indigenous and the poor while concealing their serious environmental consequences— and it is women who ultimately pay the price.

As the Manifesto of the 28th Encuentro Nacional de Mujeres notes, transnational corporations

> exploit our soils, extract common goods such as oil or minerals in a great scale, pollute land and water with cyanide, destroy the glaciers, invade with transgenic seeds and agrotoxics the land devoted to agriculture, disarticulate regional economies, displace communities, and repress those who object to this destruction. (XXVIII Encuentro Nacional de Mujeres 2013)

In Argentina, the "extractive agroexport model" turned 4 million hectares of soy cultivation in 2004 into 20 million in 2013 and allowed the use of pesticides that cause illnesses, malformations, and deaths. In Ecuador, with $3.5 billion in expected investment from Canadian corporations, big mining projects are underway. Women from the Encuentro noted that "San Juan is literally running out of water," and they denounced the damaging consequences of mega-mining and justified their choice to host their 2013 annual meeting in that city (*La Nación* 2013b).

As corporate agriculture and mining expanded in Latin America, they have caused conflicts and human rights violations in Mexico, Brazil, Paraguay, Ecuador, Bolivia, and Argentina, as peasant communities working on subsistence farming are taken from their land (Antonopoulos 2009b). In Argentina alone, 9 million hectares are being taken from peasants—mostly indigenous, many of them women—by the state and private firms (*Russia Today* 2013). Evictions or coerced vile price sales are helped by "harassment . . . violence, pressure, intimidation, and punishment" (Núñez, interviewed, July 23, 2013). At times, it is government officials who sell the peasants' ancestral land to wealthy investors. Those displaced find themselves forced to work for the new owners. At one of the Encuentros, Juana Inderecio described how they "stay at the side of the road, without access to water," only to face police repression (Zicavo 2010). Violent, unjust, and cruel, the ongoing dispossession of peasants brings memories of the indigenous people exploited, enslaved, and murdered in the past to make room for mining or agricultural production, and it falls disproportionally upon women to care for their ill, poisoned family members—just as it does to find water that is not polluted and still available despite these corporate activities (True 2012, 87).

Made temporarily milder for poor families through cash transfers or microcredit, the long crisis now exposes the fragility of Latin America's social fabric and the deep and lasting effects of neoliberal transformations over the lives of millions. Moreover, it is women, especially poorer women, who bear the environmental, health, and economic costs with their unpaid labor. The unrecognized, non-remunerated reproductive labor of women might have subsidized not only corporate profit, but also the illusions of social mobility and the prosperity of the "Pink Tide" governments themselves.

If Latin America's commodity boom attenuated the consequences of the crisis, by 2014 the boom had waned, funding for social policies had faltered, and the crisis had made a comeback. Reviving fears of the 2001 crisis, Standard & Poor declared Argentina to be on a "selective default" as of July 30 (Lahrichi 2014; Salvia 2014). Although President Fernández de Kirchner's anti-imperialist rhetoric depicts the default as an artificial operation of "vulture" American investors, levels of poverty in the nation are up to eight times higher than those officially reported, affecting at least one-third of the population—despite the monetary allowances received by at least 22 percent of families. As the crisis returns with a vengeance, a new cycle of unemployment, poverty, and extra-economic dispossession, commodification, and proletarization is under way (Kornblihtt 2014). Addressing their conditions as workers, as taking on the burden of domestic labor, as well as the violence exhibited on their bodies, many Latin American women convey a difficult present and an uncertain future (Seligson, Smith, and Zechmeister 2012, 73).

Bringing to light women's unpaid labor is crucial, as time surveys show (ECLAC 2013a, 122). "Including care in the economic analysis" while exploring its links to structural oppression and violence against women makes visible women's material contributions to the reproduction of society and the production of wealth. However, such knowledge will not be truly useful unless it is accompanied by collective and political mobilization to bring change. Remarkably, during this protracted crisis, women across Latin America have mobilized to make exploitation and violence visible, as well as to counter them. As critical feminist scholarship has shown, in light of the role of women's unpaid labor in (involuntarily) subsidizing capital's expansion, women from all walks of life—such as the thousands attending the Encuentros, the Mujeres de negro in Mexico, and myriad other groups—help us understand the rationale of violence subjecting them to new cycles of dispossession and the commodification of life triggered by crises. Moreover, these women teach us about the extent to which the global economy relies on their unpaid labor and extra-economic appropriation in twenty-first-century capitalism. Women's double exploitation shows that capital thrives not only in economic relations, but also in the extra-economic appropriation of surplus, as in the case of unpaid household work. In mobilizing and resisting, as Mohanty suggested (2003, 530), "our minds must be as ready to move as capital is, to trace its paths and to imagine alternative destinations."

PART III

Scandalous Sex

PART III.

Scandalous Sex

CHAPTER 9

Exploits and Exploitations

A Micro and Macro Analysis of the "DSK Affair"

CELESTE MONTOYA

On May 14, 2011, Dominique Strauss-Kahn, the director of the International Monetary Fund and probable Socialist candidate for the French presidency, was arrested on a plane at New York City's JFK Airport. In a dramatic scene, he was led away by police, disheveled and in handcuffs. He was charged with the sexual assault of Nafissatou Diallo, a 32-year-old Guinea native and housekeeper at the Sofitel New York, the hotel where Strauss-Kahn had been staying. Several days later, he resigned, much to the shock of France and the world. However, within months the case was dropped. The prosecution began to lose faith in the credibility of the victim and their ability to successfully prosecute the criminal case against this high-profile defendant.

Despite its sensationalization, the "DSK Affair" was not particularly extraordinary. A wealthy and powerful white man was accused of sexual assault by a black female domestic worker. While early attention was placed on Dominique Strauss-Kahn, the case ultimately came to focus on the credibility of the victim. Thus the alleged perpetrator's troubling sexual history was dismissed and all the structural inequalities within which male violence has long been rooted were ignored. In a classic reversal, her motives were put into question, and the very vulnerabilities that contributed to her assault were used against her. No longer a sympathetic victim, she was cast in the role of a lying, manipulative opportunist and her attacker the victim of her deceit, targeted for his position of wealth and power.

These intersecting power differentials of gender, socioeconomic class, race, and nationality take on a whole new dimension when focusing on the actual identities of these actors. The alleged assailant is the director of the International Monetary Fund and possible presidential contender for France's 2012 election, and the alleged victim is a migrant and asylum recipient native to Guinea, one of the poorest countries in the world, both a former colony of France and a recipient of IMF funding. When put into juxtaposition and analyzed with a feminist lens, we see strong parallels as well as connections between the micro-level examples of the power asymmetries in the "DSK Affair" and the macro-level examples found in the global political economy.

Not unlike the rape narrative described here, critics of development politics discuss the ways in which neoliberal development policy is gendered, raced, and classed. Furthermore, such critics have gone so far as to characterize capitalist exploitation as both a form and instigator of violence. For example, Gibson-Graham (1996) discusses the "rape script" of globalization by which "capitalist penetration" cannot be avoided or contested. Beyond these general analogies, however, are the more telling links between the broader structural patterns of colonial legacies and neoliberal exploitation and widespread and increased violence against women. Linking together the micro-level and macro-level exploitations more directly is the narrative of feminized migration. Neoliberal practices imposed upon developing countries limit the opportunities for societal groups to survive, placing pressure on these groups (and increasingly the women of these groups) to migrate. Migration, although sometime touted as a source of gender liberation, is one that leaves many immigrant women vulnerable to sexual exploitation and other forms of violence.

Dominique Strauss-Kahn is not the perfect embodiment of neoliberalism. Almost paradoxically, he seemed to be leading the IMF in a different direction, away from structural adjustment and austerity measures and with a more meaningful emphasis on human development. Yet, at the same time, he was an active participant in the financial industry's culture of misogyny and sexual exploitation. The Oscar-winning documentary *Inside Job* provides a brief insight into a world where strip clubs and prostitution are not only rampant, but a normalized part of finance, where madams are given blank invoices to charge sexual services as "consultations" or "market research." These individual instances of sexual exploitation, violence, and abuse cannot and should not be understood as distinct from the policies that have facilitated similar systemic patterns at a global scale.

The global order being perpetuated by big finance is one that sets up the macro-level circumstances that create the vulnerabilities, which can then be taken advantage of in sometimes violent manners. While Dominque Strauss-Kahn might have been attempting to reform the global order that has played such a pivotal role in facilitating the exploitation of women, this does not mean that he is not complicit in said exploitation in his personal endeavors.

This chapter examines the analogies and connections between the macro-level power politics of neoliberal exploitation and the micro-level power politics in the exploits of Dominque Strauss-Kahn, the IMF's former director. The chapter is organized into two sections. In the first section, I provide a micro-level analysis of the "rape script" and apply it to the "DSK Affair." In addition to providing an overview of the contradictory narratives by the alleged victim, perpetrator, and the media, as well as the varied responses to such narratives, I deconstruct the gendered, raced, and classed power dynamics that characterize the case, highlighting the ways in which it follows a common narrative for sexual assault. In the second section, I deconstruct the case in a different manner, relating specific micro-level details to their macro-parallels in the global arena, so as to demonstrate how the intersectional power dynamics of the "DSK Affair" mirror and are in fact made possible by trends in the broader international political and economic environment. Finally, I focus on connections between these levels of analysis, pushing beyond the narrative similarities to discuss the more direct implications of the neoliberal global order on violence against women.

THE "DSK AFFAIR" AND ITS ENACTMENT OF A COMMON RAPE SCRIPT

The "DSK Affair," on its surface, exemplifies many of the power differentials surrounding sexual assault cases, not only in the scenario recounted by the alleged victim, but in the aftermath. In these particular events, we see an all too common narrative play out: one in which a person in a position of power and privilege takes advantage of and exploits the weaknesses of a person in a vulnerable position. It follows a "rape script," a gendered grammar of violence with rules and a structure that assign people to positions within the script (Marcus 1992). In the "rape script," men are the subjects of violence against women. Whether or not this violence is deemed as legitimate depends on the intersections of gender with race and class. The intersections determine which bodies are understood as sexually available, and ultimately which bodies can be considered as rapable (MacKinnon 1997; Bourke 2007). Violence that contradicts classic power patterns, such as a darker man raping a white woman or a working-class man raping an upper middle-class woman, are deemed illegitimate and worthy of punishment. Violence that upholds power dimensions, such as intra-racial or intra-class violence, or intersecting hierarchies, such as a white man raping a darker woman or a wealthy man raping a poorer woman, is significantly more difficult to prosecute. In traditional societal construction, there are certain contextual circumstances in which women's resistance to violence is considered not only unthinkable but is condemned when it occurs (Markus 1992).

While the feminist movement has done much to challenge these scripts in the past two decades, the scripts have not been completely eradicated. Instead they have taken on subtler and more insidious forms, most specifically with regard to the notion of "credibility." Because rape is defined by consent (or the lack thereof), sexual assault cases become a process of judging one person's word against another, or weighing one person's reputation against that of another (Lees 1997). Randall (2010) argues that although the archetype of the "ideal" sexual assault victim has been expanded somewhat over the years, it still exists and functions so as to disqualify many complainants' accounts of sexual assault. The excavation of personal records has been and remains a central strategy of the defense (Sheehy 2002; Randall 2010). "Good" victims are those who are deemed pure and demure, who are able to demonstrate that they fought to the best of their ability, and who are able to consistently recount the struggle. "Bad" victims are those women whose lives, backgrounds, and characteristics depart from the narrow confines of ideal victims (Randall 2010). A victim's "moral character" and "behavior" influence the prosecutors' judgments regarding the credibility of complainants (Spears and Spohn 1997; Haskell 2003).

Race and class also play into the notion of credibility. Being white and middle class contributes to a victim's credibility, whereas being poor may elicit the response that the woman made the accusation for monetary or other gains (Phipps 2009). Racialized and marginalized women are less easily identified as "ideal" victims and are more easily stigmatized as "bad" or "undeserving" victims (Randall 2010). Credibility testing can be compounded by cultural and language problems (Razack 2002). The power dynamics inherent in "credibility" often result in a woman's vulnerabilities being used against her. Victim blaming is a persistent means of reinforcing structural inequalities and allowing sexual assault to continue undiminished. The "DSK Affair" illustrates many of the power dynamics theorized and demonstrated in the research of feminist scholars. What began as the very public recognition and disruption of the dominant rape script quickly devolved into its re-entrenchment.

The Victim's Narrative and Narratives of the Victim

In the original reports to detectives and the assistant district attorneys, Nafissatou Diallo provided her narrative of the alleged attack and her subsequent actions. On May 14, 2011, Diallo was working the Saturday morning shift, where she was assigned to clean the rooms on the 28th floor. A few minutes after noon she sees a room service attendant leaving Suite 2806, who assures her that the room is empty and ready to be cleaned. She opens the door, announces herself and then begins checking the rooms. When she approaches the bedroom she again announces herself and is confronted by a naked white-haired man approaching from a nearby bathroom. She apologizes and turns to leave. He grabs her breasts then slides around her to close the door to the suite. She pleads with him, "Sir, stop this! I don't want to lose my job." He responds, "You don't have to lose your job." He tells her that she is beautiful and pulls her onto the bed, pinning her to the edge, and attempts to force her to perform oral sex. She resists, pushes him away, and tells him that her supervisor is right there, which he dismisses. He becomes more aggressive, pushing her to the bathroom and pinning her to a wall and trying to pull down her pantyhose, of which she is wearing two pairs. He slides his hand beneath the pantyhose and grabs her hard. Again she tries to resist and he pushes her to her knees, wrenching her shoulder and then forcing himself into her mouth. Afterward she flees to the main hallway and hides in one of the rooms she previously cleaned. Not long afterward, she observes him leaving the suite and entering the elevator. Unsure as to what to do and afraid that she might lose her job, she attempts to return to work, but she feels nauseated and disoriented. A few minutes later, her supervisor arrives and upon encountering the shaken employee eventually coaxes a reluctant Diallo to share her story. The head of housekeeping and then security are called, and they encourage Diallo to make a police report.

Soon after the arrest, prosecutors very publicly announced that they had a strong case against the director of the International Monetary Fund. They had a victim who had consistently recounted the events, several witnesses who encountered her very soon after the attack who can recount her reaction, and physical evidence that demonstrated a sexual encounter with the alleged assailant. DSK's DNA is found in semen on Diallo's uniform and in the epithelial cells on her pantyhose and panties. Doctor's observed "redness" in her vaginal area about five hours after the attack, and she has a ligament tear in her shoulder. The evidence is compelling, and on May 18, DSK resigns his IMF directorship "with infinite sadness" in an effort "to protect this institution." In his resignation letter he denies "with the greatest possible firmness all of the allegations that have been made."

What seemed to be an airtight case, however, became questionable when prosecutors began to express doubt publicly. On June 30, 2011, prosecutors sent a letter to DSK's attorney, reporting that "during the course of this investigation, the complainant was untruthful with assistant district attorneys about a variety of topics concerning her history, background, present circumstances and personal relationships." On August 23, 2011, the charges were officially dropped, with a statement from Manhattan District Attorney Cyrus R. Vance, Jr.: "I determined that I was no longer convinced beyond a reasonable doubt that I know what happened—not that something didn't happen, but whether we, as an office, knew beyond a reasonable doubt what happened. We did not have that quantum of evidence." In court papers, the prosecuting team noted that their decision to drop the charges reflected doubts about the woman's overall credibility, not "factual findings." Prosecutors said that they still believed there was evidence to support the notion that DSK had forced the woman to perform oral sex, but that inconsistencies in her past and in her account of the moments following the episode could make it extremely difficult to persuade jurors to believe her (Associated Press 2012). This statement is telling. It was not that the evidence of the case or of the assailant (which will be discussed later) but the victim herself that weakened the case. What had happened?

Diallo's early relationship with the prosecuting team was a favorable one. It began to sour, however, when facts began to emerge about fabrications in her past and in her statement testimony. The first blow came when Diallo admitted that she had entered the country illegally on another women's visa and then later applied for asylum using a false story. She had been coached by an unidentified "immigration consultant" who made her memorize a story in which she claimed to be fleeing political and sexual persecution from Guinea. Diallo's actual story might have been enough to make these claims; she had been unwillingly subjected to female circumcision as a child and later, as a teenager, was raped by two soldiers for violating curfew. She fled Guinea after her husband died of AIDs and with the hope of sending for her daughter so that she might avoid a similar fate of poverty and violence. The "consultant" insisted that she needed a more compelling tale, one she used to successfully gain asylum and later recounted convincingly to the prosecution team. In the scripted story, she claimed that she and her husband faced retaliation from a ruthless regime that they opposed, her husband was tortured and left to wither away in prison as a political dissident, Diallo was beaten and gang-raped by soldiers who ripped her two-year-old daughter from her arms. In addition to the asylum story, Diallo admitted to cheating on her taxes (claiming a friend's child as her own) and lied about her income to attain low-income housing.

While none of these factors diminished the evidence in Diallo's case, once she could no longer be constructed as an "ideal" victim, the prosecution and the media (who had been leaked information) lost any sympathy they had previously held for her. Many of the societal positions that rendered her vulnerable in the first place were turned against her. According to Diallo, these lies had been all about securing a safe future for her daughter and herself. The unpleasant truth is that it is not uncommon for refugees to receive similar coaching to exaggerate and even fabricate claims as a means of navigating an onerous asylum process. Asylum seekers must present a convincing case of how the violence they have experienced is persecutory and it must meet a fairly high threshold; very few cases are successful. "Distinctions are drawn about the type of violence that is worthy of an asylum grant, the type of victim a 'credible' asylum seeker must be, and the violence experienced by an asylum seeker versus the violence experienced by an undocumented immigrant" (Nayak 2015). The asylum system as it is creates incentives for claimants to carefully craft their stories so as to provide the most compelling case (Nayak 2015). Gender-based claims are particularly difficult to navigate, in part because of the universal experiences of violence against women.

Exacerbating the situation were several misunderstandings that were publicized. Not long after the June 30th letter, the media began circulating a story that prosecution had a full transcript of a phone call Diallo had made to an incarcerated man within a day of the assault in which she commented that her alleged attacker was rich and that she knew what she was doing. This new angle shifted the narrative toward painting Diallo as an opportunist. It was later revealed that there were two phone calls, both initiated by Amara Tarawally (the inmate). In the first call Diallo simply tells Tarawally about the assault, recounting details consistent with her official report. In the second phone call, Tarawally suggests that she could get money from this, but Diallo responds that she will let the lawyer deal with that issue. In this instance, the officers' interpretation of the conversation reflects and reinforces the rape myth in which lower class women accuse upper class men for monetary. They focus on the script they know, the discussion of money, even though it is not initiated by Diallo, and ignore the parts of the story that illustrate her vulnerability and that support earlier testimony. This narrative was reinforced when Diallo's lawyer filed a civil suit against Strauss-Kahn in August, before the criminal charges were officially dropped. Sensing trouble in the criminal case, it was a sound strategy, one often used for victims of sexual assault because such cases have a lower standard of proof than do criminal trials and become an alternative mode of recourse for crime victims when the criminal case route is exhausted. The case was filed with the State Supreme Court in the Bronx, the complainant's home community, where the odds for a sympathetic jury were greater than in Manhattan. In sexual assault cases, however, choice of venue becomes an additional reason to question the motivations of the accuser, particularly in highly publicized cases where the defendant is very wealthy. Such questions were raised in this case, as the lawyers for Strauss-Kahn stated that they had always maintained that the motivations of the accuser included making money (Rashbaum and Eligon 2011).

The case was settled in 2012 for an undisclosed amount. According to one of her attorneys, "the agreement to settle the matter will provide her with a new beginning so that she and her daughter can move forward and begin the process of healing." He also noted that Diallo has been unable to work, disabled by a shoulder injury she suffered in the assault.

DSK's Narrative and Narratives of DSK

Strauss-Kahn has persistently maintained his innocence. Several months later, in his first public interview, he stated, "What happened involved neither violence nor constraint nor aggression nor any offense." According to him, Diallo looked "surprised but in no way terrified."[5] He has characterized it as "a hurried sexual encounter" with a woman half his age whom he had never met (Palvia 2011). In a somewhat apologetic tone, he framed his actions, not as rape, but as "moral failing." "What happened was not only an inappropriate relation, but more than that, a mistake vis-à-vis my wife, my children and my friends, the French . . . I regret it infinitely."

While the media and ultimately the prosecution focused much scrutiny on the victim's credibility, there was also significant public attention directed at the high-profile Dominique Strauss-Kahn. Two competing narratives emerged, one of DSK as a sexual aggressor and unrepentant serial sexual harasser, the other as "*le grand séducteur*" for whom consent, as per the "rape script," is never an issue. But the line between the two was often blurred, as demonstrated in Christophe Deloire and Christophe Dubois's 2006 book *Sexus Politicus* in which they dedicate a chapter to DSK's proclivity for "seduction to the point of obsession." In 2007, when Dominique Strauss-Kahn became the French candidate for the IMF, increased media attention was drawn to his sex life. Jean Quatremé, a journalist for *Libération*, states that "[t]he only real problem with Strauss-Kahn is his attitude to women. Too insistent, he often comes close to harassment. It is a problem known to the media but that nobody talks about" (translated and quoted in *New York Times* 2011).

In 2008, Strauss-Kahn admitted an affair with Piroska Nagy, a Hungarian economist in a subordinate position at the IMF. The affair was ruled to be an "error of judgment" but not sexual harassment, despite the fact that Nagy wrote a letter to the IMF warning them of his behavior and stating that the relationship was not entirely consensual: "I was damned if I did and damned if I didn't, [he is] a man with a problem that may make him ill-equipped to lead an institution where women work under his command." During this time there were numerous reports, as well as first-hand accounts, of his advances on women. One French female politician, Socialist MP Aurélie Filipette, said that she had once been the object of a "very heavy-handed flirt" and that she made sure to never be alone with him in a closed room. Danielle Evenou, the wife of a former Socialist minister and a well-known French actress, said flippantly in a radio interview, "Who hasn't been cornered by Dominque Strauss-Kahn?" A more damning account of DSK's behavior was reported by French writer Tristane Banon, in the aftermath of his arrest. She alleged that Strauss-Kahn attacked her when she was interviewing him in 2003. She reports that during an interview with him in an empty apartment, he forced her to the floor, tried to open her jeans and bra, and put his fingers in her mouth and underwear. She claims to have had to fend him off with kicks and punches. While Strauss-Kahn has admitted to making sexual advances, he claims that he only tried to kiss her and stopped when she objected. He has dismissed her claims of assault as "imaginary" and slanderous. Banon lodged her complaint after his arrest in New York, explaining that her mother and others had discouraged her from coming forward earlier because of his powerful political stature. French prosecutors decided against pursuing charges, citing that the case had exceeded the statute of limitation for sexual assault charges.

While there is persuasive evidence characterizing DSK as a sexually aggressive man with a penchant for sexual harassment, his persistent characterization as *"le grand séducteur"* implies consent on the woman's part and ignores the pattern of behavior, as well as the positionality of the women with whom he allegedly engages in "consensual" sexual activity. An alternative account of the assault is told by biographer Michel Taubmann, ostensibly from the perspective of Dominique Strauss-Kahn, whom he interviewed extensively.

Emerging from the shower as naked as Adam, the director general of the IMF was confronted with Nafissatou Diallo, whom he had never seen before. He watched her walk down the corridor. Nafissatou Diallo turned around. She stares him straight in the eyes. Then she unashamedly looked at his private parts. The flesh is weak. Dominque Strauss Kahn saw this as proposition. Rarely in his life has he refused the possibility of a moment of pleasure. (Translated and quoted in Lichfield 2011)

The picture painted is one of Strauss-Kahn as a lover of pleasure, a sexual opportunist, or perhaps even a sexual hedonist, but not a predator. More troubling than this caricature of *"le grand séducteur"* were more blatant iterations of the rape script, such as that exemplified by leftist editor Jean-Francois Kahn: "Why all the fuss? It's merely a bit of hanky panky with the help" and his reference to the incident as *"troussage de domestique,"* roughly translated as "trussing of a domestic" and used to refer to the situation of an employer having forced sex with a servant. This characterization relies on either the assumption of consent or a dismissal of the need for consent, a persisting perception of non-rapability.

Contributing to this dismissive attitude regarding the seriousness of DSK's actions is an established culture in which sexual exploitation is not only allowed, it is expected. As discussed earlier in the chapter, high finance, an industry that is highly male dominated, is one in which money, power, and sex are combined into exploitative practices where prostitution becomes a normalized part of doing business. This type of behavior is replicated not only within Western countries, but in Western-dominated global "aid" institutions. An example of this came to light in the based-on-true-life movie *The Whistleblower*, when UN peacekeepers and contractors were implicated in the sexual exploitation of the vulnerable populations whom they were sent to help.

As a wealthy white man in a very powerful position, the power dynamics align such that the "rape script" for Dominique Strauss-Kahn legitimates sexual violence. For this reason, it has been very difficult to sustain any of the charges made against him. Regardless of the varied intersectional privileges retained by various victims, he is always put into a position of credible access. While there have been attempts to disrupt this script, such as the coverage of his initial arrest, the protest of various women's organizations, and the civil suit, he has yet to be held fully accountable for any of these sexual assaults.

At the same time, he has been held more accountable than most. The fact that he and fellow economic reformer Eliot Spitzer are two of the few actors associated with the financial industry who have faced political repercussions for their sexual behavior has been fodder for conspiracy theories. While it is curious that two of the few oppositional voices to neoliberal practices should have their "indiscretions" aired above those of others who are likely involved in similar activities, it should not diminish the seriousness of their behavior. Rather, this might serve to highlight the veil of power that contributes to and protects exploitative practices at both micro and macro levels. Furthermore, it demonstrates that even critics of neoliberalism fail to recognize the full implications of the harm being done to certain segments of the population. That they would engage in the exploitation of women whose very vulnerability to sexual exploitation is created by the system they are fighting against demonstrates not just a personal hypocrisy, but an incomplete analysis of the gendered (and raced and classed) repercussions of the global order.

POWER DIFFERENTIALS IN THE MACRO-NARRATIVE

Beyond the obvious individual-level power differentials in the "DSK Affair," the case also parallels and connects to the narratives of the global political economy. Dominique Strauss-Kahn, as a French national and contender for the presidency, stands as a symbol of colonial power and the hegemonic West. While attempting to reform its policies, DSK still stood as head of the IMF, an organization with a long history of harmful and exploitative practices. Nafissatou Diallo, on the other hand, as a native of Guinea, represented the developing world at which this Western power is directed. Furthermore, as an asylum-seeker employed in domestic work, she represented the disadvantaged populations displaced by colonial legacies and structural adjustment policies. In this section, I identify the parallels between micro- and macro-level power differentials. This type of analysis has multiple implications. Examining the macro level provides geopolitical context, which illustrates the particular positioning of Diallo and Strauss-Kahn and allows insight into the complexities of the case at the micro level. Moving from the micro to the macro level provides a vivid analogy for the gendered, raced, and classed exploitations of the global economy.

In this section of the chapter, I provide a brief overview and discussion of the IMF, its policies and practices, and related critiques regarding its role in perpetuating inequalities between its recipients and the West through the enactment of debt politics, as well as within individual countries through structural adjustment policies. Included in this discussion is the role played by neoliberal policies, such as those enacted by the IMF, in the feminization of labor and migration. These feminizations have contributed to the increased vulnerabilities of women in transnational flows of labor, facilitating the types of exploitations and assaults that occurred in the "DSK Affair." Next, I extend this analysis to look at the case of Guinea and its relationship in the global political economy, as a former French colony and as an IMF recipient. Through this examination we can see the larger global processes that are at work in the "DSK Affair."

The IMF and the Neoliberal Rape Script

[The DSK Affair] ironically underscores years of failed economic policies championed by the IMF on the African continent, the very reason that increasing numbers of Africans have become vulnerable second class citizens in Western capitals, often exploited as sex slaves, maids, and nannies by powerful capitalist oligarchs.

—Sahara Reporters 2011

The International Monetary Fund and the World Bank were both established in the post-World War II era to promote international trade and monetary cooperation by loaning money to governments in times of severe economic crisis. The IMF is made up of 184 countries, but votes are allocated according to each country's contribution. Thus, the organization's direction is often dictated by the five countries that contribute the most money and control 50% of the votes: France, Germany, Japan, the United Kingdom, and the United States.

Feminist and postcolonial critiques have been aimed at the organization not only for its hegemonic power configuration, but for the neoliberal policies it imposes on lender states in form of structural adjustment programs. Structural adjustment policies (SAPs) are the policy changes required by the IMF and the World Bank as conditions for getting loans. They are market-oriented adjustments that include internal reforms, especially privatization and deregulation, as well as the reduction of trade barriers. Many critics see these reforms as exploitative, because they position stronger states and/or multinational corporations to access valuable resources (including both natural and human resources), often at significantly lowered prices. Other policy aims include cutting state expenditures (commonly referenced as austerity measures) that may come in the form of cutting back on social welfare policies, including health care, education, and social safety nets. These types of reform tend to hit poorer citizens, not only because they result in fewer government-provided public goods, but because they have been associated with lower wages, poorer working conditions (due to decreased bargaining power for workers), fewer public sector jobs, and environmental degradation.

A critique levied by Spurr (1993) and again by Chang and Ling (2011) is that globalization and its neoliberal policies reiterate colonialist rhetoric. Globalization creates exploitative relationships that benefit only a small segment of the world to the detriment of the remaining majority. Critics dismiss structural adjustment policies, such as those advocated by the World Bank and the IMF, as neo-colonial attempts to "sustain and reinforce conditions that will invite foreign investors to exploit either the labor or natural resources of a country to produce foreign currency for balance of payment purposes and to repay national debt ... [which] encourage[s] the use of a country's resources for export development rather than for domestic development" (Fall 2001, 71).

Chang and Ling (2011, 34) invoke the "rape script" language discussed in the introduction of this chapter in their description of how liberals "outrightly embrace one-way penetration of the local by the global." Use of the sexual assault metaphor and of a "rape script" reveals many parallels. Some countries, characterized by wealth and political power, are the perpetrators of violence against other poor and developing countries. Whether or not that violence is perceived as legitimate depends on the contextual political positions. As long as the violation follows traditional power differentials (particularly in regard to Western hegemonies), it is permissible. If the violation challenges these hierarchies, it is condemned. Furthermore, the scrutiny is almost always placed on the developing countries: What did they do to put themselves in their current situation? What can they do to prevent future instability and poverty? There is little questioning of how the past or current actions of Western capitalist nations have contributed to the perpetual underdevelopment of the poorest countries. Consent is implied, and resistance to Western interventions is frequently condemned.

Somewhat ironically, Dominque Strauss-Kahn was working to change some of these practices. As a social democrat, he believed in balancing the free market polices of globalization with those aimed at preserving some degree of social equality. In a speech on November 1, 2010, he spoke of globalization as having "delivered a lot" and helping "hundreds of millions of people break the bonds of poverty." But he also spoke of globalization as having a "dark side," "lurking behind it was a large and growing chasm between rich and poor." Such a growth model was "unbalanced and unsustainable." Not long before his arrest, in a speech at the Brookings Institution, he quoted Keynes: "The outstanding faults of the economic society in which we live are its failure to provide for full employment and its arbitrary and inequitable distribution of wealth and incomes."

Gendered Impacts, Direct and Indirect

Feminist critiques of the IMF and its policies abound. The gendered costs of structural adjustment are now well documented (Beneria and Feldman 1992; Sparr 1994; Haddad et al. 1995; Pyle 1999; Sassen 2000; Beneria 2003; Pyle and Ward 2003). While the poor are generally among the hardest hit by SAPs, women are disproportionally impacted because of the gendered patterns associated with such policies. Cuts in public sector jobs, especially in education and health services, increase levels of female unemployment. Wage gaps widen, as women are pushed into informal sectors and their unpaid work increases. Education slows, food consumption decreases, girls' health and mortality worsens, women become reliant on credit as they become poorer, women take on more household responsibilities and are subject to greater domestic violence and stress. Care work is simultaneously assumed and devalued, meaning that women are required to pick up the slack when social programs are cut, at the same time that they are compelled to seek income-generating work. Essentially, women absorb the costs of cuts in state expenditure. As characterized by Diane Elson (1998, 71), women's supply of non-market work has been regarded as "infinitely elastic."

Global restructuring and SAPs have been linked to the feminization of migration (Enloe 1989; Castle and Miller 2003; Mills 2003; Pyle and Ward 2003; Hart 2005; True 2012). Women are pushed to migrate when colonial and capitalist processes disrupt or destroy former livelihoods and are pulled to migrate to places where women are preferred workers (Peterson and Runyan 2010). Enloe (1989, 186) points directly to international debt politics in her discussion of how some countries have come to rely on feminized migrant labor, whose overseas earnings help "keep foreign creditors and their financial policeman, the International Monetary Fund, content." In the last several decades, female domestic workers have joined migrant worker streams that have outpaced those of male migrants. Mills argues that "[s]tructural adjustment plans mobilize women's unpaid labor as domestic nurturers and economizers to subsidize costs for international capitalism and to guarantee the debts incurred by poor states" (2003, 47). Or put another way, SAPs transform women into an "arsenal of exportable goods" (Hart 2005, 2). Women in the developing world are sent to wealthier countries where there is a shortage of domestic services.

Research on gendered migration shows that crossing borders can be empowering, opening up new opportunities to challenge established gender norms; however, it can also lead to new dependencies and the reinforcement of existing gender boundaries and hierarchies (Morokvasic 2007). The feminization of migration is characterized by an increasing number of migrant women in precarious and low-paid jobs in manufacturing and service (Anderson 2000; Ehrenreich and Hochschild 2003). Morokvasic (2007, 71) notes that "[t]he preservation of hierarchies of class and gender means that—whatever gains that may be achieved by immigrants—they are offset by the loss of status, overwork, declassing, and exploitation. Depending on the context and the sector of work, there is also a high real risk of being confronted with experiences of extreme humiliation and violence." Many migrant workers are undocumented, which renders them dangerously vulnerable due to a lack of political recourse against employers (Anderson 1997; Misra et al. 2006).

Transnational migrants represent a pool of vulnerable, feminized labor in the lowest wage sectors of the world's wealthiest economies (Mahler 1995; Kwong 1998; Sassen 1998; Foner 2000; Mills 2003). Feminized migrant labor is characterized not only by lower wages and limited job security, but by the racialization and sexualization of female workers (Chang and Ling 2011; Ehrenreich and Hochschild 2003; Mills 2003). Domestic workers are typically isolated with unregulated work conditions sometimes characterized by substandard living quarters, harassment, and abuse. While much of this literature focuses on manufacturing jobs or domestic care work (conducted in individual households), housekeepers in hotels are also at risk for sexual exploitation. Hotel housekeeper and hotel security experts report having to deal with sexual harassment and assaults made by male guests (Greenhouse 2011). Housekeepers, many of whom are low-paid immigrants, might be offered money or simply taken advantage of. Some hotels even hire security guards with the explicit responsibility of watching over the housekeeping staff.

Nafissatou Diallo, first as an undocumented migrant and later as an asylum seeker, was relatively lucky to find a job that was as well paid as her position at the Sofitel, and she appears to have been well supported by her fellow employees and supervisors in making the criminal complaint. Yet it was still a position in which there are implicit vulnerabilities created by the highly differential social location of the domestic workers and hotel guests. A not insubstantial footnote to the story was that Diallo was wearing two pairs of pantyhose when the assault took place. The mostly female housekeeping staff had recently been required to start wearing skirts instead of pants. Wearing two pairs of pantyhose was a means of preserving "modesty" in a job that often calls for bending over. The change was made ostensibly for its gendered aesthetic appeal.

Guinea

> Whereas most African families live on one dollar per day, Mr. Kahn was soaking in luxury in a lavish $3,000 per night hotel suite. That amount alone, without even one French cigar, croissant or a shot of cognac added to the bill, equals the sustenance of 3,000 African families in Guinea today.
>
> —Sahara Reporter 2011

While the larger global patterns of gendered and racialized migration might be enough to link the micro and macro components of the "DSK Affair," Diallo's positioning as a migrant from Guinea, a country once colonized by France and a recipient of IMF funding, adds another dimension to analysis linking her interpersonal interaction with Strauss-Kahn to its uncanny parallel and connection to their intersectional global positioning. Guinea was once a part of French West Africa, an area colonized by France in the 1890s. It declared its independence from France in 1958 and has since had a fairly steady history of authoritarian rule. It was only in 2010 that the country held its first free and fair elections, led by a transitional government under the leadership of General Sekouba Konate. Guinea is, by many indicators, one of the poorest countries in the world. Its 2011 estimated GDP purchasing power parity is $11.53 billion, which ranks it as 149th in the world, with a GDP per capita estimated at $1,100, 210th in the world. It is estimated that almost half of the population lives under the poverty line.

The living conditions for Guineans are among the worst in the world. Life expectancy is 58, ranking Guinea as 191 out of 221 countries (CIA Factbook 2012). Women are particularly hard hit in many regards. Fertility is high at 5.04, as is maternal mortality at 680 per 100,000 births (CIA Factbook 2012). Female illiteracy was estimated at over 80 percent in 2002, with women averaging seven years of school (CEDAW 2007). Low education and illiteracy rates are a major contributing factor to women's low levels of employment and wages. Sexual assault rates, like in many other countries in Sub-Saharan Africa, are considered to be high (US State Department 2011). Although there is national legislation guaranteeing the equality of men and women in Guinea, women (especially rural women) continue to experience discrimination under traditional law, which bars them from owning land and thus limits their economic opportunities.

As one of the world's poorest countries, Guinea has been a regular recipient of foreign aid. From 1985 to 2002, as stipulated by providers, Guinea engaged in a process of economic liberalization. Between 2003 and 2006, growth subsided, and with the 2007 global economic crisis, the economy deteriorated further. This contributed to the violent coup that followed the death of long-time President Lansana Conte, which led to significant reductions in aid. In opposition to the new regime, international donors, including the IMF, World Bank, and the G-8, dramatically cut back on development programs. With the new democratically elected government, foreign aid and international investment is expected to return, along with intense scrutiny from aid providers and international investors.[1]

Migration from West Africa is fairly high and is driven by a variety of factors, including population pressure, poverty, poor economic performance, and continual conflict (Adepoju 2005). Rates of migration are hard to determine, and are usually estimated using temporal population comparison. At times, Guinea has been a destination for refugees fleeing war in other countries, such as Liberia. In Guinea, a 2007 study estimated an inflow of 405,772 immigrants, approximately 4.81 percent of the population, and an outflow of 520,835 emigrants, approximately 6.18 percent of the population (Haas 2007); however, this was before the coup. There is little information regarding migration flows during the political unrest, but it is reasonable to assume an increase in emigration. Even without political unrest, the push factors increased during this time with the withdrawal of aid. According to the Global Commission on International Migration (2005), women migrants in West Africa are increasingly drawn to the wage labor market as a survival strategy to augment meager family income. It further reports that migratory streams in West Africa are increasingly feminized with independent female migration a major survival strategy in response to deepening poverty in the region.

While much of the Western African migration flows stay within the region, there is movement to the developed world, including to Western European countries and the United States. Relatively little is known about the status of African female migrants in the United States. What is known shows that many of these migrants are trading one difficult location for another. While the tribulations of this new space may not compare to those left behind, they are still arduous. Migrants are safer, but they are not necessarily safe (Arthur 2009, 81). Many migrants, especially those who are unskilled, poorly educated, foreign-born women of color, occupy a peripheral status in their host country. Thus, the experience of Nassifatou Diallo is likely not that different from other Guinean or Western African woman who have been dislocated by global restructuring—the biggest distinction being that her case was cast into the public spotlight because of the powerful position of her accused assailant.

Nafissatou Diallo is just one of many women impacted by violence on both sides of her migrant experience. The violence she had experienced within her home country, both physical and economic, becomes part of the push factors initiating the desire to migrate. Women often flee from conditions of violence and oppression experienced within and by their home states but also in fleeing the effects of structural adjustment policies (Taylor and Jamieson 1999; Bernat and Zhilina 2010; True 2012). On the other side of the migration route, the gendered and racialized vulnerability is actualized in both the act of sexual violence and the subsequent lack of justice experienced in her new host country. Strauss-Kahn carried out the micro-level side of a macro-level narrative, ironically started by the institution he was trying to reform.

DISCUSSION

The domestic migrant woman worker is almost invisible in the face of international politics and economics, just as the austerity politics, for which DSK has been held up as personally responsible as IMF Chief, have reinforced the invisibility of women who have been negatively affected by his personal and public actions.

—True (2012)

Juxtaposing the macro-level politics of IMF, and neoliberal exploitation more broadly, with the micro-level exploits of its former director, Dominique Strauss-Kahn, highlights the power differentials that structure local and global society. Not only are these hierarchies shown to be parallel, they are in fact connected. The neo-colonial policies of Western elites have enacted the "rape script" of the global economy. These global assaults create and maintain the inequalities that allow for the "rape script" to continue undiminished in the lives of the most vulnerable. In the case of Strauss-Kahn, although he attempted to change the global rape script in his reform of IMF development policies, he directly enacted it in his actions toward Nafissatou Diallo.

The connections between micro-level violence and the macro workings of the global political economy are entirely too prevalent. In her pivotal 2012 book, *The Political Economy of Violence against Women*, Jacqui True provides a compelling argument on the numerous ways in which the current global political economic order is implicated in widespread and pervasive violence against women. She demonstrates the ways in which the global financial crisis, brought on by the liberalization of the financial system, international development loans, and the collapse of credit, has had a disproportionate impact on women (True 2012, 95). Unfortunately, the continued commitment to austerity, despite evidence of its detrimental effects, continues to perpetuate physical and economic violence against women and undercuts efforts to combat it. Gendered violence has become so widespread and pervasive that it, in and off itself, is rarely a compelling case for asylum—thus the need for the coaching and embellishments that ultimately led to the discreditment of Diallo in the criminal case.

The need to disrupt the micro and macro rape scripts is pivotal if there is any hope in combating the gendered violence that continues across all geographic and social borders. Despite the fact that violence against women has garnered a more secure position on the global political agenda, efforts have remained more rhetoric than reality. There is an inherent contradiction found in the fact that those state and international institutions taking up the antiviolence mantel (including the United States and the United Nations) are also the biggest promoters of a neoliberal order that has had very real, gendered, racialized, and violent consequences.

The grand narrative guiding the story of DSK and Diallo has many points in which interventions might be made. In order to make these interventions, however, it must be read not as just a micro-level story of unique individuals and circumstances, but as part of widespread patterns of abuse and violence where the exploitation starts with policies enacted by private and governmental financial institutions. The power differentials between those making global economic decisions and those most significantly (and detrimentally) impacted by it remain vast. Even when the decision makers are ostensible reformers, as was the case for Dominque Strauss-Kahn, they are still embedded in social locations of privilege that are raced, gendered, and classed, as well as reflective of geopolitical location. Such positioning can lead to micro- and macro-exploitation, or, at the very least, a blindness to such exploitations. Unraveling the grand narrative of exploitation and violence requires more than just reflexivity on the part of these decision-makers, but a more inclusive democratic process in which a diversity of social and geopolitical locations are represented. While there has been a wave of such movements, from Occupy to the Indignados and beyond, there is still much to be done before the status quo has been shaken. Critical feminist organizations and analysis are a pivotal part of this organized opposition, as they help to extend the analysis of implications. It is not enough to make the distinction between the 1 percent and the 99 percent, but instead to spell out the ways in which economic exploitation is visited upon different communities, particularly the most vulnerable.

NOTE

1. Guinea is of particular interest to investors for its natural resources, which include vast iron ore reserves, as well as bauxite, gold, and diamond reserves.

CHAPTER 10

We, Neoliberals

AIDA A. HOZIĆ

INTRODUCTION

We should probably not be surprised that scandals—particularly sexual scandals—have become *the* language of political and economic restoration in the aftermath of the 2008 financial crisis. Scandals and financial crises have frequently gone hand in hand, and not simply because lust and greed historically have been associated with each other (Folbre 2009). Rather, as Mary Poovey (2008) has persuasively argued, financial crises are first and foremost crises of representation, revealing the gap between fact and fiction inherent in all credit instruments. When made visible, this gap, which Poovey calls "the problematic of representation," can seriously threaten social and political stability since it questions "the prevailing model of value, the conventions that facilitate trust, and the signs that convey creditworthiness—monetary, social, legal, and political" (Poovey 2008, 6). (Sexual) scandals—like imaginative writings that Poovey examines, such as novels and romances—help bridge that gap. They do not just smooth over the fissures of representation but displace existing anxieties, set limits to transgressions, and reinforce boundaries between public and private lives. Most important, while contention over gender roles, which are central to the constitution and justification of public and private spheres, stands at the heart of scandals in societies experiencing crisis, the relevance of gender itself can be obscured by the noise that scandals generate. Ironically, therefore, scandals have powerful stabilizing effects on social norms and gender relations. Despite

[margin annotations: "Crisis reveals" with arrow; "gap betw Fact and fiction"]

all the huffing and puffing, they ultimately deliver power back to the powerful.

Since 2008, two types of scandals have proliferated through media outlets situated at the epicenters of the crisis, the United States and Europe. On the one hand, there has been a constant stream of sexual scandals linking powerful men (Dominique Strauss-Kahn, the head of IMF; Swedish King Gustaf; Anthony Wiener, US congressman; Silvio Berlusconi, former Italian prime minister; Spanish King Juan Carlos; Mark Sanford, South Carolina governor; David Petraeus, US general and director of the CIA— to name just a few) to prostitution, adultery, exhibitionism, and/or sexual assault. On the other hand, there has been a never-ending series of scandals over excessive state and corporate surveillance and/or their inverse— attacks by hackers (WikiLeaks, the Anonymous, the Snowden Affair, the hacking of Sony/Hollywood emails, continuously reported hacks of US servers by Russia, China, and North Korea). The two types of scandals have also frequently overlapped. For instance, Julian Assange, founder of WikiLeaks, was charged with sexual assault in Sweden; revelations about Silvio Berlusconi's bunga-bunga parties in Italy dovetailed with publication of his telephone surveillance transcripts; Bradley Manning, the US private who supplied WikiLeaks with government documents, has since changed his sex and has become Chelsea Manning; General David Petraeus was sentenced to two years probation and $100,000 for sharing classified information with his biographer and lover Dr. Paula Broadwell; John R. Schindler, professor at the US Naval War College and a vocal critic of Eric Snowden in the American media, was forced to resign because of leaked text messages and photos he took of his own private parts. These overlaps should not surprise us. As scripts of transgression and disclosure, scandals are symptoms of reclamations of political and economic authority and renegotiations over the public/private divide. Thus, even when they are not explicitly sexual, scandals are always deeply, structurally gendered since their exposés intrinsically challenge the accepted meanings of concepts traditionally linked with women, such as privacy, home, family, intimacy, or affection.

In this chapter, I explore the institution of scandal by focusing on the phone-hacking affair in the United Kingdom, which seriously rattled Rupert Murdoch's media empire in 2011. I am interested in two related questions: What are the conditions that make scandals propagate? And what role do scandals play in societies in crisis, especially financial crisis? The phone-hacking scandal—while neither explicitly sexual nor as potentially damaging to established powers as the Snowden affair—illustrates extremely well some of the frequently overlooked dynamics of scandals, or as Michel Foucault (1990, 11) would put it, the "polymorphous techniques of power" that scandals generate. The chapter reviews the key elements of the phone-hacking scandal in the United Kingdom and places them in the context of global media industry restructuring. It sets the stage for some probing questions about the way in which scandals and economic *recovery* have played off each other in the aftermath of the global financial crisis.

Scandal vs. recovery

THE SCANDAL (OR IT'S A SMALL, SMALL WORLD)

Even by the standards of British tabloid journalism, this was a scandal.

In 2005, Buckingham Palace got a whiff that representatives of the media might have gained access to private voice mail accounts of royal family members. The incidents seemed trivial at first. A few senior staff members noticed that their phone messages were appearing and disappearing at random. At about the same time, *The News of the World*, one of the oldest British newspapers, owned by Rupert Murdoch, published stories about Prince Harry and Prince William containing information known only to a very small circle of people within the palace. The stories themselves were banal enough ("Prince William had a knee injury") but the royals, ever concerned about possible leaks, contacted Scotland Yard and demanded an inquiry. Several months later, in August 2006, as a result of the inquiry, a private investigator hired by *The News of the World*, Glenn Mulcaire, and the royal editor of the paper, Clive Goodman, were arrested and charged with "conspiracy to intercept communications without lawful authority" (Van Natta, Becker, and Bowley 2010).

Scotland Yard's investigation revealed that phone hacking of the royal family was just the tip of an iceberg. The police seized several thousand phone numbers from Mulcaire that might have been hacked. But the inquiry was never broadened to include them. Only a few other celebrity victims were named, and just a few select others were notified that they might have been subject to hacking (Davies 2014). Indeed, as *The New York Times* wrote in 2010, in the first extensive US article about press phone-hacking in the United Kingdom, subsequent reviews of "court documents and interviews with investigators and reporters" clearly showed "that Britain's revered police agency failed to pursue leads suggesting that one of the country's most powerful newspapers was routinely listening in on its citizens" (Van Natta, Becker, and Bowley 2010). Even the public seemed unmoved by the apparent invasion of privacy into the lives of others. In the aftermath of the financial crisis, 2010 elections, and debates about austerity—revelations about eavesdropping on the rich and famous were nothing but background noise.

All that changed in July 2011, when it was revealed that in 2002 *The News of the World* hacked into the voice mail of a murdered schoolgirl, Milly Dowler, interfering with a police inquiry and giving false hope to her parents that she might still be alive. From that point on, it was obvious that the phone-hacking operations at *The News of the World* were not limited to a select few, but targeted anyone who could increase the paper's circulation, including dead children. The news of widespread hacking by the press was even more difficult to process since the editor at the time of Milly Dowler's disappearance, Rebekah Brooks, Rupert Murdoch's favorite associate and his "adopted daughter," had for years led the campaign of "naming and shaming" against alleged sex offenders and pedophiles in her newspapers. The irony of such blatant exploitation of violence against children for profit was not lost on the British public, and the outrage snowballed into a rare public "naming and shaming" of Rupert Murdoch and his family: the shutting down of *The News of the World*; indictments against Rebekah Brooks, her editorial successor Andy Coulson, and several other staff members; and commencement of a lengthy parliamentary inquiry into "culture, practices and ethics of the press" in the United Kingdom, known as the Leveson Inquiry.[1]

The Milly Dowler scandal and the Levenson Inquiry brought to light not just the extent of phone-hacking operations at *The News of the World* and the questionable morals governing the British press, but the hitherto unimaginable degree of intimacy between the press, the politicians, and the police. Scotland Yard officers were accepting bribes from the press and were concealing their own investigative leads in exchange for good media coverage. Andy Coulson, former editor of *The News of the World*, was director of Communications for the Conservative Party and then for Prime Minister David Cameron. Rebekah Brooks seemed to be an intimate friend of every British prime minister (and their wives) over the past two decades—Tony Blair, Gordon Brown, and David Cameron. Her cache of text messages to Cameron disclosed that they were in touch at least twice a week, discussing politics, horses, and country suppers in their common neighborhood of Chipping Norton in the Cotswolds. The neighborhood crowd—"the Chipping Norton Set"—included, apart from Brooks and Cameron, Rupert Murdoch's daughter Elisabeth and her (then) husband Mathew Freud (the most powerful PR man in Britain); Steve Hilton, Cameron's director of Strategy, and his wife Rachel Whetstone, at the time a senior Google executive; Emily Oppenheimer Turner, a diamond heiress; and an assembly of other media, political, and corporate figures from the British "1 percent." Writing about the intricate lines of power running through the Cotswolds, Marina Hyde (2011) thus rightly observed that "historians assessing this period will find even cabinet papers infinitely less revealing than guest lists" at cozy parties in the bucolic English countryside.

THE BACKDROP (OR "IT IS A WAR OUT THERE")

To assess the scope and the relevance of the phone-hacking scandal for analysis of the financial crisis and its aftermath, we must zoom even further out, beyond the Cotswolds, and look at the global media landscape as its background. In August 2007, News Corp, a media conglomerate ran by Rupert Murdoch, purchased Dow Jones, a financial information company and publisher of *The Wall Street Journal*. For more than three months (and many years before that), the Bancrofts—the family who had owned Dow Jones for more than a century—resisted the sale to Murdoch. Eventually, a combination of business pressures and Murdoch's exceedingly generous offer (5.6 billon dollars, $60 a share—67 percent higher than the Dow Jones share price when it became public) tipped the balance, giving Murdoch ownership of one of the most coveted brand names in the financial and media world (Ellison 2010).

This, of course, was the summer when the first signs of the coming financial crisis were already visible on the horizon. For a moment that summer, Murdoch fantasized about how to buy Merrill Lynch's 20 percent stake in Bloomberg, which would have given him control over worldwide financial information. The moment passed, but the crisis did not (Wolff 2008a, 2008b). By October 2007, Merrill Lynch, the world's largest brokerage firm, reported a loss of $7.9 billion, resulting from its overexposure to subprime mortgages. A year later, in July 2008, Merrill sold it shares in Bloomberg to Bloomberg itself. And then, on September 15, 2008, on the day when Lehman Brothers went belly-up, Bank of America purchased Merrill Lynch. In the next months, the world's financial markets went into a complete seizure. World trade was in free fall, and millions of jobs—from the United States to China—were lost.

The crisis had a negative effect on media industries as well. Print media were hit particularly hard. Already shaken by the rise of web portals, and the shift of news readership to the Internet, newspapers—in the United States especially—now faced a precipitous drop in advertising revenue as well. Between 2008 and 2010, eight American newspaper chains declared bankruptcy, prompting the US Congress to begin "debating whether the financial problems in the newspaper industry pose a public policy issue that warrants federal action" (Kirchhoff 2010). Even Murdoch's News Corp was affected by the crisis. In 2009, Murdoch was forced to write off $3 billion in losses, half of his purchasing price of *The Wall Street Journal*. It was estimated at the time that the purchase had cost him $5 billion of his personal fortune (Shafer 2010).

The newspapers in Britain were not doing much better either. Murdoch's Fleet Street assets—*The News of the World, The Sun, The Times*, and *Sunday Times*—were accumulating losses in the billions of pounds, and analysts were warning that the print media were dragging the entire company down (Arango and Pérez-Peña 2009). Murdoch, however, remained convinced that the business was not the problem, but the newspapers themselves— "They started to speak more to elites, or worse, to only other journalists, rather than to the people who read, or who ought to be reading, them" (as quoted in Starkman 2013). According to Michael Wolff (2010), Murdoch's biographer and an astute observer of his business moves, the media magnate continued to strategize how to buy *The New York Times* and, by 2010, waged a full-fledged war on The Old Grey Lady, as the *Times* is also known. "Observing Murdoch battle the Sulzbergers [owners of *The New York Times*]," wrote Wolff, "is a little like watching the Corleones pick on the Royal Tenenbaums" (2010).

Following the dictum of "when markets are low—buy," Murdoch's News Corp embarked on a political journey to take over satellite broadcaster British Sky Broadcasting (BSkyB) in 2010. News Corp already owned 39.1 percent of the company; the new bid was to acquire the remaining 60.1 percent. The combined control over BSkyB and the print media in the United Kingdom was predicted to bring Murdoch's annual revenues to £7.5 billion, dwarfing the revenue of the British Broadcasting Corporation (BBC), estimated at £4.8. The European Commission approved the bid in November 2010 but it required approval of the British authorities also. In the United Kingdom, however, Murdoch's attempt to gain control over a quarter of the news market faced significant opposition from other media companies. Publishers of *The Guardian, Telegraph, Daily Mirror*, and *Daily Mail* and cable/broadcasters British Telecom, Channel 4, and the BBC joined forces against Murdoch in an unprecedented show of unity, mobilizing and leading public opinion to oppose the bid (Sabbagh 2010).

The Guardian, in particular, shielded from the vagaries of the marketplace by its owner, the Scott Trust (estimated at $1.4 billion), aggressively sought to protect the kind of journalism in the public interest that they believed Murdoch's expansive empire was trying to undermine.[2] Opting against the subscription model for digital viewing, pushed for by Murdoch's newspapers and eventually adopted even by *The New York Times*, *The Guardian* focused on expansion of its readership. The paper embraced technological change, opening its web edition to reader participation

("Comment is free"), live-blogging events, and nurturing imaginative visualization of news and data. At the same time, however, *The Guardian* continued to invest in old-fashioned, labor-intensive investigative journalism, such as the dogged pursuit of the phone-hacking story for several years by one of its venerable reporters, Nick Davies. As the paper that provided a platform—and shelter—for WikiLeaks and Edward Snowden files, *The Guardian* sought to affirm its left-wing political orientation while simultaneously gaining a foothold in the American news market (Wolff 2015).

The war for and over media space translated into coverage of the financial crisis and its aftermath. The business press had largely failed to forewarn its readers about the risks inherent in expanding financialization, choosing instead to celebrate bullish markets that supported their advertising revenue. Business journalists were accused "of being as voluntarily embedded with some financial institutions as some reporters were with the military" (Bromley 2015, 63). Media analysts noted the tendency to cover the crisis in terms of victims and villains, to frame the aftermath through discourse of austerity, and to ignore strikes, protests, and demonstrations against austerity measures. Murdoch's media led the charge against stimulus packages in the United States and Australia, associating government spending, and the politicians promoting it, with socialism and communism. For their part, Murdoch's opponents—including *The New York Times*, which remains closely tied to Wall Street, but especially *The Guardian*—have remained open to the writings of the economists critical of austerity, such as Joseph Stiglitz and Paul Krugman.

This was then the backdrop to the phone-hacking scandal and "all the news that fit the press" that were obtained illegally by the News Corp's lieutenants—a dead girl's voice mails, Hugh Grant's telephone conversations with Jemima Khan, medical records of Gordon Brown's infant son, Prince Harry's visits to strip bars, Sir Paul McCartney's message to his ex-wife Heather Mills, Cherie Blair's pregnancy, and thousands of others like them—possibly even mobile phone messages of 9/11 victims and their families. This was the news that, according to Murdoch, people wanted to have more of, amidst wars, financial crises, and regular democratic exercises called elections. And these were the conversations—whether or not the BSkyB deal would be approved, what cabinet ministers would be in favor of Murdoch's bid, should Andy Coulson become the prime minister's director of communications—that entertained the guests at the Cotswold's dinner parties. Simmering behind the headlines was a battle of the global media giants over ownership, platforms, and the type of news that the public in the world's richest democracies deserved to have. But scratch that surface, and there was yet another layer to discussions over supper in the countryside, as will be further explored in the next section—an intra-elite conflict over the spoils of the global economy, the makeup of great power alliances, and the future course of "disruptive innovation" affecting millions of lives all over the world.

ANATOMY OF A SCANDAL

Scandals, wrote John B. Thompson (2000), have become an endemic feature of American political culture. In one of the first systematic studies of scandals, written shortly after President Clinton's impeachment and the Monica Lewinsky affair, Thompson sought to explain the expansion of this new political genre in the United States with changes in the media landscape. In his view (2000, 6), the development of new media had "transformed the nature of visibility and altered the relations between public and private life." Public figures have become so public and so visible that "their capacity to draw a line between their public persona and their private life is much more limited" (2000, 6). But scandal also, noted Thompson, told us something about broader social struggles that are "fought out in the symbolic realm, in the to and fro of claims and counter-claims, of revelations, allegations and denials" (2000, 6). In their current incarnation, scandals are symptomatic of a decline of ideological politics, an emphasis on the character of leaders, and the growing legalization of politics. "Thanks to these developments," concluded Thompson (2000, 262), "scandals have taken on fresh significance as credibility tests in the context of struggles between political parties which could no longer count on traditional class loyalties and which were no longer divided by strong ideological differences."

In the aftermath of the Iraq war and the financial crisis, Thompson's observations recalling the "end of history" no longer seemed able to explain the new wave of scandals in public life. Thus, building upon Thompson's work but also contradicting his main claims, Robert M. Entman (2012) chose to focus more on the silencing effects of scandals in politics than on the scandals themselves. Making a distinction between scandals and *potential* scandals (or between scandals and scandalous obfuscations, in the terminology of this volume), Entman noticed how scandals were, therefore, by no means commensurate with the scale of normative offense or to public outrage—they were intentionally construed. Scandals *cascade* "across a hierarchy of networks" but "must feed back to the upper levels (government elites and media organizations)" to fully materialize (2012, 187). It is only with the support of elites—or, better, under the conditions of great polarization among the elites—that potentially scandalous events turn into public scandals.

According to Entman, the financial meltdown of 2008 was an excellent example of a scandal that did not happen, precisely because misconduct was hidden in plain sight. Unlike the scandalizing publicity that was showered over the Federal Emergency Management Agency (FEMA) in the aftermath of Hurricane Katrina, few if any high-ranking government officials were criticized for the outbreak of the financial crisis or the handling of its aftermath. There was, says Entman (2012, 9), a lot of indignation, but for the most part, blame was placed "on an ambiguous and largely anonymous set of targets like 'Wall Street greed' and 'executive bonuses.'"

Applying Entman's analysis to the scandals of the global financial crisis, it appears that the most widely publicized scandals were nothing but distractions from scandalous activities that were allowed to lie dormant. In addition, as the British phone-hacking scandal seems to suggest, these very public scandals were quite indicative of the degree of conflict among the elites in the epicenter. If the financial crisis was a shock that pushed even the most neoliberal, market-oriented governments toward Keynesianism in 2008, fears of inflation—and of devalued wealth for the richest among the rich—led to a turn toward austerity just two years later (Irwin 2013). But the move was not widely popular—either among public sector dependents, disproportionately comprising women and minorities, or among those whose fortunes were in any way linked to mass consumption markets rather than rents. Inflation, noted Jared Bernstein (2014), echoing Paul Krugman (2014),

> erodes asset values, not unlike a tax on capital gains, and generally speaking, those who depend on portfolios vs. paychecks are going to be less sensitive to unemployment. So, as Paul [Krugman] stresses, they have a class interest to advocate for heading off inflation, even if it's a phantom menace, while at the same time worrying not so much about the impact of tightening on those who depend on a tight job market.

The deeply political aspect of these (class) conflicts, damaging to democratic processes, thus found itself an outlet in scandals and in resituating of the public/private divide.

WE, OTHER NEOLIBERALS (OR WE, NEOLIBERALS?)

So what role do scandals play in this crisis-ridden neoliberal age?

Perhaps Michel Foucault's analysis of Victorian age, that age of scandals par excellence, may help us with an answer. The first chapter of Foucault's

The History of Sexuality, Volume One, is entitled "We, Other Victorians" (1990). The title, it has been noted, may not have been the most accurate translation of the French original—"Nous autres, victoriens" (Kelly 2013). Different locations of the comma in the French and English titles suggest two possible—and very different—interpretations of the relation between Foucault's contemporaries and the Victorian age.

On the one hand, Foucault was admittedly influenced by Steven Marcus's (1966) book *The Other Victorians*, which explored the underbelly of Victorian culture by focusing on public and private writings about sex, and on liminal figures of that period—the prostitute, the client, the hysteric, the pimp. Foucault seemed particularly fascinated by Marcus's references to a nineteenth-century book called *My Secret Life*, penned by an anonymous author as (in Foucault's words) "a meticulous narrative of a life which was essentially devoted to sexual pleasures" (1978, 5). Following up on Marcus, then, the first interpretation of Foucault's title would suggest identification with these reluctant, different, or outright subversive Victorians who indulged in a life of bodily pleasures and desires and—scandalously—spoke freely about it.

On the other hand, Foucault, unlike Marcus, was reluctant to view these "other Victorians" as persons "of the shadows, situated on some 'other side' in an age of prudishness" (1978, 5). Foucault argued that without underestimating the importance of "the silences, the barriers, the evasions," we, just like Victorians, live in a "society of speaking sex" (1978, 6). Ours is "a kingdom imagined by Diderot in *Les Bijoux Indiscrets*; a certain, nearly invisible mechanism makes sex speak in a virtually inexhaustible chatter." And we seek knowledge from that chatter, expecting sex "to tell us about ourselves (1978, 6)." Thus, it seems easy to argue, the second interpretation of the title—"We, Victorians"—may be just as plausible as the first one.

The ambivalence in the title was probably intentional. The first chapter of *The History of Sexuality, Volume One*, which sets the tone for the entire three-volume project, presents Foucault's argument against the common view of the Victorian era as "this hypocritical, prudish bourgeois society, miserly with its pleasures, obstinate in its refusal to either recognize or name them" (1978, 6). For if "the repressive hypothesis," as Foucault calls it, were true—"then the mere fact that one is speaking about it [sex] has the appearance of deliberate transgression" (1990, 6). Instead of this facile exercise in liberation (and not just sexual), Foucault proposes to

examine the case of a society which has been loudly castigating itself for its hypocrisy for more than a century, which speaks verbosely of its own silence, takes great pains to relate in detail the things it does not say, denounces the powers its exercises, and promises to liberate itself from the very laws that have made it function. (1990, 8)

Thus the key question, he concludes, is not "Why are we repressed?" but rather, "Why do we say, with so much passion and so much resentment against our most recent past, against our present, and against ourselves, that we are repressed?" (1990, 8).

Foucault's argument against "the repressive hypothesis" of the Victorian age—and contemporary comparisons to it—is, therefore, threefold. First, Foucault objects to the oversimplified portrayal of the Victorian era as the period of prohibition, censorship, and denial. Instead, he sees that period, which spoke most loudly through its scandals, as producing discourses about sex—and through those discourses (scientific, educational, psycho-analytic), new and complex domains of sexuality. Second, Foucault rejects "talk about repression" among his contemporaries as a meaningless challenge to power, which imagines itself as anticipation of the coming freedom. "Ours is, after all," he writes, "the only civilization in which officials are paid to listen to all and sundry impart the secrets of their sex." Third, and most important, Foucault opposes the notion of power that is "spontaneously conceived as [. . .] law, as interdiction, as prohibition, and repression" (1978, 8). Quite the contrary, he writes, "we are dealing not nearly so much with a negative mechanism of exclusion as with the operation of a subtle network of discourses, special knowledges, pleasures, and powers." In fact, "power is tolerable only on condition that it mask a substantial part of itself. [. . .] For it, secrecy is not in the nature of an abuse; it is indispensable to its operation" (1990, 86).

And so, it would be a mistake to view scandals—the quintessential narratives of transgressions and disclosures—as instances that simply reveal the hidden workings of power, although, at times, it may appear that they do so. "As scandal recasts secret activities into a public story of exposure," writes William A. Cohen (1996, 9) in his analysis of Victorian scandals, "it makes questions about truth almost impossible to answer, however deliberately it mobilizes truth-determining institutions (police interrogation, trial procedures, legislative inquiries)." As they reshuffle the boundaries between private and public/secret and transparent domains of life, scandals simultaneously proclaim them, produce them, and reify them. To view them as moments of truth or straightforward instances of the unmasking of authority would be to ignore that they are themselves constituted by and constitutive of authority. Even more important, it would mean to ignore the importance of the public/private divide—and its gendered instantiations—for the depoliticized, unquestioning functioning of the capitalist economy.

Namely, as Mark Rupert (1995) has observed, capitalist hegemony depends on a clear-cut separation of private and public, economics and politics: production of hegemony is a process of continuous abstraction, objectification, and estrangement of politics from economics, and of public from private interests. The divide has become only more important in this age of "communicative capitalism" (Dean 2001), which perpetuates itself by feeding publicity with secrets, thus recreating the fantasy that privacy could actually exist as a domain untouched by corporate or state power. The paradox of living on social networks (contingent on expensive hardware), while demanding the right to privacy, parallels discussions among TED women (see True, Chapter 3 of this volume) on whether or not "women can have it all," careers and family life, as if this were a choice available to everyone. Thus, particularly for the privileged, "ideologies and institutions of intimacy," write Laurent Berlant and Michael Warner (2000, 317), "are increasingly offered as a vision of the good life [. . .], the only (imaginary) place where good citizens might be produced away from the confusing and unsettling distractions and contradictions of capitalism and politics." The salvation from the vagaries of the neoliberal economy is supposed to be found in a secured, reconstructed domain of privacy and intimacy—rather than in a radical transformation of public life. For the poor, however, intimacy is increasingly disallowed. As Tepe-Belfrage and Montgomerie explain in Chapter 5 of this volume, when austerity calls, like in the United Kingdom after the global financial crisis (GFC), even spare bedrooms in public housing projects can become taxable property.

Thus, Foucault's recourse to Victorians in *The History of Sexuality* carries a potentially apt warning for the analysis of scandals in the neoliberal age. Do scandals enunciate the liminal figures of our era—hackers, whistle-blowers, immigrants, "black lives matter," welfare mothers, and other public sector dependents, as theorized in many of the chapters in this volume? Or do they instead, through their "polymorphous techniques of power," generate the pleasures associated with access to secret knowledge for the rich and the middle classes, only to turn us all into willing, consensual neoliberals? A critical feminist response to this question would be that any renegotiation of the public/private divide necessarily evokes a repositioning of gender roles—but not necessarily for the better. Indeed, it is amazing how easily it is forgotten that it was precisely the domain of private, intimate, and domestic that was once granted to women—only to keep them in their (political) place, all the while supporting the capitalist economy with their unpaid labor (Mies 1986; Okin 1989). The apotheosis of privacy—as a response to either sexual scandals or excesses of surveillance after the financial crisis—does not bode well for gender politics and/or democratic politics at all.

EPILOGUE

The phone-hacking scandal, which gradually unraveled thanks to *The Guardian*'s relentless investigation, prevented the purchase of BSkyB by Rupert Murdoch's News Corp in 2011. The scandal led to the resignation of one of Murdoch's most trusted adjutants, Les Hinton, from the position of a publisher of *The Wall Street Journal*. Sir Paul Stephenson, head of the Metropolitan Police (Scotland Yard), the highest-ranking policeman in the United Kingdom, was also forced to leave his post; Murdoch's son, James, lost his position on the Board of the News Corp and gave up his title as the executive chairman of News Corp's UK publishing unit. News Corp itself was split into a publishing and an entertainment unit. A few private indiscretions were eventually disclosed also—Rebekah Brooks and Andy Coulson admitted to having an affair while they were editors of *The News of the World*. Both were married at the time. And, collapsing affairs of the state and business into the affairs of the heart, Rupert Murdoch divorced his 38-years-younger wife Wendy Deng because she allegedly had an affair with the former British Prime Minister Tony Blair.

As you sow, so shall you reap, it would seem. But not quite. By 2015, Rupert Murdoch was once again in negotiations to buy BSkyB. The newly re-elected British Conservative government under David Cameron was much more likely to approve the deal. Rebekah Brooks was found not guilty on all charges. Andy Coulson was released after serving 5 months of his 18-month prison sentence for phone hacking. News Corp was in a much better financial situation after the split. James Murdoch became the CEO of 21st Century Fox, as his father prepared for departure from the helm of the company. Rebekah Brooks was once again taking part in business strategy meetings of the Murdoch conglomerate.

As a result of the scandals that it uncovered—WikiLeaks, phone hacking, Eric Snowden—and its savvy web presence, *The Guardian* has become the second most popular English-language newspaper website in the world. In his farewell address after 20 years as the editor of *The Guardian*, Alan Rusbridger (2015) said that he was leaving the company more financially secure than in many moments in its past. Two-thirds of its readership was now outside the United Kingdom. The newspaper won a Pulitzer Prize for its work on the Snowden files. A documentary film based on Snowden's relationship with *The Guardian* and its reporter Glen Greenwald won an Oscar in 2015.

The arc created by the phone-hacking scandal and its closure four years later resembles the morality play of fall, rise, and redemption that Elisabeth Prügl describes in Chapter 2 of this volume. The phone-hacking scandal has not just come and gone—it has produced new monetary gains, mostly benefiting its main protagonists, while the structures of the newspaper industry (and the financial community that feeds it) have remained largely unchanged. Instead of disclosing power, scandals seem to hide it. Through their chatter, economic order has been restored without notice. Another crisis may yet unfold.

NOTES

1. The findings of the Leveson Inquiry are now available through the UK Government Web Archive at http://www.levesoninquiry.org.
2. For an excellent expose of *The Guardian*'s editorial and business policy over the last two decades, see farewell address of its long-term editor Alan Rusbridger (2015).

CHAPTER 11

Gender, Finance, and Embodiments of Crisis

PENNY GRIFFIN

INTRODUCTION

Marieke de Goede has argued that, to build a more accurate and holistic view of how "seemingly disinterested financial language is firmly rooted in gendered cultural practices," we need a broader understanding of financial crisis as a complex social phenomenon, culturally mediated, represented, and visualized in certain ways (2005, 42). Gendered cultural practices (including gendered recruitment and promotion practices, discriminatory forms of lending, gendered assessments of credit worthiness, visual and written summations of crisis, and so on) are, this chapter argues, best understood by deconstructing the relationship between financial crisis, visual culture, and the concept of embodiment. Analysis of popular and visual culture in and of the global financial crisis reveals the gendered power of the ideas, assumptions, and justifications about the world that have governed the origins and future trajectory of contemporary global finance.

Conventional and widely disseminated accounts of crisis have consisted of three types of approach to crisis, focusing on structural, institutional, and behavioral explanations of and for the crisis (see Griffin 2013a). Such accounts have dominated cultural representations of crisis, frequently offering a picture of the economic world as a sequence of abstract events, unrelated to the everyday practices of social and cultural reproduction, and imagining financial crisis through various representations of masculinities and femininities (men in suits, bears in suits, suits in rubbish bags, male "banksters," women cleaning, women swimming above financial sharks, ballerinas atop bulls, and so on), as this chapter discusses. On the other hand, and as the editors of this volume highlight, critical inquiry into the logics and effects of the global financial crisis entails asking questions about the discursive foundations of the crisis, including the place of the human body in the crisis.

The notion of embodiment implies the presence of tangibility, visibility, or material form. Examining the global financial crisis as embodied requires, at least to some extent, interrogating the "concreteness" of the crisis and its expression in human, physical form. Using representations of the crisis in popular and visual culture as a tool to deliberate on the nature of gendered social and economic relations during and beyond the crisis, this chapter applies a deconstructive method in order to understand how visual and popular culture sources have reproduced certain gendered meanings in and about global finance. All research employs grammatical, rhetorical, and narrative structures that bestow meaning, create value, and constitute knowledge, intentionally or not (Shapiro 1986). A deconstructive approach to global finance and financial crisis requires a commitment to challenging the (often shielded) claims to objectivity, certainty, accuracy, and truth that have characterized conventional accounts of the global financial crisis. This chapter thus rejects the claims to objectivity, certainty, accuracy, and truth that typify conventional approaches to economic behavior, as evidenced in mainstream economics and business school approaches, but also seeks to understand how these claims work to stabilize and render coherent otherwise contestable meanings and identities, such as the financial wisdom and economic "common sense" that have driven dominant responses to crisis. While deconstructing gendered relations of power does not tell us anything necessarily about the many and varied axes of discrimination through which global finance has made sense of the world (including discriminations and discursive privileges based on race, class, or [dis]ability, for example), this chapter hopes to contribute to the opening of a space to consider the variety of cultural and disciplinary exclusions that discipline bodies and minds in the global political economy. It hopes, specifically, to encourage sensitivity to the breadth of relations of power that enable certain behaviors, assumptions, and representations in the global political economy, and asks that we consider as widely as possible the constitution and effects of dominant, heteronormative, discursive structures (since discriminations rarely fit neatly into easily labeled and tidily separated conceptual boxes). Contextualizing and then deconstructing particular, and "popular," crisis texts (understood broadly) enables the analyst to highlight the incoherencies, inconsistencies, and problematic assumptions that conventional approaches and accounts have otherwise rendered indiscernible.

VISUAL AND POPULAR CULTURE AND THE GLOBAL FINANCIAL CRISIS

International political economy (IPE) is highly attentive to understanding the power relationships involved in capitalist culture(s) and their relationship to wider structures of domination. IPE scholars often offer critical analyses of culture as the environment where meanings are made and shared. Unlike international relations (IR), however, which has in recent years become increasingly attentive to the significance of visual sources of meaning and relations of power, IPE rarely treats popular and visual cultures as trustworthy or legitimate objects and sources of inquiry, taking "a rather narrow view on the kinds of evidence appropriate" for analyzing meaning, if, indeed, the question of "meaning" arises at all (Weldes 2006, 177). Although "popular visual language is increasingly the language that amateurs and experts rely upon in order to claim contemporary literacy," and despite much politics being "conducted through popular visual language" (Weber 2008, 137), IPE scholars have been hesitant to explore the power (political, economic, social, and cultural) that visual and popular culture wields on and through world politics. There is much "culture" in IPE, and significant critical IPE scholarship has been dedicated to analyzing the concept of "culture." There remains, however, much less engagement with ideas about textuality, identity, and difference, and, while other disciplines have produced lively and extensive debates on visual and popular culture, IPE scholars have fashioned relatively few. IPE thus continues to be somewhat ignorant of the meanings circulating in and through popular and visual culture that might be relevant to understanding the realm of the "economic."

Analysis of visual and popular culture in the global financial crisis can say something important about the gendered power relations that have underpinned the global financial industry and the representative practices that have enabled those power relations to continue relatively unchallenged. As Bleiker articulates, representation "is always an act of power" and this power "is at its peak if a form of representation is able to disguise its subjective origins and values" (Bleiker 2001, 515). Global finance and its institutions, key actors, practices, and discourses has proven adept at disguising the subjective origins of their key forms, guiding assumptions, and practices.

Global finance has not been built accidentally upon exclusivist forms of masculinity and does not by coincidence marginalize the types of bodies that do not perform such "masculine" traits as decisiveness, competitiveness, risk-taking, aggression, and individualism. The global financial industry represents the development of a type of Western/Northern "epistemic community" produced by particular capitalist histories, offering incentives and rewards for certain types of behavior (aggression, competitiveness, individualism, risk-taking, moral "flexibility," etc.) (Griffin 2013a). From a model of "gentlemanly capitalism," evolved to eliminate from financial practice its less honorable associations with gambling, to the cut-throat narratives of "greed is good" finance and, more recently, the evolution of "diversity management," gender quota strategies and the myth of "the financially prudent woman" (see Prügl 2012 and Chapter 2 of this volume), the global financial industry conveys limits to human behavior based on gendered assumptions about the capacity and predictability of human bodies. While financial success has historically been modeled on (white, professional) men's ability to face unpredictable futures "boldly, rationally, and responsibly" (de Goede 2004, cited in Griffin 2013a, 19), a more recent focus on women as potentially corrective bodies in the global financial system has been profoundly, and problematically, essentialist, seeking to exploit women's "innate" and "feminine" gifts for responsibility, domesticity, and circumspection.

The use of symbols of masculinity, and its threatened emaciation, throughout the crisis is not, this chapter argues, a sideline to understanding the core reasons for, the effects of, and proposed solutions to the global financial crisis. Rather, key visual moments in the history of the crisis tell us a great deal about the nature of and proposed responses to the crisis and, perhaps most significant, who enjoys the power to make their meanings circulate in the world of economic relations. As Carver notes, international politics "is rarely done in any direct sense by philosophers but rather by people whose intellectual horizons are largely formed by TV, movies, visual reports in the news and rather more remotely, textual journalism and verbal briefings" (2010, 426). Pervasively narrated, and thus reproduced, in everyday ways (across the news media, for example, or in film, on television, and through social networking and blog sites), the global financial crisis has been constituted as much by popular imagery as it has by official policy and governance rhetoric. This chapter takes a number of visual sources, from both news media publications and otherwise highly subversive public protest movements, and examines how and where they have deployed gender symbolism in their coverage of global finance and crisis and to what effect(s). The images selected for consideration here include representations of Tarantino-style male "banksters" prowling the streets (*The Economist*), unhappy bears dressed as downtrodden bankers (*Time*), and great white sharks threatening to swallow whole the lone female swimmer/US economy (*The Economist*).[1] These images are, of course, only pictures. Emanating from sources that are considered to benefit from a certain expertise in matters economic, however, the visual symbols chosen not only reflect a world of gendered financial expectations; by reproducing the channels of visual and linguistic authority through which this world signifies economic sense, they actively sustain it.

Conventional Approaches to the Global Financial Crisis

Discourses, practices, and representations of global finance are always embodied in some sense, be it physically, materially, emotionally, or theoretically, "both in the modelling of types of masculinity considered best able to embody the strength, intelligence and virility to succeed in a cutthroat, aggressive and individualistic industry" and also "in the accounts, practices and communities of those committed to the centrality of the market as the only distributor of (scarce) resources" (Griffin 2013a, 17). The foundations of (neoliberal) global finance are intrinsically gendered, since they are predicated on masculinist subjectivities, particularly those based on the privileging and experiences of middle-class, white, Western men. Understanding the constitution and effects of the financial crisis requires interrogating the taken-for-grantedness of conventional accounts of the global financial crisis, while also asking how knowledge is conditioned (historically, socially, and culturally) and informed by patterns of power, value, interests, and identities.

Dominant approaches to the financial crisis have consisted of three types of account: those that focus on structural explanations of the crisis, those that focus on an institutional account, and those that champion behavioral explanations (see Griffin 2013a).

Structural explanations of the crisis, emanating largely from critical (Marxist) accounts, focus on crisis as a result of structural flaws in local or global capitalisms. Herein, the crisis is the result of structural transformations in capitalism, including, for example, financial deregulation, the rise of the multinational corporation, the "spatial restructuring" of capitalist production (see, e.g., McNally 2009), and the financialization of the world economy. Such transformations have destabilized the world economy to the point of economic crisis (Griffin 2013a, 18–20).

Institutional accounts, however, do not focus on the systemic whole, isolating instead failures in particular industries and market practice. As also for mainstream economics, this approach fails (purposefully, since its advocates are inherently concerned with the maintenance of the current, albeit improved, system) to see causation as internal to the system, and focuses on so-called external causes, such as government interference, exogenous events, a few bad apples, and so on. Of the three approaches, the institutional explanation has probably been most often articulated across governance discourses and by financial leaders and politicians, who have sought to blame market actors for the crisis and have located the solution to the crisis in actor-led, national, institutional reforms seeking particular market improvements (see Best 2010 and Griffin 2013a, 20–22).

The third type of account of crisis to dominate both official and popular reporting has been behavioral explanations for the crisis. Emphasizing the "human factor," such explanations have been the most explicitly sexualized of crisis accounts (although structural and institutionalist accounts are as gendered in their reliance on the preexisting framework of masculinized economic activity). These explanations have been embedded prominently in the cover imagery of major news sources, such as the "high end" magazines *Time* and *The Economist*, and are reproduced later in this chapter in Figures 11.1, 11.2, 11.3, 11.4, 11.5, and 11.6. They include representations that describe personal fault, moral delinquency, greed, fraud, and "executive culpability," but they have also linked explanations for the crisis with biological assumptions about masculinity and femininity (see Griffin 2013a, 23–25). Thus, "hormonal" explanations for "irresponsible," blameworthy, and even criminal behavior have been offered, while a focus on the "more prudent investment styles of women" (Prügl 2012 and Chapter 2 of this volume) and their comparative "level-headedness" has allowed people's bodies to be read as blameworthy and thus problematic. This is evident in accounts of the "death of macho," illustrated by male executives perilously close to disaster (Salam 2009), discussions of fraud published alongside images of Tarantino-esque male "banksters" (Figure 11.1), and in analysis of the United States' sluggishly slow recovery, symbolized by a "wimpy" male bicep (Figure 11.6).

Gender in/and the Global Financial Crisis

Adducing "masculinity as a variable that may have caused the financial crisis" inserts gender into discussions of the crisis to enable, as Prügl articulates, a particular narrative "of fall, rise, and redemption," which facilitates the redemption of finance capitalism as chastened and reformed (2012, 21; see also Chapter 2 of this volume). Behavioral accounts of crisis reify the hypermasculinization of finance and distract from the real issue of critiquing the processes by which incentives are created and sustained in international capitals market, further contributing to the reproduction of a flawed and highly sexist system of economic relations (see, for example, the corseted male of global credit controls in Figure 11.2, or the plaintive male bear of the falling financial market in Figure 11.4). As Seabrooke argues, conventional accounts of the crisis, particularly discussions of re-regulation, miss how "everyday expectations about how the economy works provide constraints on the capacity of economic and political elites to change the system" (2010, 51). Even otherwise subversive engagements with global finance, such as the imagery chosen for the Occupy Wall Street campaign (which cannot be reproduced here for "various legal reasons"),[2] avoid challenging the assumed masculinity of global finance, so central to understanding the modern accumulation of wealth has "masculinity" become. These "critical" images choose the "shocking" juxtaposition of ballerina atop bull, trash bags held together with a businessman's necktie or the face of British "liberator" Guy Fawkes (Figure 11.7) to emphasize masculinity's central role in the global economy. Rather than simply replicating the assumptions and expectations about people's bodies and capacities that have centered masculine privilege in global finance, a better understanding of the crisis is, however, generated through careful examination of how, where, and to what effect(s) assumptions and expectations have been shaped, used, and reproduced by particular accounts of the crisis (including visual, popular, and official discourses).

Given the focus that has emerged on women in finance across various media, governance, and policy-based responses, it is interesting to ask what, if anything, has changed about the financial industry, financial governance, and financial relations since the global financial crisis. The simple, but depressing, answer is not much. Like the Asian financial crisis before it, at the time "one of the worst financial crises in the postwar period" (IMF 1998), the global financial crisis has instigated "increasingly populist calls for greater regulation," unleashing "a wave of populist anger that led to the imposition of price controls in the western states by the Federal Energy Regulatory Commission and later passage of Sarbanes-Oxley reforms" (Widmaier 2010, 141–142). Yet very little across the global financial industry has substantially altered. Rather, it seems that the concentration of wealth in the hands of a privileged (white, male) few seems to have deepened. As Prügl notes, there is very little evidence of chastened behavior on the part of financial institutions, with the leaders of financial investment companies showing "remarkably little repentance when called to testify on executive pay or their fraudulent double-dealings with collateralized debt obligations" (2012, 31). Money from central banks continues to be extended relatively cheaply and easily, while banking systems' capacity to move assets around has simply been relaxed, allowing them to offload "risky assets" from balance sheets and improving "tier-one capital ratios" (Ryan 2013, in Griffin 2015a). According to Grey, the combination of "massive bank bailouts, virtually free and unlimited credit for banks and financial institutions, and austerity for the working class" has only further propped up the financial system and enriched the ruling elite, "inflating financial asset values" and doing "nothing to revive the real economy" (2013). Meanwhile, across the globe "economic growth continues to stagnate," despite "vast subsidies to the banks and investment houses" (2013).

Rather than instituting radical and far-reaching financial reforms, as requested by populist demands for "a society based on human needs not hedge fund profits" (Occupy protester, in *The Atlantic* 2011), the disorientation created by crisis has thus far been very successfully harnessed and exploited by neoliberals to sediment power in the hands of an existent (male) elite. While financial reform during and "after" the financial crisis has been exceptionally thin on the ground, social reform has been exercised with apparently joyful abandon. What *has* changed during and "after" the crisis is the access of non-elites to wealth, made possible by austerity measures that have cut or capped public sector wages, increased consumption taxes, instigated far-reaching pension reforms, targeted safety nets, and revisioned the healthcare system and the labor market (Deen 2013, cited in Griffin 2015a). Almost entirely absenting consideration of gendered relations of power and their existent effects on economic formations and processes, both official and populist responses to the financial crisis and calls for reform have largely erased the disproportionate effects of the recession on women, especially poor women (see Bedford and Rai 2013; Deen 2013, Griffin 2015a). Governance responses to the crisis continue to reproduce gendered assumptions about wealth as not only desirable but also morally good within a culture of masculinized financial success. Women, encouraged to enter corporate boardrooms and trading floors by active and sometimes aggressive recruitment and quota strategies,[3] do not appear to be altering the fundamental character of financial services, and there is little evidence that the masculinized nature of the industry is changing (Griffin 2015a). The fall of "Wall Street Macho" (Salam 2009) and the rise of "Davos woman" (Elias 2013) has not "demasculinized" the mechanisms of financial governance and practice, and "women are no more visible in finance than they were before the crisis" (Prügl 2012, 31; see also Griffin 2015a).

SYMBOLISING CRISIS: DECONSTRUCTING THE POPULAR AND VISUAL LANGUAGE OF THE GLOBAL FINANCIAL CRISIS

Humans form their identities, as Storey articulates, from a varied and contradictory series of identifications, subject positions, and forms of representation (2003, 91). Human identities are not the expression of human "nature"; they are rather "a performance in culture" and meaning (and therefore the processes of meaning-making by which "events,"[4] such as a financial crisis, can be understood) are not "something fixed and guaranteed in nature" but are "always the result of particular ways of representing nature in culture" (Storey 2003, x).

The visual and popular culture of the financial crisis says something important both about how nature (the "natural event" of the financial crisis) has been represented in culture (cultural texts and practices, including, for example, the media, popular protest, social media and the blogosphere, consumer culture, etc.) and about who has the power to make their meanings circulate in the world of economic relations. The ways in which the financial crisis has been rationalized depend upon the meanings circulating in and through popular and visual culture, which enable, endorse, and reproduce particular reactions while regulating the possibility of alternative responses. This has depended on the use of a variety of (sometimes quite frequently repeated) metaphors, analogies, and representations to make sense of (and thus to circulate "common sense" about) the crisis. Metaphors, for example, of enormity have been deployed to support the case for "emergency" responses that press for martial law–style governance (for the protesters, the governance of "renegade" financial actors and institutions and, for the policymakers, the regulation of costly and cumbersome welfare systems). Presented across media, policy, and popular discourses as a singular event of epic proportions, the crisis has repeatedly been reproduced in terms of shock, devastation, anxiety, fear, anger, and shame (see, for example, Widmaier 2010). Imagery of waves, typhoons, sinkholes, capsized and sunken ships, inhospitable oceans, and high seas can be seen throughout media publications (a 2008 *Time* illustration, "Rough Seas," for example, offers the image of the sculpture of a sinking boat that sits, framed by the City's skyscrapers, in London's Thames River. This, *Time* notes, "seemed an apt metaphor for state of the global financial market"; 2008b). As Brassett and Clarke note, a rhetoric of trauma and impending (but "natural") disaster is heavily invested in the emotional categories deployed in policy discourses "that sought to address the "financial tsunami" that was threatening to engulf the world economy" (2012, 5).

This chapter is, of course, interested specifically in how the visual language of the global financial crisis, as used across the social, political, and economic landscape during and "after" the crisis, might be read as gendered. The images reproduced here have been selected from news media and popular protest sources (predominantly based in the Northern Hemisphere, but with global reach) and depict masculinity, femininity, and the world of economic activity variously. They make the world of the financial crisis meaningful in particular ways, referencing metaphors of disaster and recovery, for example (as in Figures 11.3 and 11.5), or selecting and displaying specific bodies while excluding others (e.g., Figures 11.1, 11.2, 11.6). As Storey articulates, dominant ways of making the world meaningful are "produced by those with the power to make their ways of articulating meaning circulate discursively in the world," which generates particular "hegemonic truths" that "assume an authority over the ways in which we think and act" (2003, x–xi). Our actions, our very horizons of possibility, are actively shaped by power-laden processes of meaning-making, reproduced and sustained through popular and visual culture. It is unclear, for example, how we might meaningfully engage with alternative economic practices, processes, or systems if no (or at least very few) parts of our cultural landscape make available and represent these alternatives. Terms such as "financialization," "globalization," and "deregulation" have slipped almost unnoticed into everyday languages, legislations, policies, and practices. We are less able to engage critically with the extent of a society's financialization, however, when capital mobility is so mundanely assumed to be a "natural" component of global economic relations that it is background material across sources of popular and official economic "expertise."

Embodiments of Crisis (1): Newsmedia, Finance, and the World of Men

This section looks at examples of the ways in which the global financial crisis has been represented and embodied across high-selling, "reputable" news media sources, the capacity of which to command knowledge and attract an elite readership rests firmly on their ability to accurately reflect the culture (in this case, of global finance) to which they speak. The representational practices deployed by these popular and pervasive news media sources thus rationalize the financial crisis in various ways but, most significantly for this chapter, discriminate actively and often between identifiable and sexed bodies as symbolic of economic success, regulation, and recovery in the global political economy. Analysis of these sources shows

Figure 11.1 *The Economist*'s "Banksters." Cover, July 7, 2012.
Reproduced from http://retalls.seminaritaifa.org/2012/07/12/banksters/

how the "natural event" of the financial crisis has been represented in culture, revealing a good deal about the relations of power through which meanings circulate in the world of economic relations. As shown in the imagery reproduced here (Figure 11.1), news media and popular protest sources have often sought to reaffirm the meaning of the global financial system and its practices as symbolic of white, masculine corporate power,

Figure 11.2 *The Economist*'s "A Good Time for a Squeeze." Cover, August 6, 2007.
Reproduced from http://www.readingthepictures.org/2007/08/your-turn-good-time-for-a-squeeze/

immersing their coverage of the financial crisis and beyond in images of masculinity.

The Economist, for example, a publication elsewhere "saturated with images of masculinity," as scholars have noted (Hooper 2001, 117–127), has chosen frequently to illustrate its coverage of the financial crisis with various representations of gendered hierarchy. In August 2007, a credit "corset" is shown to squeeze the male businessman (presumably) forced into it (since corsets, although worn by men, are much more often associated with women) (Figure 11.2). In November 2007, the predatory "Jaws" of the financial crisis threatens to swallow whole the vulnerable female swimmer, here representing the American economy (possibly Mother America herself) (Figure 11.3).

Figure 11.3 *The Economist*'s "America's Vulnerable Economy." Cover, November 17, 2007.
Reproduced from https://www.pinterest.com/pin/307792955755987062/

Time's coverage of financial crisis has tended to preference either abstractly or explicitly masculine symbolism (see Figures 11.4, 11.5, and 11.6. These images show dejected bears dressed as bankers, unemployed male workers queuing for food in the 1930s, and under-endowed male muscles proffering only a "wimpy" US recovery).

Figure 11.4 *Time* magazine's "Looking Beyond the Bear." Cover, March 26, 2001.
Reproduced from http://www.coverbrowser.com/covers/time/82

Claiming to be "one of the most authoritative and informative guides to what is happening in the worlds of health and science, politics, business, society and entertainment" (*Time* 2014), *Time* magazine rarely, in fact, chooses a female, of any description (woman, child, animal), in its representations of global finance or the politics of economic relations (Angela Merkel or Christine Lagarde appear sporadically). Cover illustrations on financial crisis during the twentieth century have depicted the male experience of recession (Figure 11.5), male historical figures (John Galbraith, Milton Friedman, George Schultz, Alan Greenspan, for example) and the masculine credentials of economic recovery (Figure 11.6), or they have simply deferred to the masculinized bull (of Wall Street) and the bear (of the market; see Figure 11.4).

The regular revivals of the term "Great Recession" might, suggests Rampell, "have something to do with a near-eschatological desire to witness a downturn of epic, historical proportions. After all, as long as we're suffering,

Figure 11.5 *Time* magazine's "The New Hard Times." Cover, October 13, 2008.
Reproduced from http://www.amazon.com/TIME-Magazine-October-2008-Times/dp/B001OYVGP4

we might as well brand the suffering so it'll sound more impressive to our grandchildren" (2009). Its use also enables *Time* to draw on the visual symbolism of a distinctly masculine crisis, as per this cover photograph (Figure 11.5), which depicts unemployed male workers in the United States queuing for (free) soup (use of unemployed men compliments descriptions of a "he-cession," as discussed later, which were particularly popular in 2008). In Figure 11.6, the *Time* cover suggests that the US economy is "getting stronger," so why does it still seem "weak"?

Unlike *The Economist*, *Time*'s target audience is not specifically male. Yet, like *The Economist*, the visual language of *Time*'s coverage of the global financial crisis locates finance directly in the world of men, both reflecting and sustaining gendered financial expectations. Women do appear on the cover of *Time*, but their purpose is more often to illustrate "lifestyle" features, rather than to initiate serious and sustained conversation about world politics. Thus *Time* regularly runs "women's issue" cover stories on

Figure 11.6 *Time* magazine's "The Wimpy Recovery." Cover, April 2, 2012.
Reproduced from http://bilder.bladkongen.no/upl/normal500/time-1-2012.jpg

illness, health and well-being, fashion, lifestyle, babies, hormones, dieting, and celebrities, all of which invariably feature illustrations of women's bodies. Once again, men appear in power, holding power, bearing the burden of responsibility for crisis, threatened by crisis or resolving crisis.

Both *Time* and *The Economist* consider themselves, and are often described as, elite publications. Both are put together to convey a sense of prestige and expertise, and both are directed at an international readership of elite professionals (in *The Economist's* case, a specifically male readership). Their capacity to make sense to and maintain their audience rests on their ability to accurately reflect the worlds of global finance, business, current events, and world politics to which they speak. The visual symbolism of these magazines' representations of the financial system and ongoing crisis reflects gendered financial expectations (that finance is, for example, a masculine activity, or that men are responsible for the path of and for resolving the crisis), but this symbolism is not merely the passive reflection of how things are. Rather, the visual language of powerful and pervasive news media commentary also reproduces those expectations, sustaining the gendered conditions of global finance and reaffirming finance as a stronghold of elite masculinity.

Embodiments of Crisis (2): Popular Protest and Alien Women

Official responses (found in governance and policymaking discourses) to the financial crisis have reconcentrated power in the hands of an elite few, engendering techniques of governance to facilitate "effective," but socially devastating, crisis management. Popular responses, where they have failed to take up the call to end the gendered relations from which the crisis emerged, have reified existent and gendered forms of practice, process, and structure.

The now iconic representation of a female ballerina atop the deeply masculinized Wall Street bull (the first and perhaps most celebrated Occupy Wall Street image) is powerful because it is a potent juxtaposition of meanings,[5] and it is so *because* it is gendered. The bull can of course be read, as Salverda articulates, as "a symbol of unbridled capitalism" (2006). Bulls are not, of course, cows, and their use across popular iconography through the ages (and across cultures) has been symbolic of god-like fearsomeness, aggression, and virility. The bull, as a mythically libidinous beast, thus also represents "the inherent masculinity of the financial services industry" (Salverda 2006). The ballerina of the Occupy poster, on the other hand, her posture indicating a degree of command over the beast below, is a symbol of grace, fluidity, and freedom. She "leads the way to success" because she has approached the chaos, "not with violence or vengeance, which in this case is represented by the smoky scene and masked crowd in the background," but with grace and serenity (Just a Memo 2011). Importantly, the ballerina is no matador, with his symbolic proximity to masculine prowess, conflict, and, some might say, foolhardiness. While the use of a female figure to represent nonviolence is certainly not rare, the poster has been so widely disseminated, and thus effective as a visual bookmark for the Occupy movement, because it is visually surprising—a powerful and gendered metaphor for the movement because the ballerina and the bull are widely considered to be poles apart, symbolically and physically.

Although antithetical in many ways to the dominant narratives of global finance and financial capitalism, the representational practices of popular protest movements have frequently reinforced both the assumed masculine character of financial services and the otherness of women's position in and relationship with economic discourse (as with, for example, imagery of the ballerina atop the Wall Street bull, a garbage bag, wrapped in a tie, on the floor of a stock exchange, a giant female figure striding across Manhattan, and various visual deployments of the board game Monopoly's Rich Uncle Pennybags). Problematizing the structures and mechanisms of globalized finance and its governance is no mean feat, and challenging the status of the "1 percent" may reasonably seem enough for many protest groups. Without paying attention, however, to the gendered patterns of power and reproduction that prop up economic relations and advocating instead apparently "gender-neutral" alternatives to the current capitalist system, such groups only further entrench the gendered practices that have impeded women's income and savings rates, for example, and have enabled gender bias in the policies of both private and public financial institutions (see Van Staveren 2010). While female-focused groups such as Codepink and Women Occupy have been more sensitive to women's vulnerabilities in the global economy and their voices have been important across the Occupy movement, such groups have not, perhaps unsurprisingly, sought to subvert the imagery and sexual politics of the movement itself. This has relied heavily and repeatedly on female/male and feminine/masculine binaries in its calls for an economic revolution (often deploying visual imagery of male revolutionary figures, such as Guy Fawkes, as in Figure 11.7), without calling into question the gendered relations of power evident in this symbolism.

From around 2007 to 2009, a particular panic about male unemployment (particularly in the US and Britain) led to an outbreak of descriptions of the financial crisis as a so-called "mancession" or "he-cession." A discourse of crisis emerged based on repetitions of a 1950s, male-breadwinner style of gender relations and, despite existing research showing the disproportionate job losses faced by women during the Asian financial crisis (1997–1998) (Deen 2013), reports continued to claim that the crisis was disproportionately hurting men (see also Griffin 2010, 2015a).

Subsequent, and more accurate, reporting suggests that women (and women everywhere, not just in the US, which has monopolized crisis reporting) continue to suffer disproportionately during times of slowed economic growth, precarious employment, and increased food prices (see, for example, Buvinic et al. 2009; Deen 2013). Evidence has also suggested that men actually experienced job losses during the global financial crisis at a lower rate than in earlier recessions (see Griffin 2010). As UN Assistant Secretary General John Hendra has argued, austerity measures undermine progress on equal divisions of care responsibilities across case studies,

Figure 11.7 "Guy Fawkes/V for Vendetta" Occupy Wall Street campaign poster.

pushing "the responsibility for, and cost of, social and public goods back onto households, and in effect, onto women" (interviewed in Deen 2013).

The assertion, across a number of popular newsmedia, protest, and policy channels that men were being hardest hit by the crisis and that a "he-cession" was imminent, and imminently catastrophic, reflected widely held assumptions of men's central role in local and global economic systems. There has, after 2009, been no "quiet but monumental shift of power from men to women" (as Salam suggests 2009, 66) in any society, and certainly not in global financial services. Where their survival was precarious before the crisis, women's position has become yet more uncertain. Women continue to command lower salaries and, in countries where gender gaps were beginning to narrow, austerity governance threatens to unravel previously increasing levels of gender equality (see Elson 2012; McVeigh 2013).

Of course, since men were considered more dramatically affected by the crisis, they were also more often held responsible for that crisis, in the sense of being considered to blame for the crisis (Figures 11.1, and 11.4) but also ultimately accountable for the resolution of that crisis (Figures 11.2 and 11.6). As popular protest movements called for the "robber bankers" to be jailed, discussions across popular and official discourses concerning greedy bankers and hormonally overloaded investors blamed men, or at least certain male bodies (led astray by their innate "talents"), for the crisis. The emergence, then, of narratives of women's fiscal responsibility, prudence, and trust-worthiness as a potential panacea to the crisis is perhaps not surprising. Prügl's analysis reveals how a good deal of Northern news media coverage of the financial crisis and women's "special" gifts has lifted woman "into a story that associates her with financial caution and risk aversion and calls forth her civilizing and moderating influences," making her available to mediate, where once she was ignored, "between male aspirations for profit and unpredictable economic vagaries" (2012, 23). This story does not, however, destabilize man's place at the center of the financial world, and the financial sector remains "one of the few bastions of virtually uncontested masculine privilege" (2012, 22). Gendered power relations abound in what Prügl refers to as a "new world order of patriarchal finance capitalism," driven by the continuation of sexism in the financial industry's hiring and promotion practices, "the predatory forms of lending" that have left poor women, in particular, exposed, "the privileging of financial interests" that continue "to benefit men disproportionately in regulatory practices" and businesses that "continue to be run to fit male experiences and preferences" (2012, 32–33). The reproduction of myths of women as financially prudent and more fiscally responsible than men has not served to challenge the fundamentally masculine character of the financial industry, which remains centered on white, masculine privilege. Femininity and (since gender is so rarely understood as separate from sexed bodies) women continue to play a secondary, supporting, and restraining role to the assumed centrality of masculine action ("irrationally" exuberant or chastened), which further reinforces woman's alien position in finance.

CONCLUSION

Understanding the global financial crisis as a visually significant, embodied, and sexualized crisis is crucial in fathoming the enduring constitution and effects of gendered relations of power in global finance. This chapter has argued that the crisis represents, not the failings of "greedy" or over-sexed individuals, over-zealous banks, and misguided strategies for risk management, but the weaknesses of a system predicated on the unprecedented concentration of social power among a privileged few. Although conventional accounts of global finance and the financial crisis have frequently disembodied the crisis, abstracting financial relations from the social relations that make them possible, the concept of embodiment, especially embodied representations of the human form, have been and continue to be central to understanding the constitution and ongoing effects of the financial crisis and the industries that have enabled it. An embodied crisis, it is in the visual practices of conventional accounts and understandings of the crisis that this is most clear. As shown here, the representational practices deployed by conventional accounts (in visual, oral, and written form) have manifested and continue to reveal gendered economic and power relations, dependent upon gendered distinctions between bodies as able or incapable of performing economic success, virility, regulation, and recovery. Even where conventional descriptions have not explicitly deployed images, they have often relied upon visual metaphors, analogies, and representations to make sense of (and thus to circulate "common sense" about) the crisis, calling, for example, for emergency responses to tidal waves of global economic instability.

Although, then, human bodies may, officially, be marginal to dominant (neoliberal) accounts of capital mobility, economic growth, and market recovery, the longevity of the financial system has depended upon (and continues to revolve around) rationalizing human bodies in various ways. Representing bodies, usually male and female, across their coverage, and frequently according to problematic assumptions about sex, gender, and male and female bodies' "natural" proclivities, a variety of responses to and discussions of the crisis have deployed the body as either complementary to or problematic in the global financial industry and its successes. Although the discipline of IPE, in its orthodox and critical forms, has tended to ignore the contributions of studies of visual culture, a gender perspective on the visual and popular culture of the crisis can reveal how—far from being challenged by critique and counterposition—dominant, capitalist (neoliberal) discourse has been enabled and encouraged, throughout the crisis and beyond, by specifically gendered narratives of achievement, responsibility, trustworthiness, and reliability. Rather than challenging existing logics, structures, and effects of financial "common sense," both popular reporting and official accounts of the crisis have further sedimented a (neo)liberal order of global finance, while otherwise subversive protest movements have obscured the gendered foundations of unequal power relations in the global political economy.

NOTES

1. Images not reproduced here but significant to the formulation of this chapter's analysis include illustrations of businessmen standing precariously over precipitous ledges (Salam 2009) and women mopping the floors of stock exchanges (*Time* 2008). In the former, a silver-haired male executive, cigar in hand, noose around his torso, is pulled forward toward an unknown drop. The male figure himself appears to bear no apparent terror and his expression is haughty but inscrutable. A line of smart buildings recedes from the foregrounded figure and two American flags can be made out in the background (see Griffin 2013b, 216). In the latter, a woman "mops the floor of the Frankfurt stock exchange" before the opening of markets in September 2008 (*Time* 2008a), the implication being, of course, that (lowly) women have been left to clean up the (global) mess that men have left behind.
2. Citing "various legal reasons," *Adbusters* (the magazine whose call for assembly in New York inspired the Occupy movement) would not allow us to reprint a number of their posters. With copyright now protecting the images that accompanied some of the most significant protests in the current era, it is perhaps easy to understand why the current crisis is not just a crisis of capitalism but also, as Wanda Vrasti argues in Chapter 14 of this volume, a crisis of imagination.
3. Norway's 2003 decision to impose a gender quota on corporate boards is often held up as a pioneer of the gender quota system, with similar efforts having followed in France, Malaysia, Belgium, Iceland, Italy, the Netherlands, and Spain.
4. I use "event" with caution since it is more accurate, I would argue, to articulate the financial crisis as a historical and ongoing process (much in keeping with structural explanations that focus on the changes to economic relations brought about by practices of deregulation and financialization). The language of "crisis" is, however, particularly important to understanding the neoliberal governance of crisis, since it allows for the enaction of (gendered) discourses of urgency, immediacy and muscularity (Griffin 2015b). Relying on the trope of urgency, for example, allows policymakers to substitute in-depth and "nuanced political and legal

thinking" with "muscular" interventions, a greater reliance on "executive" power and "the downgrading of impediments to robust action posed by the "soft" laws of human rights and due process," all necessitated by the apparent "emergency" of the crisis situation (Otto 2011, 77).

5. "We put together a poster for the July issue of *Adbusters*. The poster was a ballerina—an absolutely still ballerina—poised in a Zen-ish kind of way on top of this dynamic bull. And below it had the [Twitter] hashtag #OccupyWallStreet. Above, it said, 'What is our one demand?' I felt like this ballerina stood for this deep demand that would change the world. There was some magic about it" (*Adbusters* cofounder Kalle Lasn, quoted in Beirut 2012).

PART IV

Scandalizing Reimaginings

CHAPTER 12

Global Raciality of Capitalism and "Primitive" Accumulation

(Un)Making the Death Limit?

ANNA M. AGATHANGELOU

INTRODUCTION

In October 2011, Prime Minister George Papandreou asked Greek voters whether they had confidence in his leadership and whether they approved or rejected the EU bailout package and wished to return to the drachma. These two high-stakes votes took other European leaders by surprise. French President Nicolas Sarkozy, for one, saw Papandreou's decision as an "irrational" one that "surprised all of Europe." The discussion spilled over into a North American classroom, where Papandreou's decision, one student said, was not "irrational" and would not create chaos. At this, another student protested:

> There is a final solution to Europe's debt crisis; one that can solve all the continent's financial and economic woes *once and for all*. What Europe needs now is German conquest. To quell the furor we need a new Führer. Germany obviously has the formula, but it lacks the initiative. It needs a robust push, a swell of encouragement from the rest of the hurting world, to do what must be done. And what must it do? It must conquer Europe. Before you know it, what was once economic chaos will be replaced by Germanic stability, a passion for hard work, and a healthy contempt for "taking it easy." (from a Canadian classroom discussing International Relations, Fall 2013)

Figure 12.1 *Libération*'s XAOS. Cover November 2, 2011.

Germany's *Der Spiegel* newspaper published an article "Papandreou Is Right to Let the Greeks Decide," but with a deliberately chosen blue cover[1] (Figure 12.1) and under the title "Le Chaos" (in Greek, *XAOΣ*); *Fox Business* reported, "Greek Prime Minister George Papandreou seems willing to risk throwing Europe—and by extension the global economy—into chaos in an effort to save face politically" (Prial 2011). Elsewhere in the same piece, Axel Merk, president of Merk Investments and an expert on European fiscal policy, predicted,

> The people will say "no." What Papandreou's asking is, "Do you guys want to suffer and make the tough choices?" Of course the answer will be "no." Then the country will fall into anarchy and (Papandreou) will say, "It's not my fault, and it's what the people wanted."

Chaos and anarchy as concepts presuppose a previous order that can be (dis)ordered. As we know, Marx's narrative of "primitive" accumulation says communities must be freed from land and social laws to create labor populations and raw materials for production. In the case of the global economy, what might be required in the chaos ensuing from the failure of Greek leadership to act rationally? Theorists and intellectuals, as well as corporate actors, deploy chaos and anarchy to mark the boundaries of economic rationality to constitute certain publics (e.g., those supporting austerity/those resisting). In many cases, Papandreou's opinions are linearly articulated as irrational, while Merkel (the new Führer presaged by the student cited earlier?) as "Europe's misunderstood visionary" (*Financial Times* 2013) becomes the colonizer and enslaver of Greece (Terzis 2010), thus reinforcing specific visions of a global power and an economic system undergirding it.[2]

The chaos created in Europe due to the bad management of resources in countries like Greece does not make sense unless we also consider two unexplored questions. First, how is it possible to subscribe to the spirit of EU partnership of equality, which suggests the definition of a common sensibility, without exiting the state of nature that seems to prevail among the dominant discourses, producing Greece as a problem, with the possibility of undoing Germany and the global economy? Second, how is it possible to further militarize in a European Union that understands itself as democratic? I argue Greece is being turned into a laboratory where bankers, political leaders, corporations, the military, and various publics, both left and right, are experimenting with organizational forms, financial instruments, regimes of capital accumulation, and working relationships within a changing EU imperial bureaucracy. Much of the economic language that corporations, bankers, the World Bank, and the International Monetary Fund (IMF) use to describe their work and rationalize their market strategies draws on metaphors of race, biology, technology, and social difference.

Tempting as it may be, I am not making a blanket accusation of an emerging white imperial supremacy whose goal is more profits. Rather, I am attempting to show how such performances of power are informed and shaped by the changing conditions of material forces and knowledge production. In fact, many financial officers and political economic institutions are engaged in an imaginative practice that comes to understand Germany and Greece through newspaper articles, such as those from *Libération* and *Der Spiegel* cited earlier. This performative practice allows the emergence of these countries into market discourses. The notion of Germany as "visionary" and Greece as "feminized" and "lazy" shapes actors' understandings, as well as the ways they choose to live in the world (i.e., financial policies), while circumscribing the possibilities for economic reform. Such a focus on raciality in the market offers an entry point into the ways this matrix of power zones and orders the world (Agathangelou 2013, 2014), even as our awareness of it changes.

In this chapter I argue that a presumed relation of chaos/order is pivotal to the "coloniality of power" and the global raciality of capitalism. This zoning of the world as chaotic/ordered generates new assemblages of capital and raciality, displacing the many tensions and conflicts and the direct forces upon which these reorganizations and zonings depend to suture a formation that is neither stable nor fixed. I consider debates on raciality and international feminist political economy with a focus on debt, reproduction, and "primitive" accumulation. Experiments in Greece are reconfiguring the boundaries "between capitalist speculation and the incertitude of value, between free labor and slavery, between those who are inoculated and those who test the vaccine, between the contractual projection of calculable value the uninsurable risk and, not least, between life and death" (Mitropoulos 2012, 4).

Focusing on the two major memoranda signed by Greek political leaders and the European Union, IMF, and the EBank, and two documentaries, *Debtocracy* (2011) and *What's Wrong with the Greeks?* (2012), interspersed with some popular discourses (*The Vima, BILD, Focus*), I articulate an analytic of global raciality (see also Fanon 1967a, 1967b; Agathangelou and Ling 2009; Kayatekin 2009; Chakravartty and Ferreira da Silva 2013; Seth 2013), which allows me to theorize the moments when "the others of Europe," the "primitives," "the degenerates," "the Swindlers in the Euro family" (Focus 2011) are available for any kind of use but are utterly beyond "integration" or "domestication" by Europeans, as they are assumed, re-assembled and re-constituted as asocial. Drawing on these sites and from the vantage point of this analytic, I argue that the articulation of the lazy and the criminal, as well as the Führer (in the figure of Merkel), during the recent crisis discloses contemporary sexual and racialized anxieties; as such, it betrays a spirit of vanquishment manifest in the brutalities of capital's leadership and insular subjectivities assumed by whites and "whites but not quite" (Agathangelou 2004) in their exploitation of both humans and ecologies; as such, it also highlights our engagement with the ways we imagine, practice, and reconfigure global racial capitalism in its late-modern form, and the risks of speculative finance. I read the financial crisis as a political event of our times, outlining the fears circulating about "Greeks" and "fascists," connecting them to debates on international feminist political economy (Hozic 2000, 2001, 2002; Peterson 2003; Bedford and Rai 2010; Kanna 2010; Agathangelou 2011; Nguyen 2011; Roy 2012) and the production of global order/power.

If the debt in Europe turns into a constellation of present fears and plural historical trajectories about those places of "bad debt," I suggest that it has lessons for those of us thinking about radical global anti-racialized and anti-masculinist politics. If Greece is being turned into a place of no value but original accumulation, then that particular Greek-world-making project is also a *fugitive place* pointing to possibilities of thinking about the indeterminacy of social reproduction without physical force and inalienable rights.

ANTI-COLONIAL FEMINIST POLITICAL ECONOMY METHODOLOGY AND ITS ARCHIVE

Neoliberalism had its intellectual roots in a circle of German and Austrian economists of the 1920s and the 1930s. After World War II, these roots took hold in the political and economic foundations of the nascent West German government. For Foucault, the timing was not incidental. After the collapse of the Nazi regime, the new West German state had to build itself out of "nothing," or so the story goes; there was no longer any site of historical or legal legitimacy to which the government could refer, as the authority of the German state had been subsumed by the Nazi state. According to Foucault, rather than attempting to frame a new government around sovereignty with no legal or historical anchorage, the West German government opted to frame itself around the economic freedom of its subjects. By institutionalizing economic freedom as its core, the new government produced a form of legitimacy; by participating in the free economy, the people of West Germany gave their implicit consent.

Because it is the foundation of the state, the economic domain of the German market has a very different relationship with the political. Within this new configuration, the state is beholden to the market from which its sovereignty extends; the market, in effect, generates the possibility for the sustenance of the state. Accordingly, the state must serve the market, rather than the other way around, giving us a new formulation. In the words of Foucault, "the ordoliberals [German neoliberals] say we should completely turn the formula around and adopt the free market as organizing and regulating principle of the state . . . a state under the supervision of the market rather than a market under the supervision of the state" (2008, 116). *Look up this bit of Foucault*

American neoliberals stretched this logic by focusing on labor and taking the vantage point of the worker. Rather than a price at which a worker sells his or her labor, they conceived the wage as an income or revenue stream. Thus, an individual earning a wage is not selling his or her labor but rather getting a return on the investment of capital, making him or her an enterprise or entrepreneur, with his or her skills and abilities understood as capital. This economic logic was extended in the household, historically the sphere of social reproduction, making it a "unit of production in the same way as a classical firm" (Foucault 2008, 245). From this vantage, private institutions such as marriage are economic structures, which, like all partnerships, allow interests to be linked in such a way that the "transaction costs" of each particular agreement are minimized or economized. Thus, the household forms an economic trust, an investment object, to serve the mutual interests of the parties involved (de Goede, Afterword in this volume).

This latter formation reveals the flipside of law and reason, in the embrace of neoliberal governmentality. The market logic as the sole arbiter of value turns folk into privatized subjects, both in their households and in the market. The governmentality of neoliberalism is economically extended through a diffuse network of techniques operating on the fully tractable surface of economic subjectivity. With neoliberalism, in other words, we arrive at the apotheosis of political economy through the absolute economization of the political subject, through the economic necessity to care for oneself in the monogamous terror of the home and the state.

This logic is increasingly problematized as more European economies are on the brink of default, with discussion focusing on the nationalization of economies in Greece, Ireland, Spain, and Portugal. While rating agencies cite national accountability ("irresponsible" persons and "authorities" not meeting obligations; "swindlers" who cannot be trusted to manage fiscal and other public resources; "lazy" and "bankrupt Greeks"), the crisis has as much to do with German, French, British, and American publics, banks, and credit institutions. The popular discourses are smoke screens, Plumpe (2011) argues, as they prevent deliberations of emerging governance approaches and their implications on different institutions such as the household, the state, and people of different spaces.

The co-production of the neoliberal logic and the social order (i.e., the German state with the market within the EU) inscribes economic liberty to be the condition of the possibility of rights and political liberty. The emergence of this ordoliberal order draws on the market as its major vehicle of governance, as its technology for stretching its power into different sites arguing for choice. The market expansion of options in terror and violence, boundary setting, and law enforcement permits a masculine assertion of mutual benefit. For instance, German economists like Eucken and Sinn argue that it is important to "lower the prices in the south of the euro zone relative to those in the north, so as to reflect lower productivity ... [T]hat would require German inflation of 5% for ten years, or a similar level of deflation in the south, or some combination of the two" (*The Economist* 2014).

The neoliberal logics that highlight *homo oeconomicus* as an entrepreneurial subject depend on governance instruments that regulate international debts working to secure capital's rights and claims at the expense of poor states at large, lower income-generating peripheries in Europe, women, and people of color (see Morgan 2008, 14). Human capital regimes engage in activities that Mbembe (2001, 2003, 35) and Agathangelou (2009) term productive morbidity. In the margins of the European economy, in the default countries, colonial/racial analytic frameworks reveal a macabre practice and logic: necropolitics (Mbembe 2003) links debt and death; the erasure of lives allows extension of financial speculation into experimentation and re-engineering with racialized, human bodies. The new technologies of debt and credit and austerity secure the profits of banks and corporations in different strata of peripheral and postcolonial states and lead to the starvation of some populations, both citizens and migrants, to produce value out of "demiurgic surgery" and death. In the words of Mbembe,

> The traces of this demiurgic surgery persist for a long time, in the form of human shapes that are alive, to be sure, but whose bodily integrity has been replaced by pieces, fragments, folds, even immense wounds that are difficult to close. [...] the morbid spectacle of severing. (Mbembe 2003, 35).

The dissolutions of bodies into fragments open them up to ongoing displacements and the ravenous directives of capitalism rendering them vulnerable sites of surgery, experimentation and death. And even in death there is an involution of exploitative tech-neo-imperialist materialisms, histories, and politics, along with the co-opted powers of multiple fugitive and resistance movements, folded back into fetishized, racialized blood-quantum, purity and supremacy serving as sources of vitality in a global hierarchical matrix of wars and "statistical extermination[s]" (Jaimes-Guerrero 1998, 423; Weaver 2001, 248; Panourgia 2014). Generating capitalist innovations seems to require more raw matter to erect new financial regimes. Thus, the question about the chaos that is generated by particular subjects cannot be answered within the emergent regimes of speculation. It ought to be answered from the analytical lens of the zones of fungible terror. It is from this zone that the severing of bodies and death can be conjuncted with the "well-managed" budgets and lives of the dominant leaders of the European and US imperial political powers, forces, and financial regimes.

ENTERPRISE AND CHAOTIC SUBJECTS: *WHAT'S WRONG WITH THE GREEKS?*

In a documentary titled *What's Wrong with the Greeks?* Alexandra Paschalidou asks this question of her father. His response is articulated against the discourses blaming "swindlers" and "lazy" Greeks: "The problem," he says, "is not with the Greeks but rather with the economy." Further, "people should not be expected to make structural changes when they are starving." Paschalidou adds, "The lazy Greek is far from becoming an enterprise. The Greek subject is indignant of the environment and its embodiment of a violence that is committed on them" (Paschalidou 2012). She cites a demonstrator's protest: "[T] hese laws make us feel like the fleeing refugees of the Eastern bloc and also other countries trying to escape poverty or war. This is the future they have planned for us. There is no life, no future here. . . . People are trying to take their life back" (Loukia Kotronaki, cited in Paschalidou 2012). As this project entails "social catastrophe" (Sotiris 2012, cited in Paschalidou 2012), she rhetorically asks, "So, is the problem Greece, or the fact that capitalism ran into a wall?" And she answers herself: "It's not a debt or loan crisis. It is a crisis of over-gathered wealth" (Paschalidou 2012).

Against the dominant and hegemonic grammar of ordoliberals, Paschalidou articulates the tensions emerging in the promises of an economy for a productive and secure life when its primary goal in the name of innovation is profit for the few, not caring for its majority. Exposures of populations and bodies and thereby the body politic to various deaths and material risks systematically strip the body politic's power, in all but name, in this state of alert. A politically qualified state of siege or a body politic in crisis opens up the space to revoke all protections central to a democratic project. The production and performance of an imagination, a social practice dividing the visionaries from the swindlers of the global economy, enlist violence as the accumulation mechanism to settle the boundary between legitimate and illegitimate subject production and the economy. If the Greek body is a unit and a metonym for the swindler of the resources of Germany and the larger European Union, the migrant turns into a site of fungible property of a global order.

Theorizing the presence of certain "Greek" bodies requires a new grammar. In engaging with the practices of everyday life and the social production of living spaces as modes of analysis, I can theorize the ways in which "Greek" gendered bodies function as a location where global visions of slavery and settler colonialism meet. The "Greek" and "Greece" (never a homogeneous environment and corporeality) gendered form turn into imagined spaces of unending possibility—or usefulness—within the imaginaries of this neo-colonialism. Their unending potential also contains a capacity for chaos and disorder, particularly when Greeks live outside settler colonialism and slavery's property-making mandate.

The Greek sexualized body as a spatial trope has the potential for order or chaos, helping us perceive how power presents or hides itself in the landscape. What happens when we think about Greece as the "bottomless pit" (Wolfgang Schaeuble, Merkel's finance minister), or the lazy Greek as a result of ordoliberal colonial spatial patterns? How are subjectivity and space, turned into sites of siege, thereby obliterated by the economy of debt and credit? How does the ordoliberal turn constitute moments of enchantment—evading both the material labor of the human and the creativity of its own agency—non-existent? How do the rich, the poor, and the laboring classes all delude themselves turning their subjectivity also into "settler" (i.e., savages) colonial subject? In asking these questions, I do not wish to make easy parallelisms with the historical formation of settler colonialism, as easy as this may seem. Rather, I ask these questions to bring attention to how the Greek becomes constituted as a sexualized body, lazy and chaotic, making space for new conquests, economic and otherwise. The body's integrity seems to bump against the social gesturing that a sovereign corporeality limits the unbounded desire for more accumulation. Such a limit has to be punctured for the body to be opened up. The body then can turn into a site of experimentation to test how far a production of species can go (Foucault 2008). This experimentation is not disciplining, or even "regularizing," "the man-as-species" (Foucault 2008, 247). It is mere speculation. It is the imaginative and experimental acts of finance to constantly liquidate, drawing on the capacities of reason, faith, and experience, and mortgaging life (i.e., the workers and peasants are supposed to work until they die for being alive; mort-gage = dead pledge) to foretell an indeterminate future. But with increasing speculation over the biological, over life itself, engineering crisis as the basis of the economy and social order, the system may have to generate itself with the dead debris it has created.

In the ordoliberals' new geography, the private spaces of the family (Aphrodite, a metonym for the Greek sexualized subject, property, Greeks, migrants within Greece, and the economy) and the public spaces of state militarism, fundamentalist fascisms, and land theft (i.e., the sale of the islands) occupy the same space. Aphrodite, on the cover of the *Focus*

Figures 12.2 and 12.3 *Focus*'s "Swindlers and Abusers in the European Family/The traitor within the European Family." Cover February 22, 2010.
Reproduced from https://liberthalia.files.wordpress.com/2015/07/betrc3bcger-in-der-euro-familie.jpg

Focus's "Greece and our Money." Cover May 3, 2010.
Reproduced from http://www.patrasevents.gr/imgsrv/f/full/1198640.jpg

magazine (2010) (Figures 12.2 and 12.3) comes to be the metonym of this abuse and theft, a metonym of the body politic that is diseased and has generated the conditions for the production of beggars! The sexual selected site of contestation is identified both as the source of disorder (the "poison") and the "cure," whose eradication provides the remedy—as if this paradoxical logic of poison and cure, the binary logic of the Other, works in the same way. Within this innovative emerging capital and neo-colonial (nevertheless democratic) imaginary space, this logic operates as a strategy of spatial sexual control, functioning through the spatial tactic of expulsion (literal or figurative) of those bodies produced as contaminating the anticipated spaces for capital innovation where the leveraging of finance capital, hedge funds, and currency exchange requires expropriating the value of living flesh. However, conquest and the imagined white Aryan family as semi-public spaces that constitute the nation are omitted from the debates about financial crisis. Conquest is mentioned only in passing, and the family and the state exist in separate realms. For Paschalidou, the family is a social and spatial formation that functions as a modality of conquest. By investigating the formation of the family, we can sense/see where conquest and slavery come together. The family as a site unit of property, enslavement, and conquest is not a priority to Greek existence; in fact,

Greek people "fail" in attempts to constitute the family unit without debt and without turning themselves into beggars.[3]

In reading Paschalidou's film and connecting it to popular discourses of Greece, I am not pointing to an overarching plan to perpetuate racism against Greece. Rather, a repertoire of practices, competencies, and relations between sections of different parts of different states, including Greece, is being engineered when needed. Greece emerges as a problem, thereby a possible experimentation site for multiple actors, such as transnational corporations, federal laboratories, security projects in capital's shifting practices of accumulation and innovation, and their global acceptability.

While commentators note Greece's irresponsibility and what Paggalos (2010) labels the "eating together" of Greek money, they avoid critiquing capital and problematizing the crisis of over-production of capital in a globalized configuration. Though remaining outside a critique of racism and capital (and rather focusing on "eating together" culturally specific understandings), these engagements at the same time keep alive the status of the nationalized Greek for whom access to money is now an inaccessible privilege (denial of money now makes one human) and for whom military and paramilitary forces must do for now (making one secure or protecting him or her from the criminals and the beggars).[4] The fact that "fortress" and "Euro" Europe has not delivered security and wealth and has only served to criminalize what could be a powerful agent and player in European life and democracy, the figure that does not exist for political economy, the vagrant, calls for a revised approach.

Marx has identified the production of unemployed and their criminalization through vagrancy laws as central to the occluded process of primitive accumulation (Marx 1990, 873). However, this lazy rascal is one of many criminalized knowledges and practices to which people defer in times of crises, particularly the crisis of dominant power, of "modernity" and its enchantements. When popular discourses mention deficits, they do not emphasize the multiple reconfigurations of state/private relations within and outside Greece, or the globalizing projects in the form of credit and austerity measures, lower corporate taxes, and military and paramilitary projects (Pentaraki 2013, 704). In 2008, Greece distributed €28 billion to the banking sector to offset the effects of the Wall Street crash (Kaplanis 2011) and sustained its corporate tax at one of the lowest rates in the European Union, "facilitating an increase of 40 percent in corporate profits from 1995 to 2010" (Pentaraki 2013). Its military budget is one of the 20 biggest in the world, and it has one of the highest rates of inequality of all 28 EU countries, including the engineered casualization of the workforce, the gradual dismantling of labor rights, and hyper-exploitation and violence in the form of suicide, sexual violence in the household, and violence against migrants. By 2010, Greece "was already on the edge of poverty" (Theodorikakou et al. 2012), and the narrow definition of the "crisis" as an event that becomes expressed in 2010 as "sovereign debt" evades a focus on the co-generation of practices of primitive accumulation regimes and ignores the unemployed, women, wage earners, and migrants. Rather, Greece's "financial crisis" status is produced by an internationalization of the configuration of the "lazy" and "irresponsible" Greek—mediated through the carefully crafted body of the international debtor.

Marking the Greeks in this drama of a financial crisis as "the problem," to use Paschalidou's words, gestures to a deeper problem that evades dominant practices and attempts to fit what is happening into existing familiar categories. The problem is ultimately epistemological, that is, one of history and theory. Paschalidou grapples with this problematic as she recognizes that Greeks are being reinvented as a problem, thereby generating the state in a stage of siege and reinventing the global economy as in danger of being stolen. At the same time, Greece's "international" peripheral status and, within it, the lazy and swindler Greek are produced by the Europeanization of this particular configuration and representation of the racialized subject of debt. This is mediated through the global debtor, whose possibility depends on the zoning and ordering of people as good and bad debtors, on the zoning of laborers and non-laborers, of humans and slaves.

Calling this mediation of and subservience to market "necroeconomics" the process through which "death establishes the conditions of life," Montag writes, "The market reduces and rations life; he who with impunity may be allowed to die, slowly or quickly, in the name of the rationality and equilibrium of the market" (2005, 15). Death is the contested side of market relations, but he presumes this to be a new phenomenon. What is the value of centralizing the "zone of nonbeing" when thousands are condemned to die? What is finance in this phase of imperial capital reconstruction?

Financialization re-spatializes common existential concerns to generate the conditions necessary for the emergence of those deemed masters (Hernandez 2009; Lucarelli 2010). It orients itself toward derivatives, new money-forms that allow businesses and states to hedge against adverse events, ranging from exchange rate fluctuations to political turmoil, to dramatically changing weather conditions. Governments and the private sector secure derivative relations in which bodies and lands are adjusted to "operate at the most intimate of material levels, investing the transversal relations that connect and combine the entire worlds of priceable risk" (Cooper 2010, 179). Financialization recognizes reconstruction as a structuring ontologic, while simultaneously disavowing this recognition by imagining it to be a political practice, not a politico-existential relation, in all sites, even when it is difficult to hide this intensified politics that condemns people by further dividing them into "citizens" and "migrants," into bodies and flesh, into workers and non-workers, into free labor and slaves.

DEBTOCRACY: SEXUAL AND RACIAL CAPITAL EXPROPRIATIONS AND CAPTURES

The history of Greek loans, debt, and bankruptcies started in 1824, before Greece was established as a state. The first loan was issued for 800,000 British pounds sterling (GBP), but only 308,000 GBP and army supplies worth 11,900 GBP arrived in Greece. In 1843, the government defaulted on the loan. After the Greek government settled outstanding defaults in 1878, global capital markets reopened, with major players willing to provide funds. Between 1879 and 1891, Greece received loans from Harmbo of London, Banque de Paris, Brleishrober of Berlin, and Banque de Constantinople. In effect, foreigners were extracting 49 percent of the budget, and in 1893 the state went bankrupt. An 1892 loan was intended to help Greece build its economy and manage initial stages of governance, but much of it was spent on the military and the upkeep of Otto, a Bavarian prince who had been made king of Greece by the English (Lazarretou 2004; Notaras 2007; Menzel 2014).

After 1886, Greece depended on foreign investors to finance its budget deficits, but its ability to borrow money began to change:

> Higher government expenditure, mainly expenditure on the repayment of domestic debt, and its financing through foreign borrowing caused higher interest payments [which contributed] to the persistent budget deficits that prevented the return to the gold standard. Greece soon became over-indebted [and its] reputation as a borrower began to suffer. (Lazarretou 2004, 15)

In 1898, Greece was asked to create the International Committee for Greek Debt Management to monitor its economic policy.[5]

A default in 1932 caused Greece to impose a moratorium on its outstanding foreign debt until 1964 (Manolopoulos 2011; Fotiadis 2012). After the fall of the junta in 1967 and the return to democracy, the government unloaded the national debt on public utility companies. It signed a French loan (1977) requiring Greece to buy boats, cotton, and other products from Lacoste, thus ruining the Greek shipyard business, cotton manufacturing, and other industries. Similarly, loans from Mitsubishi Funds (1987) forced the purchase of external products while the local industry shrank. The national debt doubled in four years.

When Greece entered the eurozone, the economy suffered a long-term money supply shortage, as the Central European Bank did not approve issuing Greece more currency. Every year for 10 years, Greece had a 4 percent increase in GDP, a high rate for Europe; for each 4 percent GDP, the national debt increased by 18 percent, as Greece borrowed money to show increased GDP (Stafford 2011). The agriculture sector shrank to 3 percent of the GDP and manufacturing to 13 percent, while the average for the European Union was about 35 percent. As production dropped, more products were imported.

The gradual structural shift due to financialization was called "privately led social innovation" (Froud et al. 2010), but in an unequal class-sexual-racially-based society, this is a problematic form of social provisioning, as the gap between the accumulation of assets and debt will be much larger for women, migrants, and the working class. With the middle class now added to the list, Greek households have been in a state of austerity since 2000; savings rates are negative, with €28 billion in savings lost in 2009. Families do not have enough money for necessities; 77 percent of the average income went to loan repayments in 2010. Starting in 2008, the government took citizens' money, savings, pensions, and treasury reserves and printed extra money to keep banks afloat. In other words, households were integrated into the financialization of everyday activities through privatized debt (Fouskas and Dimoulas 2011; Young 2011).

The Greek state issued platitudes ("We are safe, the euro is bullet-proof") but when Greek treasury bonds came out in January 2009, nobody was buying. The government needed the people's money to cover its expenses, which in the "euro decade" reached €490 billion. Although Greece had already repaid €450 billion to service these loans, another €40 billion was due, about half of which was accumulated budget deficit. In Greece, the use of debt to sustain an economy has created a "debtocracy," to cite the 2011 documentary film by Aris Hatzistefanou and Katerina Kitidi on the historical and political causes of Greece's sovereign debt crisis.

Debtocracy requires experimentation, with sex and race used to secure speculative and monetary regimes and their "necessary" subjects. In Greece, it involves a technology shift from sovereign debt to colonizing lands, bodies, and states, and savagely reconfiguring social interactions:

The debt crisis is being used to create a grab bag for private interests to take ownership over the Greek public sector. . . . Finance today achieves what military invasion used to do in times past. So the new mode of warfare is financial, not military. It's much cheaper and it's much safer for the country doing the attack. (Hudson 2012)

This grabbing of land and labor, this pleonexia, is, as Kristeva writes, "greed ... the desire to 'possess always more'; it connotes an appetite that cannot be sated" (1982, 123). Debt is the technology that makes possible the suturing of the modern state. Importantly, it also (un)makes the precarious self-determined, self-productive, and self-transcendental self, as it is premised on investments emerging from greed and violent shifts, with fungibility constantly recomposed through austerity measures, constitutional change (Drossos 2011; Skoutaris 2014), and the "creative destruction" of migrant, middle- and working-class households.

In 2002, acting on the neoliberal fundamentalist advice of Wall Street powerhouse Goldman Sachs, Greece abandoned its national currency, the drachma, in favor of the euro. Using financial technologies called derivatives, Greece made large chunks of Greek public and household debt disappear, making national accounts look "good" to bankers eager to lend more. In this, Greece yielded to the temptation of structured finance, the synthetic informatics' instruments of which were developed in the United States and adopted by US transnational financial institutions, including Goldman Sachs, Citibank, JP Morgan Chase, and Bank of America, to generate phenomenal profits in deregulated global markets fueled by dollar-denominated liquidity, released by the US Federal Reserve through the virtual transaction of synthetic derivatives known as synthetic collateralized debt obligations (CDO).

Synthetic instruments expanded into the private sector, as European Monetary Union (EMU) member governments applied them to their more vulnerable publics (migrants, workers, women and children, nonprofit organizations) to mask public debt levels, skirt strict EMU rules, and engage in monetary easing. Across the Eurozone, opaque over-the-counter (OTC) derivative deals took place between "special purpose vehicles" (SPV)—transnational banks providing Eurozone governments with cash in return for future payments. Such repayments reduced government fiscal revenues, since the revenue from collateral assets was pledged to CDO investors.

Apparently, Goldman Sachs advised Greek financial institutions to trade in derivatives (Keiser 2010; Liu 2010), betting on the possibility that Greece would default, thus raising the country's cost of borrowing but making a tidy profit for itself and local corporations and private parties involved in the scheme. The Goldman Sachs transaction consisted of a cross-currency swap of about $10 billion of debt, issued by Greece in dollars and yen and swapped into euro. This reduced the debt and added $1 billion in funding to the European Union's Luxembourg-based statistics office for that year. Arguably, rating companies were aware of the deal but did not change credit ratings for Greece, because its risk profile had not changed; specifically, the additional unit risk was made invisible through dispersion into the "systemic risk of the euro zone" and, through it, into global systemic risk (Liu 2010, 2).

Financialization draws on violent technologies of constituting the ethnos (Athanasiou 2011; Golden Dawn 2012) while reconstituting anew its practices of original accumulation by presuming huge numbers of people as being non-burdened, irresponsible, non-obligated, and structurally as doing nothing. Those who do nothing are nothing (remembering Marx and his reference to vagrancy laws). And of course those who do nothing, who are nothing, are unpredictable and destructive. It is those who cannot register as political persons and as laborers, as they are inconsistent across time. It is no wonder that *Focus* again depicts the Aphrodite of Milos (Ἀφροδίτη τῆς Μήλου) (Figure 12.4). This time the statue is not draped in the Greek flag but rather in the ways it is draped in the Louvre. Holding a gun in the left hand (instead of the apple), Aphrodite points toward the left where Germany is (or may be). With a title that reminds us of James Bond, which reads, "Go ahead Angela, make my day: Greece's challenge to Germany—and the euro," the reader is supposed to gain some relief from this saga. Instead of recognizing that the violence that has come with the introduction of the euro may be fundamentally disruptive to the social contract called Europe, this journalist turns the statue of Aphrodite of Milos, the goddess of womanhood and love, against a gendered subject (Angela), with a gun in hand, ready to decide whether to kill her or not. Displacing though the anxiety on the Greeks that the secret (i.e., its enchantement) of capitalism will be exposed and that agencies will be generated provoking theorisations and sensibilities that speak to the naturalization of the market's entrepreneurialism and innovation, worth defending, no matter what the cost indexes a double bind: either the statue kills Angela and does away with the terror of capital, or continues to go along. However, this seeming choice is a technology that incites industry and allegiance to the Germans, whereas to the Greeks it suggests rebellion and even killing. This killing act, of course, is animated by the will of the master and never by the will of those constituted as idle species or dead flesh (Agathangelou 2011). The master uses direct force, either through rhetorics of idleness or practices of finance, as its technology of governance,

Figure 12.4 *The Economist*'s "Go ahead, Angela, make my day." Cover January 31, 2015.
Reproduced from http://el-siglo2.blogspot.com/2015/02/apres-la-victoire-de-syriza-athenes.html

and yet uses the statue to tell us that Greece is going to shoot Germany and the euro, metaphorically and materially.

Such fictions and fantasies of the Greeks indulging in laziness and dissatisfaction lead to punishments that incite terror (i.e., further austerity, starvation, sale of islands) in order to transform the Greeks into flexible and precarious sites of primitive accumulation. As economist Max Keiser says, "Greece has been sacrificed. . . . . It is dead. It is over. Forget it" (quoted on Aljazeera 2010). The financial reconfiguration of Greece entails a reinvention of the world, highlighting that the contingent outcomes of transnational power fields transform particular forms of disparities and differences. Keiser's remarks bring to the fore the costs for desiring a global capitalist economy. Greece is one of its victims, with despondency and gloom settled on the bodies of the working class, unemployed, women, and migrants, starved and gradually sinking into their graves. Importantly, Keiser's comments rightly suggest a present where imagined white regimes mark an international politico-economic space that excludes "Greece," as we already know it, as it is already dead, a site of chaos and ultimately, a site of reconstruction irrespective of the dire consequences and on who for capitalism.

MEMORANDA: EXPROPRIATION AND CAPTURE TOOLS

In Germany, the reconfiguration of capital relations, including the dramatic compression of incomes, and curbing imports and increasing exports to create large surpluses, led to a new "model" of compressed labor costs for German employers. Its application in Greece and Portugal required the big German banks to disengage, without too many losses and with guarantees, from riskier positions on "shaky" countries and firms to which they had extended credit. Through Troika (Germanized ECB, with France's Trichet at its head, IMF, and European Commission), a memorandum (i.e., conditionality) was imposed on Greece on May 5, 2011, followed by another in June.

The first memorandum advocated a "doctrine of necessity" (Skoutaris 2014), or the reforms required for labor restructuring. Making the labor force stand for the failed European monetary project signaled the surgery and engineering of a neoliberal subject responsible for his or her own future. This memorandum abolished bonuses for civil servants and pensioners in public and private sectors, canceled solidarity benefits for the poor, demanded the abolition of retirement before age 60, and reduced the minimum wage from €750 to €500 monthly.

The second memorandum built on this, aiming to completely restructure labor relations. "Agreements" at the workplace level were legally prioritized over those at the national level. Collective agreements signed by the Union of Enterprises need not be applied; these agreements "must promote competitiveness on the basis of the cost of labor and job creation." Restrictions on the number of hours of part-time work and on temporary contracts were eliminated. The trial period was one year for new jobs (previously two months), during which time, employers could dismiss workers without notice or compensation. The minimum wage was attacked, with working conditions now dependent on workers' countries of origin; premiums for overtime and unemployment benefits were reduced by €500 million. In addition to drastic changes to the pension system, the memorandum called for a sharp reduction in disability pensions, an increase in the price of health care and hospital examinations, and the privatization of strategic sectors (railways, transportation, energy, etc.), with accompanying job losses.

All this came under the pretext of "filling the coffers of the state" to "repay the debt." In fact, the aim was to offer low-priced sectors of the economy to capitalist firms with surpluses of capital who were seeking new profitable opportunities. Both memoranda articulated methods that changed those codified in labor and social legislation and institutions structured by the results of sexual, racial, and class conflict post-1974.

These memoranda bypassed governmental bodies, ignoring democratic rule. The expected failure of the concretization of the memoranda led to the resignation of George Papandreou (November 10, 2011) and the setting up, without an election, of a "technical" government under Loukas Papademos, who had studied at MIT and had worked at the Central Bank of Greece (supervising Greece's entry into the Eurozone) and at the European Central Bank, where he was vice president. The memoranda also enabled speculative operations outside national law. As Skoutaris (2014) notes, the "doctrine of necessity" pushed for a "fiscal compact" whereby markets became constitutional steering committees, and social contracts were restructured into unincorporated relations. In 2012, the Eurogroup stated,

> The Eurogroup . . . welcomes the intention of the Greek authorities to introduce over the next two months in the Greek legal framework a provision ensuring that priority is granted to debt servicing payments. This provision will be introduced in the Greek constitution as soon as possible. (Reuters, 2012)

Costas Mitropoulos, manager of the Hellenic Republic Asset Development Fund, asserted,

> Our first message to get across is; we are not the Greek state. We are an independent fund responsible for privatizations, and we now own 3 per cent of the territory of Greece. We have a mandate for three years. We are protected against political interference. (cited in Udry 2012, 9)

Using Greece as the experimentation site to push asunder the market and sovereign boundaries through the technology of debt signals capital's desire to restructure labor relations and constitutional powers. This process has dire effects on everyday life and health and moves away from growth, jobs, and wages as sources of cumulative growth. In the new productive model, "labor assumes a different role" (Lucarelli 2010, 5) by becoming more flexible. Households are restructured into sites of original accumulation, rendering subjects into mere flesh that can be exploited unconditionally or turned into profitable morbidity by presuming the human body and its necessary ecologies as "bio-fodder." The majority of Greeks are the "slaves" of speculators, notably Wall Street bankers, and are enslaved to those Greeks who have benefited: households, banks, and major corporations speculating on public debt and pocketing the surplus and the interest from national bonds.

The marking of Greece as "dead" deflects attention from the global register and transforms the problem into an individual state—one for which Greece is responsible. Rather than being located in the international and transnational governance networks, the cause of and solution for financial problems becomes technical, evading contestations over the global raciality of capitalism. The crisis that is Greece, even at the moment it is articulated as a question of financialization through debt, conjures European aspirations for differentially positioned peoples in the region, promising transcendence of locality and nationalism. The "crisis" also allows for the unhinging of the US-European model of capitalist economy from a moral good, forms of fetishism and scenes of savagery. Yet it remains entangled in discourses of race, class, and gender, which render these aspirations anything but transcendental.

Discourses of debt are evading Greece's "backwardness" and also generating it. To understand this paradox, we must recognize the broader blurring of boundaries between current "debt-slavery" in the European Union and North America and historical and current forms of forced slave labor (and/or "wage-slavery"). In many ways, accounts of Marxist feminist political economy reproduce mythologies of whiteness by erasing the specific geographies upon which racialized and gendered hierarchies are co-produced with science and the global order. As the ensuing collapse is part of the governance strategies of a global raciality of capitalism that depends on zonings and penetrations for its regeneration, discussions of slavery and its various racialized/gendered manifestations must proceed with caution. Consider, for example, IMF's Christine Lagarde, who has more sympathy for the "really poor" in Niger than the "tax-dodging" Greeks:

> No, I think more of the little kids from a school in a little village in Niger who get teaching two hours a day, sharing one chair for three of them, and who are very keen to get an education. I have them in my mind all the time. Because I think they need even more help than the people in Athens ... All these people in Greece who are trying to escape tax. (Lagarde 2012, cited in Elliott and Aitkenhead 2012)

Greece has no excuse for its "failing" economy. Rather, the enterprise's subject is at fault, as he or she has failed to meet his or her responsibilities. Of course, this failure goes hand in hand with the understanding of the criminal under the neoliberal regime: criminalized Greeks escape taxes and criminalized Greeks do not suffer. And if they do, it is their fault.

Crucial to but implicit in this passage is Lagarde's presumption of the inter-market. While the market conditions or environmental circumstances within which individuals, as enterprises, are operating are being questioned, she continues to focus on the Greek as an enterprise, assuming that "Greeks" are equal participants with the rest of the Europeans under these market conditions. She draws on colonial and classist imaginaries of the worthy poor, legacies of charity/missionary work, and the disciplinary side of (neo)liberalism and its conservative intolerance of laziness, cheating, or lack of "fair play" and respect for the "rule of law" to reinforce the sense of Western moral supremacy (as givers of charity to Niger and as paragons of fiscal virtue to Greece). Both are in a subordinate position, but they occupy different spaces in Lagarde's imaginary. Greece and Greeks are still presumed potential subjects in an inter-market where the neoliberal project can emerge. The debt of the Greek in a global racial capitalism inscribes him or her still as a subjectivity, while simultaneously drawing the border, defining a limit whose ground is an "other" and geopolitically imagined elsewhere. The state, banks, and international institutions move this emergence along, using the fewest possible resources, even when the stakes for the survival of the proletariat and the migrant are high.

This new and virulent economic politics expressed by Lagarde highlights a breach between market and household. Now "private subjects" are imagined as constituted under the paradigmatically public form of privatization, the transformation or the working out of answer innovative positions to the "limits" of capitalism. This move is critical, as it allows a turn to necropolitics. For such subjects, the economic mechanisms of competition and cost benefit analyses are fostered within their homes, within themselves. Ultimately, while debt cannot contain the *chimeras* of capitalism, it is pushing asunder the boundaries of law to constitute more people as structurally impossible. In short, debt is a sexual and racial technology of fungibility[6] enabling and excusing colonial violence and injustice in the present as the inevitable working out of a progressive capitalist world: folding conflict and violence in the market and household (*oikos*) relations by turning them into sites of original accumulation and preempting their future.

The EU report *Towards a Common Operational European Definition of Over-Indebtedness* (Davydoff et al. 2008) says over-indebtedness stems from persistent arrears, a heavy payment burden, and an inability to handle unexpected expenses. It connects low income, over-indebtedness, and its sub-elements: arrears, illiquidity, and heavy payment burden. Over-indebted households are more likely to be income-poor (less than

60 percent of median income) and in persistent poverty, with higher rates of basic deprivation (clothes, food, heat), secondary deprivation (household goods, cars), environmental deprivation (pollution, crime, the purchase of the islands to generate the money they owe), and health deprivation (limited activities due to health problems). The analysis suggests income inadequacy, rather than a high level of personal consumption, as a key factor in over-indebtedness in Greece (*Spiegel* 2011). In the households examined, more than 40 percent had experienced a major drop in income over the previous 12 months, with unemployment and pay cuts commonly cited factors. Households without access to savings or other ways of raising resources (illiquidity) were pushed into over-indebtedness, while the country's resources were spent on further privatization of social resources and military alliances.

In February 2010, Minister of Foreign Affairs Guido Westerwelle tried to sell the Eurofighter to the Greek government, while insisting on the need to drastically reduce public spending and "social expenditure." French and German banks opened lines of credit for the sale of arms from German or French industries with export guarantees (subsidizing German and French arms industries). That meant raising value-added taxes, lowering the wages of public sector workers, and "privatizing," for example, by allowing Deutsche Telekom to take over the Greek public telephone company, OTE.

The market in this newer form requires processes and political events that promise "nothing but the eternal duration of the death we are unable to acknowledge having died" (Farley 2009, 1056). This program of capital is rooted in the constitution of sexual and racial bodies as subsidies; at the same time, it erases sexual positionalities, constructing debt as the determinant of racial vassal states, rendering Greek and migrant women and children invisible within the "universal" order of dominant masculine subjects (German, French, and Greek elites). It proposes race and sex as a substitute for class and the "natural" physical and moral foundation of a neoliberal order. Systematic euro-patriotic decisions seek reconstructive projects likely to benefit the elites of Greece, Germany, and France, focusing on sex and race as a structural arrangement, so that the burden falls disproportionately on women, migrants, the working class, and youth. Prime Minister Constantinos Karamanlis (2004–2009) said to Parliament, "We have to cut public spending and we have to tidy up our house and this cannot be achieved with your empty promises" (cited in *Debtocracy* 2011). This call to the Greeks to "tidy[ing] our house" recuperates the Greeks into the European family, sustaining in place the sexual slave/master relationship, simultaneously ridding "Greece" of the possibility of mobilizing Greeks and their imprint toward a world-making justice project (Panourgià 2014).

In effect, the state and international institutions are trying to enforce a foundational servitude to debt and monetary policies, a shift made possible by a temporal ordering of debt and slavery, contingency and fungibility. Financialization and speculation place the control of resources in the hands of corporate (white) powers who rely on starvation and slaughter: "Some things are worse than death. How dark can it be? What is the blackness of blackness? . . . Is there a death that is more—and therefore worse—than death? *Primitive accumulation is mass murder beyond the limit*" (Farley 2009, 1068; emphasis mine).

PRIMITIVE ACCUMULATION: "MASS MURDER BEYOND THE LIMIT"

Ananya Roy says that capitalism is "a set of dispersed but coherent efforts to construct and make productive, a global economy where poverty is a frontier of profit and accumulation" (2012, 106). Stamp adds, "People are over-indebted if their net resources (income and realizable assets) render them persistently unable to meet essential living expenses and debt repayments as they fall due" (2009). Over-indebtedness should be distinguished from indebtedness, which refers to the use of credit, an increasingly used element of modern financial systems. The Law Reform Commission's Consultation Paper clarifies:

> Indebtedness can be said to refer to a commitment to repay moneys which a debtor has borrowed and used. In this regard, indebtedness can be seen as a necessary and healthy consequence of the provision of credit which is beneficial to society as a whole and to individuals. The majority of credit agreements are repaid without difficulty and result in benefits for all parties to the agreement. (2009, 10)

While indebtedness in itself is not problematic, the unprecedented growth in personal debt in Greece has been a concern for a decade. In 2007, 26.4 percent of Greek households were in debt; 30.9 percent in 2010. This increase, coupled with the economic recession, high levels of job loss, and significant cuts in household income, has pushed more people to borrow money to cover "urgent temporalities of need" (Roy 2012, 106). Dr. Kanakis, president of Doctors of the World, says,

> We consider the center of Greece as facing a humanitarian crisis. All the distinctive features are there; people who are hungry, homeless, who lack medication

and healthcare.... There are people who still maintain some social security rights but that is not enough, as a poor woman-pensioner indicated. She said, "I buy either food or medicine. I cannot afford both." (*Debtocracy* 2011)

Austerity measures are worsening the everyday access of people to basic necessities, thereby threatening their existence. As neurosurgeon Panos Papanicolaou tells us, all countries with IMF "support," including Greece, show a dramatic drop in average life expectancy: "The average life span in those countries fell by 5–10 years. With the cuts we are facing now, it's clear that our life expectancy will be greatly reduced" (*Debtocracy* 2011). And reconfiguration of the global raciality of capitalism depends on a dominant orientalist limit: the Third World and the presumption of reproduction. This imaginary serves the idea of infinity, whereby capitalism can always reassemble itself anew, all in the name of a world-making reproduction project.

This European-American-led world-making reproduction project endows *some* with nation, rights, democratic representation and participation, and a modular bodily capacity to generate money and surplus value, while also redeploying a hegemonic state to decide who deserves to be reproduced, who is dead, and whose flesh is under siege for generating the life and value of the very few.

Original accumulation results in the reconfiguration of territories and subjects as well as marginalization and death, even when experienced as "relief" (IMF support) and free choice. Much more is at stake than crude neoliberalism and its principles of market efficiency. Debt has become intertwined with death and with the "figure of resilience charged with converting [debt] into enterprise" (Roy 2012, 136) and the profits and the flesh that accrue to him or her. Experiments in Greece are reconfiguring the boundaries "between capitalist speculation and the incertitude of value, between free labor and slavery, between those who are inoculated and those who test the vaccine, between the contractual projection of calculable value the uninsurable risk and, not least, between life and death" (Mitropoulos 2012, 4).

Within these global power dynamics, the finance of corporeality and debt as technology of the resilient and entrepreneurial figure make sense. The enslaved body is the "primitive" form of biopower in Marx's concept of the primitive accumulation, the ground energy and social relation for the formation of property. In this sense, to be enslaved is to experience violence with impunity, outside the social contracts of Hobbes and Locke and the protections of the law. While Roy speaks of microfinance as the global asset class flying in the "face of local debtor revolts" (2012, 136), her logic applies to the Greek household, which has been turned into the experimentation deathscape demanded by debtocracy. In Greece, there is a close relationship between the banishment of those subjects at risk, or "risk failures," and those marked as "pre-black" (Mitchell 2010, 243–244). Mitchell sees "risk failures" as always "bound up with historical and spatial processes of [sexual and] racial formation" (2010, 44).

On December 23, 2008, four men attacked Konstantina Kuneva, a Bulgarian migrant worker in Athens and secretary of the Union of Housekeepers and Cleaners of Attika, with sulfuric acid. As a migrant, Konstantina was underpaid and unprotected in an undervalued sector of labor; she joined the union to fight wage slavery and was constantly threatened. As a result of the necropolitical attack, she spent days in a coma and months in intensive care. Forced to swallow the acid, she sustained serious internal injuries, particularly to her vocal cords, throat, and stomach. Meanwhile, the perpetrators remain unidentified. Significantly, the elimination of Kuneva's voice is an act of banishing from the body politic once and for all those bodies outside the "exclusionary norms of gender, capital, and nation" (Athanasiou 2011, 2).

In Greece, capital asymmetrically ascribes some corporealities with nonvalue (i.e., the inert matter), some with zero-value, and others with value. Through financial derivatives and technologies of sex and race, that is, "the product of various social technologies [and] institutional discourses, epistemologies, and critical practices" (Lauretis 1987, ix), debt's productivity is made possible through the gendered and racialized intimacy of an assemblage of bodies and countries that are liable for this debt: "In this inescapable density of social relations, default is transformed into death; the trade in debt becomes necropolitics" (Roy 2012, 144).

Until recently, Greece had the lowest suicide rate in Europe. With the majority of Greece's population becoming "owners" of debt, suicide soared. Dimitris Chistoulas, who killed himself on April 4, 2012, in Syntagma Square, left the following note:

> I find no other solution than a dignified end, before I am reduced to scavenging in the rubbish bins to feed myself. I feel that young people without a future will one day take up arms and that on Syntagma Square, they will hang the traitors to the nation by their feet.

That evening, thousands met at Syntagma and called for a gathering via social networks around a crucial slogan: "This was not a suicide. It was a murder. Let us not become used to murder." Within hours, special police arrived on BMW motorcycles (sent from Germany) to impose order, dispersing the crowd with tear gas (Udry 2012). Before committing suicide, another man said,

> I have been taking care of my 90-year-old mother for 20 years. In the last 3–4 years she has developed Alzheimer's, recently she also has been having Schizophrenic fits amongst her other grave health problems, so nursing homes won't accept her. The problem is that the economic crisis came about so fast that I didn't have the foresight to save enough money in my account. . . . I have run out of money and we can no longer afford to eat . . . I have no solution in front of me.

He asks, "Do any of you know of the answer?" (Lambadariou 2012).

NOTES

1. Blue is the color of the flag of the sovereign state of Greece, thereby gesturing to the chaos ensuing from this site.
2. Tony Corn (2010) wryly articulates the new imperial order and its shifts as "Chermany" versus "Chimerica."
3. Marx must be tossing in his grave. He was the one who argued that the production of the unemployed, idle populations, and their criminalization through vagrancy laws were pivotal to the occluded historical process of primitive accumulation (1990, 873). Marx, though, did not speak much to the racialized redeployments of vagrancy law as key sites for the mutual imbrication of race, surveillance, and labor in both colony and metropole.
labor in both colony and metropole.
4. I am not interested here in reclaiming a picture of real or non-real beggars, but rather to show how figures of swindlers and beggars circulate through publics that formed around the prerogative of surveillance and policing, waging a war and sowing death in the contemporary world. However, if this reading is to yield, however incompletely, some insight into the experiences of those labeled debtors, criminals, beggars, and swindlers, I hope that this reading can sow some productive doubt that might inform such a venture. If a debtor, or a beggar, is not an identity, but a structure of knowledge and perception, then the people whose lives might be recovered from this reading are not swindlers and beggars but something else, perhaps, a fugitive public that does not spend its creative energies and labor toward reproducing a world that inscribes death-projects.
5. One representative from each European country that intervened to suspend hostilities between Greece and Turkey in the war of 1897 (the UK, France, Germany, Italy, Russia, and Austria-Hungary) was appointed to the committee. The committee was active until World War II (see Lazaretou 2004, 14; see also Valaoritis 1902, 177–194; Andreades 1925, 305–337).
6. See Anna M. Agathangelou (2014) for a nuanced analysis of fungibility and value.

CHAPTER 13

Toward a Queer Political Economy of Crisis

NICOLA SMITH

INTRODUCTION

In this chapter I consider what it might mean to queer the political economy of crisis. I argue that—given that same-sex and other non-normative sexualities[1] are routinely erased in debates about "the economy"—it is clearly important to explore the material effects of crisis on queer lives. This is not to add queer and stir to discussions of economic crisis, for a central thrust of queer theory has been to critique notions of sexual identity as coherent and stable and for them to be organized and policed as such. Rather, a queer political economy of crisis should also interrogate how "crisis" itself is constituted through heteronormative gender logics and power relations, for "the economic, tied to the productive, is necessarily linked to the reproduction of heterosexuality" (Butler 1997, 274). In order to illuminate these themes, I explore how neoliberal policy responses to crisis in the United Kingdom are serving to disadvantage lesbian, gay, bisexual, transgender, and queer (LGBT/Q)[2] communities and others who fall outside heterosexist, married monogamy (such as single parents), and how heteronormative imaginaries of "the family" are themselves playing an important role in reproducing the neoliberal economic order.

The chapter is structured as follows. In the first section, I draw from and build upon recent queer scholarship that treats questions of economic and social justice as central to, rather than separable from, issues of sexual in/justice. I advance an agenda that not only aims to recognize the redistributive consequences of crisis on queer lives but that also inter-rogates how heteronormativity is itself deeply implicated in narratives of economic and social "crisis." In the second section, I turn to the case of the United Kingdom, where the cornerstone of the government's response to crisis has been an aggressive program of austerity measures (despite the UK already being one of the most socially and economically unequal coun-tries in the developed world; OECD 2011; Dransfield 2014). Focusing on sexuality as an axis of inequality, I chart a variety of ways in which LGBT/Q people and communities have been adversely affected by the combination of rising unemployment and spending cuts. Yet there has, on the whole, been silence about the impact of austerity on sexual in/justice; instead, it is the issue of equal marriage that has dominated LGBT/Q politics and activ-ism in recent years. As I argue in the final section, it is no accident that austerity politics have coincided with the achievement of equal marriage in the United Kingdom, nor that the British Prime Minister David Cameron has proudly proclaimed the United Kingdom to be a global showcase for LGBT/Q rights. Drawing examples from Cameron's speeches on a variety of economic and social themes—including same-sex marriage, LGBT/Q poli-tics, troubled families, and economic crisis—I contend that equal marriage is both positioned within, and made intelligible through, neoliberal and heteronormative discourses that attribute economic and social crisis to the failure of individual families and which naturalize neoliberal capitalism as a system of oppression in the process.

QUEERING CRISIS

In the preface of their special issue for *S&F Online* entitled "A New Queer Agenda," Lisa Duggan and Richard Kim (2012) ask how socioeconomic justice has *not* yet come to be identified as an "LGBT/Q issue." Given that there are so many pressing issues that affect LGBT/Q people across the world—including low wages, unemployment, housing, and health care—it is dismaying that politics and activism have so often been posi-tioned within a liberal rights framework that treats formal, legal equality as the primary goal.[3] The focus on marriage rights rather than on wider economic and social in/equality does not represent, or even recognize, the 99 percent of those who are poor, of color, immigrants, incarcerated, unemployed, or homeless (2012, 1). Jacob DeFilippis (2012b, 1) simi-larly points to a "surreal, stony silence" about the economic crisis from the LGBT/Q movement, writing that it is "beyond maddening" to see hefty economic resources being pumped into the fight for equal marriage when there are far more urgent concerns for so many. Both within and outside LGBT/Q communities, it is the poorest and least privileged to have been struck the hardest by the double hit of rising poverty and shrinking social protection. And yet the period of so-called economic crisis has coincided with the advancement of a narrowly defined "gay agenda" that speaks to and for a socioeconomic elite, rather than the disadvantaged, disenfranchised, and dispossessed (DeFilippis 2012b; Duggan and Kim 2012).

Such calls for a queer agenda for economic and social justice are significant not only for LGBT/Q activism and policy advocacy internationally, but also for the vast and diverse body of queer scholarship that grew to prominence in the 1990s and that now represents one of the major intellectual canons of the social sciences, arts, and humanities. Queer studies have often been associated with the "politics of recognition," rather than the "politics of redistribution" (Fraser 1995, 68)—or, as Judith Butler wryly puts it, with the "merely cultural" (1997, 265). This is in part because a great deal of queer theorizing has tended to elide, rather than interrogate, the intersections between economy and sexuality (Binnie 2004), and in part because, as a consequence, queer and Marxist studies have had a rather antagonistic relationship, with the former accusing the latter of ignoring sexuality and the latter charging the former of discounting materiality. But it is also the case that a variety of queer scholars have increasingly taken up issues of political economy as central to the study of sexuality, and vice versa (for a review, see Bergeron and Puri 2012). Although this project is sometimes articulated in terms of a more open dialogue with Marxism, it also owes a clear debt to the long tradition of feminist political economy that takes as its starting point the intimate relations between gender, sexuality, and capitalism (Jacobs and Klesse 2014). For example, in her calls to interrogate the "sexual order of political economy," Butler (1997, 272) explicitly highlights the importance of socialist feminist work in expanding understandings of political economy to include processes of social reproduction, so that

> gender and sexuality become part of material life, not only because of the way in which they serve the sexual division of labor, but also because normative gender serves the reproduction of the normative family ... [S]truggles to transform the social field of sexuality do not become central to political economy to the extent that they can be directly tied to questions of unpaid and exploited labor, but rather because they cannot be understood without an expansion of the "economic" sphere itself to include both the reproduction of goods as well as the social reproduction of persons.[4]

This feminist—and, increasingly, queer—project is both deconstructive and reconstructive, for it explores not only how gender, sexuality, and capitalism are co-constitutive, but also how the removal of gender and sexuality from the study of globalization and capitalism is in itself (re)productive of gendered and sexualized power relations (see, inter alia, Pettman 1997; Steans 1999; Agathangelou 2005; Penttinen 2008; Griffin 2009). Such work aims to challenge how questions of political economy have been constructed as being somehow separable from questions of sexuality and gender—a move that enables the "private" and feminized realm of social reproduction not only to be broken off from the "public" and masculine realm of political and economic power, but also to be removed from inquiry altogether (Youngs 2000; Peterson 2003; Bedford and Rai 2010). In contrast, feminist and queer scholarship aims to unpick and unpack the economy/sexuality dichotomy while also pointing toward its material effects in (re)producing unequal power relations. For example, Penny Griffin (2013a, 9) notes how the absenting of the complex ways in which the global political economy is gendered and sexualized does important political work, for it serves to naturalize the expansion of a specific mode of Western capitalism across the globe and the "highly masculinised and ethnocentric model of human activity" upon which this is founded.[5] Similarly, Anna Marie Smith (2001, 103) calls for critical scholarship to explicitly refuse the "liberal tactic" of detaching issues of economic justice from gender, sexual, racial, and other social inequalities—inequalities that are not only produced by neoliberal capitalism but that are in turn productive of it (see also Duggan 2003; Crosby et al. 2012; Rosenberg and Villarejo 2012; Wesling 2012; Winnubst 2012).

In turn, one of the major contributions that queer theory can make to feminist political economy is to open up not just sexuality but heterosexuality as a category of analysis (Danby 2007). Among other agendas (Smith and Lee 2015), queer scholarship aims to expose and challenge the routine erasure and marginalization of non-normative sexual identities and practices across a range of levels and representations—from the micro-practices of daily life to the macro-processes of global political economy (Lind 2010). This erasure not only represents a form of discursive violence in and of itself, but also masks the real and often devastating impact of economic and social injustice on queer lives (lives that, indeed, are assumed not even to exist). A queer political economy of crisis, therefore, should attend to the material effects of crisis on queer lives—such as the impact of welfare policies, access to health care, employment rights, and homelessness—which in turn cannot neatly be removed from, but rather intersect with, other deep structural inequalities such as gender, sexuality, race, dis/ability, and class (DeFilippis 2012a). This is not to add queer and stir to discussions of economic crisis, for a key aim for queer theory has precisely been to contest the coherence and stability of sexuality and, in so doing, to challenge the classification and privileging of heterosexuality as "a" sexuality in the first place—a process that, in turn, enables other forms of sexual expression and identity to be marked out against the "normal" and the "natural" (Danby 2007; Browne and Nash 2010). Rather, a queer approach to crisis can and should be inspired by the desire to advance an "ethics of recognition" (Elliot 2010, 74) that aims to render more visible non-normative sexual and gender subjectivities in order to disrupt the demarcation and consequent subtraction of identity politics from the politics of economic and social justice.

A queer political economy of crisis, moreover, encourages reflection on how "crisis" is serving to reinforce a "specific mode of sexual production and exchange that works to maintain the stability of gender, the heterosexuality of desire, and the naturalisation of the family" (Butler 1997, 274). Feminist political economists have drawn attention to the importance of both sexuality and the household but, in so doing, they have tended to "leave untouched" reproductive heterosexuality as a social institution (Lind 2010, 10), for example by conceptualizing the household as consisting of a husband, a wife, and children (Danby 2007).[6] Queer scholarship not only aims to reveal and critique the presumption of heterosexuality, but also interrogates the complex and sometimes contradictory ways in which this is built into daily practices, social norms, and public policy (Chambers and Carver 2008). Thinking queerly about crisis opens up space to consider how heteronormative gender logics might themselves play an important role in reproducing the neoliberal economic order. If understood not as the cultural expression of heterosexism but rather as "a matrix that ties sexual arrangements to economic relations to government policy" (Jakobsen 2012, 24), heteronormativity represents a logic through which reproductive heterosexuality is both privileged and normalized through the articulation and repetition of specific constructions of sexuality, intimacy, and the family that are (re)presented as natural and essential rather than as contingent and contestable. Heteronormative power relations are both intimate and politicized, feeding into and from foundational distinctions such as public/private and moral/amoral (Griffin 2011)—distinctions that are not only embodied in the institutionalization of heterosexual marriage and hierarchical sex and parenting roles (Griffin 2011) but also in the free-market rationalities of neoliberalism (Winnubst 2012). In the context of crisis, queer scholarship thus highlights the need to make connections between heteronormativity and neoliberalism by exploring how notions of individual responsibility draw upon imaginaries not just of market activity, but also of the "private" spheres of family, intimacy, and sexuality (Winnubst 2012; Hong 2012). In the remainder of this chapter, I explore and expand upon these themes by analyzing the scandalous economics of crisis in the United Kingdom, examining how neoliberal policy responses are serving to disadvantage those who fall outside of heterosexist, married monogamy while also depending upon heteronormative constructions of "the family" as both economically (un)productive and sexually/socially (re) productive.

THE SCANDALOUS ECONOMICS OF AUSTERITY IN THE UNITED KINGDOM

The current UK government[7]—a coalition between the Conservative and Liberal Democratic parties—came to power in May 2010 in the context of the United Kingdom's longest and deepest recession since the 1930s (Hay and Smith 2013). In their joint program for government, the parties set out a range of shared goals—from consumer protection and civil liberties to international development and climate change—but explicitly identified deficit reduction as *the* key priority that "takes precedence" over any other policy measures (HM Government 2010, 5). The government's first ("emergency") budget of June 2010 identified deficit reduction not just as a precondition for economic recovery but as "the most urgent task facing this country," to be achieved through a seven-year fiscal consolidation package of £113 billion per year by 2014–2015 and £128 billion per year by 2015–2016. The package relied primarily on reductions in public spending (representing 77 percent of the total consolidation), including £11 billion in welfare reform "savings" and a freeze on public sector pay (HM Treasury 2010, 1–2). This program of public spending cuts—the greatest since World War II (Stanley 2014a)—continues apace even as the United Kingdom experiences economic recovery, with the Chancellor, George Osborne, announcing that a further £25 billion in spending cuts (principally from the welfare budget) will follow the next election (BBC 2014; for full details see HM Treasury 2014).

That the austerity measures are profoundly devastating in social terms—not to mention potentially destructive of long-term economic sustainability[8]—is by now well documented (see, inter alia, Hossain et al. 2011; Ferguson and Lavelette 2013; Taylor-Robinson et al. 2013). In a review of the impact of austerity in the United Kingdom, for instance, Oxfam (2013) reports that both absolute and relative poverty levels are on the increase since 2010; that absolute poverty in particular has surged (rising by nearly 900,000 in 2012 alone); that, along with the richest tenth of the population, it is the poorest fifth who have suffered the greatest fall in net income; that by 2020 an extra 1.5 million working-age adults and an additional 80,000 children will be living in poverty (so that one-fifth of working-age adults and one-quarter of children will be in poverty); that unemployed people are losing 7 percent of their income due to the mismatch between increases in social security payments and the cost of living; that average hourly earnings for those in work have decreased in real terms by 5.5 percent since 2010; and that unprecedented numbers of people in the United Kingdom are now in need of emergency food aid, with at least half a million people using food banks every year.[9]

There is, moreover, a wealth of evidence to show that the effects both of the crisis itself and the austerity measures are highly unevenly distributed along a variety of axes such as gender, race, age, dis/ability, and class (Ginn 2013; Hudson et al. 2013; Rubery and Rafferty 2013; Belfield et al. 2014; Razzu 2014). For example, the Women's Budget Group (WBG) cites findings from the House of Commons library that no less than 80 percent of the combined expenditure saved and revenue raised through the changes to social security and personal taxation since 2010 comes from women (Women's Budget Group 2014a).[10] The WBG also finds that women's unemployment remains 50 percent higher than before the crisis (in contrast to 41 percent for men), that long-term unemployment is growing at a faster rate among women than men, and that in 2012 the gender pay gap increased for the first time in five years (from 14.5 percent to 15.7 percent) (Women's Budget Group 2014b). Similarly, a joint study by Demos and Scope finds that people with disabilities—who make up nearly one-fifth of the working-age population—have been affected disproportionately by the spending cuts (to the tune of at least £9 billion during the current Parliament), even though they are already far more likely than non-disabled people to be vulnerable to poverty, low pay, and unemployment (Wood 2012). Poverty is also "higher among all black and minority ethnic groups than among the majority white population" (Barnard and Turner 2011, 2), with significant and widening disparities in terms of employment prospects, too: for example, average unemployment for 16- to 24-year-olds from black and ethnic minority groups rose from 32 percent to 37 percent between 2010 and 2013 but remained at just 19 percent for white people of this age group (Phillips 2014).

Structural hierarchies of gender, race, class, age, and dis/ability are relevant in and of themselves to LGBT/Q politics because such inequalities cannot be removed from, but rather closely intersect with, lived experiences of sexual orientation and gender identity—something that queer people who are poor, of color, unemployed, or homeless know only too well (DeFilippis 2012b). And yet there has been little acknowledgment in the mainstream media, in policy activism, or in research practice of sexuality as an axis of economic (in)justice in the United Kingdom, or of how queer communities might experience specific forms of material disadvantage and oppression as a consequence of the crisis and cuts.

Research commissioned by UNISON, however, clearly finds that the austerity measures have had a significant and disproportionate impact on LGBT/Q people in the United Kingdom. This qualitative study—which involved 101 written contributions via a secure website and 12 in-depth follow-up interviews—documents a variety of ways in which LGBT/Q individuals, communities, and service providers have been affected. Participants pointed to financial difficulties due to redundancies, pay cuts, and changes in benefits, but also emphasized that such hardships were neither exclusive to LGBT/Q communities nor equally shared within them: rather, it was the poorest and most vulnerable from both within and outside LGBT/Q communities who were identified as being the most affected. But participants also identified a number of specific challenges being faced by LGBT/Q people as a direct result of the austerity measures, most notably the sharp reduction in specialist services—such as information, advice, and support services; health services such as sexual health, mental health, drugs and alcohol, and gender reassignment services; youth and community services; specialist forums and networks; and social cohesion projects—as a direct consequence of the spending cuts and of the instability in statutory and other funding sources. This was of great concern because LGBT/Q people are in particular need of such services due to continuing discrimination and often open prejudice in a variety of social contexts (from housing and welfare to education and the workplace) and, relatedly, because many are reluctant to use mainstream services due to fears of such discrimination and prejudice. Of concern, too, was that the decline in dedicated services means that important gains were in danger of being lost, not only in terms of addressing issues such as health promotion, homelessness, and unemployment for LGBT/Q people, but also in terms of promoting awareness of LGBT/Q issues and in challenging heterosexism and cissexism, with participants expressing considerable anxiety that homophobia, biphobia, and transphobia are on the increase.[11] In addition, participants pointed to a growing sense of invisibility and marginalization, in part because they were feeling more isolated and less connected to their community due to the closure of support groups and outreach services, and in part because they felt as if LGBT/Q issues and concerns were being treated as less important than "other" issues, or even as indulgent. This was in turn linked to public perceptions that LGBT/Q people were either no longer in need of dedicated services on the grounds that equality has been "achieved" or because stereotypes (such as that of the "Pink Pound") mean that LGBT/Q people are assumed to be in positions of socioeconomic privilege. As well as the silencing of LGBT/Q issues and concerns, participants expressed worries about the growing risk of violence toward LGBT/Q people, with an increase in homophobic and transphobic incidents linked to a combination of factors, including growing prejudice, a reduced police presence, fewer staff on public transport, and the declining availability of LGBT/Q-friendly accommodation (Mitchell et al. 2013).

In addition to the UNISON study, a number of individual LGBT/Q organizations have pointed to similar issues and concerns: for example, Stonewall Housing (2014) reports that two-thirds of people who approach the organization for advice and help identify their sexual orientation or gender identity as directly related to their housing problem, that four-fifths of the organization's advice clients are out of work, and that two-fifths are experiencing harassment.

It is striking, however, that—despite evidence that the combined effects of the economic crisis and spending cuts have been very damaging to and for queer communities—this has, on the whole, been met with silence from policymakers, the media, academics, and activists. For example, the potential impact on LGBT/Q people of the introduction of the Housing Benefit social sector size limit—which formed part of the Welfare Reform Act 2012 and entailed restrictions on the size of accommodation for working-age people in receipt of Housing Benefit living in the social rented sector— was notable by its absence in policy and media debates.[12] Although the government's consultation document on "21st Century Welfare" included responses from 325 external organizations, including disability groups and housing associations, these did not include key LGBT/Q activist organizations such as the LGBT Consortium, Stonewall, OutRage! and Press for Change (Department for Work and Pensions 2010). Similarly, the only mention made of sexuality in the subsequent equality impact assessment document by the Department of Work and Pensions (2012, 15) was to note that "[t]he Department does not have information on its administrative systems on the sexual orientation of claimants. The Government does not envisage an adverse impact on these grounds." The deep irony here is that the appropriately nicknamed "bedroom tax" could scarcely be more sexualized in its unambiguous delineation of the boundaries of a properly gendered sexuality as linked to the social and economic domain of the household. Simply put, the "tax" does not just reflect a cultural privileging of the heterosexual ideal of married monogamy but represents the forcible and state-sanctioned imposition of that ideal. Those who fall outside the norm of the nuclear family—such as single parents whose children live with them over the weekend but not during the week—are not only explicitly placed on the outside of social acceptability in terms of the configuration of their home/family/caring arrangements but are, quite literally, penalized by the state for this.[13]

And yet it is the issue of equal marriage—rather than welfare reform, spending cuts, homelessness, or unemployment—that has dominated LGTB/Q politics and activism in the United Kingdom in recent years. Albeit writing about the United States rather than the UK context, Lisa Duggan points to the emergence of what she terms "the new homonormativity" of the so-called gay agenda—that is, a politics that does not resist but, quite the opposite, actively promotes the norms and institutions of heteronormativity and which situates gay culture in the privatized and individualized realms of domesticity and consumption (Duggan 2003, 50–51). In contrast to the advancement of a collectivist program for economic and social justice that, in the UK context, would entail a critique of, and resistance to, austerity politics, the equal marriage agenda instead explicitly articulates the private, family sphere as the central locus of "gay rights" and, in so doing, "positions gay people as the perfect neoliberal subjects" (McRuer 2012, 1). Indeed, as I explore in the final section of this chapter, the equal marriage agenda has emerged as a key site upon which the neoliberal politics of heteronormativity are being (re)articulated and, as such, represents much more than "just" the co-opting of LGBT/Q politics. Rather, it is part of a broader and deeper project that reinforces and depends upon narratives of "family trouble" as explicitly linked to economic and social dis/order.

FAMILY GUY: DAVID CAMERON'S CRISIS NARRATIVES

In the remainder of this chapter, I attempt to situate the "gay agenda"—and the equal marriage agenda in particular—within the wider politics of economic and social crisis. Drawing examples from David Cameron's speeches on same-sex marriage, LGBT/Q politics, troubled families, welfare spending, and economic crisis, I explore how heteronormative constructions of "good" and "bad" families are being used to individualize economic and social disorder and thus to naturalize the profoundly political dynamics of crisis, together with its pernicious consequences for economic and social justice. Before proceeding, I should clarify that it is not the Conservative Party, but rather their Liberal Democrat coalition partners—and most notably the Equalities Minister, Lynne Featherstone—who have been instrumental in campaigning for, and pushing through, the Marriage (Same Sex Couples) Act that came into force in 2013. But, although equal marriage has undoubtedly met with some considerable resistance from within the Conservative Party, it is significant that Cameron himself has been forthright in his public support for this policy.[14] As he set out at a Lesbian, Gay, Bisexual and Transgender Reception in July 2012, for instance: "It's something I feel passionately about and I think if it's good enough for straight people like me, it's good enough for everybody and that's why we should have gay marriage and we will legislate for it" (D. Cameron 2012a). Similarly, as he argued in a Q&A with Airbus workers in December that year: "my view is that we should change the law and we should say that same-sex couples can get married . . . I think it's time to say, marriage is great and being gay shouldn't be a bar to being married" (D. Cameron 2012b).

Indeed, Cameron has not only emphasized his enthusiastic support for equal marriage as a specific policy but has also explicitly positioned this as being part of his own political vision for Britain. For example, in a speech to campaigners at a LGBT reception in July 2013, Cameron set out marriage equality as a symbol of Britain's national standing on the global stage:

> Many other countries are going to want to copy this. And, as you know, I talk about the global race, about how we've got to export more and sell more so I'm going to export the bill team. I think they can be part of this global race and take it around the world . . . It is something to celebrate that Britain is now—and it's official—the best place to be gay, lesbian or transgender anywhere in Europe. That is a great achievement. That's not my measure; that is an internationally recognised measure. (D. Cameron 2013b)

Although this welcoming of LGBT/Q communities into the Conservative Party fold[15] might seem to be a rather surprising and sexually progressive move in light of the party's long history of homophobic discourse and policy practice,[16] it also represents a very particular vision of what constitutes acceptable social and sexual "progress." For, while Cameron's support for same-sex marriage might appear to be a step forward for equality, it arguably has *nothing to do with equality* and *everything to do with marriage*. That equality is not a principal aim is quite plainly shown by the transparent lack of any kind of accompanying policy program to advance social, political, and economic equality for LGBT/Q communities. Cameron has made no attempt to situate same-sex marriage within a wider discourse of social and sexual justice, nor has he offered any kind of substantive commitment to ending social and sexual *in*justice for LGBT/Q communities.[17] Rather, this "victory" for gay rights—a "victory," moreover, that Cameron has been quick to claim as his own—is tantamount to a case of "job done," with the achievement of equality marriage treated as synonymous with the achievement of sexual equality per se.

It is a neat, if not necessarily intentional, trick, for Cameron's support for same-sex marriage represents the discursive *enclosure* of "gay rights" within an otherwise highly traditional and socially conservative pro-marriage agenda. Thus, LGBT/Q politics become articulated as follows: "[M]arriage is a great institution—I think it helps people to commit, it helps people to say that they're going to care and love for another person. It helps people to put aside their selfish interests and think of the union that they're forming" (D. Cameron 2012a); and "[T]he character of love, which marriage reflects: [is] faithful, stable, tough, unselfish and unconditional" (D. Cameron 2013b). Quite apart from the unabashed assumption here that to be married automatically qualifies one as capable of being in love, of being caring, and of being selfless—qualities that, presumably, the unmarried do not and cannot possess—what such discourses also reveal is a narrowing, and therefore limiting, of gay rights to marriage rights and of sexual equality to marriage equality. Far from representing any kind of open challenge to heteronormative power relations, gay rights are instead articulated in such a way as to reinforce and further legitimate reproductive heterosexuality as *the* natural and privileged sexuality. It is therefore through the lens of heteronormativity that marriage equality becomes intelligible (Duggan 2003; Eng 2010). This is a move, moreover, that erases the continuation and, as I outlined earlier, the heightening of structural inequality and disadvantage under the Coalition government. To quote Grace Hong, this (re)defining of sexual justice in homonormative terms itself serves to "exacerbate the conditions which lead to utter devaluation of poor, racialized, sexually and gender deviant populations . . . enabled by the limited incorporation and affirmation of certain forms of racialized, gendered, and sexualized difference" (Hong 2012, 91).

That the equal marriage agenda is helping to redraw (and ultimately to reinforce) the boundaries of heteronormativity is, therefore, only part of the story, for it is also crucial to consider how heteronormativity is itself part of the narrative through which neoliberal austerity politics are made thinkable and therefore politically possible. For, as Tracey Jensen (2012, 1–2) compellingly argues, the austerity-imperative is being expressed not just through references to the "extravagant waste" and public indebtedness of previous governments, but also through a series of metaphors surrounding the family: the "hard-working family," the "solvent family," and most of all "the responsible family." In his speech on "Troubled Families" in December 2011, for instance, Cameron argued,

> [W]e need a social recovery in Britain every bit as much as we need an economic one. So while the government's immediate duty is to deal with the budget deficit, my mission in politics—the thing I am really passionate about—is fixing the responsibility deficit. That means building a stronger society, in which more people understand their obligations, and more take control over their own lives and actions . . . Whatever you call them, we've known for years that a relatively small number of families are the source of a large proportion of the problems in society. Drug addiction. Alcohol abuse. Crime. A culture of disruption and irresponsibility that cascades through generations. (D. Cameron 2011c)

Important here, then, is how constructions of *economic* crisis are being linked to constructions of *social* decline through the drawing of explicit parallels between the "pre-crisis greed," "excessive consumption," and "moralized profligacy" of both the state and the household (Stanley 2014b). Public and private debt become coupled together as "fundamental problems" of the British economy (D. Cameron 2013a), with Britain itself likened to a "hard-working family" that is not "owed a living in the modern, global economy" but that has "to earn it—and earn it the hard way" (D. Cameron 2011a). This need for economic and social recovery in turn relies upon a conflation of what it is to be economically "broke" (Montgomerie 2013) and socially "broken," with economic and social decay both attributed to the failure of individuals, rather than to political processes and socioeconomic relations (Tepe 2014).

Again, this is a neat trick, for it enables resistance to social and economic injustice—such as the August riots of 2011—to be dismissed as the product of individual pathology:

> [W]hat we know for sure is that in large parts of the country this was just pure criminality . . . This was about behavior: people showing indifference to right and wrong, people with a twisted moral code, people with a complete absence of self-restraint. (D. Cameron 2011b)

Crucially, it is not (just) individuals per se, but rather individual *families* who are constructed as lying at the heart of this: "Broken Britain" *is* the "broken family." As Cameron explained in his speech on the August riots,

> The question people asked over and over again last week was "where are the parents? Why aren't they keeping the rioting kids indoors?" Tragically that's

been followed in some cases by judges rightly lamenting: "why don't the parents even turn up when their children are in court?" Well, join the dots and you have a clear idea about why some of these young people were behaving so terribly. Either there was no one at home, they didn't much care or they'd lost control. Families matter. I don't doubt that many of the rioters out last week have no father at home. Perhaps they come from one of the neighbourhoods where it's standard for children to have a mum and not a dad, where it's normal for young men to grow up without a male role model, looking to the streets for their father figures, filled up with rage and anger. (D. Cameron 2011b)

Family trouble is therefore identified not just as a symptom—or even as a symbol—of social and economic crisis, but rather is located as its root cause: "We need a social fight-back . . . [I]f we want to have any hope of mending our broken society, family and parenting is where we've got to start" (D. Cameron 2011b).

Such references to parenting are especially important because of the imaginaries of the Child that they conjure up. As Lee Edelman (2004, 2) contends, appeals to the Child powerfully shape the very logic within which politics is made thinkable, for it represents futurity and therefore the very possibility of social, economic, and political "progress." The Child therefore conserves "the absolute privilege of heteronormativity" (Edelman 2004, 2). One of the core principles of homophobia is precisely the notion that "same-sex sexuality is aligned with death, distanced as it is from the biological possibility of 'natural' reproduction" so that queerness is itself positioned as antithetical to futurity (and thus the very possibility of politics and progress) (Downing 2013, 138–139). The modern, and moral, subject thus becomes intelligible not only as a productive subject but also as a *re*productive subject—a subject who is both consumer and parent or, put another way, in "possession" of both property *and* children in order to achieve full political, economic, and cultural recognition *as* a subject under neoliberal capitalism. The property-less and child-less, in contrast, become constituted as non-subjects: surplus, abject, and unintelligible (Eng 2010; Hong 2012). Under neoliberal capitalism, it is above all the "surplus" body (Hong 2012, 87)—neither economically productive nor socially reproductive—that is represented as queer: that is, as "valueless, unprotectable, vulnerable, and dead" (Hong 2012, 92).

As Cameron set out in his speech on "The Values That Underpin Our Long-Term Economic Plan" in March 2014,

If we don't get to grips with the deficit now we are passing a greater and greater burden of debt to our children. We are saying that more and more

of their hard earned future income should be wasted on paying off the bill
we leave them. Do we really want to be the ones who responded to a crisis
by putting off to tomorrow what we had to do today? Can we really teach
our children the importance of being responsible and at the same time shirk
the most fundamental responsibility of all? ... Imagine looking your children in the eye and trying to explain why we crippled their future with our
debt. I couldn't do that. And I'm sure you couldn't either. We all want the
same for our children: a secure future and a chance to make something of
their lives. But they won't get that future unless we cut the deficit now.
(D. Cameron 2014)

This discourse—a direct call to arms to the productive and reproductive citizen to safeguard "our children" (and thus the future itself)—is a
discourse that shifts responsibility for economic and social crisis away
from government and squarely onto the shoulders of the most vulnerable in society. It renders the "surplus" bodies—or, put another way,
all of those actually existing human beings who find themselves living
under the crushing weight of gendered, racialized, classed, and sexualized hierarchies—individually culpable for the structural context in which
they find themselves. As Jacob DeFelippis (2012a, 4) notes, this tactic of
blaming the victim—that is, of blaming the individual for economic and
social decline and, consequently, of the poor for their own poverty—has
powerful parallels with the homophobic and racist discourses that blamed
the spread of AIDS on the very people dying of the disease. But death can
also be "slow death" (Berlant 2007, 754) through the wearing out and running down of people and populations for whom depletion, debilitation, and
deterioration come close to defining both their lived experience and their
historical existence (Berlant 2007). If nothing else, then, a queer critique of
crisis should refuse—and refuse unequivocally—to collude with neoliberal
discourses that not only mark out populations for slow death in this way
(Puar 2012), but that also naturalize, normalize, and therefore invisibilize
this very process.

CONCLUSION

I want to end with a quote from Matthew Watson (2014, 2), who writes that

[e]conomic crises are there to be won and lost; argued over and written about;
defined into and out of existence; influenced, shaped and reconstituted ...
The ultimate political effects of a crisis are always every bit as much about the

narration of the underlying condition as about its materiality: crises must be felt as well as lived.

"Crisis" is often understood as a material fact—as some kind of exogenous reality that must be responded to—rather than as a discursive construction through which neoliberal capitalism is being reforged. But neoliberal discourse might instead be understood as internal to the crisis itself, a part of the way in which the crisis becomes articulated and understood, indeed a language through which "crisis" becomes recognized as such (Hay and Smith 2013). In this chapter I have drawn on queer and feminist theory to explore how neoliberal constructions of economic crisis are not only gendered but also sexualized. In so doing, I have sought to contribute to the overarching project of this edited collection by connecting sexual politics with the scandalous economics of crisis in the United Kingdom. More specifically, I have interrogated how the consequences of, and very constitution of, neoliberal crisis are reproductive of heteronormative gender logics and power relations, which in turn serve to naturalize and normalize structural inequality and disadvantage. Crisis *is* felt, but it is also lived. And, as this chapter and this volume contend, it is a scandal.

ACKNOWLEDGMENTS

I would like to thank Jacqui True, Aida Hozic, Ian Bruff, and Michelle Pace for their invaluable comments on earlier versions of this chapter, and also Donna Lee for the many conversations we had about the "bedroom tax" that in part inspired this piece.

NOTES

1. The term "non-normative sexualities" refers not only to people who self-identify as LGBT/Q but also to people whose sexual and/or gender identities and practices do not neatly fit into such categories. In this chapter I use "LGBT/Q" and "queer" to denote non-normative sexualities and genders, but I do so in full recognition that the meanings of, and relationship between, identity markers such as "LGBT," "queer," and "non-normative sexualities" are highly politically contested. For a discussion of the dangers and difficulties of using, and *not* using, identity markers, see Engel (2007).
2. The "Q" in LGBT/Q is sometimes used to denote "questioning."
3. For an extended discussion of the equal marriage agenda as an example of liberal identity politics in the United States, for instance, see Duggan (2003).

4. Social reproduction refers not only to the biological reproduction of human-beings but also to the reproduction both of the labor force and of the "institutions, processes and social relations associated with the creation and maintenance of communities—and, upon which, ultimately all production and exchange rests" (Bakker and Silvey 2008, 2–3).

5. See Griffin (2009) for an in-depth analysis of World Bank discourses, for instance.

6. See Danby (2007) and Barker (2012) for queer reviews of the feminist political economy literature on the household and caring labor, respectively.

7. At the time of writing (May 2014).

8. Criticisms of the economic viability of the UK government's approach have not just come from the left: for example, the International Monetary Fund's chief economist, Olivier Blanchard, has described George Osborne as "playing with fire" (Conway 2013).

9. Similarly, the Institute for Fiscal Studies has found that—in contrast to a decade ago, when income standards were rising year-on-year and poverty levels were falling—both the poor and other income groups have become worse off, on average, since 2010 (Cribb et al. 2013, 1).

10. As Polly Trenow from the WMB remarks: "the government is redistributing between the sexes—taking money from women to give to men" (Women's Budget Group 2014b, 1).

11. As Jacqui True (2012) so powerfully argues, increases in instances of gendered and sexualized violence—including domestic/family violence, (male) suicides, depression and mental illness, workplace bullying, and homophobic hate crimes—cannot simply be dismissed as isolated, individual acts. Rather, they are part of a global political economy of violence that has been further exacerbated by economic crisis and austerity.

12. Many thanks to Donna Lee for pointing me toward this example.

13. The "spare room subsidy" has been criticized by the UN Special Rapporteur on the Right to Adequate Housing, Raquel Rolnik, for representing a human rights violation (Gentleman 2013).

14. Although he is reported as having expressed private regret over the unanticipated party political fallout this led to (Watt 2013).

15. For instance, Cameron has stressed "the immense contribution that lesbian, gay, bisexual and transgender people make in every part of our country, in the arts, in media, in sport, in business, in finance . . . I want to thank you for the immense contribution that you make to our country" (D. Cameron 2012a).

16. For instance, Margaret Thatcher's homophobia has received little attention in the literature on Thatcherism, and yet it was under her leadership that Section 28 of the Local Government Act of 1988 was brought into force. This stated that a local authority "shall not intentionally promote homosexuality or publish material with the intention of promoting homosexuality" or "promote the teaching in any maintained school of the acceptability of homosexuality as a pretended family relationship" (Moran 2002, 205).

17. This is perhaps not surprising for a man who had repeatedly opposed gay rights when in opposition, including voting against the repeal of Section 28 in 2003 (Watt 2009).

CHAPTER 14

Self-Reproducing Movements and the Enduring Challenge of Materialist Feminism

WANDA VRASTI

The feminist movement is basically an anarchist movement which does not want to replace one (male) power elite by another (female) power elite, but which wants to build up a non-hierarchical, non-centralized society where no elite lives on exploitation and dominance over others.

—Maria Mies (1986), 37

The situation of women is different from that of any other social group. This is because they are not one of a number of isolable units, but half a totality: the human species. Women are essential and irreplaceable; they cannot therefore be exploited in the same way as other social groups can. They are fundamental to the human condition, yet in their economic, social and political roles, they are marginal. It is precisely this combination—fundamental and marginal at one and the same time—that has been fatal to them.

—Juliet Mitchell (1966)

It has often been said that what we are witnessing today is not only an economic crisis of systemic proportions, it is also a crisis of the imagination. "Economic dogma has taken hold of the public discourse for three decades, and has destroyed the critical power of political reason. The collapse of the global economy has exposed the dangers of economic dogmatism, but its ideology has already been incorporated into the automatism of living society," writes Italian autonomist writer Franco (Bifo) Berardi in his latest book, *On Poetry and Finance* (2012, 7). Marxist writer Mark Fisher (2009) has named this "automatism," "capitalism realism," a generalized belief that capitalist market relations are the most "rational" way of organizing society despite mounting evidence to the contrary. According to Fisher, this kind of lack of imagination is indicative of the powerlessness and isolation that individuals experience under capitalism.

At the same time, the argument has also been made that the present crisis is, in fact, a crisis of social reproduction (also a crisis of masculinity). Whereas the Great Recession of the 1970s struck at the heart of the productive sphere, the 2008 crisis affected mostly people's ability to reproduce their standards of living: make payments on their homes, pay their debts, put themselves through school, and meet basic needs. The two are not unrelated. The solution chosen for the 1970s crisis of profitability was not the traditional approach of destroying capital to make room for a renewed era of growth, but quite the opposite: capital was freed from its last spatio-temporal boundaries and regulatory shackles and was allowed to compete globally. The strengthening of capital at the expense of labor in the last 40 years resulted everywhere in the Western hemisphere in reduced wages, broken solidarities, and precarious living standards, compensated only by financial mechanisms of speculation and indebtedness, which were sooner or later bound to implode. By the time the crisis finally hit, in 2008, postwar structures of solidarity and social democratic institutions of support had been hollowed out so thoroughly by neoliberal planning that there was little in place to help people cope with the effects of the crash (Silva 2013).

These two readings of the crisis—as a crisis of the imagination and a crisis of social reproduction—are, in fact, complementary. The crisis of imagination begs the question: *Which notions of progress are still operative today? What types of utopias or futures can we deduce from the present situation?* To this, the crisis of social reproduction responds: *A politics of resistance today is necessarily also a politics of reconstruction and reproduction.* Anti-capitalist struggle today must propose a form of life opposed to the individualizing morality of debt and work. Rebuilding old structures of solidarity and developing new capacities for collective self-reproduction are paramount to this task. Only when living in common will become an enjoyable, feasible, and sustainable activity will market rationality cease to look like the only "rational" option.

So far, this volume has focused on the intersection of gender and crisis, looking at how the crisis has impacted women and gender relations, or how gender has been mobilized to "clean up" after the crisis. Not so much attention has been paid to the potential that feminism holds for pushing back the crisis. But feminism, as the Maria Mies quote opening this chapter suggests, has always harbored a utopian impulse that reaches far beyond redressing the gender imbalance in public and economic affairs. Feminism is an expansive political project with complex views on political practice, economic organization, culture, sexuality, ecology, language, and knowledge, as expressed in the second opening quote by Juliet Mitchell. Despite appearing to be concerned only with the welfare of a particular set of individuals (women), feminism is a complete political provocation. Particularly materialist feminism, also known as second-wave feminism (as developed in Italy, Germany, and the United States in the 1970s), reaches far beyond issues of identity and representation to deal with social and natural life in an interconnected way. In this chapter, I revisit some of the key contributions of materialist feminism and try to tease out some provocative lessons for this double crisis of imagination and reproduction. Although this type of feminism has been criticized, especially by third-wave feminists, for essentializing the specificity of women, the feminist standpoint continues to be a valid ground from which to critique the separations and hierarchies of our times. The recent (re-)publication and warm reception of Silvia Federici's *Revolution at Point Zero: Housework, Reproduction and Feminist Struggle* (2012) and Lise Vogel's *Marxism and the Oppression of Women: Towards a Unitary Theory* (2014) indicate that the challenge of materialist feminism is in no way a dated one.

To guide us through this journey, I chose Silvia Federici's concept of the "self-reproducing movement," which calls for a unity between political action and the work of social reproduction understood broadly: "We need to create forms of life in which political activism is not separated from the task of our daily reproduction" (Federici, cited in Vishmidt 2013). I take this idea, which I believe contains some of the most provocative advances in feminist criticism and politics, and trace it back through various feminist movements and interventions from the 1970s, such as the Wages for Housework campaign, artist Mierle Laderman Ukeles's "Manifesto of Maintenance Art," and Marge Piercy's anarcha-feminist science fiction novel, *Woman on the Edge of Time* (1976). In the final section, I try to show how this distinctively feminist approach went "mainstream" a couple of years ago when the Occupy camps privileged reproduction over disruption as their main tactic of protest against a political culture of individuation and social disintegration. From this, I derive the conclusion that in the midst of a crisis of reproduction, which dissolves existing social bonds of care and trust, the feminist perspective and the practices elaborated from it are indispensable tools for combating the isolation and fracture imposed by capitalism on all levels of human experience.

FEMINISM AND THE SELF-REPRODUCING MOVEMENT

Marxist feminist author Silvia Federici, best known for her books *Caliban and the Witch* (2004) and *Revolution at Point Zero* (2012), as well as for her involvement in the Wages for Housework campaign of the 1970s, has recently introduced the term, "self-reproducing movement," to highlight the centrality of reproductive work for building a sustainable culture of resistance. This is in line with the quintessential materialist feminist recognition about the centrality of unpaid women's work to the reproduction of capitalism and the insistence that every movement against capital must include, if not begin from, the contestation of this sexual division of labor by making reproductive work a central, equally shared, and valued activity (Della Costa and James 1972; Mies 1986, 2005; Fortunati 1996; Federici 2004, 2012; James 2012). Noteworthy about this approach is also the idea that female work is indispensable and un-merchandisable. Not only will the question of reproductive work not disappear with women's entry into the workforce or their equal standing before the law but, perhaps, there is also something worthwhile about these arduous, repetitive, and ephemeral tasks that Hannah Arendt ([1958] 1998), for instance, groups under the category of simple, metabolic labor. What if reproductive work, in fact, contains many of the resources and relations we need to connect to the world? What if, what is generally considered low-skill subsistence labor, precisely the type of work modernity promises to help us overcome, contains the seeds for a politics of autonomization away from an alienated being of our species? A politics of this sort could not be legislated or accomplished with the tools of conventional politics. What would be needed is a "revolution of everyday life," a general movement toward the transformation of all social forms (family, education, knowledge, production, reproduction, etc.) supportive of the value structure endemic to capitalism. Federici's "self-reproducing movement" is only the latest contribution in what is essentially a long lineage of New Left politics and tactics stretching from the late 1960s all the way to the Occupy/Indignados movement(s) from a couple of years ago.

I quote here from two interviews in which Federici explains the concept and its background:

> We have seen even before the Occupy movement—but the Occupy movement has made it visible—the need and desire for a kind of politics that recalls something of a feminist politics: the refusal to separate the political and the personal, the affective and the political. We used to discuss in New York particularly with people of the younger generation of activists the idea of creating

a self-reproducing movement. We conceptualize this as a movement that would not continuously surge and collapse, surge and collapse but would actually have a continuity through all its transformations. This continuity would be precisely the ability to also place the needs of people and the relationship of people at the center of the organizing. (cited in Brunner 2012)

In New York, for instance, a broad discussion has been taking place for some years now among people in the movement on the need to create "communities of care" and, more generally, collective forms of reproduction whereby we can address issues that "flow from our everyday life" [. . .]. We have begun to recognize that for our movements to work and thrive, we need to be able to socialize our experiences of grief, illness, pain, death, things that now are often relegated to the margins or the outside of our political work. We agree that *movements that do not place on their agendas the reproduction of both their members and the broader community are movements that cannot survive, they are not "self-reproducing," especially in these times when so many people are daily confronting crises in their lives.* (cited in Haiven 2011a; emphasis added)

Feminist politics has always moved from an assumption of the unity between the personal and the political, as captured in the slogan, "the revolution begins at home." But as Silvia Federici points out, since the 2008 crisis at the very latest, the politics of reproduction is no longer exclusively a women's question. As capital spreads its crisis tendency to the sphere of reproduction, enclosing people's homes, savings, and access to health care, effectively undermining their capacity to live and labor, radical politics had to respond with a counter-movement that prioritizes the production of life (the need for food, education, care, mutual aid, sociality) above all else. The self-reproducing movement, then, is a concept for our times.

For Federici, the self-reproducing movement is also a practical concern. Where many of our present oppositional strategies involve one-off spectacular events, such as demonstrations and strikes, greater attention to everyday needs would help resistance extend to all moments of life, across the entire fabric of our communities. Protest, then, would become a "round-the-clock bodily presence," such as the Occupy camps (Caffentzis 2012):

We need to build a movement that puts on its agenda its own reproduction. The anti-capitalist struggle has to create forms of support and has to have the ability to collectively build forms of reproduction. [. . .] We have to ensure that we do not only confront capital at the time of the demonstration, but that we confront it collectively at every moment of our lives. What is happening internationally proves that only when you have these forms of collective reproduction, when you have communities that reproduce themselves collectively, you have struggles that are moving in a very radical way against the established order, as for example the struggle of indigenous people in Bolivia against water privatization or in Ecuador against the oil companies' destruction of indigenous land. (Federici 2005)

Struggles in the sphere of reproduction, then, are essentially struggles for "commoning" the resources and capacities needed to produce life. They are also struggles against the separation between individuals and means of production, needs and capacities, production and social reproduction, and within individuals themselves reproduced under capitalism (Endnotes 2010, 80–81). This merging of feminist principles and political practices of "commoning" has taken several forms over the years. We find it in social movements, prefigurative communities, solidarity economies, local initiatives, art projects, literature, and more. Not all of them were explicitly feminist, but to the extent that they draw on a feminist critique of capitalism and imperialism, we can locate the roots of such critique in the Wages for Housework campaign.

WAGES FOR HOUSEWORK

Alienated by the macho revolutionary culture of the student and worker movement, especially their ignorance of domestic labor as central to the reproduction of the quintessential capitalist commodity—labor-power, feminists of the 1970s went on to create their own organizations, tactics, and communities. These were generally more committed to principles of egalitarianism, consensus decision-making, and an ethics of care. Their intention was to revolutionize daily life starting from the realm of necessity. Eating, cleaning, housing, care, and education were important to them, not because they were women's work, but because this is where the reproduction of life and social relations takes place. The home is both the place where the most pernicious divisions among the working class begin and where we find a potential for love and care exceeding capitalist rationality.

The Wages for Housework movement kicked off in Italy with the publication of Mariarosa Della Costa and Selma James's pamphlet, "The Power of Women and the Subversion of the Community" in 1972. The piece argued that housework and childbirth are material activities producing use value as well as the commodity known as labor-power. This intervention provided a much-needed materialist analysis of women's work, which positioned women not simply as victims of patriarchal domination in the home, but also as workers exploited by capital, on par with men (Vogel

2014, 21–22). Different from male labor, though, women's work did not receive a wage. Carried out under the pretense of love, it was unrecognized and invisible labor, impossible to regulate, bargain or struggle over. But Marxist feminists insisted that there is nothing natural or harmless about this (hetero)sexual division of labor. To begin having a conversation about the working conditions of women in the home, these feminists insisted that women would first have to be acknowledged as workers, hence the controversial demand for wages. Only once this common ground was established could women begin contesting and even refusing the divisions under which their labor takes place. This means, Wages *for* Housework could be read as a "transitional demand" toward Wages *against* Housework.

While we continue to reap the fruits of these debates today, there has always been a great deal of disagreement over the actual merit of demanding Wages for Housework. For Silvia Federici (1975), at least, the demand should be understood literally. Far from cheapening women's work, as the common complaint goes, holding a wage would grant women a tremendous leverage in their fight against capitalism and a collective basis from which to struggle. It would also recognize women as a constitutive part of the working class. Kathi Weeks (2011) also insists on the performative dimension of this demand, which, she argues, should be understood as an instigation to collective action and an assertion of collective power previously not granted to women. Without a common and combative slogan, like Wages for Housework, that could articulate the position of women in the capitalist economy and bring women into the streets, women would be condemned to remaining "nagging bitches, not workers in struggle" (Federici 1975). As a movement, the struggle for Wages for Housework was only in its last instance about a "lump of money." En route to that destination, it was also a collective process of becoming, a process of political education, a political perspective, and a transitional demand "for the power to make further demands" (Weeks 2011, 133–134).

The Wages for Housework movement impressed more through its critique than its tactics. While the student movement was busy occupying buildings, running pirate radio stations, and stating various forms of direct action, the feminist movement (*Lotta Feminista*) ran demonstrations and political economy debates that became increasingly abstract and divorced from the larger feminist movement. So we could ask: *Was this actually a self-reproducing movement that folded the daily needs of everyday life into a form of protest or was it simply a movement that placed the critique of social reproduction at its center?*

Although the answer would have to lean toward the second option, Wages for Housework provided a theoretical framework for connecting the reproduction of life to the reproduction of struggle. The movement represented a powerful break with the culture of dissidence of the day (the juvenile anti-authoritarianism of the Beatniks, the culture jamming of the Situationists, the politics of refusal of the Italian Autonomists, and the guerrilla tactics of the Black Panthers), best described by Jacque Camatte's sentiment, "This World We Must Leave" (1995). Women could not leave this world. Their economic dependence on men, their reproductive capacities and obligations, and their sociocultural position of inferiority did not afford them the luxury of romantic revolt. While men were "on the road," engaged in a life of the mind or preparing guerrilla tactics, most women were homebound, tied to familial obligations. This is why feminists were also rarely impressed with utopias of a society of less work when this utopia had nothing to say about women's work or about the length of their workday. Any attempt to transcend the sphere of necessity that does not take into account the sexual division of labor makes the work of caring for basic human needs the natural and invisible responsibility of women. A feminist utopia is one that starts from the realm of necessity, and tries to collectivize and valorize it. A great example of this critique put into practice, even if only art practice, was Mierle Lademan Ukeles's "Manifesto for Maintenance Art."

"MANIFESTO OF MAINTENANCE ART" (1969)

Following the birth of her first child, Ukeles became acutely aware of the separation of artwork from everyday activities and the blindness to child care, housework, and other routine maintenance activities. As a reaction to the opposition and hierarchies separating art and life, nature and culture, public and private, Ukeles wrote a manifesto explaining:

Two basic systems: Development and Maintenance. The sourball of every revolution: after the revolution, who's going to pick up the garbage on Monday morning?

Development: pure individual creation; the new; change; progress; advance; excitement; flight or fleeing.

Maintenance: keep the dust off the pure individual creation; preserve the new; sustain the change; protect progress; defend and prolong the advance; renew the excitement; repeat the flight;

[...]

Maintenance is a drag; it takes all the fucking time (lit.).

The mind boggles and chafes at the boredom.

The culture confers lousy status on maintenance jobs = minimum wages, housewives = no pay.

clean your desk, wash the dishes, clean the floor, wash your clothes, wash your toes, change the baby's diaper, finish the report, correct the typos, mend the fence, keep the customer happy, throw out the stinking garbage, watch out don't put things in your nose, what shall I wear, I have no sox, pay your bills, don't litter, save string, wash your hair, change the sheets, go to the store, I'm out of perfume, say it again—he doesn't understand, seal it again—it leaks, go to work, this art is dusty, clear the table, call him again, flush the toilet, stay young. (Ukeles 1969)

In classic modernist fashion, where art is no longer the realization of some aesthetic principles, but the assertion of life *as* art (e.g., Duchamp's toilet), Ukeles claims:

Art: "Everything I say is Art is Art. Everything I do is Art is Art."

Ukeles' proposition is simple: her art will consist of nothing more than making maintenance work visible in an art context. The separation between Ukeles, the housewife, and Ukeles, the artist, disappears once her domestic work is brought into the museum.

I will simply do these maintenance everyday things, and flush them up to consciousness, exhibit them, as Art. I will live in the museum as I customarily do at home with my husband and my baby, for the duration of the exhibition. (Right? or if you don't want me around at night I would come in every day) and do all these things as public Art activities: I will sweep and wax the floors, dust everything, wash the walls (i.e. "floor paintings, dust works, soap-sculpture, wall-paintings") cook, invite people to eat, make agglomerations and dispositions of all functional refuse. (Ukeles 1969)

As simple as it sounds, this is a revolutionary move in that it breaks with the arrogance of much of our social organization and value structure for which maintenance work is a natural fact of life that more or less takes care of itself. It is perhaps also revolutionary in that it cuts Ukeles's workload in half.

Additionally, Ukeles also proposes to interview workers of various occupations as well as museum visitors about what they think maintenance is, "what is the relationship between maintenance and freedom," and "what is the relationship between maintenance and life's dreams." Taking it from the sociological to the material or from the figurative to the literal, the exhibition also includes a sanitation component. Every day, containers of various types of refuse will be delivered to the museum for processing and disposal. This way, the museum participates directly in the work of maintaining the city that maintains it. Fittingly, Ukeles has been the (unsalaried) Artist of the New York City Department of Sanitation since 1977.

As with Wages for Housework and the entire tradition of materialist feminism, the ambition here is not to do away with the time-consuming and arduous labor of reproduction but to reorganize it along more participatory and egalitarian lines. Instead of transcending the realm of necessity into a world of boundless leisure and contemplation, the feminist utopia is something more telluric. The ambition is to put an end to the separation of production from reproduction and art from life through self-activity and self-provisioning.

WOMAN ON THE EDGE OF TIME (1976)

It is no easy task to imagine what such an ambitious vision would look like. Provocations like Wages for Housework, the "Manifesto of Maintenance Art," and prefigurative activist communities of the 1970s (see Barbara Epstein's *Political Protest and Cultural Revolution: Nonviolent Direct Action in the 1970s and 1980s* [1993]) provide some intimation of what such "revolutions of everyday life" could look like but their success is always limited by conditions not of their own choosing. Literature has it a lot easier in this regard. Of all modes of representation, literature, perhaps even more so than art, has the advantage that it can "present a 'speaking picture' of the good society; to show in concrete detail what it would be like to live in such a society, and so make us want to achieve it" (Kumar 2010, 555). This is why science fiction writing is the natural home of the utopian imagination.

After a certain period of quiet, during the 1970s, utopian science fiction experienced a revival in the hands of feminist writers. They took the fantasies of technological liberation dominating the genre around the turn of the century and constructed a social vision structured around ecology, egalitarianism, and "attention to emotions" (Crawford 2003, 213). Almost all feminist utopias from the period focus on small-scale communities, where work is shared equally, gender divisions are superfluous, and isolation is no longer the overriding emotion of modern life. While most "serious" thinkers of the postwar period steered clear of utopia, claiming it was laden with authoritarian impulses and lazy politics, feminist writers used utopian writing to lay bare the gendered and imperialist dimension of world politics in the starkest colors: "We see in fiction what we refuse to see in the real world" (Miller cited in Crawford 2003, 210). Utopia, in their hands, became more than an exercise in painting an image of the future. It was equally about teasing out the latent possibilities and immanent desires buried in the present.

The most cited example in this category is usually Ursula Le Guin's *The Dispossessed* (1974), the story of an anarchist community that runs against the limits of its own vision, requiring a jolt of dynamism to renew itself. Salvation eventually arrives in the form of a male romantic hero. My personal favorite, however, is the lesser-known, *Woman on the Edge of Time* (1976) by Marge Piercy. This book is perhaps more literarily conventional and problematically "agrarian" than the technologically savvy and socially complex, *The Dispossessed*, but it is also more revolutionary in its conclusions and more explicitly feminist in its orientation. In it, Piercy engages in, to use a phrase from Marx, an "insistent ruthless critique of everything"—capitalism, patriarchy, racism, medical science, the welfare state, heterosexual love, the nuclear family, language, and our deepest fantasies of progress and security, only to follow it up with what Neeta Crawford calls a "ruthless imaginative reconstruction of everything" (2003, 199). The result is a somewhat more technologically simplistic society but one that is highly sophisticated in dealing with problems of exclusion, competition, and jealousy and whose constant aim it is to keep resocializing people to be good to one another (Piercy 2003).

Woman on the Edge of Time tells the story of Consuelo (Connie) Ramos, a poor Chicana woman living in New York in the 1970s, who has the rare gift of communicating with other dimensions. About the same time that Connie is diagnosed with mental illness and committed to a high-security mental institution, she begins taking up contact with Luciente, a creole woman from the future society of Mattapoisett.

At first, these trips are disappointing to Connie. Mattapoisett reminds her too much of the rural Mexico her family tried so hard to escape. There are no flying cars and certainly no material abundance. Tedious, repetitive work has been largely automated, but equally hard labor, like agriculture and child rearing, are still done "by hand" and shared equally across all members of society. In fact, farming and parenting are the most esteemed types of work in Mattapoisett. Everyone involved in child rearing is technically a "mother," and there are dozens of festivities celebrating women's roles. Instead of trying to overcome gender inequality by granting women the same privileges and competencies as men, as Le Guin does in *The Dispossessed*, for instance, Piercy celebrates the specificity of women and brings female knowledge and social roles to the center of society, where they can shape the value structure and social organization of a whole.

Mattapoisett is a thoroughly communist society. Basic needs are provided for by each according to their abilities, to all according to their needs. All work is socially useful and personally meaningful. So is education, which is integrated into all areas of life and always aligned with socially useful ends, except for the sabbatical, which is reserved for pleasure and travel. A rigid division of labor is overcome by merging manual and mental labor, arts and sciences, production and social reproduction, politics and parenting. Collective decisions are taken by a grand council of "laymen" elected by lot. But Mattapoisett is also more than that.

In Mattapoisett, "[w]e're all peasants," Luciente explains (1976, 64). "We learned a lot from societies that people used to call primitive. Primitive technically. But socially sophisticated. [. . .] We tried to learn from cultures that dealt well with handling conflict, promoting cooperation, coming of age, growing a sense of community, getting sick, aging, going mad, dying. . . ." People in Mattapoisett are educated with other people in mind: they know how to look after children, heal people, help people die peacefully, and negotiate conflicts. They are also skilled in arts and crafts, which come in handy especially during the culture's numerous festivals and celebrations. As with all peasant societies, knowledge of plants, animals, and climate stems from a practical concern with survival on a resource-scarce planet. Technology is not avoided but integrated into a different kind of value structure, where connectivity and sustainability take precedence over comfort and abundance.

Woman on the Edge of Time blends together elements from peasant societies, creole and indigenous cultures, and the American counterculture to construct a thoroughly anti-racist, anti-sexist, and anti-ageist society. The result is not a perfect society. Needs and conflicts persist, but then "some problems you *solve* only if you stop being human, become metal, plastic, robot computer" (1976, 114). We recognize here traces of Maria Mies and Veronika Bennholdt-Thomsen's work on the "subsistence perspective" (2005), or John Berger's writing on peasants from the *Into Their Labors* trilogy (see especially the introduction to vol. 1, *Pig Earth*, from 1979). All these works belong to a minor strand of left-libertarian writing, which proceeds from the limitations of the body, the planet, and the future to plead not for some political realism but to oppose fictions about the transcendence of the (corpo)real.

Of course, Connie's present stands in stark contrast to all of this. Connie comes from a long lineage of humiliation and abuse at the hands of family members, lovers, employers, landlords, social workers, and more recently, doctors. In the hospital, Connie is reduced to bare life, her voice dismissed, signs of life mistaken for signs of disobedience. She is "a sane woman labeled insane, a survivor reduced to a victim" (Moylan 1986, 123). The greatest threat she faces, though, stems from modern society's quest for perfectibility: Connie is supposed to undergo several invasive medical experiments to make her "safe for society." To save herself and her friends in the ward, Connie poisons the entire award-winning medical team supposed to administer these operations, condemning herself to a life inside institutions. This ultimately "terroristic" act is aligned with Mattapoisett's uncertain future. In killing a certain version of the present, she open up the possibility of a different future. The price for the Mattapoisett way of life is paid with Connie's own life.

Woman on the Edge of Time is perhaps the most detailed account of a self-reproducing movement. But this world is not just served to us. We are at once seduced by Mattapoisett and left to wonder, like Connie, what we are prepared to do to bring this future into existence. In raising the question of direct action and even violence, Piercy suggests that the self-reproducing movement, with its attention to emotions and focus on reproduction and socialization, is perhaps not an entirely pacifist proposition. This world still needs to be renewed from the inside and secured from the outside. The self-reproducing movement, for Piercy at least, is a movement of permanent struggle against its own stagnation and against external forces of reaction. We might say, in this case, that the self-reproducing movement is, in fact, a form of permanent revolution.

THE OCCUPY ENCAMPMENTS (2011–2012)

Another home for the self-reproducing movement are prefigurative communities and radical events. Prefigurative communities are usually activist groups who live out the change they want to see in the world in the form of communes, direct action, and camps, like the ones we saw in public squares a few years ago. Prefiguration started in the 1970s as a reaction to instrumental politics and its separation between rulers and ruled, theory and strategy, reason and emotion. A common home for prefigurative practices are radical events, like the French Revolution, the Paris Commune, or May 1968. These are moments when the flow of history is interrupted and political action becomes immediate and sensuous (Haiven 2011b). One acts "as if one is already free" (Graeber 2009, 203). Political channels of political communication and decision-making are sidestepped for people to work out the details of the future society in the here and now. Such an instance was the Occupy movement that took hold of major cities in North America and Western Europe in 2011–2012.

In this section, I want to focus specifically on the example of the Occupy camps as a real-life example of a self-reproducing movement, however short-lived. The concrete utopia enacted in the Occupy camps was, of course, never as detailed and complex as those represented in science fiction, but they managed to take the anti-authoritarian sensibility seen in *Woman on the Edge of Time* out into the streets and give it a concrete social and spatial dimension. They created a utopianism for the here and now.

Let us take, for instance, the camp at Liberty Plaza in New York. It was a kind of "living installation or social sculpture" (Schwendener 2011) made of assembly and lecture spaces, information booths and media centers, cooking tents, day care corners, barter tables, a library space, drum circles, and an endless array of banners and posters separating it from the curious eyes of tourists, press, and police officers. Inside the camp, magical things happened: people made their first contact with direct democracy; homeless people found food and shelter; work was cooperative; art and music were made; social cohesion emerged in the place of isolation and depression. In the words of a participant in the May 1968 events in Paris, people were "living beyond their intellectual, emotional and sensorial limits: each person existed above and beyond himself" (cited in Haiven 2011b, 71).

Also important, the camps invited people to live *in public*, to do things usually reserved for the private sphere, such as cooking, cleaning, and caring, or things deemed suspicious or dangerous in public, like assembling, camping, and celebrating. Taking public squares and filling them with networks of mutual aid and voluntary cooperation, free food and education, spontaneous creativity and participatory structures was a good reminder of just how militarized and corporatized public space had become in recent years. In this sense, perhaps the camps were less an occupation than a *liberation* of space from the hands of corporate interests and riot police.

Another distinctive mark of Occupy was the public display of collective enjoyment. Carnival, street theater, drumming circles, surrealist and situationist artistic practices had been staples of the alter-globalization movement since the 1990s to the exasperation of police and public officials, who never knew how to respond to this "nonviolent warfare" other than by using force and demagogy. Among protesters, however, these rituals of collective enjoyment forged a sense of solidarity and social cohesion at a time when the moralization of debt and the humiliation of precarious living were working to isolate people from each other.

There was a tremendous emotion around it [the camps]—the joy of finding you were not alone, the shame that was shed as the prisoners of debt stepped out of the shadows, the ferocity of solidarity when so many of us were attacked by the police, the dizzying hope that everything could be different, and the exhilaration in those moments when it was. (Solnit 2012)

Although not an openly feminist movement, Occupy borrowed many of the lessons feminists have developed and refined since the 1970s, such as "an egalitarian vision of society," "consensus-based decision making, the distrust of leaders (formal or charismatic) and the idea that you need to prefigure the world you want to create through your actions and organization," "an ethics of care and sisterhood and a respect for animals and nature" (Federici in Haiven 2011a). Attention to social reproduction was, naturally, a key part of it. Occupy placed the needs of and relationships between people at the center of organizing. Food and shelter were the most immediate concerns as the occupations were trying to become self-reliant enclaves and outlast police repression. But cooking and cleaning were never deemed more important than maintaining the library, running general assemblies, or celebrating the occupation. All aspects of the camp were considered equally important, and there was no distinction between caring for the personal and organizing for the political.

But the camps were also the most controversial elements of the movement, and feminists were among the most vocal in pointing them out. As experiments in collective living, they reproduced many of the power differentials and exclusions we find in society at large. Although they tried to overcome these problems by constantly tweaking the methods of communication and collective decision-making, the movement as a whole still prioritized the prefigurative over the strategic component. To put it crudely, what the society of the future would look like was more important than how we would get there. This neglect of strategic action left the movement politically inchoate and vulnerable to police repression. As soon as the camps were cleared out, the movement had trouble finding another common point of reference. And although the Occupy "spirit" retreated into the neighborhoods and remains active in anti-debt campaigns, anti-foreclosure mobilization, and other community initiatives, it lacks the force and vitality it once did. We might, then, ask the question: *How can we claim that the Occupy camps were an example of a self-reproducing movement given their brief life span? Did perhaps the vitality of the camps contribute more to their unsustainability than to their capacity for reproduction?*

For some answers, I turn to Max Haiven's definition of the radical event, which will help put the Occupy movement in quite a different light than Federici's self-reproducing movement:

Radical events of collective action are animated by and refract a "flash" of a utopia of unalienated labor. [. . .] Here collectivities, to the extent that they are able to create temporary (even partial and problematic) conditions of autonomy, create their own form of life and collaborate "biopolitically" on their own accord. These events are, at least in one valence, radical experiments with organizing social cooperation another way. As such, they (often inadvertently) open themselves to the raw "magma" of human cooperation or the "social flow of doing." It is precisely this openness that marks the event as "radical," as fundamentally at odds with a form of capitalist biopolitics that tyrannically seeks monopoly over the possibilities of social cooperation. (2011b, 70)

Radical events, then, are moments when politics explodes from its "representational" casket, erasing the lag between speech and behavior, theory and action, public and private. Divisions of labor, hierarchies and socially assigned roles, official channels of communication, and the very category of "the public" as an entity that needs representation by either political or media vehicles dissipate. Radical events release individuals and collectivities from the "done" of their being into an unalienated social flow of "doing," to use John Holloway's distinction (2002). The normal order of things dissolves, however briefly, to reveal vulnerable cracks and surprising possibilities. In such days of intense social activity, time moves faster, events seems more real, experiences arrive unmediated, and people become makers of their own history: "the production and reproduction of reality is totally unalienated and monstrously democratic" (Haiven 2011b, 75).

A politics of this intensity is bound to be short-lived. The immediacy of the radical event, what Haiven calls its "obstreperous temporality," which the Occupy movement certainly had plenty of, leaves little room for strategic planning and calculated action. Its recklessness and abandon remind one more of a sexual encounter than a political program, as suggested by this Paris 1968 slogan: "The more I make love, the more I want to make revolution. The more I make revolution, the more I want to make love." This is, then, the ultimate paradox of the self-reproducing movement: in trying to overcome the problem of alienation by closing the distance between speech and action, public and private, strategy and utopia, present and future, it undermines its own chances for reproduction. Its radicality becomes an all-consuming form of expenditure.

Still, despite this cautionary tale, I would like to insist that the Occupy movement and, in particular, the camps had a long-term affective impact. For change to be effective, it must be affective. A successful social movement cannot just offer a critique of the present, it must also substantiate theory with an experience people can relate to and have a part in. "It's one thing to say, 'Another world is possible.' It's another to experience it, however momentarily" (Graeber 2002, 72).

If one of the greatest forces behind the political apathy of our generation is that "[w]e have lost the pleasure of being together" (Berardi and Lovink 2011), cooking together in the camps, building shelter, learning the rules of open communication, and sharing free goods was the most effective way of counteracting the isolation and the feeling of powerlessness contributing to our domination. The camps were zones of utopian sentience, without which it is hard to imagine the Occupy movement gaining as much traction as it did. The longevity of the movement was probably not helped by the camps, which attracted the most attention while also being the movement's most vulnerable target. But neither would Occupy have had such resonance had there not been the concrete utopias of the camps to give people a sensorial taste and participatory stake in its oppositional vision. So, perhaps, when we talk about the self-reproductive capacities of a movement, we should also consider their relevance for a common memory and a radical imagination of what is possible (Haiven 2011b).

CONCLUSION: WHAT DOES IT MEAN TO BE A FEMINIST TODAY?

In a recent article in the *New Left Review*, Nancy Fraser (2009) argued that feminism, and second-wave feminism in particular, has unwittingly played into the hands of free-market capitalism. "Feminism's ambivalence," as she calls it, on issues relating to wage labor, the welfare state, and the politics of equality amidst difference, has been resolved in neoliberalism's favor. The attack on the family wage or the critique of the normalizing role of the welfare state has helped break up solidaristic attachments and push a politics of individuation and flexibilization that equates women's liberation with private consumptive satisfactions. There has always been a fear that broad movements like feminism could be coopted and defanged by having their anti-capitalist and anti-authoritarian components reduced to a narrow concern with cultural equality and representational correctness. There might be something to this, judging by how much more militant the feminist movement used to be in the 1970s. But, as I have tried to show in this chapter, this is not the only possible trajectory for feminism.

The appeal of something like the self-reproducing movement rests on the life-affirming and life-creating force of a feminism that starts with gender but does not end there. Placing care and reproduction at the center of life, where it belongs, has the power of bringing people together and in contact with a dimension of collective living otherwise banished from life under capitalism.

And while it is true that the instances reviewed here have had varying degrees of success—many turning out to be less sustainable and practical than expected—the case could still be made that radical politics today has to incorporate an attention to principles and values traditionally associated with feminism: basic need provision, socialization, and an attention to emotion. To the extent that feminist politics and, above all, feminist tactics (consensus democracy, prefigurative communities, revolutions of everyday life, Wages for Housework) have been intended as an antidote for isolation (i.e., the isolation women have felt in the home), it only makes sense that these tactics be rediscovered today, when the neoliberal march of capitalism secures its victory by keeping people divided and defeated. The innovation of a self-reproducing movement that unites protest action with the activities of daily care and need provision is to bridge, even momentarily, the fracture that capitalism creates between the doing and the done, self and other, subject and object, and, in so doing, to inject energy and joy where otherwise would only be resignation and cynicism.

Afterword

Gendering the Crisis

MARIEKE DE GOEDE

INTRODUCTION

In January 2014, at the annual New Year's cabaret of Dutch bank ABN-Amro, former minister of finance and head of the ABN-Amro Board of Directors, Gerrit Zalm, performed a "comic" New Year's sketch dressed as his fictional sister, Priscilla. Priscilla—a broad dame in a shiny blue dress and butterfly glasses—appears to be a former prostitute and current manager of a brothel. Her business, she recounts, is a flourishing company in an age-old business sector, with high profits, a good cost/income ratio, and—unlike the bank—an "excellent" gender balance. "Women on top is not a problem in my business," Priscilla states proudly. Complaining that her bank manager brother has always denied her existence, Priscilla recounts how he has nevertheless sought her business advice on numerous occasions, given the fact that their work in the market in professional services is, after all, to some extent comparable. In fact, Priscilla recounts, the best practices now being implemented across the bank were done so on her advice. Those new, post-crisis best practices include, for example, placing the interests and desires of customers first; only taking known and calculable risks; and taking professional responsibility for a "satisfying outcome" for the client. Placing customer satisfaction first is a century-long practice in her business, Priscilla concludes, and it is high time, in the wake of the financial crisis, that the banking business should follow this example (Willems 2014).

Let's think through Zalm's remarkable and not-quite-funny speech from the perspective of "scandalous economics." Dutch bank ABN-Amro had the ambition to become a world-leading player on the global investment markets before the onset of the 2008 credit crisis, aggressively pushing itself into global derivatives markets, including trade in the mortgage-backed collateralized debt obligations (CDOs) that later took some of the blame for exacerbating the crisis. CDOs are exotic financial products that allow speculators to bet on the direction of price developments of mortgage securities, without actually purchasing the underlying securities, or the under-underlying mortgages. These instruments were increasingly traded at the onset of the 2008 crisis by speculators betting on the default of mortgage securities, and retrospectively came to be seen as having caused, or at least exacerbated, the crisis (FCIC 2011; Lewis 2011). In 2007, ABN-Amro was prey to a takeover from the international banking consortium Fortis/RBS/Santander, which paid a record €71 billion for the bank. Not long after the takeover, however, the bank's balance sheets were shown to be weak, placing the entire banking consortium at risk of failure. One factor in this near-failure was ABN-Amro's participation in a CDO deal issued by Goldman Sachs. In this synthetic CDO deal, called ABACUS, ABN-Amro had assumed the risk of default for a referenced portfolio of mortgage-backed securities. ABACUS, which the *New York Times* calls an "exotic, complex instrument" "virtually unheard of outside of financial circles," would later become the subject of a fraud investigation by the US Securities and Exchange Commission, leading to the first (and so far, the only) conviction of individual liability for fraud in the aftermath of the crisis. In 2013, Goldman Sachs middle-manager Fabrice Tourre was found guilty of having made materially misleading statements when marketing ABACUS to European investors (Thomas 2010; De Goede 2015b). In 2008, ABACUS led to a loss of US$804 million for ABN-Amro and the RBS consortium. ABN-Amro was nationalized in October 2008, as the Dutch government feared for the stability of the entire national financial system.

It is against the background of ABN-Amro's controversial speculations and spectacular rescue that former finance minister Zalm—who enjoys a solid, even sober, reputation in The Netherlands—is pursuing an agenda of restoring the bank's reputation and profits. What are we to make, then, of his sexualized act at the New Year's conference, where he sought to affirm the bank's new business ethics of professionalism, responsibility, and sustainability, by impersonating a madam? Why did he think that such an explicitly gendered act would appeal to employees in the challenging project of restoring the bank's reputation after a crisis that disproportionality affected low-income and single-parent families? In an interesting role reversal of the age-old connection between financial and sexual excess, Zalm's impersonation is remarkable for seeking to restore stability and professionalism through an appeal to the business ethics of professional prostitutes, who supposedly take only "known and calculable risks"— unlike pre-2008 investment banks. But the broader and more important question, perhaps, is how gender and finance are newly interwoven in the political practices of representing financial crisis and in the post-2008 political search for new stabilities. What kind of responses are made more or less likely through the gendered representations of financial crisis and its rescue?

The chapters collected here, in their many diverse ways, show how the financial crisis has gendered roots and impacts, how crisis representations are gendered in novel ways with political consequences, and how particular narratives of contemporary power-feminism obscure enduring inequalities of opportunity and foster neoliberal imaginations of full and flexible market availabilities. If perhaps we once considered representations of financial excess in terms of whoring and female fickleness remnants of past political imaginations (Pocock 1975), we now know that in the current crisis, gender is back—with a vengeance. *Scandalous Economics* details and documents the diverse ways in which gender figures in the crisis and in contemporary economics more generally. Across the political spectrum, from the ABN-Amro chairman's New Year's sketch, to the critically acclaimed documentary *Inside Job*, from the post-crisis box office hit *The Wolf of Wall Street*, to the ABACUS court case, sexualized imaginations and a focus on scandals play a key role (for other compelling examples of gendered visualizations in finance in economy and culture, see Penny Griffin, Chapter 11 in this volume). If there is a new acknowledgment of the "female virtues" of sensibility and stability in some of these examples, like in Zalm's New Year's sketch and the post-crisis praise for Merkel and Lagarde—documented by Adrienne Roberts in Chapter 4 of this volume—these function to limit political response and critical questioning. The contrast between masculine cultures of finance and feminine values of good housekeeping and business ethics acknowledge gender while seeking to maintain the status quo.

In this brief closing chapter, I delve into these examples and ask what is rendered visible and invisible through these particular representations of sex and scandal. What mode of subjectivity is enabled and foreclosed, and what modes of ethics are appealed and denied? I argue that gendered representations of crisis primarily serve to redraw the boundaries between morality and excess, *without* a fundamental rethinking of the use and usefulness of securitizing common household debts and the legitimacy of speculative vehicles. The political project of restoring financial-economic moralities works through an appeal to clearly bound gender roles. Such representations of clear boundaries between societal roles obscure the complex and distributed nature of responsibility for systemic crisis, however. They deny the complex ethical considerations entailed in the daily performativities of finance (Butler 2010; Callon 2010), and entail a limited way of thinking ethically.

SEX, SCANDAL, AND THE NORMAL

The examination of practices of "scandalous economics" is of pressing importance in the context of the current credit crisis. As Brigitte Young, among others, has documented, the securitization of common household debts, including mortgages and credit card bills, has had very specific gender dynamics and gender fallouts (see also Hozić and True, Chapter 1 of this volume). These practices brought mundane household debts within the scope of global commodification and securitization, and depended on particular, cultural work of understanding homes as investment objects (Langley 2007; Young 2009; chapters in this volume). The gender dimensions of these developments have to some extent been paradoxical. If the housing boom expanded credit to low-income and single-parent families, traditionally outside the scope of formal finance, its aftermath has hit these constituencies the hardest. As Melinda Cooper (2015, 280) has put it, "For a brief moment, the private-sector expansion of uninsured money and uninsured credit embraced the nonstandard subjects who had once been summarily excluded from the New Deal social consensus. . . . Not surprisingly, however, the rates of interest it extracted from these nonstandard borrowers were extremely high." When CDOs like ABACUS eventually triggered a perhaps inevitable collapse of this fragile and globally interconnected chain of securitization, it was low-income women and minority households—who had recently been drawn into mortgage markets with "teaser rates" and easy credit checks—who were most at risk of default and eviction (Aitken 2006; Bruff and Wöhl, Chapter 6 of this volume).

Against this background, and in light of the role of ABACUS in the failure of Dutch bank ABN-Amro, it is all the more remarkable that its new chairman seeks to restore its values through a mock-appeal to the professional ethics of prostitution. Taming the lost morality of finance in this example requires not the mastery of financial man, but the madam's business ethics. The significance of sexualized representations of crisis is both how they represent excess and diagnose the aberrant condition, and how they implicitly suggest and discursively enable an appeal to normalities. There is a rich literature at the intersection of cultural studies and political history that has detailed and analyzed the ways in which public discussions and literary representations of eighteenth-century credit structures and early modern crises like the South Sea Bubble centered around sexual metaphors and female allegorical "figures of disorder" (Ingrassia 1998, 24; also Lloyd 1984; Crosthwaite, Knight, and Marsh 2012). Descriptions of credit, Ingrassia (1998, 26) argues, embodied "many associations of negative and stereotypically female qualities [such as] avaricious sexuality, emotional instability [and] hysteria." These representations, moreover, enabled the slow discursive articulation of rational financial man as the one to "tame" fickle credit and render her useful and industrious (see especially, Pocock 1975). In Chapter 2 of this volume, Elisabeth Prügl uses the notion of "myth" to analyze how notions of woman function in financial discourses to "help make sense of something new and unknown." Writes Prügl: "Myth always has an intention, a motivation. It produces an alibi that hides the historicity of things, fixes human beings in their places. . . ." Sexualized representations of credit and crisis, while having roots in eighteenth-century political discourses, are still at the heart of the way we understand finance today. The gendered representation of financial crises as instances of madness, delusion, hysteria, and irrationality—as moments where rational financial man has lost sense of himself—has a particular historical durability. As I have argued elsewhere, such representations simultaneously construct the sphere of financial normality or rationality (de Goede 2005, especially chapter 2).

These normalities, by definition, are posited retrospectively. Only in looking back on the spiral of financial innovation and the invention of increasingly complex—and costly—ways of speculating on the performance of residential mortgage loans, can we identify a line that was crossed, or a sense of ethical behavior that was damaged. As Janet Roitman (n.d.) has put it, "Crisis, as an historical concept, refers to the retrospective effects of events and to their constitutive presuppositions." Representations of bodily excess, all too often, enable such post-crisis representations of boundaries crossed. The constitutive presuppositions of crisis discourse include the existence of clearly demarcated worlds of regular and regulated financial trading that is virtuous and industrious. In truth, it is important to realize that such worlds have rarely existed in financial history, which has always struggled with articulating the legitimate boundaries of financial trading and containing the so-called "animal spirits" of speculation (Tellmann 2013). Financial speculation and innovation always operate at the limits of law, pushing the boundaries of what is understood to be regular and regulated in a relentless drive for profit opportunities. In the context of the present crisis, this means that pronouncements on the legitimacy of speculative vehicles such as mortgage-backed CDOs (like ABACUS), which operated at the limits of law and allowed speculators to take large bets on the imminent decline of housing markets, are drawn only in retrospect (Langley 2014). Importantly, such boundaries rely on political-moral arguments, rather than purely juridical ones—and it is precisely in this moral dimension that appeals to gender play an important role (Alessandrini 2011).

In the rich though troubling political tradition of signifying financial crisis through sexual excess, the recent credit crisis offers some remarkable new examples. Consider the 2013 film *The Wolf of Wall Street*, directed by Martin Scorsese. Based on Jordan Belfort's narrative account, the film recounts Belfort's rise and fall as financial investment manager and large-scale speculator—moving from the penny stock business, to owning a major and respectable-looking Wall Street firm (called Stratton Oakmont), to being convicted and sentenced for securities fraud. The film's depictions of sexual excess and drug abuse have been much commented on: aggressive sales tactics are celebrated, office parties involve free hookers for all, and the main protagonist boasts about taking enough drugs "to sedate the majority of New York's population." To some viewers, the film offers a realistic though glamorized insight into the world of 1990s Wall Street speculation, a sexualized trading room culture, and widespread, normalized drug abuse (as discussed, for example, in Leyshon and Thrift 1997; McDowell 1997).

However, viewed from its post-crisis 2013 release date, there are other significant aspects of the film that exceed the question of whether it more or less accurately represents the 1990s trading room culture. The film's depiction of sexual transgression go hand in hand with powerful narrations of clear and deliberate transgressions of the boundary between normal trading and fraudulent excess; between regular speculation and deliberate client scamming. In several scenes in the film, the Belfort character speaks directly into the camera to explain how his fraudulent schemes worked. The scenes do not last long, and quickly trail off to merge back into the more spectacular scenes of office partying and drug abuse. For example, about halfway through the film, Belfort explains directly into the camera what an initial public offering (IPO) is, and how his company defrauded investors by secretly channeling shares to befriended buyers at a set price when Stratton Oakmont was involved in an IPO. But then the Belfort character says, "Look, I know you're not following what I'm saying, right? That's OK. The real question is this: 'was all this legal?' Absolutely f** not. But we were making more money than we knew what to do with." Scenes like these are important, because they convey the message that Belfort knew what he was doing, and that the fraud was both intentional and clear-cut.

Belfort's direct narrations into the camera explaining his fraudulent schemes are key to the film and constitutive of its political message. In this film, financial transgression and sexual transgression go hand in hand, implicitly depicting an era in which the boundaries between normal trading and fraud were clearly drawn. Because Belfort repeatedly but *knowingly* transgresses the boundaries of legitimate trading, the film encourages nostalgia for a mythical era in which lines between fraud and excess were firm and clear. In this reading, the film's success in the midst of the 2008 credit crisis appeals to viewers' longing for mundane, industrious, normalities. Today, the complexity of instruments such as derivatives means that the boundary of legitimate trading and "true" valuation have become barely recognizable. As Randy Martin (2013, 90) has described the social logic of the derivative, "price is contested at every moment of its articulation. Derivatives stand as an enhanced medium of this open and ceaseless contestation." *Contra* the ceaseless contestation of value in the derivative logic, post-crisis re-anchoring of value proceeds through social and moral ordering, rather than through a purely calculative one (see also Tepe-Belfrage and Montgomerie, Chapter 5 of this volume). At the same time, by suggesting that Belfort's frauds were both intentional and outrageous, it offers a simple morality in which the lines between legitimate and illegitimate behavior are clearly knowable, if not always respected. A return to moral ordering is rendered a logical post-crisis response. Rather than a fundamental rethinking of the societal value of financial instruments such as CDOs, or signaling the need for thorough economic restructuring, the political message of *the Wolf of Wall Street* is one that seeks to subjugate individual fraud and excess.

However, the current crisis involves diffuse complexities that are not reducible to simple fraud, but that are closely interrelated with contested historical ideological developments, underlying culturally specific notions of homeownership, contingent financial product development, and the important role of ever-faster technological financial trading (e.g., Langley 2008, 2014; Lenglet 2011). Within this modulating complex, the lines between legitimate financial product innovation and simple customer fraud are extremely difficult to draw in the aftermath of crisis—both politically and judicially. The seeming simplicities of Belfort's scams lure the viewer into an easy politics of blame and rescue (see also de Goede 2015a). As one critic of the film concluded, usually "Wall Street's sins are more subtle. . . . [T]he selling of a synthetic collateralized debt obligation is nearly impossible to convey on screen" (Nocera 2013, 1). According to this journalist, *The Wolf of Wall Street* cannot readily be read as a post-crisis Wall Street critique, because Belfort's firm Stratton Oakmont was a small fish compared to the big, traditional Wall Street firms. "For all the considerable pain Stratton Oakmont inflicted on its investors," Nocera (2013) writes, "it doesn't even begin to approach the kind of pain the real Wall Street can inflict. Firms like Stratton Oakmont don't bring the financial system to the precipice. They can't cause a global recession." It is telling that the biggest post-crisis Wall Street firm steers away from visualizing the thorny questions concerning the legitimacy of speculation, and instead focuses on a case of mid-level fraud.

It is not just the glamorous and popular *Wolf of Wall Street*, however, that comprehends and politicizes the current crisis through the imagery and sensationalism of sexual transgression. Curiously, the Oscar-winning documentary *Inside Job*, which overall provides an intelligent critique of the crisis and the complex "chain of securitization" underpinning it, also comprises a long scene in which the sexual excess of Wall Street speculators is discussed. This part of the film documents Wall Street's intimate ties with prostitution networks, interviews "madam" Kristin Davis, who claims to have catered to the highest levels of investment bank professionals, and suggests the pervasiveness of charging visits to strip clubs to corporate accounts. The film suggests the inherently "perverse" mind of financial traders, prone to excessive risk-taking and cocaine abuse, lodged in the structures of their brains and demonstrable in MRI scans. Though I am not contesting the existence of such practices on Wall Street—as in some other societal sectors—these easy gestures toward sex and scandal do little to render insightful the complex gender dynamics of Wall Street and the politics of global securitization (McDowell 1997; Fisher 2012). At the same time, they deflect the viewers' concern away from larger questions of the legitimacy of speculation, suggesting instead that Wall Street cultures of excess and expense accounts are the problem. If anything, this part of the film exposes the conservative imagination of current capitalist critique, which articulates moral outrage through sexual transgression, and implicitly seeks to re-anchor itself in a template of traditional family values (Cooper 2015; Tepe-Belfrage and Montgomerie, Chapter 5 of this volume; Smith, Chapter 13 of this volume).

There are numerous examples, then, that illustrate that historically durable equation of financial crisis and sexual excess. I have argued that such cultural strategies and (metaphorical) parallels work politically to suggest that it is possible to easily and firmly draw boundaries between norm and excess, between legitimacy and fraud, between public and private. Lost.

moralities are represented in terms of sexual transgressions, and appeals to re-regulation and re-normalization of financial sectors imply the restoration of moral, gendered orders.

DISTRIBUTED RESPONSIBILITY

In contrast to such understandings of clear lines between good and bad, morality and immorality, normality and fraud, financial practice usually entails more complex distributions of responsibility and inequity, in which it is not easy to draw a line between the permissible and fraud or immorality. In order to start considering such complexities, one journalist's investigation into the life of one of the mortgage bonds that was caught up in the ABACUS securitization is illustrative (Eavis 2013). This bond, called GSAMP Trust 2007-NC1, collected a series of individual residential mortgages issued by sub-prime mortgage lenders, to be repackaged and sold as highly rated investments for (international) institutional investors. In this bond, the mortgages were sold by a firm called New Century and were issued to individual low-income house buyers, including, for example, a woman named Wendy Fillmore and her husband, who bought a home in Las Vegas in 2006. Less than six years later, the house is valued at about half of the mortgage value, leaving the Fillmores with considerable debt on paper and unable to move. Peter Eavis's (2013) investigation of GSAMP Trust 2007-NC1 is interesting not just because it renders visible the real pain and human impact of the crisis fallout, but also because it offers a view of the distant connections and distributed responsibilities of mortgage securitization. This view moves away from post-crisis politics that blames marginal financial subjects for knowingly taking on unmanageable debts (Aitken 2006), and offers a more complex image in which (un)ethical decisions were made at each link in the chain of securitization, which ties the Fillmore's mortgage to European pension holders. The complex chain of securitization of GSAMP Trust 2007-NC1 connects low-income Las Vegas residents, through sub-prime mortgage lenders like New Century, with major Wall Street trading firms like Goldman Sachs, which securitized loans and marketed them to traditional European investment banks (increasingly eager to speculate on the performances of US mortgages), to Dutch and German pension holders.

Surely, Wall Street greed and the relentless capitalist drive to stretch the boundaries of the judicially permissible in a search for profits should be recognized and critiqued. But cutting through sensationalist depictions of Wall Street sex and scandal is important in order to foster a more complex picture of political responsibility. The focus on sexual excess and deviant Wall Street cultures can work as a strategy of obfuscation that deflects attention away from larger systemic questions (Hozić and True, Chapter 1 of this volume). Jane Bennett offers the notion of distributed responsibility to conceptualize politics in the face of complex and distributed system. Such a notion, she writes, "does attenuate the blame game, but it does not thereby abandon the project of identifying . . . the sources of harmful effects. To the contrary, such a notion broadens the range of places to look for sources" (Bennett 2010, 37). Drawing firm boundaries around gender identities through sensationalist depictions of transgressions, as both *The Wolf of Wall Street* and *Inside Job* ultimately do, underplays the complexity of the "long term strings of events" that Bennett (2010, 37) seeks to uncover and include in the work of accountability.

CRITIQUE BEYOND REFOUNDATION

As Cooper (2015) has shown, speculative critiques tend to display foundational tendencies in contrast to the fluctuating logic of the derivative and the supposedly anti-foundational tendencies of global capital. Speculative critique habitually seeks to re-anchor value in preexisting notions of land or labor (e.g., Ott 2011). Cooper writes, "moments of social democratic consensus such as that achieved during the New Deal always come at the price of new lines of exclusion and new inscriptions of social value—divisions of labor and welfare that invariably anchor value in the proper reproduction of sex and race (i.e., in the proper form of the family)" (2015, 31). It is in this context that the nexus between financial crisis, sexual excess, and scandal is most politically significant: it displays a pervading nostalgia for clearly ordered worlds. In a moment of crisis, it seems that values have to be re-anchored not purely in economic or juridical terms, but in their appeal to society's moral orders.

In contrast to the re-foundational tendencies of historical challenges to speculation, Cooper (2015) poses the question of how to "think a truly ambitious anticapitalist critique" (see also Vrasti, Chapter 14 of this volume). *Scandalous Economics* offers a multiplicity of answers and very diverse starting points to these questions. For example, Adrienne Roberts in Chapter 4 challenges what she calls the "instrumentalist" deployment of gender equality agendas, and seeks to articulate "feminist criteria" on which alternatives to capitalism and agendas of anti-capitalism may build, including notions of inclusiveness, transparency, and effectiveness (drawn from Prügl and True 2014). A different strategy of critique was formulated by Gibson-Graham in *The End of Capitalism* (1996), where they plead for the exploration of "disharmony"—or the multiple ways in which economic practice already comprises a "rich diversity of capitalist and noncapitalist activities," which need to be rendered visible (1996, vii, xi).

I suggest that it is helpful in this context to reconsider Judith Butler's formulations of ethics and agency, understood as the "force of citationality" (1990, 220). Butler's formulations point in a political direction that is quite different from the formulation of clear professional standards and benchmarks. For Butler, ethics are located at the site of citationality: the site where the daily order is reproduced, and where the (financial) professionals—subjected in their role—have the power to challenge or jam or reorient their professional practice. For Butler, political agency does not preexist its emergence through discursive structure: citationality is both the condition of the emergence of agency, and the practice through which a force of agency can assert itself. "Agency is in the hiatus of iterability, the compulsion to install an identity through repetition, which requires the very contingency, the undetermined interval, that identity seeks to foreclose" (Butler 1990, 220). Rather than articulating clearly defined gender identities, for Butler, the politics of gender is in the unpredictable "interval" between norm and its continuous but contingent repetition in practice. As Butler (2010, 155) has put it in a more recent article that engages directly with the way in which her work has been appropriated within political economy: it is possible to imagine a subject who reroutes her daily practice to make a claim that breaks with existing "loyalty and power": "such a subject breaks out of the established framework within which public politics proceeds, facilitating a certain crisis in the framework, posing anew the question of what can and cannot intelligibly take place within that framework." In this manner, Butler (2010, 149) draws attention to the multiple "seams and fissures" of economy and finance, and seeks to use these as anchor points of critique.

Butler's formulations seem very abstract, but we might think through them to consider some practical examples of contingent but forceful assertions of agency within what journalist Michael Lewis has called "the CDO machine." Karen Ho (2009) has documented the repetitive, homosocial processes of subjectification that financial professionals undergo: including particular schooling, training, late-night work cultures, and near-impossible demands of speediness and precision. Breaking out of such cultures and challenging them from within requires risky performances that break with the norm. We might think of the work of industry whistle-blowers as a form of challenge that pivots on the resistance of tight subjectifications, and that seeks to reiterate and reformulate the boundaries of normal practice. Whistle-blowers do not become outcasts overnight: normally, they have a longer history of challenging their professional practices internally, articulating to their bosses the problematic ethical implications of particular (valuation) practices, and attempting to redirect the professional assemblage in which they are taking part. Researcher Kate Kenny, in a recent investigation on whistle-blowers in *The Guardian*, says she was "surprised by the amount of work that goes into being a whistle blower ... [such as] the constant reading of documents, rebutting of arguments, exposing of lies and learning about the law" (quoted in Smith 2014, 41; cf. Kenny 2010). Here, there is a slow challenge to and reiteration of norms that precedes the full-blown exclusion of the whistle-blower as outcast.

Slowly, and in the context of ongoing investigations, we now learn that at least some individuals participating in the CDO machine repeatedly voiced critique and questions over the ways in which mortgages were approved, bundled, and securitized. The Financial Crisis Inquiry Report (FCIC 2011) documents the case of Richard Bowen, business chief underwriter at Citigroup, who repeatedly voiced his worry to his superiors that the loans being pooled into securitized products did not meet internal guidelines and quality standards. In 2006, Bowen sent an email to the bank's executives with the heading "URGENT—READ IMMEDIATELY" to voice his concerns. The bank management did not respond, but Bowen was downgraded in his performance review and in his bonus (FCIC 2011, 19). Another example is that of Alanye Fleischmann, former securities lawyer at Chase bank, who during 2006 started raising concerns with her superiors about the quality of the loans that were being approved for securitization—which she considered to be "the bottom of the mortgage barrel" (Taibbi 2014). After having voiced these concerns internally numerous times to no avail, in early 2007 Fleischmann wrote a memo to one of Chase's managing directors, documenting the problems in the securitization process, which she believed amounted to securities fraud. As Fleischmann put it to the *Rolling Stone* journalist who has recently revealed her story: "It used to be if you wrote a memo, they had to stop, because now there's proof that they knew what they were doing" (quoted in Taibbi 2014). Less than two years after writing the memo, Fleischmann was quietly laid off. Though she has spoken to the US Securities and Exchange Commission and the Department of Justice on numerous occasions, she feels that, to date, little has been done with the information she has provided. As a final example, we can consider the insider challenge that came from a due diligence firm called Clayton, which worked to examine and rate the mortgage loans that went into processes of securitization. During 2006 and 2007, Clayton began to reject substantial percentages of loans for this purpose, because the loans were of poor quality and documentation concerning income and the long-term ability to repay was insufficiently convincing. However, of the 28 percent of loans judged to be of poor quality and unfit for securitization, nearly 40 percent were waived in for securitization by the banks (FCIC 2011, 166–167). Put simply, in their drive to maximize profit and create securitized products to sell globally, investment banks ignored and sometimes bluntly shut out the critical voices within who were signaling problems with the processes. The "scandalous economics" at work in the relentless drive to securitization are exposed through the warnings and recollections of critical voices on the inside.

The examples of insider challenges and whistle-blowers are different from articulating anti-capitalist projects and standards. But these examples do show how financial subjects can play a role in challenging and possibly rerouting the daily practices through which their own subjectivity emerges. Here, individuals are challenging their particular subjectifications and are attempting to enact ethics in their mundane professional practice. Thus, they illustrate a notion of ethics that a sense of complexity and distributed responsibility engenders. As Bennett has put it, "perhaps the ethical responsibility of an individual human now resides in one's response to the assemblages in which one finds oneself participating: Do I attempt to extricate myself from assemblages whose trajectory is likely to do harm?" (2010, 37). Some financial participants, including Bowen, for example, attempted to extricate himself and reorient the assemblages he found himself participating in—even if the value of that attempt is being recognized only years later. In this reading, a performative ethics is about a continuous reflection on and challenge to the daily iterative practices in which we all participate. It is about recognizing and exploiting the interval that routine citationality affords.

CONCLUDING

Scandalous Economics is a book about gender and the financial crisis—showing the multiple interrelations between financial practices and gendered effects; the unequal inclusion of women in contemporary economic hierarchies; the troubling interrelations between masculine power abuse and the lack of credibility given to (female) migrant narratives (as in the "DSK Affair"); and the many enduring cultural representations that equate financial crisis with sexual excess, and that seek to re-anchor normality in traditional gender divisions. But Scandalous Economics does more than focus on gender as a problem of power and equality. It shows the limited nature of the responses to crisis that have been enabled on the basis of these gendered discourses, as, for example, in the case of the EU "troika" handling of the Greek crisis, in which, as Anna Agathangelou shows in Chapter 12 of this volume, the Greeks were feminized and victimized, while being forced to accept a set of austerity measures through a process that in no way can be considered democratic (also Bruff and Wöhl, Chapter 6 of this volume). In other words, the importance of this volume is not only in the work it does on gender and economics—work that proves itself to have acute importance in the wake of the current crisis—but also in the way it analyzes limited and impoverished policy responses to the financial crisis. As illustrated by Zalm's New Year's sketch impersonating a madam, the post-crisis politics of restoring gendered moral orders is directly related to a limited ethical repertoire. Retreating behind entrenched gendered boundaries is a sign of the limited imagination with which contemporary politics and business have dealt with the crisis fallout.

BIBLIOGRAPHY

Ackerly, Brooke, Maria Stern, and Jacqui True (eds.). 2006. *Feminist Methodologies for International Relations*. Cambridge: Cambridge University Press.

Adams, Renee B., and Daniel Ferreira. 2009. "Women in the Boardroom and Their Impact on Governance and Performance." *Journal of Financial Economics* 94, no. 2 (November): 291–320.

Adams, Tim. 2011. "The Testosterone Trap." *The Australian Magazine*, September 24.

Adbusters. 2011. "On September 17th Take Out the Trash." September 25. https://www.adbusters.org/content/september-17th-take-out-trash.

Adepoju, Aderanti. 2005. "Migration in West Africa." A paper prepared for the Policy Analysis and Research Programme of the Global Commission of International Migration.

Adichie, Chimamanda. 2012. "This Year's Biggest 'He Said, She Said': The Rape Case against DSK Was Tossed—But Would a Jury Have Believed Him or the Victim." *Newsweek*, January 2.

Adler, Roy P., and Ron Conlin. 2009. "Profit, Thy Name Is . . . Woman? The Consistent Correlation between Women Executives and High Profitability." *Miller-McCune*, February 27.

Agathangelou, Anna. 2004. *The Global Political Economy of Sex: Desire, Violence, and Insecurity in Mediterranean Nation States*. London: Palgrave Macmillan.

Agathangelou, Anna M. 2009. "Necro-(neo)Colonizations and Economies of Blackness: Of Slaughters, 'Accidents', 'Disasters' and Captive Flesh." In *International Relations and States of Exception: Margins, Peripheries and Excluded Bodies*, eds. Sheila Nair and Shampa Biswas, pp. 186–209. New York: Routledge.

Agathangelou, Anna M. 2011. "Bodies to the Slaughter: Global Racial Reconstructions, Fanon's Combat Breath, and Wrestling for Life." *Somatechnics Journal* 1, no. 1: 209–248.

Agathangelou, Anna M. 2012. "The Living and Being of the Streets: Fanon and the Arab Uprisings." *Globalizations* 9, no. 3: 451–466.

Agathangelou, Anna M. 2013. "Neoliberal Geopolitical Order and Value: Queerness as a Speculative Economy and Anti-Blackness as Terror." *International Journal of Feminist Politics* 15, no. 4: 453–476.

Agathangelou, Anna M. 2014. "Wither Anarchy? Harvesting the 'Global' Bio-tech Body, Indian Markets and Biomedical Technologies." In *The Global Politics of Science and Technology*, Vol. 2, *Global Power Shift*, eds. M. Mayer et al., pp. 1–23. Berlin; Heidelberg: Springer-Verlag.

Agathangelou, Anna M., and L. H. M. Ling. 2009. *Transforming World Politics: From Empire to Multiple Worlds*. New York; London: Routledge.

Agence France-Presse. 2012. "Women Could Save Japan's Economy: IMF's Lagarde." *Raw Story*, October 13. http://www.rawstory.com/rs/2012/10/13/women-could-save-japans-economy-imfs-lagarde/.

Agriantoni, C. 1986. *The Beginnings of Industrialization in 19th Century Greece*. Athens: Commerical Bank of Greece [in Greek].

Ahamed, Liaquat. 2009. *Lords of Finance: The Bankers Who Broke the World*. New York: Penguin.

Aitken, Rob. 2006. "Capital at its Fringes." *New Political Economy* 11, no. 4: 479–498.

Alessandrini, Donatella. 2011. "Regulating Financial Derivatives? Risks, Contested Values, and Uncertain Futures." *Social & Legal Studies* 20, no. 4: 441–462.

Aljazeera. 2010. "Max Keiser on the Greek Debt Crisis." February 2. https://www.youtube.com/watch?v=0p0lRXm9Qsk.

Allen, Katie. 2009. "Could Crash Spell Doom For City's Boys' Club? Years of Macho Culture Ended in Financial Implosion. Now MPs Are to Examine Sexism in the Square Mile, but Is It Ready to Change?" *The Observer*, July 26.

Allen, Katie. 2014. "Austerity in Greece Caused More Than 500 Male Suicides, Say Researchers." *The Guardian*, April 21.

Amin, Samir. 2011. "Audacity, More Audacity." *The Bullet: Socialist Project* no. 577. December 6. http://www.socialistproject.ca/bullet/577.php.

Anaximenes of Miletus. ca. 585–525 B.C. http://www.drury.edu/ess/History/Ancient/anaximenes.html.

Anderson, Bridget. 1997. "Servants and Slaves: European Domestic Workers." *Race & Class* 39: 37–49.

Anderson, Bridget. 2000. *Doing the Dirty Work? The Global Politics of Domestic Labour*. London; New York: Zed Books.

Andreades, A. 1925. *Lectures on Public Finances: National Loans and Greek Public Economics, Part I and II*. Athens: Library of Historical Studies.

Antonakis, Nicholas. 1997. "Military Expenditure and Economic Growth in Greece, 1960–90." *Journal of Peace Research* 34, no. 1: 89–100.

Antonopoulos, Rania. 2009a. *The Current Economic and Financial Crisis: A Gender Perspective*. The Levy Economics Institute of Bard College, Working Paper No. 562 (May).

Antonopoulos, Rania. 2009b. *The Unpaid Care Work—Paid Work Connection*. Policy Integration and Statistics Department Working Paper No. 86. International Labour Office, Geneva.

Arango, Tim, and Richard Pérez-Peña. 2009. "Murdoch's Soft Spot for Print Slows News Corp." *New York Times*, February 22. http://www.nytimes.com/2009/02/23/business/media/23paper.html?pagewanted=all.

Arendt, Hannah. 1998 [1958]. *The Human Condition*. 2nd ed. Chicago: University of Chicago Press.

Arthur, John. 2009. *African Women Immigrants in the United States*. New York: Palgrave Macmillan.

Ashcraft, Richard. 1996. "Lockean Ideas, Poverty and the Development of Liberal Political Theory." In *Early Modern Conceptions of Property*, eds. John Brewer and Susan Staves, pp. 43–61. London: Routledge.

Aslanbeigui, Nahid, and Gale Summerfield. 2000. "The Asian Crisis, Gender and the International Financial Architecture." *Feminist Economics* 6, no. 3: 81–103.

Assassi, Libby. 2009. *The Gendering of Global Finance*. London: Palgrave Macmillan.

Associated Press. 2012. "DA Speaks on Why He Dropped NYC Strauss-Kahn Case." January 18.

Athanasiou, Athena. 2011. "Becoming Precarious through Regimes of Gender, Capital, and Nation." *Cultural Anthropology Online*, October 28. http://www.culanth.org/field-sights/250-becoming-precarious-through-regimes-of-gender-capital-and-nation.

Athanassiou, Ersi. 2009. "Fiscal Policy and the Recession: The Case of Greece." *Intereconomics* 44, no. 6: 364–372.

Atlantic, The. 2011. "The Signs and Slogans of Occupy Wall Street." October 11. http://www.theatlantic.com/video/index/246518/the-signs-and-slogans-of-occupy-wall-street/.

Austin, Regina. 2004. "Of Predatory Lending and the Democratization of Credit: Preserving the Social Safety Net of Informality in Small-Loan Transactions." *American University Law Review* 53, no. 6: 1217–1257.

Baden, Sally. 2013. "Women's Collective Action in African Agricultrual Markets: The Limits of Current Development Practice for Rural Women's Empowerment." *Gender & Development* 21, no. 2: 295–311.

Bagati, Deepali, and Nancy M. Carter. 2010. "Leadership Gap in India Inc.: Myths and Realities." http://www.catalyst.org/knowledge/leadership-gap-india-inc-myths-and-realities.

BagNews. 2007. "Your Turn: Good Time for a Squeeze." August 8. http://www.bagnewsnotes.com/2007/08/your-turn-good-TIME-for-a-squeeze/.

Bair, Sheila. 2012. *Bull by the Horns: Fighting to Save Main Street from Wall Street and Wall Street from Itself.* New York: Simon & Schuster.

Bakker, Isabella. 2003. "Neoliberal Governance and the Reprivatization of Social Reproduction." In *Power, Production and Social Reproduction*, eds. Isabella Bakker and Stephen Gill, pp. 66–82. New York: Palgrave Macmillan.

Bakker, Isabella. 2007. "Social Reproduction and the Constitution of a Gendered Political Economy." *New Political Economy* 12, no. 4: 541–556.

Bakker, Isabella, and Stephen Gill. 2003. "Global Political Economy and Social Reproduction." In *Power, Production and Social Reproduction*, eds. Isabella Bakker and Stephen Gill, pp. 3–16. Basingstoke; New York: Palgrave Macmillan.

Bakker, Isabella, and Stephen Gill (eds.). 2003. *Power, Production and Social Reproduction.* Basingstoke: Palgrave Macmillan.

Bakker, Isabella, and Rachel Silvey. 2008. "Introduction: Social Reproduction and Global Transformations—From the Everyday to the Global." In *Beyond States and Markets: The Challenges of Social Reproduction*, eds. Isabella Bakker and Rachel Silvey, pp. 1–16. London: Routledge.

Balibar, Etienne. 2010. "Europe Is a Dead Political Project." *The Guardian*, May 25. http://www.guardian.co.uk/commentisfree/2010/may/25/eu-crisis-catastrophic-consequences.

Ballinas, Víctor. 2013. "Continúan los *feminicidios* en Ciudad Juárez." *La Jornada*, March 11. http://www.jornada.unam.mx/2013/03/11/politica/018n1pol.

Ballve, Teo. 2011. "Women Take Reins of Power in Latin America, but not in U.S." *The Progressive*, January 16. http://www.teoballve.com/article/women-take-reins-of-power-in-latin-america-but-not-in-us/.

Banerjee, S. B. 2008. "Live and Let Die: Colonial Sovereignties and the Death Worlds of Necrocapitalism." *Reartikulacija* 3. http://www.reartikulacija.org/?p=259.

Bansak, Cynthia. A., Mary E. Graham, and Alan A. Zebedee. 2011. "The Effects of Gender Composition of Senior Management on the Economic Fallout." *Applied Economics Letters* 18, no. 16: 1603–1607.

Barber, Brad M., and Terrance Odean. 2001. "Boys Will be Boys: Gender, Overconfidence, and Common Stock Investment." *The Quarterly Journal of Economics* 116, no. 1 (February): 261–292.

Bárcena, Alicia, and Sonia Montaño, Paulina Pavez, Corina Rodríguez, and Alejandra Valdez. 2013. "Los bonos en la mira: aporte y carga para las mujeres." *Observatorio de Igualdad de Género de América Latina y el Caribe. Informe Anual 2012.* Santiago de Chile: Naciones Unidas.

Barker, Drucilla K. 2012. "Querying the Paradox of Caring Labor." *Rethinking Marxism* 24, no. 4: 574–591.

Barnard, Anne, Adam Nossiter, and Kirk Semple. 2011. "From African Village to Center of Ordeal." *New York Times*, June 14.

Barnard, Helen, and Claire Turner. 2011. *Poverty and Ethnicity: A Review of Evidence.* York: Joseph Rowntree Foundation.

Barrett, Paul M. 2013. "Blythe Masters, JPMorgan's Credit Derivatives Guru, Is Not Sorry." *Bloomberg Business,* September 12.

Barry, Ursula, and Pauline Conroy. 2014. "Ireland in Crisis. Women, Austerity and Inequality." In *Women and Austerity: The Economic Crisis and the Future for Gender Equality,* eds. Maria Karamessini and Jill Rubery, pp. 186–206. London: Routledge.

Barthes, Roland. 1957. Le mythe, aujourd'hui. In *Mythologies.* N.p.: Éditions du Seuil, pp. 193–247.

Bartzokas, A. 1992. "The Developing Arms Industries in Greece, Portugal and Turkey." In *Restructuring of Arms Production in Western Europe,* eds. M. Brzoska and P. Lock, pp. 166–177. New York: Oxford University Press.

Barua, Abhijit, Lewis F. Davidson, Dasaratha V. Rama, and Sheela Thiruvadi. 2010. "CFO Gender and Accruals Quality." *Accounting Horizons* 24, no. 1 (March): 25–39.

Basch, Linda. 2009. "More Women in Finance, a More Sustainable Economy." *Christian Science Monitor*, June 24.

BBC. 2014. "Osborne Says £25bn More Cuts Needed." *BBC* sec. Politics, January 6. http://www.bbc.co.uk/news/uk-politics-25617844.

Becker, Gary. 1957. *The Economics of Discrimination.* Chicago: University Press.

Beckmann, Daniela, and Lukas Menkhoff. 2008. "Will Women Be Women? Analyzing the Gender Differences among Financial Experts." *Kyklos* 61, no. 3: 364–384.

Bedford, Kate, and Shirin M. Rai. 2010. "Feminists Theorize International Political Economy." *Signs: Journal of Women in Culture and Society* 36, no. 1: 1–18.

Bedford, Kate, and Shirin M. Rai. 2013. "Feminists Theorize International Political Economy." *E-international Relations,* March 30. http://www.e-ir.info/2013/03/30/feminists-theorize-international-political-economy/.

Beirut, Michael. 2012. "The Poster That Launched a Movement (Or Not)." April 30. http://designobserver.com/feature/the-poster-that-launched-a-movement-or-not/32588/.

Belfield, Chris, Jonathan Cribb, Andrew Hood, and Robert Joyce. 2014. *Living Standards, Poverty and Inequality in the UK: 2014.* IFS Reports (R96). London: Institute for Fiscal Studies. doi: 10.1920/re.ifs.2014.0096.

Bélanger, Danièle, and Linh Trang Giang. 2013. "Precarity, Gender and Work: Vietnamese Migrant Workers in Asia." *Diversities* 15, no. 1: 5–20.

Bello, Walden. 1998. "Back to the Third World? The Asian Financial Crisis Enters Its Second Year." *Focus on the Global South,* July 23. http://focusweb.org/node/198.

Bellotti, Magui. 2002. "17 Encuentro Nacional de Mujeres: Lo personal es político." *Brujas* 21, no. 29: 42–55.

Benería, Lourdes. 1992. "The Mexican Debt Crisis: Restructuring the Economy and the Household." In *Unequal Burden: Economic Crises, Persistent Poverty and Women's*

Work, eds. Lourdes Benería and Shelley Feldmann, pp. 83–104. Boulder, CO: Westview Press.

Benería, Lourdes. 1999. "Globalization, Gender and the Davos Man." *Feminist Economics* 5, no. 3: 61–83.

Benería, Lourdes. 2003a. *Gender, Development and Globalization*. London: Routledge.

Benería, Lourdes. 2003b. "Economic Rationality and Globalization: A Feminist Perspective." In *Feminist Economics Today: Beyond Economic Man*, eds. Marianne A. Ferber and Julie A. Nelson, pp. 115–133. Chicago: University of Chicago Press.

Benería, Lourdes, and Shelly Feldman. 1992. *Unequal Burden: Economic Crisis, Persistent Poverty and Women's Work*. Boulder, CO: Westview Press.

Benitez, Milva, and Josefina López MacKenzie. 2011. "Las niñas desaparecen como gallinas." *plazademayo.com*, December 22. http://www.plazademayo.com/2011/12/las-ninas-desaparecen-como-gallinas/.

Bennett, Catherine. 2009. "Comment: So you think women would have saved us. Think again: We are told that what the world needs is more females at the top. So, I give you Hazel, Tessa, Harriet . . ." *The Observer*, February 22.

Bennett, Jane. 2010. *Vibrant Matter: A Political Ecology of Things*. Durham, NC: Duke University Press.

Berardi, "Bifo" Franco. 2012. *The Uprising: On Poetry and Finance*. Los Angeles, CA: Semiotext(e).

Berardi, "Bifo" Franco, and Geert Lovink. 2011. "A Call to the Army of Love and to the Army of Software." *Revolution by the Book: The AK Press Blog*, October 12. http://www.revolutionbythebook.akpress.org/on-occupy-franco-bifo-berardi-and-geert-lovink/.

Berger, John. 1979. *Pig Earth*. New York: Vintage Books.

Bergeron, Suzanne. 2004. "The Post Washington Consensus and Economic Representations of Women in Development at The World Bank." *International Feminist Journal of Politics* 5, no. 3: 397–419.

Bergeron, Suzanne, and Jyoti Puri. 2012. "Sexuality between State and Class: An Introduction." *Rethinking Marxism* 24, no. 4: 491–498.

Berlant, Lauren. 2007. "Slow Death (Sovereignty, Obesity, Lateral Agency)." *Critical Inquiry* 33 (4): 754–780.

Berlant, Lauren, and Michael Warner. 2000. "Sex in Public." *Intimacy* (A Critical Inquiry Book), ed. Laurent Berlant. Chicago: University of Chicago Press.

Bernanke, Ben S. 2015. *The Courage to Act: A Memoir of a Crisis and Its Aftermath*. New York: W. W. Norton.

Bernat, Francis P. and Tatyana Zhilina. 2010. "Human Trafficking: The Local Becomes the Global." *Women and Criminal Justice* 20, no. 1–2: 2–9.

Bernstein, Jared. 2014. "Inflation Erodes Assets: That's Why Some People Fear It." *On the Economy: Jared Bernstein's Blog*, August 22. http://jaredbernsteinblog.com/inflation-erodes-assets-thats-why-some-people-fear-it/.

Best, Jacqueline. 2010. "The Limits of Financial Risk Management: Or What We Didn't Learn from the Asian Financial Crisis." *New Political Economy* 15, no. 1: 29–50.

Best, Jacqueline, and Matthew Paterson (eds.). 2010. *Cultural Political Economy*. London; New York: Routledge.

Bexell, Magdalena. 2012. "Global Governance Gains and Gender: UN-Business Partnerships for Women's Empowerment." *International Feminist Journal of Politics* 14, no. 3: 389–407.

Bezanson, Kate, and Meg Luxton (eds.). 2006. *Social Reproduction: Feminist Political Economy Challenges Neo-Liberalism*. Montreal; Kingston: McGill-Queen's University Press.

Bieling, Hans-Jürgen. 2012. "European Governance: On the Relationship between Democratic and Non-democratic Deliberation within the European Multi-level System." *World Political Science Review* 8, no. 1: 201–216.

Binnie, Jon. 2004. *The Globalization of Sexuality*. London: SAGE.

Blackburn, Robin. 2006. "Finance and the Fourth Dimension." *New Left Review* 39 (May/June): 39–70.

Blackburn, Robin. 2008. "The Subprime Crisis." *New Left Review* 50 (March/April): 63–105.

Bleiker, Roland. 2001. "The Aesthetic Turn in International Political Theory." *Millennium: Journal of International Studies* 30, no. 2: 509–533.

Blyth, Mark. 2013. *Austerity: The History of a Dangerous Idea*. New York: Oxford University Press.

Bodnar, Janet. 2006. *Money Smart Women: Everything You Need to Know to Achieve a Lifetime of Financial Security*. Chicago, IL: Kaplan.

Boseley, Sarah. 2014. "Scheme Offering Shopping Vouchers to Mothers Who Breastfeed To Be Extended." *The Guardian*, November 21. http://www.theguardian.com/lifeandstyle/2014/nov/20/shopping-vouchers-breastfeeding.

Bouchet, Michel-Henry, and Robert Isaak. 2011. "Is the Financial Crisis a Male Syndrome?" Businessweek, November 29. www.businessweek.com/authors/3298-michel-henry-bouchet-and-robert-isaak.

Bourdieu, Pierre. 1987. "The Force of Law: Toward a Sociology of the Juridical Field." *Hastings Journal of Law* 38: 805–853.

Bourke, J. 2007. *Rape: A History from 1860 to Present*. London: Virago Press.

Bowden, Mark. 2008. "Mr. Murdoch Goes to War." *The Atlantic*, July/August. http://www.theatlantic.com/magazine/archive/2008/07/mr-murdoch-goes-to-war/306867/.

Bowman, Andrew, Ismail Ertürk, Julia Fround, Sukhdew Johal, John Law, Adam Leaver, Michael Moran, and Karel Williams. 2014. *The End of the Experiment: From Competition to the Foundational Economy*. Manchester: Manchester University Press.

Bramall, Rebecca. 2013. *The Cultural Politics of Austerity: Past and Present in Austere Times*. Basingstoke: Palgrave Macmillan

Brassett, James, and Chris Clarke. 2012. "Performing the Sub-Prime Crisis: Trauma and the Financial Event." *International Political Sociology* 6, no. 1: 4–20.

Brassett, James, and Lena Rethel. 2015. "Sexy Money: The Hetero-Normative Politics of Global Finance." *Review of International Studies* 41, no. 3: 429–449.

Braunstein, Elissa, and James Heintz. 2008. "Gender Bias and Central Bank Policy: Employment and Inflation Reduction." *International Review of Applied Economics* 22, no. 2: 173–186.

Bridgforth, Glinda, and Gail Perry-Mason. 2003. *Girl, Make Your Money Grow! A Sister's Guide to Protecting Your Future and Enriching Your Life*. New York: Harlem Moon and Broadway Books.

Brill, Steven. 2009. "What's a Bailed-Out Banker Really Worth?" *New York Times*, December 29. http://www.nytimes.com/2010/01/03/magazine/03Compensation-t.html.

Broadbent, Kaye. 2013. "'Because we have husbands with full time jobs . . .' The State, Household and Home Care Work in Japan." In *The Global Political Economy of the*

Household in Asia, eds. Juanita Elias and Samanthi J. Gunawardana, pp. 127–144. Basingstoke: Palgrave MacMillan.

Bromley, Michael. 2015. "From Wall Street to Main Street." In *The Media and Financial Crises: Comparative and Historical Perspectives*, eds. Steve Schifferes and Richard Roberts, pp. 59–72. Abingdon; Oxfordshire: Routledge.

Brooks, Rosa. 2014. "Recline, Don't 'Lean In' (Why I Hate Sheryl Sandberg)." *Washington Post*, February 25. http://www.washingtonpost.com/blogs/she-the-people/wp/2014/02/25/recline-dont-lean-in-why-i-hate-sheryl-sandberg/.

Brown, Wendy. 1995. *States of Injury: Power and Freedom in Late Modernity*. Princeton, NJ: Princeton University Press.

Browne, Kath, and Catherine J. Nash. 2010. *Queer Methods and Methodologies: Intersecting Queer Theories and Social Science Research*. Burlington, VT: Ashgate Publishing.

Bruff, Ian. 2011. "Overcoming the State/Market Dichotomy." In *Critical International Political Economy: Dialogue, Debate and Dissensus*, eds. Stuart Shields, Ian Bruff, and Huw Macartney, pp. 80–98. Basingstoke: Palgrave Macmillan.

Bruff, Ian. 2014. "The Rise of Authoritarian Neoliberalism." *Rethinking Marxism* 26, no. 1: 113–126.

Brunner, Christoph. 2012. "Debt, Affect and Self-Reproducing Movements: Interview with Christian Marazzi, George Caffentzis and Silvia Federici on the latest events in Quebec," June. http://eipcp.net/n/1339011680.

Bryan, Dick, Randy Martin, and Mike Rafferty. 2009. "Financialization and Marx: Giving Labor and Capital a Financial Makeover." *Review of Radical Political Economics* 41, no. 4: 458–472.

Bryan, Dick, Randy Martin, Johnna Montgomerie, and Karel Williams. 2012. "An Important Failure: Knowledge Limits and the Financial Crisis." *Economy and Society* 41, no. 3: 299–315.

Butler, Judith. 1990. *Gender Trouble: Feminism and the Subversion of Identity*. New York: Routledge.

Butler, Judith. 1997. "Merely Cultural." *Social Text* 52–53: 265–277.

Butler, Judith. 2010. "Performative Agency." *Journal of Cultural Economy* 3, no. 2: 147–161.

Buvinic, Mayra, Shwetlena Sabarwal, and Nistha Sinha. 2009. *The Global Financial Crisis: Assessing Vulnerability for Women and Children*. Policy Brief prepared for the World Bank, March. http://www.worldbank.org/financialcrisis/pdf/Women-Children-Vulnerability-March09.pdf.

Caffentzis, George. 2012. "In the Desert of Cities: Notes on the Occupy Movement in the US." January 8. http://www.reclamationsjournal.org/blog/?p=505.

Çagatay, Nilufer, Diane Elson, and Caron Grown. 1996. "Introduction: Special Issue on Gender, Adjustment, Macroeconomics." *World Development* 23, no. 11: 1827–1938.

Caglar, Gülay, Elisabeth Prügl, and Susanne Zwingel (eds.) 2013. *Feminist Strategies in International Governance*. London: Routledge.

Callon, Michael. 2010. "Performativity, Misfires and Politics." *Journal of Cultural Economy* 3, no. 2: 163–169.

Camatte, Jacques. 1995. *This World We Must Leave: And Other Essays*. Los Angeles, CA: Semiotext(e).

Cameron, Angus. 2008. "Crisis? What Crisis? Displacing the Spatial Imaginary of the Fiscal State." *Geoforum* 39, no. 3: 1145–1154.

Cameron, Angus, Anastasia Nesvetailova, and Ronen Palan. 2011. "Wages of Sin? Crisis and the Libidinal Economy." *Journal of Cultural Economy* 4, no. 2: 117–135.

Cameron, David. 2011a. "Speech on the Big Society—Speeches—GOV.UK." https://www.gov.uk/government/speeches/speech-on-the-big-society.

Cameron, David. 2011b. "PM's Speech on the Fightback after the Riots—Speeches—GOV.UK." https://www.gov.uk/government/speeches/pms-speech-on-the-fightback-after-the-riots.

Cameron, David. 2011c. "Troubled Families Speech—Speeches—GOV.UK." https://www.gov.uk/government/speeches/troubled-families-speech.

Cameron, David. 2012a. "Prime Minister's Speech at Lesbian, Gay, Bisexual and Transgender Reception—Speeches—GOV.UK." https://www.gov.uk/government/speeches/prime-ministers-speech-at-lesbian-gay-bisexual-and-transgender-reception.

Cameron, David. 2012b. "Transcript of Prime Minister's Speech & Q&A at Airbus Plant—Speeches—GOV.UK." https://www.gov.uk/government/speeches/transcript-of-prime-ministers-speech-qa-at-airbus-plant.

Cameron, David. 2013a. "Economy Speech Delivered by David Cameron—Speeches—GOV.UK." https://www.gov.uk/government/speeches/economy-speech-delivered-by-david-cameron.

Cameron, David. 2013b. "Prime Minister Thanks Campaigners and Workers for Helping to Bring about Equal Marriage Legislation—Speeches—GOV.UK." https://www.gov.uk/government/speeches/prime-minister-thanks-campaigners-and-workers-for-helping-to-bring-about-equal-marriage-legislation.

Cameron, David. 2014. "The Values That Underpin Our Long-Term Economic Plan—Speeches—GOV.UK." https://www.gov.uk/government/speeches/the-values-that-underpin-our-long-term-economic-plan.

Cameron, G. 2008. "Oikos and Economy: The Greek Legacy in Economic Thought." *Journal of Existential and Phenomenological Theory and Culture* 3, no. 1: 112–133.

Carroll, Toby. 2012. *Delusions of Development: The World Bank and the Post Washington Consensus in Southeast Asia*. Basingstoke: Palgrave Macmillan.

Carver, Terrell. 2010. "Cinematic Ontologies and Viewer Epistemologies: Knowing International Politics as Moving Images." *Global Society* 24, no. 3: 421–431.

Casey, Michael J. 2013. "In the Next Crisis, Women Will Likely Dominate the Committee to Save the World." *Wall Street Journal*, September 16. http://blogs.wsj.com/moneybeat/2013/09/16/in-the-next-crisis-women-will-likely-dominant-the-committee-to-save-the-world/.

Castellanos Serrano, Cristina, and Elvira Gonzáles Gago. 2013. "Wirtschaftskrise, Politik, Protest und Geschlecht in Spanien." In *Macht oder ökonomisches Gesetz? Zum Zusammenhang von Krise und Geschlecht*, eds. Ingrid Kurz-Scherf and Alexandra Scheele, pp. 206–225. Münster: Westfälisches Dampfboot.

Castle, Stephen, and Mark J. Miller. 2003. *The Age of Migration*. Houndmills: MacMillan Press.

Catalyst. n.d. "Quick Take: Women in Financial Services." http://www.catalyst.org/publication/245/women-in-financial-services.

Catalyst. 2004. *The Bottom Line: Connecting Corporate Performance and Gender Diversity*. New York: Catalyst.

Chacko, G., C. L. Evans, H. Gunawan, and A. Sjöman. 2011. *The Global Economic System: How Liquidity Shocks Affect Financial Institutions and Lead to Economic Crises*. Upper Saddle River, NJ: Pearson FT Press.

Chakravartty, Paula, and Denise Ferreira da Silva. 2012. "Accumulation, Dispossession, and Debt: The Racial Logic of Global Capitalism: An Introduction." *American Quarterly* 64, no. 3 (September): pp. 361–385.

Chambers, Samuel A., and Terrell Carver. 2008. *Judith Butler and Political Theory: Troubling Politics*. London: Routledge.

Chan, Kam Wing. 2010. "The Global Financial Crisis and Migrant Workers in China: 'There Is No Future as a Labourer; Returning to the Village Has No Meaning.'" *International Journal of Urban and Regional Research* 34, no. 3: 659–677.

Chang, Kimberly A., and L. H. M. Ling. 2011. "Globalization and Its Intimate Other." In *Gender and Global Restructuring: Sightings, Sites, and Resistance*, eds. Marianne H. Marchand and Anne Sisson Runyan, pp. 27–43. London; New York: Routledge.

Chant, Sylvia, and Caroline Sweetman. 2012. "Fixing Women or Fixing the World? 'Smart Economics,' Efficiency Approaches, and Gender Equality in Development." *Gender & Development* 20, no. 3: 517–529.

Chernow, Ron. 1997. "Grim Reckoning in Japan and Beyond." *New York Times*, November 17.

Chorley, Matt. 2012. "IoS exclusive: Problem Families Told—'Stop Blaming Others.'" *The Independent*, June 10.

Chowdhury, Abdur. 2011. "'Til Recession Do Us Part': Booms, Busts, and Divorce Rate in the United States." *Working Chapter 2011-05*. College of Business Administration, Marquette University.

Cimacnoticias. 2013. "Documentan activistas desaparición de 24 mil mujeres migrantes en el sexenio de Calderón." *Emeequis*, February 13. http://www.m-x.com.mx/2013-02-13/documenta-activistas-desaparicion-de-24-mil-mujeres-migrantes-en-el-sexenio-de-calderon/.

Clinton, Hillary. 2011. *Women and the Economy Summit Keynote Address: "Some Leaders Are Born Women."* September 16. http://www.ncapec.org/docs/Publications/APEC%20Women%20and%20the%20Economy%20Summit.pdf.

Coates, J. M. 2009. "Second-to-Fourth Digit Ratio Predicts Success among High-Frequency Financial Traders." *Proceedings of the National Academy of Sciences* 106, no. 2: 623–628.

Coates, J., and J. Herbert. 2008. "Endogenous Steroids and Financial Risk-Taking on a London Trading Floor." *Proceedings of the National Academy of Sciences* 105, no. 16: 6167–6172.

Codrington, Graeme. 2012. "Banksters—The Most Recent Crisis Explained Simply by The Economist." July 6. http://www.newworldofwork.co.uk/2012/07/06/banksters-the-most-recent-crisis-explained-simply-by-the-economist/.

Cohen, S. M. 2006. "Anaximenes." Philosophy lecture. http://faculty.washington.edu/smcohen/320/anaximen.htm.

Cohen, William A. 1996. *Sex Scandal: The Private Parts of Victorian Fiction*. Durham, NC: Duke University Press.

Cohen, William D. 2010. "Does Wall St Need an Estrogen Injection?" *New York Times*, April 1.

Collignon, Stefan. 2012. "Fiscal Policy Rules and the Sustainability of Public Debt in Europe." *International Economic Review* 53, no. 2: 539–567.

Collignon, Stefan, and Daniela Schwarzer (eds.). 2003. *Private Sector Involvement in the Euro: The Power of Ideas*. London: Routledge.

Collignon, Stefan, Piero Esposito, and Hanna Lierse. 2012. "European Sovereign Bailouts, Political Risk and the Economic Consequences of Mrs Merkel." In *The European Rescue of the European Union? The Existential Crisis of the European Political Project*, eds. E. Chiti, A. J. Menéndez, and P. G. Teixeira, pp. 295–326. ARENA Report 3/12. Oslo: Centre for European Studies.

http://www.reconproject.eu/projectweb/portalproject/Report19_
EuropeanRescueEuropeanUnion.html.

Conway, Ed. 2013. "IMF Inflicts 'Double Blow' on George Osborne." *Sky News*, April 16. http://news.sky.com/story/1078887.

Cooper, Melinda. 2010. "Turbulent World's Financial Markets and Environmental Crisis." *Theory, Culture & Society* 27, no. 2–3: 167–190.

Cooper, Melinda. 2015. "Shadow Money and the Shadow Workforce: Rethinking Labor and Liquidity." *South Atlantic Quarterly* 114, no. 2: 395–423.

Cooper, Melinda, and Angela Mitropoulos. 2009. "The Household Frontier." *Ephemera, Theory and Politics in Organization* 9, no. 4: 363–368.

Corn, Tony. 2010. "The Clash of the Caliphates: Understanding the Real War of Ideas." *Small Wars Journal*, March. http://smallwarsjournal.com/blog/journal/docs-temp/715-corn.pdf.

Coyle, Diane (ed.). 2012. *What's the Use of Economics: Teaching the Dismal Science after the Crisis*. London: London Publishing Partnership.

Crawford, Neta C. 2003. "Feminist Futures: Science Fiction, Utopia, and the Art of Possibilities in World Politics." In *To Seek Out New Worlds: Science Fiction and World Politics*, ed. Jutta Weldes, pp. 195–220. New York: Palgrave.

Credit Suisse Research Institute. 2012. *Gender Diversity and Corporate Performance 2005–2011*. Zurich: Credit Suisse.

Cribb, Jonathan, Andrew Hood, Robert Joyce, and David Phillips. 2013. *Living Standards, Poverty and Inequality in the UK: 2013*. IFS Report (R81). London: Institute for Fiscal Studies.

Crosby, Christina, Lisa Duggan, Roderick Ferguson, Kevin Floyd, Miranda Joseph, Heather Love, Robert McRuer, et al. 2012. "Queer Studies, Materialism, and Crisis A Roundtable Discussion." *GLQ: A Journal of Lesbian and Gay Studies* 18, no. 1: 127–147.

Crosthwaite, Paul, Peter Knight, and Nicky Marsh. 2012. "Imagining the Market: A Visual History." *Public Culture* 24, no. 3–68: 601–622.

Crouch, Colin. 2011. *The Strange Non-Death of Neoliberalism*. London: Polity.

Cruz Vargas, Juan Carlos. 2012. "Sufren violencia en México 46 de cada 100 mujeres mayores de 15 años: Inegi." *Proceso*, July 16. http://www.proceso.com.mx/?p=314286.

Dales, Laura. 2013. "Single Women and Their Households in Contemporary Japan." In *The Global Political Economy of the Household in Asia*, eds. Juanita Elias and Samanthi J. Gunawardana, pp. 110–126. Basingstoke: Palgrave Macmillan.

Danby, Colin. 2007. "Political Economy and the Closet: Heteronormativity in Feminist Economics." *Feminist Economics* 13, no. 2: 29–53.

Dauvergne, Peter, and Genevieve LeBaron. 2014. *Protest Inc: The Corporatization of Activism*. Cambridge: Polity Press.

Davies, Bob. 1997. "The IMF Sees Asian Fallout Concentrated in the Region." *The Asian Wall Street Journal*, December 22.

Davies, Nick. 2014. *Hack Attack: How the Truth Caught Up with Rupert Murdoch*. New York: Faber & Faber.

Davydoff, D., E. Dessart, G. Naacke, N. Jentzsch, F. Figueira, M. Rothemund, W. Mueller, H. E. Kempson, A. Atkinson, A. D. Finney, and L. Anderloni. 2008. "Towards a Common Operational Definition of Over-Indebtedness." *Commissioned Report*. European Commission. http://research-information.bristol.ac.uk/en/publications/towards-a-common-operational-european-definition-of-overindebtedness%2886d863ee-51ad-4a83-b541-3b65130128ff%29/export.html.

Dean, Jodi. 2001. *Publicity's Secret: How Technoculture Capitalizes on Democracy*. Ithaca, NY: Cornell University Press.

de Beauvoir, Simone. 1989. *The Second Sex*. New York: Random House, Vintage Books Edition.

De Brauw, Alan, Daniel O. Gilligan, John Hoddinott, and Roy Shalini. 2012. "The Impact of Bolsa Família on Women's Decision-Making Power." *Social Sciences Research Network*, February 3. http://ssrn.com/abstract=1999073.

Debtocracy (Documentary). 2011. Editor/Script: K. Kitidi, A. Chatzistefanou. http://www.debtocracy.gr/indexen.html.

Deen, Thalif. 2013. "Q&A: Women Hardest Hit by Growing Austerity Measures." *Inter Press Service (IPS) News Agency*, June 10. http://www.ipsnews.net/2013/06/qa-women-hardest-hit-by-growing-new-austerity-measures/.

Deere, Carmen Diana, and Cheryl R. Doss. 2006. "The Gender Asset Gap: What Do We Know and Why Does It Matter?" *Feminist Economics* 12, no. 1–2: 1–50.

Deere, Carmen Diana, Gina Alvarado, and Jennifer Twyman. 2010. *Poverty, Hardship, and Gender Inequality in Asset Ownership in Latin America*. Center for Gender in Global Context, Michigan State University.

DeFilippis, Joseph. 2012a. "Common Ground: The Queerness of Welfare Policy." *S&F Online* 10, no. 1–2. http://sfonline.barnard.edu/a-new-queer-agenda/common-ground-the-queerness-of-welfare-policy/.

DeFilippis, Joseph. 2012b. "Introduction." *S&F Online* 10, no. 1–2. http://sfonline.barnard.edu/a-new-queer-agenda/introduction/.

De Goede, Marieke. 2000. "Mastering 'Lady Credit.'" *International Feminist Journal of Politics* 2, no. 1: 58–81.

De Goede, Marieke. 2004. "Repoliticizing Financial Risk." *Economy and Society* 33, no. 2: 197–217.

De Goede, Marieke. 2005. *Virtue, Fortune, and Faith: A Genealogy of Finance*. Minneapolis: University of Minnesota Press.

De Goede, Marieke. 2006. *International Political Economy and Poststructural Politics*. Basingstoke: Palgrave.

De Goede, Marieke. 2009. "Finance and the Excess: The Politics of Visibility in the Credit Crisis." *Zeitschrift für Internationale Beziehungen* 16, no. 2: 299–310.

De Goede, Marieke. 2015a. "Financial-Economic Assemblages and Distributed Responsibility." In *Documenting World Politics*, eds. Rens van Munster and Casper Sylvest, pp. 58–77. London: Routledge.

De Goede, Marieke. 2015b. "Speculative Values and Courtroom Contestations." *South Atlantic Quarterly* 114, no. 2: 355–375.

Deleuze, Gilles. 1995. *Negotiations 1972–1990*. Trans. Martin Joughin. New York: Columbia University Press.

Della Costa, Mariarosa, and Selma James. 1972. *The Power of Women and the Subversion of Community*. Bristol: Falling Wall Press. April 1.

Deloitte Center for Corporate Governance. 2011. *Women in the Boardroom: A Global Perspective*, November.

Dominguez, Edmé, Rosalba Icaza, Cirila Quintero, Silvia López, and Asa Stenman. 2010. "Women Workers in the Maquiladoras and the Debate on Global Labor Standards." *Feminist Economics* 16, no. 4: 185–201.

Dos Santos, Paulo L. 2009. "On the Content of Banking in Contemporary Capitalism." *Historical Materialism* 17, no. 2: 180–213.

Dowd, Maureen. 2011. "Powerful and Primitive." *New York Times*, May 18.

Downing, Lisa. 2013. *The Subject of Murder: Gender, Exceptionality, and the Modern Killer*. Chicago: University of Chicago Press.

Dransfield, Sarah. 2014. "A Tale of Two Britains: Inequality in the UK | Oxfam GB." *Policy & Practice*. http://policy-practice.oxfam.org.uk/publications/a-tale-of-two-britains-inequality-in-the-uk-314152.

Drezner, Daniel W. 2014. *The System Worked: How the World Stopped Another Great Depression*. New York: Oxford University Press.

Drossos, Yiannis Z. 2011. *Greece: The Sovereignty of the Debt, The Sovereigns over the Debts and Some Reflections over the Law*. Working Papers Series, 2011/#7. Institute for Global Law and Policy, Harvard Law School. http://www.scribd.com/doc/67037360/GREECE-THE-SOVEREIGNTY-OF-THE-DEBT-THE-SOVEREIGNS-OVER-THE-DEBTS-AND-SOME-REFLECTIONS-ON-LAW-by-PROF-YIANNIS-DROSOS-HARVARD-LAW-SCHOOL.

Duggan, Lisa. 2003. *The Twilight of Equality? Neoliberalism, Cultural Politics, and the Attack on Democracy*. Boston: Beacon Press.

Duggan, Lisa. 2012. "After Neoliberalism? From Crisis to Organizing for Queer Economic Justice." *S&F Online* 10, no. 1–2. http://sfonline.barnard.edu/a-new-queer-agenda/after-neoliberalism-from-crisis-to-organizing-for-queer-economic-justice/.

Duggan, Lisa, and Richard Kim. 2012. "Preface: A New Queer Agenda." *S&F Online* 10, no. 1–2. http://sfonline.barnard.edu/a-new-queer-agenda/preface/.

Duggan, Paul. 2011. "In Sex-Crime Prosecutions, Credibility a Thorny Issue." July 2.

Dunaway, Wilma A. 2001. "The Double Register of History: Situating the Forgotten Woman and Her Household in Capitalist Commodity Chains." *Journal of World-Systems Research* 7, no. 1: 2–29.

Dymski, Gary A. 2009. "Racial Exclusion and the Political Economy of the Subprime Crisis." *Historical Materialism* 17, no. 2: 149–179.

Dymski, Gary, Jesus Hernandez, and Lisa Mohanty. 2013. "Race, Gender, Power, and the US Subprime Mortgage and Foreclosure Crisis: A Meso Analysis." *Feminist Economics* 19, no. 3: 124–151.

Easterly, William. 2001. *The Elusive Quest for Growth: Economists' Adventures and Misadventures in the Tropics*. Cambridge, MA: MIT Press.

Eavis, Peter. 2013. "A Toxic Bond That Keeps Causing Pain." *International Herald Tribune*, August 14.

ECLAC (United Nations Economic Commission for Latin America and the Caribbean). 2005. *The Millennium Development Goals: A Latin America and Caribbean Perspective*. United Nations, Santiago de Chile. http://archivo.cepal.org/pdfs/2005/S2005581.pdf.

ECLAC. 2011. *Social Panorama of Latin America 2010*. Santiago de Chile: United Nations.

ECLAC. 2013a. *Social Panorama of Latin America 2012*. Santiago de Chile: United Nations.

ECLAC. 2013b. "Femininity Rate of Indigence and Poverty, by Geographical Area," Table 1.7.4. *Annual Report 2012*. United Nations, Santiago de Chile.

ECLAC. 2013c. *Statistical Yearbook for Latin America and the Caribbean 2013*. Santiago de Chile: United Nations.

ECLAC. 2014. *Social Panorama of Latin America 2013*. Santiago de Chile: United Nations.

Economist, The. 2007. "America's Vulnerable Economy." November 17. http://www.economist.com/node/21520418.

Economist, The. 2009. "Female Power." December 30. http://www.economist.com/node/15174418.

Economist, The. 2014. *The Economist* Tumblr. http://theeconomist.tumblr.com.

Economist, The. 2014. "The Sputtering Engine: Is Germany's Economy Getting Too Weak to Pull Europe Out of Its Crisis?" November 22. http://www.economist.com/news/europe/21633832-germanys-economy-getting-too-weak-pull-europe-out-its-crisis-sputtering-engine.

Eddo-Lodge, Reni, Rachel Hills, Laurie Penny, and Jacob Tobia. 2015. "The 1970s Feminist Who Warned against Leaning In." *BuzzFeed,* March 3. http://www.buzzfeed.com/rachelhills/the-1970s-feminist-who-warned-against-leaning-in.

Edelman, Lee. 2004. *No Future: Queer Theory and the Death Drive.* Durham, NC: Duke University Press.

Ehrenreich, Barbara, and Arlie Russell Hochschild. 2003. *Global Woman: Nannies, Maids and Sex Workers in the New Economy.* London: Metropolitan Books.

Eisenstein, Zillah. 2014. "An Alert: Capital Is Intersectional; Radicalizing Piketty's Inequality." *Feminist Wire,* May 26. http://www.thefeministwire.com/2014/05/alert-capital-intersectional-radicalizing-pikettys-inequality/.

Elborgh-Woytek, Katrin, Monique Newiak, Kalpana Kochhar, Stefania Fabrizio, Kangni Kpodar, Philippe Wingender, Benedict Clements, and Gerd Schwartz. 2013. *Women, Work, and the Economy: Macroeconomic Gains from Gender Equity.* IMF Staff Discussion Note SDN/13/10.

Elias, Juanita. 2011. "The Gender Politics of Economic Competitiveness in Malaysia's Transition to a Knowledge Economy." *The Pacific Review* 24, no. 5: 529–552.

Elias, Juanita. 2013a. "Davos Woman to the Rescue of Global Capitalism: Postfeminist Politics and Competitiveness Promotion at the World Economic Forum." *International Political Sociology* 7, no. 2: 152–169.

Elias, Juanita. 2013b. "The State and the Foreign Relations of Households: The Malaysia-Indonesia Domestic Worker Dispute." In *The Global Political Economy of the Household in Asia,* eds. Juanita Elias and Samanthi J. Gunawardana, pp. 28–42. Basingstoke: Palgrave Macmillan.

Elias, Juanita, and Samanthi Gunarwardena (eds.). 2013. *The Global Political Economy of the Household in Asia.* Basingstoke: Palgrave.

Eligon, John. "Strauss-Kahn Is Released as Case Teeters." *New York Times.* July 1.

Elliot, Patricia. 2010. *Debates in Transgender, Queer, and Feminist Theory: Contested Sites.* Farnham: Ashgate.

Elliott, Larry, and Decca Aitkenhead. 2012. "It's Payback Time: Don't Expect Sympathy—Lagarde to Greeks: Take Responsibility and Stop Trying to Avoid Taxes." *The Guardian,* May 25. http://www.theguardian.com/world/2012/may/25/payback-time-lagarde-greeks.

Ellison, Sarah. 2010. *War at the Wall Street Journal: Inside the Struggle to Control an American Business Empire.* Boston: Houghton Mifflin Harcourt.

Elson, Diane. 1989a. "How Is Structural Adjustment Affecting Women?" *Development* 32, no. 1, pp. 67–74.

Elson, Diane. 1989b. "The Impact of Structural Adjustment on Women." In *The IMF the World Bank and the African Debt: The Social and Political Impact,* ed. B Onimode. London: Zed.

Elson, Diane. 1998. "Talking to the Boys: Gender and Economic Growth Models." In *Feminist Visions of Development,* ed. C. Jackson and R. Pearson, pp. 155–170. London: Routledge.

Elson, Diane. 2002. "The International Financial Architecture: A View from the Kitchen *Femina Politica.* http://www.cepal.org/mujer/curso/elson1.pdf.

Elson, Diane. 2010. "Gender and the Global Economic Crisis in Developing Countries: A Framework for Analysis." *Gender and Development* 18, no. 2: 201–212.

Elson, Diane. 2012. "Women Are Paying the Price for Economic Austerity." *The Conversation*, October 11. http://theconversation.com/women-are-paying-the-price-for-economic-austerity-9139.

Elson, Diane. 2014. "Economic Crises from the 1980s to the 2010s: A Gender Analysis." In *New Frontiers in Feminist Political Economy*, eds. Shirin M. Rai and Georgina Waylen, pp. 189–212. Abingdon: Routledge.

Emeequis. 2013. "Documentan activistas desaparición de 24 mil mujeres migrantes en el sexenio de Calderón." February 13.

Encuentro Nacional de Mujeres. 2013. "XXVIII Encuentro Nacional de Mujeres San Juan–2013. Discurso de apertura." November 23. http://28encuentronacionaldemujeres.es.tl/DISCURSO-DE-APERTURA.htm.

Encuentro Nacional de Mujeres (Posadas). 2012. "Qué son los Encuentros Nacionales de Mujeres," *blog post*. http://27encuentronacionaldemujeresposadas.wordpress.com/about/.

Endnotes 2010. "Communisation and Value-Form Theory." *End Votes*, Vol. 2. London.

Eng, David L. 2010. *The Feeling of Kinship: Queer Liberalism and the Racialization of Intimacy*. Durham, NC: Duke University Press.

Engel, Antke. 2007. "Challenging the Heteronormativity of Tolerance Pluralism. Articulations of Non-Normative Sexualities." *Redescriptions: Political Thought, Conceptual History and Feminist Theory* 11, no. 1: 78–98.

England, Paula. 1993. "The Separative Self: Andocentric Bias in Neoclassical Assumptions." In *Feminist Economics Today: Beyond Economic Man*, eds. Marianne A. Ferber and Julie A. Nelson, pp. 37–53. Chicago: University of Chicago Press.

Enloe, Cynthia. 1989. *Bananas, Beaches, and Bases*. Berkeley; Los Angeles: University of California Press.

Enloe, Cynthia. 1989. "Maid for Export." *New Statesman & Society* 2, no. 78: 29–31.

Enloe, Cynthia. 2014. *Seriously! Investigating Crashes and Crises as if Women Mattered*. Berkeley; Los Angeles: University of California Press.

Entman, Robert M. 2012. *Scandal and Silence: Media Responses to Presidential Conduct*. Cambridge, UK; Malden, MA: Polity Press.

Epstein, Barbara. 1993. *Political Protest and Cultural Revolution: Nonviolent Direct Action in the 1970s and 1980s*. Berkeley: University of California Press.

Epstein, Gerald. 2005. "Introduction: Financialization and the World Economy." In *Financialization and the World Economy*, ed. Gerald Epstein, pp. 3–16. Northhampton: Edward Elger Publishing.

Ermer, Elsa, Leda Cosmides, and John Tooby. 2008. "Relative Status Regulates Risky Decision Making about Resources in Men: Evidence for the Co-Evolution of Motivation and Cognition." *Evolution and Human Behavior* 29: 106–118.

Ernst & Young. 2009. *Groundbreakers: Using the Strength of Women to Rebuild the World Economy*. N.p.: EYGM.

Ertel, Manfred. 2009. "Cleaning Up the Men's Mess: Iceland's Women Reach for Power." *Spiegel Online—International*, April 22.

Espino, Alma, Valeria Esquivel, and Corina Rodríguez Enríquez. 2012. "Crisis, regímenes económicos e impactos de género en América Latina." In *La economía feminista desde América Latina. Una hoja de ruta sobre los debates actuales en la región*, ed. Valeria Esquivel. *ONU Mujeres*.

Evans, Jessica, and Stuart Hall. 1999. *Visual Culture: The Reader*. London; New York: Sage.

Faiola, Anthony, and Steven Mufson. 2011. "France's LaGarde Bids for Top IMF Job." *Washington Post*, May 25.

Famá, María Victoria. 2012. "Otra vez sobre violencia y mujeres." In *Si no se cuenta, no cuenta: Información sobre la violencia contra las mujeres*, ed. Diane Alméras and Coral Calderón Magaña, pp. 25–27. Santiago: ECLAC.

Fanlfik, Patricia. 2007. *Victim Responses to Sexual Assault: Counterintuitive or Simply Adaptive?* Alexandria: American Prosecutors Research Institute.

Fanon, Frantz. 1967a [1961]. *The Wretched of the Earth*. New York: Grove.

Fanon, Frantz. 1967b [1952]. *Black Skin, White Masks*. New York: Grove.

Fanon, Frantz. 1970 [1959]. *A Dying Colonialism*, trans. H. Chevalier. New York: Pelican.

Farley, Anthony. 2009. "Shattered." *Albany Law Review* 72: 1073–1076.

Fawcett Society. 2013. *A Life Raft for Women's Equality*. London: Fawcett Society.

Federici, Silvia. 1975. "Wages against Housework." Bristol: Power of Women Collective and Falling Wall Press. http://caringlabor.wordpress.com/2010/09/15/silvia-federici-wages-against-housework/.

Federici, Silvia. 2004. *Caliban and the Witch: Women, the Body and Primitive Accumulation*. Brooklyn, NY: Autonomedia.

Federici, Silvia. 2005. "Precarious Labor: A Feminist Viewpoint." http://inthemid-dleofthewhirlwind.wordpress.com/precarious-labor-a-feminist-viewpoint/

Federici, Silvia. 2012. *Revolution at Point Zero: Housework, Reproduction and Feminist Struggle*. Oakland, CA: PM Press.

Feminist Economics. 2013. "Special Issue: Critical and Feminist Perspectives on Financial and Economic: Crises Heterodox Macroeconomics Meets Feminist Economics." Volume 19, no. 3.

Feminist Review. 2015. "Special Issue: Feminism and the Politics of Austerity." Issue 109.

Ferber, Marianne A., and Julie A. Nelson (eds.). 2003. *Feminist Economics Today: Beyond Economic Man*. Chicago: University of Chicago Press.

Ferguson, Iain, and Michael Lavalette. 2013. "Crisis, Austerity and the Future (s) of Social Work in the UK." *Critical and Radical Social Work* 1, no. 1: 95–110.

Financial Crisis Inquiry Commission (FCIC). 2011. *Final Report of the National Commission on the Causes of the Financial and Economic Crisis in the United States*, January. Washington, DC. http://www.gpo.gov/fdsys/pkg/GPO-FCIC/pdf/.GPO-FCIC.pdf.

Financial Times. 2013. "Merkel Is Europe's Misunderstood Leader." September 13. http://www.ft.com/intl/cms/s/7ee4be9a-243a-11e3-8905-00144feab7de,Authoris ed=false.html?_i_location=http%3A%2F%2Fwww.ft.com%2Fcms%2Fs%2F0%2F7ee4be9a-243a-11e3-8905-00144feab7de.html%3Fsiteedition%3Dintl&sit eedition=intl&_i_referer=http%3A%2F%2Fsearch.ft.com%2Fsearch%3FqueryTe xt%3Dmerkel%2Bis%2Bmisunderstood#axzz3OfvoYyA6.

Fine, Ben. 2010. "Locating Financialisation." *Historical Materialism* 18, no. 2: 97–116.

Fischer-Lescano, Andreas, and Lukas Oberndorfer. 2013. "Fiskalvertrag und Unionsrecht. Unionsrechtliche Grenzen völkervertraglicher Fiskalregulierung und Organleihe." *Neue Juristische Wochenschrift* 1–2: 9–14.

Fisher, Mark. 2009. *Capitalism Realism: Is There No Alternative?* London: Zero Books.

Fisher, Melissa S. 2012. *Wall Street Women*. Durham, NC: Duke University Press.

Fitzpatrick, P. 2012. "Foucault's Other Law." In *Re-reading Foucault: On Law, Power and Rights*, ed. Ben Golder. Oxford: Routledge.

Focus. 2011. "Betruger in der Euro Familie: Bringt uns Griechenland um unser Geld- und was ist mit Spanien, Protugal, Italien?" February. http://www.anorak.co.uk/304113/news/304113.html/.

Fogg, Ally. 2013. "Don't Give Me This 'If Lehman Sisters Had Been in Charge ...' Nonsense." *The Guardian*, September 17.

Folbre, Nancy. 1994. *Who Pays for the Kids? Gender and the Structures of Constraint*. New York: Routledge.

Folbre, Nancy. 2009. *Greed, Lust and Gender: A History of Economic Ideas*. Oxford: Oxford University Press.

Foner, Nancy. 2000. *From Ellis Island to JFK: New York's Two Great Waves of Immigration*. New Haven, CT: Yale University Press.

Forbes. 2013. "Talking To Nancy Gibbs, Time Magazine's New Managing Editor." September 17. http://www.forbes.com/sites/jeffbercovici/2013/09/17/talking-to-nancy-gibbs-time-magazines-new-managing-editor/.

Fortunati, Leopoldina. 1996. *The Arcane of Reproduction: Housework, Prostitution, Labor and Capital*. New York: Autonomedia.

Fotiadis, Apostolis. 2012. "Greece 2011: Society against Neoliberalism." *Betiko*, January. http://fundacionbetiko.org/wp-content/uploads/2012/11/grecia-2011-sociedad-contra-neo-liberalismo-Apostolis-Fotiadis.pdf.

Foucault, Michel. 1978. "The West and the Truth of Sex." *SubStance* 6–7, no. 20, Focus on the Margins (Autumn): 5–8.

Foucault, Michel. 1990. *The History of Sexuality; Volume One: An Introduction*. London: Verso.

Foucault, Michel. 2004. *Securite, territoire, population: Cours au College de France (1977–1978)*. Paris: Gallimard.

Foucault, Michel. 2008. *The Birth of Biopolitics, Lectures at the College de France, 1978–79*. New York; London: Palgrave.

Foucault, Michel, Paul Rabinow, and Nikolas Rose (eds.). 2003. *The Essential Foucault: Selections from the Essential Works of Foucault 1954–1984*. New York: New Press.

Fouskas, Vassilis K., and Constantine Dimoulas. 2012. "The Greek Workshop of Debt and the Failure of the European Project." *Journal of Balkan and Near Eastern Studies* 14, no. 1: 1–31.

Fox, Katherine. 2014. "Breaking Up the Bloke-Fest: Anne-Marie Slaughter Joins Some of Australia's Most Powerful Women to Talk Change." *Women's Agenda*, November 18. http://www.womensagenda.com.au/talking-about/top-stories/breaking-up-the-bloke-fest-anne-marie-slaughter-joins-some-of-australias-most-powerful-women-to-talk-change/201411174913#.VVvcNLCUfWq.

Frank, Thomas. 1997. *The Conquest of Cool: Business Culture, Counterculture, and the Rise of Hip Consumerism*. Chicago: University of Chicago Press.

Fraser, Nancy. 1995. "From Redistribution to Recognition? Dilemmas of Justice in a 'Post-Socialist' age." *New Left Review* 212: 68–93.

Fraser, Nancy. 2009. "Feminism, Capitalism and the Cunning of History." *New Left Review* 56 (March–April). http://newleftreview.org/II/56/nancy-fraser-feminism-capitalism-and-the-cunning-of-history.

Fraser, Nancy. 2013a. *Fortunes of Feminism: From State-Managed Capitalism to Neoliberal Crisis*. New York: Verso.

Fraser, Nancy. 2013b. "How Feminism Became Capitalism's Handmaiden and How to Reclaim It." *The Guardian*, October 14.

Fraser, Nancy. 2014. "Behind Marx's Hidden Abode: For an Expanded Conception of Capitalism." *New Left Review* 2, no. 86: 55–72.

Friedman, Elisabeth Jay. 2007. "How Pink Is the 'Pink Tide?'" *NACLA* 40, no. 2: 16.

Froud, Julie, Michael Moran, Adriana Nilsson, and Karel Williams. 2010. "Wasting a Crisis? Democracy and Markets in Britain after 2007." *The Political Quarterly* 81, no. 1: 25–38.

Fukuda-Parr, Sakiko, James Heintz, and Stephanie Seguino. 2013. "Critical Perspectives on Financial and Economic Crises: Heterodox Macroeconomics Meets Feminist Economics." *Feminist Economics* 19, no. 3: 4–31.

Galbraith, James. 2014. *The End of Normal: The Great Crisis and the Future of Growth*. New York: Simon & Schuster.

Garrett, Paul. 2007. "'Sinbin' Solutions: The 'Pioneer' Projects for 'Problem Families' and the Forgetfulness of Social Policy Research." *Critical Social Policy* 27, no. 2: 203–230.

Geithner, Timothy. 2014. *Stress Test: Reflections on Financial Crises*. New York: Crown.

Gelsthorpe, Loraine. 2010. "Women, Crime & Control." *Criminology & Criminal Justice* 10, no. 4: 375–386.

Gentleman, Amelia. 2013. "'Shocking' Bedroom Tax Should Be Axed, Says UN Investigator." *Guardian*, September 11.

Germain, Randall. 2010. *Global Politics and Financial Governance*. Basingstoke: Palgrave Macmillan.

Gherardi, Natalia. 2012. "La violencia contra las mujeres en la región." In *Si no se cuenta, no cuenta: Información sobre la violencia contra las mujeres*, eds. Diane Alméras and Coral Calderón Magaña, pp. 13–176. Santiago: ECLAC.

Gibson-Graham, J. K. 1996. *The End of Capitalism (As We Knew It): A Feminist Critique of Political Economy*. Oxford: Blackwell.

Gibson-Graham, J. K. 2005. "Surplus Possibilities: Postdevelopment and Community Economics." *Singapore Journal of Tropical Geography* 26, no. 1: 4–26.

Gibson-Graham, J. K. 2006. *The End of Capitalism (As We Knew It): A Feminist Critique of Political Economy*. Minneapolis: University of Minnesota Press.

Gill, Stephen, and Claire Cutler (eds.). 2014. *New Constitutionalism and World Order*. Cambridge: Cambridge University Press.

Gill, Stephen, and David Law. 1993. "Global Hegemony and the Structural Power of Capital." In *Gramsci, Historical Materialism and International Relations*, ed. Stephen Gill, pp. 93–124. Cambridge: Cambridge University Press.

Ginn, Jay. 2013. "Austerity and Inequality: Exploring the Impact of Cuts in the UK by Gender and Age." *RASP-Research on Ageing and Social Policy* 1, no. 1: 28–53.

Ginty, Molly. 2010. "In Subprime Fallout, Women Take a Heavy Hit." *Women's ENews*, January 14.

Gladman, Kimberly, and Michelle Lamb. 2013. *Governance Metrics International Ratings, 2013 Women on Boards Survey*. March. www.gmi3D.com.

Glick, Peter, and David E. Sahn.1997. "Gender and Education Impacts on Employment and Earnings in West Africa: Evidence from Guinea." *Economic Development and Cultural Change* 45, no. 4: 793–823.

Godoy, Emilio. 2010. "Latin America: Five Million Women Have Fallen Prey to Trafficking Networks." *Inter Press Service*, September 22. http://www.ipsnews.net/2010/09/latin-america-five-million-women-have-fallen-prey-to-trafficking-networks/.

Goldberg, Lauren. 2006. "Dealing in Debt: The High-Stakes World of Debt Collection after FDCPA." *Southern California Law Review* 79, no. 3: 711–752.

Golden Dawn. 2012. "The Manifesto of Golden Dawn." http://xaameriki.wordpress. com/the-manifesto-of-golden-dawn/.

Goldman Sachs. 2005. *Womenomics: Japan's Hidden Asset.*

Goldman Sachs. 2009. *Power of the Purse: Gender Equality and Middle Class Spending.* http://www2.goldmansachs.com/our-thinking/women-and-economics/power-of-purse.pdf.

Goldman Sachs. 2010. *Womenomics 3.0: The Time Is Now.*

González Gago, Elvira, and Marcelo Segales Kirzner. 2014. "Women, Gender Equality and the Economic Crisis in Spain." In *Women and Austerity: The Economic Crisis and the Future for Gender Equality*, eds. Maria Karamessini and Jill Rubery, pp.228–247. London: Routledge.

Graeber, David. 2002. "The New Anarchists." *The New Left Review* 13: 61–73.

Graeber, David. 2009. *Direct Action: An* Ethnography. Oakland, CA: AK Press.

Graeber, David. 2011. *Debt: The First 5000 Years.* Melville House.

Gramsci, Antonio. 1971. *Selections from the Prison Notebooks.* London: Lawrence & Wishart.

Grant, Melissa Gira. 2013. "Sheryl Sandberg's 'Lean In' Campaign Holds Little for Most Women." *Washington Post*, February 25. http://www.washingtonpost.com/opinions/sheryl-sandbergs-lean-in-campaign-holds-little-for-most-women/2013/02/25/c584c9d2-7f51-11e2-a350-49866afab584_story.html.

Greenhouse, Steven. 2011. "Sexual Affronts Are a Known Hotel Hazard." *New York Times.* May 20.

Greenspan, Alan. 2013. *The Map and the Territory: Risk, Human Nature and the Future of Forecasting.* New York: Penguin.

Grey, Barry. 2013. "Global Economic Crisis: No End in Sight: World Bank Cuts Forecast for Global Economic Growth." *Global Research*, January 18. http://www.global-research.ca/global-economic-crisis-no-end-in-sight/5319555.

Griffin, Penny. 2009. *Gendering the World Bank: Neoliberalism and the Gendered Foundations of Global Governance.* Basingstoke: Palgrave Macmillan.

Griffin, Penny. 2010. "Why Gender Matters in/to the Global Economy." *e-International Relations*, June 21. http://www.e-ir.info/2010/06/21/why-gender-matters-into-the-global-economy/.

Griffin, Penny. 2011. "Sexuality, Power and Global Social Justice." In *Global Social Justice*, eds. Heather Widdows and Nicola Smith, pp. 138–150. London: Routledge.

Griffin, Penny. 2013a. "Gendering Global Finance Crisis, Masculinity, and Responsibility." *Men and Masculinities* 16, no. 1: 9–34.

Griffin, Penny. 2013b. "Deconstruction as 'Anti-Method.'" In *Critical Approaches to Security: An Introduction to Theory and Methods*, ed. Laura J. Shepherd, pp. 208–222. London; New York: Routledge.

Griffin, Penny. 2015a. "Crisis, Austerity and Gendered Governance: A Feminist Perspective." *Feminist Review.*

Griffin, Penny. 2015b. *Popular Culture, Political Economy and the Death of Feminism: Why Women Are in Refrigerators and Other Stories.* Abingdon; Ozon; New York: Routledge.

Guardian, The. 2011. "Goldman Sachs: Full Senate Report." April 4.

Gunawardana, Samanthi J., and Juanita Elias. 2013. "Conclusion: The Significance of the Household to Asia's Transformation and to Studies of the Global Political Economy." In *The Global Political Economy of the Household in Asia*, eds. Juanita Elias and Samanthi J. Gunawardana, pp. 227–231. Basingstoke: Palgrave Macmillan.

Haas, Hein de. 2007. "Irregular Migration from West Africa to the Maghreb and the European Union: An Overview of Recent Trends." Report prepared for International Organization for Migration, Geneva.

Habermas, Jürgen. 2011. *Die Verfassung Europas*. Frankfurt: Suhrkamp.

Habermas, Jürgen. 2015. "Why Angela Merkel Is Wrong on Greece?" *Social Europe*, June 25. http://www.socialeurope.eu/2015/06/why-angela-merkels-is-wrong-on-greece/.

Haddad, Lawrence, Lynn R. Brown, Andrea Richter, and Lisa Smith. 1995. "The Gendered Dimensions of Economic Adjustment Policies: Potential Interactions and Evidence to Date." *World Development* 23, no. 6: 881–896.

Haiven, Max. 2011a. "Occupy and the Struggle over Reproduction: An Interview with Silvia Federici." *Rabble.ca*, December 8. http://rabble.ca/news/2011/12/occupy-and-struggle-over-reproduction-interview-silvia-federici.

Haiven, Max. 2011b. "Are Your Children Old Enough to Learn about May '68: Recalling the Radical Event, Refracting Utopia, and Commoning Memory." Cultural Critique 78: 60–87.

Hall, David. 2008. "Economic Crisis and Public Services." *Public Services International Research Unit Note 1*, December 17. www.psiru.org/reports/2008-12-crisis-1.doc.

Han, Jongwoo, and L. H. M. Ling. 1998. "Authoritarianism in the Hypermasculinized State: Hybridity, Patriarchy, and Capitalism in Korea." *International Studies Quarterly* 42, no. 1: 53–78.

Hansen, Lene. 2006. *Security as Practice: Discourse Analysis and the Bosnian War*. New York: Routledge.

Harcourt, Wendy. 2014. "Women and the European Crisis." *The Economic and Labour Relations Review* 25, no. 3: 455–464.

Harding, Sandra. 1986. *The Science Question in Feminism*. Ithaca, NY: Cornell University Press.

Häring, Norbert, and Hans Christian Müller. 2012. "Wenn Ökonomen aufeinanderprallen." *Handelsblatt*, September 13. http://www.handelsblatt.com/politik/oekonomie/nachrichten/verein-fuer-socialpolitik-wenn-oekonomen-aufeinanderprallen/7130168.html.

Harman, Chris. 1984. "Women's Liberation and Revolutionary Socialism." *International Socialism* 2, no. 23: 3–41.

Hart, Mechthild. 2005. "Women, Migration, and the Body-Less Spirit of Capitalism." *Journal of International Women's Studies* 7, no. 2: 1–16.

Harvey, D. 1989. *The Condition of Postmodernity: An Enquiry in the Origins of Cultural Change*. Cambridge: Blackwell.

Haskell, Lori. 2003. *First Stage Trauma Treatment: A Guide for Mental Health Professionals Working with Women*. Toronto: Centre for Addiction and Mental Health.

Hausman, Ricardo, Laura D. Tyson, and Saadia Zahidi. 2009. *The Global Gender Gap Report*. Geneva: World Economic Forum.

Hausman, Ricardo, Laura D. Tyson, and Saadia Zahidi. 2010. *The Global Gender Gap Report*. Geneva: World Economic Forum.

Hawley, Charles. 2010. "The World from Berlin: German Attacks on Greece 'Doubly Harmful.'" *Spiegel/Online: Focus*. http://www.spiegel.de/international/europe/the-world-from-berlin-german-attacks-on-greece-doubly-harmful-a-680283.html.

Hay, Colin, and Nicola Smith. 2013. "The Resilience of Anglo-Liberal in the Absence of Growth: The UK and Irish Cases." In *Resilient Liberalism in Europe's*

Political Economy, eds. Vivien Schmidt and Mark Thatcher, pp. 289–313. New York: Cambridge University Press.

Hayek, F. A. 1944. *The Road to Serfdom*. Chicago: University of Chicago Press.

Hayek, F. A. 1960. *The Constitution of Liberty*. London: Routledge & Kegan Paul.

Hayek, F. A. 1973. "Economic Freedom and Representative Government." *Institute of Economic Affairs*, Fourth Wincott Memorial Lecture, Occasional Papers no. 39.

He, Xin, J. Jeffrey Inman, and Vikas Mittal. 2008. "Gender Jeopardy in Financial Risk Taking." *Journal of Marketing Research* 45, no. 4 (August): 414–424.

Hellen, Nicholas. 2014. "Rise of New Underclass Costs £30bn." *The Sunday Times*, August 17.

Henley, Jon. 2013. "Recessions Can Hurt, but Austerity Kills." *The Guardian*, May 16. http://www.theguardian.com/society/2013/may/15/recessions-hurt-but-austerity-kills.

Hernandez, Cesar C. G. 2009. "La Migra in the Mirror: Immigration Enforcement, Racial Profiling, and the Psychology of One Mexican Chasing after Another." *Albany Law Review* 72, no. 4: 891–897.

Hess, Amanda. 2011. "Why Should Women Read *The Economist*?" November 12. http://magazine.good.is/articles/why-should-women-read-the-economist.

Hill, Elizabeth. 2013. "Extreme Jobs and the Household: Work and Care in the New India." In *The Global Political Economy of the Household in Asia*, eds. Juanita Elias and Samanthi J. Gunawardana, pp. 194–210. Basingstoke: Palgrave Macmillan.

Hindle, Tim. 2010. "Ladies in Waiting." *QFinance* (May).

Hirsh, Michael. 1998. "Where's the Panic? The Global Crisis May Not Be Over but It Sure Feels like It." *Newsweek*, November 30.

HM Government. 2010. *The Coalition: Our Programme for Government*. London: Cabinet Office.

HM Treasury. 2010. *Budget 2010*. London: The Stationery Office.

HM Treasury. 2014. *Budget 2014*. London: The Stationery Office.

Ho, Karen. 2009. *Liquidated: An Ethnography of Wall Street*. Durham, NC: Duke University Press.

Holloway, John. 2002. *Change the World without Taking Power: The Meaning of Revolution Today*. London: Pluto Press.

Hong, Grace Kyungwon. 2012. "Existentially Surplus Women of Color Feminism and the New Crises of Capitalism." *GLQ: A Journal of Lesbian and Gay Studies* 18, no. 1: 87–106.

Hooper, Charlotte. 2000. "Masculinities in Transition: The Case of Globalization." In *Gender and Global Restructuring: Sightings, Sites, and Resistances*, eds. Maranne Marchand and Anne Sisson Runyan, pp. 59–73. New York: Routledge.

Hooper, Charlotte. 2001. *Manly States: Masculinities, International Relations and Gender Politics*. New York: Columbia University Press.

Hossain, Naomi, Bridget Byrne, Aidan Campbell, Elizabeth Harrison, Bebinn McKinley, and Pasha Shah. 2011. *The Impact of the Global Economic Downturn on Communities and Poverty in the UK*. York: Joseph Rowntree Foundation.

Hozić, Aida. 2000. "Making of the Unwanted Colonies: Un-Imagining Desire." In *Political Theory and Cultural Studies*, ed. Jodi Dean, pp. 228–240. Ithaca, NY: Cornell University Press.

Hozić, Aida. 2001. "Political Economy of Global Culture." In *Culture, Politics, Nationalism*, eds. Michael Brint and Reneo Lukic, pp. 55–78. London: Ashgate.

Hozić, Aida. 2002. "Zoning, or, How to Govern (Cultural) Violence." Cultural *Values* 6, no. 1–2: 183–195.

Hudson, Maria, Gina Netto, Filip Sosenko, Mike Noon, Philomena de Lima, Alison Gilchrist, and Nicolina Kamenou-Aigbekaen. 2013. "In-Work Poverty, Ethnicity and Workplace Cultures." Joseph Rowntree Foundation. http://diversityuk.org/wp-content/uploads/2013/11/poverty-ethnicity-workplace-culture-full.pdf.

Hudson, Michael. 2012. "Michael Hudson Interviewed by Paul Jay: The Greek Experiment and the Financial War." http://www.happensingreece.com/mike-hudson-interviewed-by-paul-jay-the-greek-experiment-and-the-financial-war-video/.

Huffington, Ariana. 2014. *Thrive: The Third Metric to Redefining Success and Creating a Life of Well-Being, Wisdom, and Wonder*. New York: Crown.

Hunt, Ken. 2009. "In the Company of Men; What Really Leads Economies into Recession: Corporate Greed, Unscrupulous Lenders, Poorly Understood Financial Products? It May Actually Be a Case of Too Many Y Chromosomes." *The Globe and Mail (Canada)*.

Hyde, Marina. 2011. "Murdoch and Politicians: A Special Relationship That Has Only Ever Worked One Way." *The Guardian*, July 8. http://www.theguardian.com/commentisfree/2011/jul/08/relationship-only-ever-worked-one-way.

International Labor Organization (ILO). 2008. *ILO Action against Trafficking in Human Beings*. Geneva. http://www.ilo.org/wcmsp5/groups/public/@ed_norm/@declaration/documents/publication/wcms_090356.pdf.

ILO. 2010. *Women in Labour Markets: Measuring Progress and Identifying Challenges*. Geneva: International Labor Organization.

ILO. 2011. *The Global Crisis*. Geneva: International Labor Organization.

ILO. 2012. *ILO Global Estimate of Forced Labour*. http://www.ilo.org/wcmsp5/groups/public/---ed_norm/---declaration/documents/publication/wcms_182004.pdf.

ILO. 2013. *Women and Men in the Informal Economy: A Statistical Picture*. Geneva: International Labor Organization.

Ingrassia, Catherine. 1998. *Authorship, Commerce and Gender in Early Eighteenth-Century England*. Cambridge: Cambridge University Press.

International Monetary Fund (IMF). 1998. "Financial Crises: Causes and Indicators." *World Economic Outlook*, May. http://www.imf.org/external/pubs/ft/weo/weo0598/.

Inman, Phillip. 2011. "Bank of England Governor Blames Spending Cuts on Bank Bailouts." *The Guardian*, 1 March.

Irwin, Neil. 2013. *The Alchemists: Three Central Bankers and a World on Fire*. New York: The Penguin Press.

Ishikura, Yoko. 2014. "Closing the Gender Gap in East Asia." *World Economic Forum Blog*, May 20. http://forumblog.org/2014/05/closing-gender-gap-east-asia/.

Issing, O. 2009. "Why a Common Eurozone Bond Isn't Such a Good Idea." *Europe's World* (Summer): 77–79.

IWPR. 2012. *The Gender Wage Gap: 2011*. IWPR #C350, September. Institute for Women's Policy Research.

Jacobs, Susie, and Christian Klesse. 2014. "Introduction: Special Issue on 'Gender, Sexuality and Political Economy.'" *International Journal of Politics, Culture and Society* 27, no. 2: 129–152.

Jakobsen, Janet R. 2012. "Perverse Justice." *GLQ: A Journal of Lesbian and Gay Studies* 18, no. 1: 19–45.

Jakobsen, Janet R. 2014. "Economic Justice after Legal Equality: The Case for Caring Queerly." In *After Legal Equality: Family, Sex, Kinship*, ed. Robert Leckey, pp. 77–96. London: Routledge.

James, Selma. 2012. *Sex, Race and Class: A Selection of Writings from 1952–2011*. Oakland, CA: PM Press.

Janssen, R. 2010. "Greece and the IMF: Who Exactly Is Being Saved?" (July), *Center for Economic and Policy Research*. http://www.scribd.com/doc/34895662/Greece-and-the-IMF-Who-Exactly-is-Being-Saved.

Jensen, Erik. 2010. "Macho Boys' Club 'Cost Anglicans Millions.'" *Sydney Morning Herald*, December 4.

Jensen, Tracey. 2012. "Tough Love in Tough Times." *Studies in the Maternal* 4, no. 2: 1–26.

Jessop, Bob. 2001. "What Follows Fordism? On the Periodization of Capitalism and Its Regulation." In *Phases of Capitalist Development: Booms, Crises, and Globalization*, eds. Robert Albritton et al., pp. 282–299. Basingstoke: Palgrave.

Jessop, Bob. 2012. "Narratives of Crisis and Crisis Response: Perspectives from North and South." In *The Global Crisis and Transformative Social Change*, eds. Peter Uttig, Shahra Razavi, and Rebecca Varghese Buchholz, pp. 23–42. London: Routledge.

Jessop, Bob, and Stijn Oosterlynck. 2008. "Cultural Political Economy: On Making the Cultural Turn Without Falling into Soft Economic Sociology." *Geoforum* 39, no. 3: 1155–1169.

Jessop, Bob, Christoph Scherrer, and Brigitte Young (eds.). 2015. *Financial Cultures and Crisis Dynamics*. Abingdon: Routledge.

Johne, Marjo. 2011. "The Financing Gender Gap," *The Globe and Mail*, 4 March. http://www.theglobeandmail.com/report-on-business/small-business/sb-money/valuation/the-financing-gender-gap/article4258902/, accessed May 12, 2012.

Jones, Gavin W. 2009. "Women, Marriage and Family in Southeast Asia." In *Gender Trends in Southeast Asia: Women Now, Women in the Future*, ed. T. Devasahayam, pp. 12–30. Singapore: ISEAS.

Joseph, Jonathan. 2013. "Resilience as Embedded Neoliberalism: A Governmentality Approach." *Resilience: International Policies, Practices and Discourses* 1, no. 1: 38–52.

Joseph Rowntree Foundation (JRF). 2014. *Austerity in the UK*. http://www.jrf.org.uk/sites/files/jrf/JRF_Investigations_%20Austerity_2859_aw%20(4)%20(1).pdf.

Joy, Lois, Nancy Carter, Harvey M. Wagner, and Sriram Narayanan. 2007. *The Bottom Line: Corporate Performance and Women's Representation on Boards*. New York: Catalyst.

Just a Memo. 2011. "Of Occupy Wall Street, Art and Design." http://justamemo.com/2011/10/06/of-occupy-wall-street-art-and-design/.

Jütting, Johannes, and Juan R. de Laiglesia (eds.). 2009. *Is Informal Normal?: Towards More and Better Jobs in Developing Countries*. OECD Publishing. doi:10.1787/9789264059245-2-en.

Kabeer, Naila, Simeen Mahmud, and Sakiba Tasneem. 2011. *Does Paid Work Provide a Pathway to Women's Empowerment? Empirical Findings from Bangladesh*. IDS Working Paper, Vol. 2011, No. 375. Institute of Development Studies. http://www.ids.ac.uk/idspublication/does-paid-work-provide-a-pathway-to-women-s-empowerment-empirical-findings-from-bangladesh.

Kanna, Ahmed. 2010. "Flexible Citizenship in Dubai: Neoliberal Subjectivity in the Emerging 'City-Corporation.'" *Cultural Anthropology* 25, no. 1: 100–129.

Kannankulam, John, and Fabian Georgi. 2014. "Varieties of Capitalism or Varieties of Relationships of Forces? Outlines of a Historical Materialist Policy Analysis." *Capital & Class* 38, no. 1: 59–71.

Kaplanis, Yiannis. 2011. "An Economy That Excludes the Many and an Accidental Revolt." In *Revolt and Crisis in Greece: Between a Present Yet to Pass and a Future Still To Come*, eds. Antonis Vradis and Dimitris Dalakoglou, pp. 215–228. Oakland; Edinburgh: AK Press.

Karaiskaki, T. 1995. "Dramatic Population Decline." *Kathimerini*, May 28.

Karamessini, Maria, and Jill Rubery (eds.). 2014. *Women and Austerity: The Economic Crisis and the Future for Gender Equality*. Abingdon: Routledge.

Katsimi, Margarita, and Thomas Moutos. 2010. "EMU and the Greek Crisis." *European Journal of Political Economy* 26, no. 4: 568–576.

Katz, Cindi. 2001. "Vagabond Capitalism and the Necessity of Social Reproduction." *Antipode* 33, no. 4: 709–728.

Kay, Katty, and Claire Shipman. 2009. "Fixing the Economy? It's Women's Work." *Washington Post*, June 12.

Kayatekin, Serap A. 2009. "Between Political Economy and Postcolonial Theory: First Encounters." *The Cambridge Journal of Economics Symposium on Political Economy and Postcolonial Theory* 33, no. 6: 1113–1118.

Keiser, Max. 2011. "Greece Debt Crisis—On the Edge with Max Keiser." *RT TV*, August 12. https://www.youtube.com/watch?v=nOjkGVmR3Eg.

Kelly, Mark G. E. 2013. *Foucault's History of Sexuality, Volume I, The Will to Knowledge*. Edinburgh: Edinburgh University Press.

Kenny, Kate M. 2010. "Beyond Ourselves: Passion and the Dark Side of Identification in an Ethical Organization." *Human Relations* 63, no. 6: 857–873.

Kiersey, Nicholas J. 2009a. "Scale, Security, and Political Economy: Debating the Biopolitics of the Global War on Terror." *New Political Science* 31, no. 1: 27–47.

Kiersey, Nicholas J. 2009b. "Neoliberal Political Economy and the Subjectivity of Crisis: Why Governmentality Is Not Hollow." *Global Society* 23, no. 4: 363–386.

Kindleberger, C. P. 2000. *Manias, Panics, and Crashes: A History of Financial Crises*. 4th edition. New York: John Wiley and Sons.

Kirchhoff, Suzanne M. 2010. *The U.S. Newspaper Industry in Transition*. Washington DC: Congressional Research Service. http://fas.org/sgp/crs/misc/R40700.pdf.

Kittay, Eva Feder. 1988. "Woman as Metaphor." *Hypatia* 3: 63–86.

Kiyosaki, Kim. 2006. *Rich Woman: A Book on Investing for Women*. Scottsdale, AZ: Rich Press.

Klatzer, Elisabeth, and Christa Schlager. 2011. "Europäische Wirtschaftsregierung— eine stille neoliberale Revolution?" *Kurswechsel* 29, no. 1: 61–81.

Klein, Naomi. 2007. *The Shock Doctrine: The Rise of Disaster Capitalism*. New York: Picador.

Knights, David, and Maria Tulberg. 2014. "Masculinity in the Financial Sector." In *Oxford Handbook of Gender in Organizations*, eds. Savita Kura, Ruth Simpson, and Ronald J. Burke, pp. 1–15. Oxford: Oxford Handbook Online.

Knowles, J., E. Pernia, and M. Racelis. 1999. "Social Consequences of the Financial Crisis in Asia." Asian Development Bank staff paper, no. 60. Manila: Asian Development Bank.

Kofman, Eleonore. 2014. "Gendered Migrations, Social Reproduction and the Household in Europe." *Dialectical Anthropology* 38, no. 1: 79–94.

Konings, Martijn. 2010. "Neoliberalism and the American State." *Critical Sociology* 36, no. 5: 741–765.

Kornblihtt, Juan. 2014. "No es una crisis cambiaria." *Razón y Revolución*, January 14. http://www.razonyrevolucion.org/ryr/index.php?option=com_content&view=article&id=2653:no-es-una-crisis-cambiaria&catid=48:agro.

Kosík, Karel, and James H. Satterwhite (eds.). 1994. *The Crisis of Modernity: Karel Kosík's Essays and Observations from the 1968 Era* (States and Societies in East-Central Europe: Contributions to Political Thought). Washington, DC: Rowman and Littlefield.

Kreitner, Roy. 2000. "Speculations of Contract, or How Contract Law Stopped Worrying and Learned to Love Risk." *Columbia Law Review* 100, no. 4: 1096–1138.

Krippner, Greta. 2011. *Capitalizing on Crisis*. Cambridge, MA; London: Harvard University Press.

Kristeva, Julia. 1982. *Powers of Horror: An Essay on Abjection*. New York: Columbia University Press.

Kristof, Nicholas. 2009. "Mistresses of the Universe." *New York Times*, February 7.

Krugman, Paul. 2009. "How Did Economists Get It So Wrong?" *New York Times*, September 2. http://www.nytimes.com/2009/09/06/magazine/06Economic-t.html?pagewanted=all&_r=0.

Krugman, Paul. 2014. "Hawks Crying Wolf." *New York Times*, August 21. http://www.nytimes.com/2014/08/22/opinion/paul-krugman-hawks-crying-wolf.html?hp&action=click&pgtype=Homepage&module=c-column-top-span-region&region=c-column-top-span-region&WT.nav=c-column-top-span-region&_r=0.

Krugman, Paul. 2015. "Seriously Bad Ideas." *New York Times*, June 12. http://www.nytimes.com/2015/06/12/opinion/paul-krugman-seriously-bad-ideas.html.

Kumar, Alok. 2010. "Self-Selection and the Forecasting Abilities of Female Equity Analysts." *Journal of Accounting Research* 48, no. 2 (May): 393–435.

Kumar, Krishan. 2010. "The Ends of Utopia?" *New Literary History* 41, no. 3: 549–569.

Kwong, Peter. 1998. *Forbidden Workers: Illegal Chinese Immigrants and American Labor*. New York: New Press.

Lagarde y de los Rios, Marcela. 2009. "Preface: Feminist Keys for Understanding Femicide." In *Terrorizing Women: Femicide in the Americas*, eds. Rosa-Linda Fregoso and Cynthia Bejarano, pp. xi–xxv. Durham, NC: Duke University Press.

Lahrichi, Kamilia. 2014. "Poverty Keeps Growing in Buenos Aires as Argentina Wakes Up in Default." *International Finance*, August 25. http://www.international-financemagazine.com/article/Poverty-keeps-growing-in-Buenos-Aires-as-Argentina-wakes-up-in-default.html

La Jornada. 2011. "Registra Juárez en 2010 la cifra más alta de feminicidios en 18 años." January 2. http://www.jornada.unam.mx/2011/01/02/politica/006n1pol.

Lambadariou, D. 2012 "Greek Debt Crisis: Mother and Son Commit Suicide in Athens." *The Huffington Post*. May 24, 2012. http://www.huffingtonpost.com/2012/05/24/greek-financial-crisis-suicide_n_1543050.html.

La Nación. 2013a. "Matan a una mujer cada 35 horas por violencia de género." February 27.

La Nación. 2013b. "Agredieron a participantes del Encuentro Nacional de Mujeres en San Juan." November 25.

Langley, Paul. 2007. "The Uncertain Subjects of Anglo-American Financialization." *Cultural Critique* 65, no. 1: 67–91.

Langley, Paul. 2008. *The Everyday Life of Global Finance: Saving and Borrowing in Anglo-America*. Oxford: Oxford University Press.

Langley, Paul. 2012. "The Fear Index and Frankenstein Finance." *Cultural Anthropology Online*, May 15. http://www.culanth.org/fieldsights/341-the-fear-index-and-frankenstein-finance.

Langley, Paul. 2014. *Liquidity Lost: The Governance of the Global Financial Crisis.* Oxford: Oxford University Press.

Lapavitsas, Costas. 2011. "Theorizing Financialization." *Work, Employment & Society* 25, no. 4: 611–626.

Lapavitsas, Costas (ed.). 2013. *Financialization in Crisis.* Chicago: Haymarket Books.

Lapavitsas, Costas. 2014. *Profiting without Producing: How Finance Exploits Us All.* London; New York: Verso.

Latin American Public Opinion Project (LAPOP). 2012. *The AmericasBarometer.* www. LapopSurveys.org.

Latinobarometro. 2006. *Latinobarómetro 2006* (electronic dataset). Corporación Latinobarometro, Santiago de Chile. http://www.latinobarometro.org/latLicense.jsp.

Lauretis, Theresa. 1987. *Technologies of Gender: Essays on Theory, Film, and Fiction.* Bloomington; Indianapolis: Indiana University Press.

Lavinas, Lena. 2013. "21st Century Welfare." *New Left Review* 84: 5–42.

Law Reform Commission. 2009. Consultation Paper on personal debt management and debt enforcement. Dublin: Law Reform Commission.

Lazarretou, Sophia. 2004. *The Drachma, Foreign Creditors, and the International Monetary System: Tales of a Currency during the 19th and the Early 20th Century.* Bank of Greece Working Paper No. 16.

LeBaron, Genevieve. 2010. "The Political Economy of the Household: Neoliberal Restructuring, Enclosures, and Daily Life." *Review of International Political Economy* 17, no. 5: 889–912.

Lee, Hyunok. 2012. "The Political Economy of Cross-Border Marriage: Economic Development and Social Reproduction." *Feminist Economics* 18, no. 2: 177–200.

Lee, Hwok-Aun, and Rene E. Ofreneo. 2014. "From Asian to Global Financial Crisis: Recovery Amidst Expanding Labour Precarity." *Journal of Contemporary Asia* 44, no. 4: 688–710.

Lee, Micky. 2014. "A Feminist Political Economic Critique of Women and Investment in the Popular Media." *Feminist Media Studies* 14, no. 4: 270–285.

Lees, Sue. 1997. *Ruling Passions: Sexual Violence, Reputation and the Law.* Philadelphia: Open University Press.

Le Guin, Ursula K. 1974. *The Dispossessed.* New York: Harper & Row.

Lenglet, Marc. 2011. "Conflicting Codes and Codings: How Algorithmic Trading is Reshaping Financial Regulation." *Theory, Culture & Society* 28, no. 6: 44–66.

Leroy Cerqueira, Emmanuelle. 2013. "Brazil Debates Human Trafficking for Sexual Exploitation—Part II." *Global Voices.* http://globalvoicesonline.org/2013/01/09/brazil-debates-human-trafficking-for-sexual-exploitation-part-ii/.

Levitas, Ruth. 2012. "There May Be 'Trouble Ahead': What We Know about Those 120, 000 'Troubled' Families." *Policy Response Series No. 3.* Poverty and Social Exclusion in the UK Project. http://www.poverty.ac.uk/policy-response-working-papers-families-social-policy-life-chances-children-parenting-uk-government.

Lewis, Michael. 2011. *The Big Short: Inside the Doomsday Machine.* New York: W. W. Norton.

Leyshon, Andrew, and Nigel Thrift. 1997. *Money/Space: Geographies of Monetary Transformation.* London: Routledge.

Leyshon, Andrew, and Nigel Thrift. 1999. "Lists Come Alive: Electronic Systems of Knowledge and the Rise of Credit-Scoring in Retail Banking." *Economy and Society* 28, no. 3: 434–466.

Lichfield, John. 2007. "French IMF Candidate an 'Insistent' Womanizer." *Independent.* July 14.

Lichfield, John. 2011. "'The Flesh is Weak'-DSK Ally Says Hotel Maid Encouraged Tryst." *Independent.* December 1.

Lim, Joseph Y. 2000. "The Effects of the East Asian Crisis on the Employment of Women and Men: The Philippine Case." *World Development* 28, no. 7: 1285–1306.

Lind, Amy. 2010. "Introduction: Development, Global Governance and Sexual Subjectivities." In *Development, Sexual Rights and Global Governance*, ed. Amy Lind, pp. 1–20. London: Routledge.

Ling, L. H. M. 2004. "Cultural Chauvinism and the Liberal International Order: 'West versus Rest' in Asia's Financial Order." In *Power Postcolonialism and International Relations: Reading Race, Gender and Class*, eds. Geeta Chowdhry and Sheila Nair, pp. 115–141. London: Routledge.

Liu, Henry. 2010. "The Post-Crisis Outlook: Greek Tragedy." *Asian Times*, May 21. http://theglobalrealm.com/2010/05/27/the-post-crisis-outlook-%E2%80%93-part-8/.

Lloyd, Genevieve. 1984. *The Man of Reason: 'Male' and 'Female' in Western Philosophy.* London: Methuen.

Lucarelli, Stefano. 2010. "Financialization as Biopower." Edu Factory: Conflicts and Transformations of the University, June 16. http://www.edu-factory.org/edu15/index.php?option=com_content&view=article&id=36 0:financialization-as-biopower&catid=38:documentation&Itemid=56.

Luxemburg, R. 2004. *The Accumulation of Capital.* New York: Routledge.

MacKinnon, Catherine. 1997. "Rape: On Coercion and Concent." In *Writing on the Body: Female Embodiment and Feminist Theory*, eds. K. Conboy, N. Medina, and S. Stanbury, pp. 42–58. New York: Columbia University Press.

Mahmud, T. 2012. "Is It Greek or Déjà Vu All Over Again? Neoliberalism and Winners and Losers of International Debt Crises." *Loyola University Chicago Law Journal* 42: 629–712.

Mahler, Sarah J. 1995. *American Dreaming: Immigrant Life on the Margins.* Princeton, NJ: Princeton University Press.

Manolopoulos, Jason. 2011. *Greece's "Odious" Debt.* London; New York: Athem Press.

Manpower Group. 2011. "Manpower Group Outlines How Asian Companies Can Increase the Number of Women in Leading Roles for Economic Advantage." Jakarta Press Release, June 13. http://uk.reuters.com/article/2011/06/13/idUS118361+13-Jun-2011+PRN20110613.

March, James G., Lee S. Sproull, and Michael Tamuz. 1991. "Learning from Samples of One or Fewer." *Organization Science* 2, no. 1: 1–13.

Marchand, Marianne H., and Anne Sisson Runyan (eds.). 2010. *Gender and Global Restructuring: Sightings, Sites, and Resistance.* London: Routledge.

Marcus, Steven. 1966. *The Other Victorians: A Study of Sexuality and Pornography in Mid-Nineteenth-Century Britain.* New York: Basic Books.

Marie, Anna, Jaimes-Guerrero. 1998. "Savage Hegemony: From 'Endangered Species' to Feminist Indigenism." In *Talking Visions: Multicultural Feminism in a Transnational Age*, ed. Ella Shohat, pp. 323–423. New York: MIT Press.

Markus, Sharon. 1992. "Fighting Bodies, Fighting Words: A Theory and Politics of Rape Prevention." In *Feminists Theorize the Political*, eds. Judith Butler and Joan Scott, pp. 385–403. New York: Routledge.

Marlow, Susan, and Dean Patton. 2005. "All Credit to Men? Entrepreneurship, Finance, and Gender." *Entrepreneurship Theory and Practice* 29, no. 6: 717–735.

Martin, Denise, and Paula Wilcox. 2013. "Women, Welfare and the Carceral State." In *Criminalisation and Advanced Marginality: Critically Exploring the Work of Loic Wacquant*, eds. Peter Squires and John Lea, pp. 151–176. Bristol: Policy Press.

Martin, Randy. 2013. "After Economy? Social Logics of the Derivative." *Social Text* 31, no. 1: 83–106.

Marx, Karl. 1986 [1867]. *Capital 1*, Chapter 26. London: Penguin Books.

Marx, Karl. 1990. *Capital: A Critique of Political Economy* vol. 1, trans. Ben Fowkes. New York: Penguin Classics.

Marx, Karl. 2011. *Capital Volume One*. New York: Courier Dover Publications.

Mbembe, Achille. 2001. *On the Postcolony*. Berkeley: University of California Press.

Mbembe, Achille. 2003. "Necropolitics." *Public Culture* 15, no. 1: 11–40.

Mbembe, Achille. 2012. "Theory from the Antipodes: Notes on John and Jean Comaroff's TFS." *Cultural Anthropology*, February 25. http://www.culanth.org/?q=node/506.

McDowell, Linda. 1997. *Capital Culture: Gender at Work in the City*. Oxford: Blackwell Publishers.

McKinsey and Company. 2007. *Women Matter: Gender Diversity, a Corporate Performance Driver*. London: McKinsey & Company.

McLean, Bethany, and Joe Nocera. 2010. *All the Devils Are Here: The Hidden History of the Global Financial Crisis*. New York: Portfolio/Penguin.

McNally, David. 2001. *Bodies of Meaning: Studies on Language, Labor, and Liberation*. Albany: State University of New York Press.

McNally, David. 2009. "From Financial Crisis to World-Slump: Accumulation, Financialisation, and the Global Slowdown." *Historical Materialism* 17, no. 2: 35–83.

McRobie, Heather. 2012. "When Austerity Sounds like Backlash: Gender and the Economic Crisis." *OpenDemocracy 50:50*, September 18. https://www.opendemocracy.net/5050/heather-mcrobie/when-austerity-sounds-like-backlash-gender-and-economic-crisis.

McRobie, Heather. 2013a. "Is Gendered Austerity Finally on the Political Agenda?" *Open Democracy 50:50*, September 24. https://www.opendemocracy.net/5050/heather-mcrobie/is-gendered-austerity-finally-on-political-agenda.

McRobie, Heather. 2013b. "Austerity and Domestic Violence: Mapping the Damage." *Open Democracy 50:50*, December 3. https://www.opendemocracy.net/5050/heather-mcrobie/austerity-and-domestic-violence-mapping-damage.

McRuer, Robert. 2012. "Cripping Queer Politics, or the Dangers of Neoliberalism." *S&F Online* 10, no. 1–2. http://sfonline.barnard.edu/a-new-queer-agenda/cripping-queer-politics-or-the-dangers-of-neoliberalism/.

McVeigh, Tracy. 2013. "Spending Cuts Hit Women Worse, Says Report." *The Observer*, September 22. http://www.theguardian.com/society/2013/sep/21/spending-cuts-women-report.

Menzel, Kostantinos. 2014. "Born in Debt: Greece's History of Borrowing." *Greek Reporter*, January 26. http://greece.greekreporter.com/2014/01/26/born-in-debt-greeces-history-of-borrowing/.

Mies, Maria. 1986. *Patriarchy and Accumulation on a World Scale: Women in the International Division of Labor*. London: Zed Books.

Mies, Maria, and Veronika Bennholdt-Thomsen. 1999. *The Subsistence Perspective: Beyond the Globalised Economy*. London: Zed Books.

Mills, Mary Beth. 2003. "Gender and Inequality in the Global Labor Force." *Annual Review of Anthropology* 32: 41–62.

Misiones Cuatro. 2012. "Encuentro Nacional de Mujeres—Una marea de mujeres marchó por sus derechos en las calles de Posadas." Octubre 9. http://www.misionescuatro.com/ampliar.php?id=39966&titulo=Una-marea-de-mujeres-march%F3-por-sus-derechos-en-las-calles-de-Posadas.

Misra, Joya. 2003. "The Intersection of Gender and Race in the Labor Market." *Annual Review of Sociology* 29: 487–513.

Misra, Joya, Jonathan Woodring, and Sabine N. Merz. 2006. "The Globalization of Care Work: Neoliberal Economic Restructuring and Migration Policy." *Globalizations* 3, no. 3: 317–332.

Mitchell, Juliet. 1966. "Women: The Longest Revolution." *New Left Review* 40, November–December. http://newleftreview.org/I/40/juliet-mitchell-women-the-longest-revolution.

Mitchell, Katharyne. 2010. "Pre-Black Futures." *Antipode* 41 (Supplement 1): 239–261.

Mitchell, Martin, Kelsey Beninger, Nilufer Rahim, and Sue Arthur. 2013. *Implications of Austerity for LGBT People and Services*. London: UNISON.

Mitropoulos, Angela. 2012. *Contract and Contagion: From Biopolitics to Oikonomia*. New York: Minor Compositions.

Mohanty, Chandra. 2003. "'Under Western Eyes' Revisited." *Signs* 28, no. 2: 499–535.

Mohanty, Chandra. 2013. "Transnational Feminist Crossings: On Neoliberalism and Radical Critique." *Signs* 38, no. 4: 967–991.

Montag, Warren. 2005. "Necro-economics." *Radical Philosophy* 134 (November–December): 7–17.

Montgomerie, Johnna. 2013. "Household Debt: The Silent Dimension of the Financial Crisis." *SPERI*. http://speri.dept.shef.ac.uk/2013/08/28/household-debt-silent-dimension-financial-crisis/.

Montgomerie, Johnna, and Brigitte Young. 2010. *Home Is Where the Hardship Is: Gender and Wealth (Dis)Accumulation in the Subprime Boom*. CRESC Working Paper Series, Working Paper No. 79.

Montoya, Celeste. 2012. *From Global to Grassroots: The European Union, Transnational Advocacy, and Combating Violence against Women*. New York: Oxford University Press.

Mooney, Gerry, and Lynn Hancock. 2012. "Beyond the Penal State: Advanced Marginality, Social Policy and Anti-Welfarism." In *Criminalisation and Advanced Marginality: Critically Exploring the Work of Loic Wacquant*, eds. Peter Squires and John Lea, pp. 107–128. Bristol: Policy Press.

Moran, Leslie. 2002. *The Homosexual(ity) of Law*. London: Routledge.

Moran, Patricia, Deborah Ghate, and Amelia van der Merwe. 2004. *What Works in Parenting Support? A Review of the International Evidence*. Report by the Policy Research Bureau. London: The Department for Education and Skills.

Morgan, Robin. 2008. "Goodbye to All That (#2)." Women's Media Center. http://www.womensmediacenter.com/feature/entry/goodbye-to-all-that-2.

Morokvasic, Mirjana. 2007. "Migration, Gender, Empowerment." In *Gender Orders Unbound: Globalization, Restructuring, and Reciprocity*. Obladen; Farmington Hills: Barbara Budrich Publishers.

Morrall, Amanda. 2008. "Emotions Upset Market Theories." *The Press*, March 18. (Christchurch, NZ).

Morris, Norval, and David Rothman (eds.). 1997. *The Oxford History of the Prison: The Practice of Punishment in Western Society*. Oxford: Oxford University Press.

Morris, Virginia B., and Kenneth M. Morris. 2003. *A Woman's Guide to Investing*. New York: Lightbulb Press.

Moser, Caroline. 1989. "The Impact of Recession and Structural Adjustment on Women: Ecuador." *Development* 1: 11–17.

.Motta, Sara, Cristina Fominaya, Catherine Eschle, and Laurence Cox. 2011. "Feminism, Women's Movements and Women in Movement." *Interface: A Journal for and about Social Movements* 3, no. 2: 1–32.

Moylan, Tom. 1986. *Demand the Impossible: Science Fiction and the Utopian Imagination.* New York: Methuen.

Muravyev, Alexander, Oleksandr Talavera, and Dorothea Schäfer. 2009. "Entrepeneurs' Gender and Financial Constraints: Evidence from International Data." *Journal of Comparative Economics* 37, no. 2: 270–286.

Murthy, Ranjani K., Josephine Sagayam, and Sudha Nair. 2008. "Gender, Efficiency, Poverty Reduction, and Empowerment: Reflections from an Agriculture and Credit Programme in Tamil Nadu, India." *Gender & Development* 16, no. 1: 101–116.

Nandy, Ashis. 1983. *The Intimate Enemy: Loss and Recovery of Self under Colonialism.* New Dehli: Oxford University Press.

National Council for Research on Women. 2009. *Women in Fund Management.* New York: National Council for Research on Women.

Nayak, Meghana. 2015. *The Politics of Gender-Based Asylum.* New York: Oxford University Press.

Nelson, Julie. 2012. *Are Women Really More Risk-Averse Than Men?* INET Research Note #012. September. Institute for New Economic Thinking.

New Economics Foundation (NEF). 2013. *The Austerity Story.* http://b.3cdn.net/nefoundation/a12416779f2dd4153c_2hm6ixryj.pdf.

New York Times. 2009. "The Great 'He-Cession.'" *New York Times: Idea of the Day,* June 29.

New York Times. 2011. "Dominque Strauss-Kahn: What's in a Reputation." May 11.

Nguyen, Mimi Thi. 2011. "The Biopower of Beauty: Humanitarian Imperialisms and Global Feminisms in an Age of Terror." *Signs* 36, no. 2: 360–383.

Niederle, Muriel, and Lisa Vesterlund. 2007. "Do Women Shy Away from Competition? Do Men Compete Too Much?" *Quarterly Journal of Economics* 122, no. 3 (August): 1067–1101.

Niessen, Alexandra, and Stephan Ruenzi. 2009. *Sex Matters: Gender Differences in a Professional Setting.* CFR Working Paper No. 06-01. University of Cologne: Center for Financial Research. http://www.cfr-cologne.de/download/workingpaper/cfr-06-01.pdf.

Nocera, Joe. 2013. "Sex, Drugs and IPOs." *New York Times,* December 22.

Nordén, Lars. 2010. "Individual Home Bias, Portfolio Churning and Performance." *European Journal of Finance* 16, no. 4 (June): 329–351.

Notaras, Gerasimos. 2007. "Born in Debt: Modern Greece's 180-Year History of Borrowing." *World Crunch.*

Núñez, Rolando. 2013. (Interviewed) "Argentina: Hay 'toda una trama' para obligar a campesinos a abandonar sus tierras." *RT Publicado,* July 23. http://actualidad.rt.com/actualidad/view/100808-argentina-ampesinos-indigenas-abandonar-tierras.

Oberndorfer, Lukas. 2011. "Economic Governance rechtswidrig? Eine Krisenerzählung ohne Kompetenz." *AK-Infobrief eu & international* 3: 7–12.

Oberndorfer, Lukas. 2014. "Will the Juncker Commission Continue to Entrench Neoliberal Policies?" *Social Europe Journal,* October 22. http://www.social-europe.eu/2014/10/juncker-commission/.

Oberndorfer, Lukas. 2015. "From New Constitutionalism to Authoritarian Constitutionalism: New Economic Governance and the State of European Democracy." In *Asymmetric Crisis in Europe and Possible Futures: Critical Political Economy and Post-Keynesian Perspectives*, eds. Johannes Jäger and Elisabeth Springler, pp. 186–207. Abingdon: Routledge.

O'Connor, Sarah. 2008. "Icelandic Women Clean up the 'Male Mess.'" *Financial Times*, October 13.

OECD. 2011. *Divided We Stand: Why Inequality Keeps Rising: Country Note: United Kingdom*. http://www.oecd.org/unitedkingdom/49170234.pdf.

OECD. 2012. *Closing the Gender Gap: Act Now*. http://www.oecd.org/gender/closingthegap.htm.

Okin, Susan Moller. 1989. *Justice, Gender and the Family*. New York: Basic Books.

Orman, Suze. 2007. *Women and Money: Owning the Power to Control Your Destiny*. New York: Spiegel and Grau.

Ott, Julia. 2011. *When Wall Street Met Main Street: The Quest for an Investors' Democracy*. Cambridge, MA: Harvard University Press.

Oxfam. 2013. "The True Cost of Austerity and Inequality: UK Case Study." http://www.oxfam.org/sites/www.oxfam.org/files/cs-true-cost-austerity-inequality-uk-120913-en.pdf.

Oxfam. 2014. *The True Cost of Austerity and Inequality: Ireland Case Study*. Oxford: Oxfam.

Paggalos, Th. 2010. "Response to Andreas Papandreou." *Blog post*. http://axiologisibouleytwn.wordpress.com/.

Palvia, Will. 2011. "The Mystery of Room 2820; and Other Unanswered Questions in the DSK Affair." *The Times* (London), November 29.

Panitch, Leo, and Martijn Konings. 2009. "Myths of Neoliberal Deregulation." *New Left Review* 2, no. 57: 67–83.

Pankhurst, Helen. 2002. "Passing the Buck? Money Literacy and Alternatives to Credit and Saving Schemes." *Gender & Development* 10, no. 3: 10–21.

Panourgià, Neni. 2014. "Of Salt Mines and Salt Cemeteries: Greek Complicity in an International System of Injustice." *Chronos* 10. http://www.chronosmag.eu/index.php/n-panourgia-of-salt-mines-and-salt-cemeteries.html

Pantazis, Christina. 2008. "Criminalisation." *Criminal Justice Matters* 74, no. 1: 10–12.

Papadimetiou, D. 2011. "The Debt Crisis in Greece." Councellor: Finn Østrup, Center for Financial Law and Merc. Finance and Strategic Management CBS, August.

Parr, Sadie. 2011. "Family Policy and the Governance of Anti-Social Behaviour in the UK: Women's Experiences of Intensive Family Support." *Journal of Social Policy* 40, no. 4: 717–737.

Parr, Sadie, and Judy Nixon. 2008. "Rationalising Family Intervention Projects." In *ASBO Nation: The Criminalisation of Nuisance*, ed. Peter Squires, pp. 161–178. Bristol: Policy Press.

Paschalidou, Alexandra. 2012. "What's Wrong with the Greeks." Swedish Documentary on Behalf of SVT Swedish television. https://www.youtube.com/watch?v=mMQF2rSHnbw.

Paulson, Henry M. 2010. *On the Brink: Inside the Race to Stop the Collapse of the Global Financial System*. New York: Business Plus.

Pearson, Ruth. 2012. *Women, Work and Gender Justice in the Global Economy*. New York: Routledge.

Pearson, Ruth, and Caroline Sweetman (eds.). 2011. *Gender and the Economic Crisis*. Oxfam Working in Gender and Development Series. London: Practical Action.

Peck, Jamie. 2008. "Remaking Laissez-Faire." *Progress in Human Geography* 32, no. 1: 3–43.

Peck, Jamie. 2010. *Constructions of Neoliberal Reason*. Oxford: Oxford University Press.

Pedroza, Paola. 2011. *Microfinanzas en América Latina y el Caribe: El sector en cifras 2011*, IADB. http://idbdocs.iadb.org/wsdocs/getdocument.aspx?docnum=35385530.

Pellegrino, Greg, Sally D'Amato, and Anne Weisberg. 2011. *The Gender Dividend: Making the Business Case for Investing in Women*. Deloitte. http://www2.deloitte.com/content/dam/Deloitte/global/Documents/Public-Sector/dttl-ps-thegenderdividend-08082013.pdf.

Pentaraki, Maria. 2013. "If We Do Not Cut Social Spending, We Will End Up like Greece: Challenging Consent to Austerity through Social Work Action." *Critical Social Policy* 33, no. 4: 700–711.

Penttinen, Elina. 2008. *Globalization, Prostitution and Sex-Trafficking: Corporeal Politics*. London: Routledge.

Perfect, David. 2011. *Gender Pay Gaps*. Manchester: Equality and Human Rights Commission.

Perrons, Diane. 2012. "'Global' Financial Crisis, Earnings Inequalities and Gender: Towards a More Sustainable Model of Development." *Comparative Sociology* 11, no. 2: 202–226.

Peterson, V. Spike. 2003. *A Critical Rewriting of Global Political Economy: Integrating Reproductive, Productive and Virtual Economies*. London: Routledge.

Peterson, V. Spike and Ann Sisson Runyan. 2010. *Global Gender Issues in the New Millennium*. 3rd edition. Boulder: Westview Press.

Pettman, Jan Jindy. 1997. "Body Politics: International Sex Tourism." *Third World Quarterly* 18, no. 1: 93–108.

Pettman, Jan Jindy. 2003. "Gendering Globalization in Asia through Miracle and Crisis." *Gender, Technology and Development* 7, no. 2: 171–187.

Phillips, Louise. 2014. *Labour Market Statistics by Ethnic Group: January 2014*. London: Department for Work and Pensions.

Phipps, Alison. 2009. "Rape and Respectability: Ideas about Sexual Violence and Social Class." *Sociology* 43, no. 4: 667–683.

Piercy, Marge. 1976. *Woman on the Edge of Time*. New York: Knopf.

Piercy, Marge. 2003. "Utopian Feminist Visions." Video interview with Oliver Ressler for the installation "Alternative Economics, Alternative Societies." Recorded on Cape Cod, http://www.ressler.at/utopian_feminist_visions/.

Piketty, Thomas. 2014. *Capital in the Twenty-First Century*. Cambridge, MA: Harvard University Press.

Plumpe, Werner. 2011. "Stable Instabilities: Capitalism in Historical Perspective." *Eurozine*. http://www.eurozine.com/articles/2011-12-15-plumpe-en.html.

Pocock, J. G. A. 1975. *The Machiavellian Moment: Florentine Political Thought and the Atlantic Republican Tradition*. Princeton, NJ: Princeton University Press.

Polanyi, Karl. 1944 [1957]. *The Great Transformation: The Political and Economic Origins of Our Time*. Boston: Beacon Press.

Polanyi, Karl. 2001. *The Great Transformation: The Political and Economic Origins of our Time*. 2nd edition. Boston: Beacon Press.

Pollard, Jane. 2013. "Gendering Capital: Financial Crisis, Financialization and (an agenda for) Economic Geography." *Progress in Human Geography* 37, no. 3: 403–423.

Poovey, Mary. 2008. *Genres of the Credit Economy: Mediating Value in the Eighteenth-and Nineteenth-Century Britain*. Chicago: University of Chicago Press.

Poster, Mark. 1988. *Critical Theory of the Family*. New York: Seabury Press.

Poulantzas, Nicos. 1973. *Political Power and Social Classes*. London: New Left Books.

Poulantzas, Nicos. 1978. *State, Power, Socialism*, trans. Patrick Camiller. London: New Left Books.

Poulantzas, Nicos. 2000. *State, Power, and Socialism*. Verso.

Prial, Dunstan. 2011. "Greek Prime Minister Risks Chaos to Save Face." *Fox Business News*, November 1. http://www.foxbusiness.com/markets/2011/11/01/greek-prime-minister-risks-chaos-to-save-face/.

Prügl, Elisabeth. 1999. *The Global Construction of Gender: Home-Based Work in the Political Economy of the 20th Century*. New York: Columbia University Press.

Prügl, Elisabeth. 2012. "'If Lehman Brothers Had Been Lehman Sisters . . .': Gender and Myth in the Aftermath of Financial Crisis." *International Political Sociology* 6, no.1: 21–35.

Prügl, Elisabeth, and Jacqui True. 2014. "Equality Means Business? Governing Gender through Transnational Public-Private Partnerships." *Review of International Political Economy* 21, no. 6: 1137–1169.

Puar, Jasbir K. 2012. "Coda: The Cost of Getting Better Suicide, Sensation, Switchpoints." *GLQ: A Journal of Lesbian and Gay Studies* 18, no. 1: 149–158. doi: 10.1215/10642684-1422179.

Pyle, Jean L. 1999. "Third World Women and Global Restructuring." In *Handbook of the Sociology of Gender*, ed. J. Chavetz, pp. 80–104. New York: Kluwer.

Pyle, Jean L., and Kathryn Ward. 2003. "Recasting Our Understanding of Gender and Work during Global Restructuring." *International Sociology* 18, no. 3: 461–489.

Quatreme, Jean. 2007. "FMI: Sarkozy propulse DSK et enterre Fabius." *Libération*, July 9.

Raghavan, Anita. 2009. "Terminated: Why the Women of Wall Street Are Disappearing." *Forbes Magazine*, March 16.

Rai, Shirin M., and Georgina Waylen. 2013. "Feminist Political Economy: Looking Back, Looking Forward." In *New Frontiers in Feminist Political Economy*, eds. Shirin M. Rai and Georgina Waylen, pp. 1–18. Abingdon: Routledge.

Rai, Shirin M., Catherine Hoskyns, and Dania Thomas. 2014. "Depletion: The Cost of Social Reproduction." *International Feminist Journal of Politics* 16, no. 1: 86–105.

Rake, Katherine. 2009. *Are Women Bearing the Burden of the Recession?* London: Fawcett Society.

Rampell, Catherine. 2009. "'Great Recession': A Brief Etymology." *New York Times*, March 11. http://economix.blogs.nytimes.com/2009/03/11/great-recession-a-brief-etymology/?_php=true&_type=blogs&_r=0.

Randall, Melanie. 2010. "Sexual Assault Law, Credibility, and "Ideal Victims": Consent, Resistance, and Victim Blaming. *Canadian Journal of Women and the Law* 22, no. 2: 397–433.

Rankin, Katherine. 2001. "Governing Development: Neoliberalism, Microcredit, and Rational Economic Woman." *Economy and Society* 30, no. 1: 18–37.

Rankin, Katharine. 2013. "A Critical Geography of Poverty Finance." *Third World Quarterly* 34, no. 4: 547–568.

Rashbaum, William K., and John Eligon. 2011. "Hotel Housekeeper Sues Strauss-Kahn." *New York Times*, August 8.

Razack, Sherene H. 2002. "Gendered Racial Violence and Spatialized Justice." In *Race, Space and the Law: Unmapping a White Settler Society*, ed. Sherene H. Razack, pp. 121–156. Toronto: Between the Lines.

Razzu, Giovanni. 2014. *Gender Inequality in the Labour Market in the UK*. Oxford: Oxford University Press.

Read, Jason. 2013. "Negative Solidarity: Towards a Definition of the Concept." *Unemployed Negativity*, August 11. http://www.unemployednegativity.com/2013/08/negative-solidarity-towards-definition.html.

Redaccion3. 2012. "Liempe estuvo en el Encuentro Nacional de Mujeres." October 9. http://corrienteup.org/2012/10/liempe-estuvo-en-el-encuentro-nacional-de-mujeres/

Resko, Stella. 2010. *Intimate Partner Violence and Women's Economic Security*. El Paso, TX: LFB Scholarly Publishing.

Reuters. 2012. "Eurogroup Statement on Greek Package." February 21. http://uk.reuters.com/article/eurogroup-greece-statement-idUKL5E8DL02G20120221.

Ripol, Vilma. 2013. "Se comprometieron a profundizar la lucha contra la violencia de género al culminar el Encuentro Nacional de Mujeres." *Telam*, November 25.

Roberts, Adrienne. 2012. "Financial Crisis, Financial Firms . . . and Financial Feminism? The Rise of 'Transnational Business Feminism' and the Necessity of Marxist-Feminist IPE." *Socialist Studies* 8, no. 2: 85–108.

Roberts, Adrienne. 2013. "Financing Social Reproduction: The Gendered Relations of Debt and Mortgage Finance in 21st Century America." *New Political Economy* 18, no. 1: 21–42.

Roberts, Adrienne. 2014. "The Political Economy of 'Transnational Business Feminism': Problematizing the Corporate-led Gender Equality Agenda." *International Feminist Journal of Politics*. doi: 10.1080/14616742.2013.849968.

Roberts, Adrienne, and Susanne Soederberg. 2012. "Gender Equality as 'Smart Economics'? A Critique of the 2012 World Development Report." *Third World Quarterly* 33, no. 5: 949–968.

Robertua, Verdinand. 2012. *Violence against Women and Economic Globalization: Case Study of Ciudad Juarez, Mexico* (Master's thesis, Linköping University). http://www.urn.kb.se/resolve?urn=urn:nbn:se:liu:diva-80403.

Robison, Richard. 1996. "The Politics of 'Asian Values.'" *The Pacific Review* 9, no. 3: 309–327.

Rodger, John. 2008. *Criminalising Social Policy: Anti-social behaviour and welfare in a decivilised society*. Cullompton: Willan.

Rodrigues, João, and José Reis. 2012. "The Asymmetries of European Integration and the Crisis of Capitalism in Portugal." *Competition and Change* 16, no. 3: 188–205.

Rogers, Chris. 2014. *Capitalism and Its Alternatives: A Critical Introduction*. London; New York: Zed Books.

Roitman, Janet. n.d. "Crisis." *Political Concepts: A Critical Lexicon*. http://www.politicalconcepts.org/issue1/crisis/.

Romero, Mary. 2013. "Nanny Diaries and Other Stories: Immigrant Women's Labor in the Social Reproduction of American Families." *Revista de Estudios Sociales* 45 (January–April): 186–197. Bogotá.

Rosenberg, Jordana, and Amy Villarejo. 2012. "Queerness, Norms, Utopia." *GLQ: A Journal of Lesbian and Gay Studies* 18, no. 1: 1–18.

Rosin, Hanna. 2010. "The End of Men." *The Atlantic*, July/August. http://www.theatlantic.com/magazine/archive/2010/07/the-end-of-men/8135/.

Roth, Louise Marie. 2006. *Selling Women Short*. Princeton, NJ: Princeton University Press.

Roy, Ananya. 2012. "Subjects of Risk: Technologies of Gender in the Making of Millennial Development." *Public Culture* 24, no. 1: 131–166.

Rubery, Jill. 2011. *Women and Recession: Volume 20*. New York: Routledge Revival.

Rubery, Jill, and Anthony Rafferty. 2013. "Gender, Recession and Austerity in the UK." In *Women and Austerity: The Economic Crisis and the Future for Gender Equality*, eds. Maria Karamessini and Jill Rubery, pp. 123–143. London: Routledge.

Ruiz, Miriam. 2013. "Corrupción oficial genera tráfico de mujeres en México." *CIMAC*, January 15. México. http://www.cimacnoticias.com.mx/node/27975.

Rupert, Mark. 1995. *Producing Hegemony: The Politics of Mass Production and American Global Power*. Cambridge: Cambridge University Press.

Rusbridger, Alan. 2015. "Farewell, Readers." *The Guardian*. May 29. http://www.theguardian.com/media/2015/may/29/farewell-readers-alan-rusbridger-on-leaving-the-guardian.

Russia Today. 2013. "Argentina: Hay "toda una trama" para obligar a campesinos a abandonar sus tierras." July 23.

Ruwanpura, Kanchana. 2013. "It's the (Household) Economy Stupid! Pension Reform, Collective Resistance and the Reproductive Sphere in Sri Lanka." In *The Global Political Economy of the Household in Asia*, eds. Juanita Elias and Samanthi J. Gunawardana, pp. 145–161. Basingstoke: Palgrave Macmillan.

Ryan, Peter. 2013. "Five Years after Lehman Brothers Collapse, An Analyst Warns the Global Financial Crisis Is Far from Over." *ABC News*, September 26. http://www.abc.net.au/news/2013-09-26/warnings-that-the-worst-of-the-financial-crisis-is-not-over/4981944.

Sabbagh, Dan. 2010. "British Media Join Forces against Murdoch Takeover of BSkyB." *The Guardian*, October 11. http://www.theguardian.com/media/2010/oct/11/murdoch-bskyb-british-media-unite.

Sahara Reporters. 2011. "IMF Chief, Strauss-Kahn's Alleged Sex Attack Victim Is African Woman from Guinea." May 16. http://saharareporters.com/news-page/imf-chief-strauss-kahns-alleged-sex-attack-victim-african-woman-guinea.

Salam, Reihan. 2009. "The Death of Macho: The Era of Male Dominance Is Over." *Foreign Policy* 173 (July–August): 65–70.

Salverda, Tijo. 2006. "Behavioral Economics." http://au.askmen.com/money/investing_300/360_what-is-behavioral-economics.html.

Salvia, Agustín. 2014. "El 22 por ciento de los hogares recibe algún programa social." *La Nacion*, September 14.

Samaritans. 2014. *Men, Suicide and Society: Why Disadvantaged Men in Mid-Life Die by Suicide*. http://www.samaritans.org/about-us/our-research/research-report-men-suicide-and-society.

Sandberg, Sheryl. 2013. *Lean In: Women, Work and the Will to Lead*. New York: Knopf.

Sapienza, Paola, Luigi Zingales, and Dario Maestripieri. 2009. "Gender Differences in Financial Risk Aversion and Career Choices Are Affected by Testosterone." *Proceedings of the National Academy of Sciences* 106 (August 24): 15268–15273.

Sassen, Saskia. 1998. *Globalization and Its Discontents: Essays on the New Mobility of People and Money*. New York: New Press.

Sassen, Saskia. 2000. "Women's Burden: Counter-Geographies of Globalization and the Feminization of Survival." *Journal of International Affairs* 53, no. 3: 503–524.

Scherer, Michael. 2010. "The New Sheriffs of Wall Street." *Time*, May 13.

Schuberth, Helene, and Brigitte Young. 2011. "The Role of Gender in Financial Market Regulation." In *Questioning Financial Governance from a Feminist Perspective*, eds. Brigitte Young, Isa Bakker and Diane Elson, pp. 132–145. London: Routledge.

Schuman, Michael. 2013. "Will 2014 Finally Really Truly Bring an End to the Financial Crisis?" *Time* Business, December 13. http://business.TIME.com/2013/12/13/will-2014-finally-really-truly-bring-an-end-to-the-financial-crisis/.

Schwartz, Herman M. 2009. *Subprime Nation: American Power, Global Capital and the Housing Bubble*. Ithaca, NY: Cornell University Press.

Schwartz, Herman M., and Leonard Seabrooke. 2009. *The Politics of Housing Booms and Busts*. London: Palgrave.

Sassen, Saskia. 1998. *Globalization and Its Discontents: Essays on the New Mobility of People and Money*. New York: New Press.

Schwendener, Martha. 2011. "What Does Occupy Wall Street Mean for Art?" *Village Voice*, October 19. http://www.villagevoice.com/2011-10-19/art/what-does-occupy-wall-street-mean-for-art/.

Seabrooke, Leonard. 2010. "What Do I Get? The Everyday Politics of Expectations and the Subprime Crisis." *New Political Economy* 15, no. 1: 51–70.

Seguino, Stephanie. 2000. "Gender Inequality and Economic Growth: A Cross Country Analysis." *World Development* 28, no. 7: 1211–1230.

Seguino, Stephanie. 2010. The Global Economic Crisis, Its Gender and Ethnic Implications, and Policy Responses. *Gender and Development* 18, no. 2: 179–199.

Seidelmann, R. 2009. "The EU's Neighbourhood Policies." In *The European Union and Global Governance*, ed. M. Telò, pp. 261–282. London: Routledge.

Seligson, Mitchell A., Amy Erica Smith, and Elizabeth J. Zechmeister. 2012. *The Political Culture of Democracy in the Americas, 2012: Towards Equality of Opportunity*. Nashville: Vanderbilt University. Latin American Public Opinion Project (LAPOP).

Seth, Sanjay (ed.). 2013. *Postcolonial Theory and International Relations: A Critical Introduction*. New York and London: Routledge.

Sexton, J. 2010. "People-of-Color-Blindness: Notes on the Afterlife of Slavery." *Social Text* 28, no. 2: 31–56.

Shafer, Jack. 2010. "Murdoch's Disastrous Triumph." *Slate*, June 1. http://www.slate.com/articles/news_and_politics/press_box/2010/06/murdochs_disastrous_triumph.html.

Shannon, Victoria. 2010. "Equal Rights for Women? Survey Says: Yes, but . . ." *New York Times*, July 10. http://www.nytimes.com/2010/07/01/world/01iht-poll.html?pagewanted=all&_r=3&.

Shapiro, Michael J. 1986. "Metaphor in the Philosophy of the Social Sciences." *Cultural Critique* 2: 191–214.

Sheehy, Elizabeth. 2002. "Evidence Law and the 'Credibility Testing' of Women." *Queensland University of Technology Law and Justice Journal* 157, no. 2: 173.

Shepherd, Laura J. 2013. *Gender, Violence and Popular Culture: Telling Stories*. Abingdon; Oxon; New York: Routledge.

Silva, M. Jennifer. 2013. *Coming Up Short: Working-Class Adulthood in an Age of Uncertainty*. Oxford: Oxford University Press.

Silvey, Rachel. 2000. "Stigmatized Spaces: Gender and Mobility under Crisis in South Sulawesi, Indonesia." *Gender Place and Culture* 7, no. 2: 143–161.

Silvey, Rachel, and Rebecca Elmhirst. 2003. "Engendering Social Capital: Women Workers and Rural–Urban Networks in Indonesia's Crisis." *World Development* 31, no. 5: 865–879.

Singh, Ajit, and Josephine Ann Zammit. 2000. "International Capital Flows: Identifying the Gender Dimension." *World Development* 28, no. 7: 1249–1268.

Skoutaris, Nikos. 2014. "Constitutional Change through Euro-Crisis Law." Workshop at European University Institute, October 18. http://eurocrisislaw.eui.eu/wp-content/uploads/2014/10/Session-VI_Nikos-Skoutaris.pdf.

Slavnic, Zoran, and Susanne Urban. 2008. "Socio-Economic Trends in the Swedish Taxi Sector—Deregulation, Recommodification, Ethnification." *International Journal on Multicultural Societies* 10, no. 1: 76–94.

Slaughter, Anne-Marie. 2012. "Why Women Still Can't Have It All." *The Atlantic Monthly*, July–August. http://www.theatlantic.com/magazine/archive/2012/07/why-women-still-cant-have-it-all/309020/.

Smith, Andrew. 2014. "Blowing It." *The Guardian Weekend Magazine*, November 22.

Smith, Anna Marie. 2001. "Missing Poststructuralism, Missing Foucault: Butler and Fraser on Capitalism and the Regulation of Sexuality." *Social Text* 19, no. 2: 103–125.

Smith, Nicola. 2015. "Queer in/and Sexual Economies." In *Queer Sex Work*, eds. Mary Laing, Katy Pilcher, and Nicola Smith. London: Routledge.

Smith, Nicola, and Donna Lee. 2015. "What's Queer about Political Science?" *British Journal of Politics & International Relations* 17, no. 1: 49–63.

Sneader, Kevin. 2014. "Why Corporate Asia's Gender Gap Matters." *World Economic Forum Blog*, May 20. http://forumblog.org/2014/05/women-boardroom-east-asia-2014/.

Soederberg, Susanne. 2014. *Debtfare States and the Poverty Industry: Money, Discipline and the Surplus Population*. London: Routledge.

Solnit, Rebecca. 2012. "Success Is for the Stubborn." September 16. http://www.tom-dispatch.com/post/175593/tomgram%3A_rebecca_solnit%2C_success_is_for_the_stubborn/.

Sommer, Jeff. 2010. "How Men's Overconfidence Hurts Them as Investors." *New York Times*, March 14.

Spar, Deborah L. 2009. "One Gender's Crash: An Economic Crisis Women Might Have Helped to Avert." *Washington Post*, January 4.

Spar, Deborah L. 2013. *Wonder Women: Sex, Power and the Quest for Perfection*. New York: Sarah Crichton Books, Farrar, Straus and Giroux.

Sparr, Pamela (ed.). 1994. *Mortgaging Women's Lives: Feminist Critiques of Structural Adjustment*. London: Zed Press.

Spears, Jeffrey, and Cassia Spohn. 1997. "The Effect of Evidence Factors and Victim Characteristics on Prosecutors' Charging Decisions in Sexual Assault Cases." In *Justice Quarterly. Spiegel*. 2011. "Greece Must Live Up to Its Commitments." Interview with Bundesbank

Spitzer, Denise L., and Nicola Piper. 2014. "Retrenched and Returned: Filipino Migrant Workers during Times of Crisis." *Sociology* 48, no. 5: 1007–1023.

Stafford, Sophia. 2011. "The Greek Bankruptcy and Bailout: A History Review." http://sofisintown2.blogspot.com.au/2011/06/greek-bankruptcy-and-bailout-history.html.

Stamp, Stuart. 2009. *A Policy Framework for Addressing Over-indebtedness*. Dublin: Combat Poverty Agency.

Standing, Guy. 2014. *The Precariat: The New Dangerous Class*. London: Bloomsbury Academic.

Stanley, Liam. 2014a. "'We're Reaping What We Sowed': Everyday Crisis Narratives and Acquiescence to the Age of Austerity." *New Political Economy*. doi: http://dx.doi.org/10.1080/13563467.2013.861412.

Stanley, Liam. 2014b. "The Idea of Austerity: An Alternative History." Presented at the University of Sheffield Political Economy Research Series, Sheffield, January 23.

Starkman, Dean. 2013. "Murdoch's Straw Snobs." *Columbia Journalism Review*, January 8. http://www.cjr.org/the_audit/murdochs_straw_snobs.php.

Stavrianos, L. S. 2000. *The Balkans since 1453*. London: C. Hurst.

Steans, Jill. 1999. "The Private Is Global: Feminist Politics and Global Political Economy." *New Political Economy* 4, no. 1: 113–128.

Stonewall Housing. 2014. "Home." http://www.stonewallhousing.org/.

Storey, John. 2003. *Inventing Popular Culture: From Folklore to Globalization*. Malden, MA: Blackwell.

Storey, John. 2012. *Cultural Theory and Popular Culture*. Harlow: Pearson.

Strange, Susan. 1997. *Casino Capitalism*. Manchester: Manchester University Press.

Stringer, Anne. 2000. *Women inside in Debt: The Prison and Debt Project*. Adelaide: Women in Corrections: Staff and Clients Conference convened by the Australian Institute of Criminology in conjunction with the Department for Correctional Services SA. http://www.aic.gov.au/media_library/conferences/womencorrections/stringer.pdf.

Stuckler, David, and Sanjay Basu. 2013. *The Body Economic: Eight Experiments in Economic Recovery, from Iceland to Greece*. London: Allen Lane.

Sullivan, Kevin, and Mary Jordan. 2009. "In Banking Crisis, Guys Get the Blame; More Women Needed in Top Jobs, Critics Say." *Washington Post*, February 11.

Sum, Ngai-Ling. 2013. "A Cultural Political Economy of Crisis Recovery: (Trans-) National Imaginaries of 'BRIC' and the Subalterns in China." *Economy and Society* 42, no. 4: 543–570.

Sunderland, Ruth. 2009a. "The real victims of this credit crunch? Women." *The Observer*, January 18.

Sunderland, Ruth. 2009b. "We Need More Heavy-Hitters at Davos: This Mess Was Made by Men. Now Let the Women Have Their Say." *The Observer*, February 1.

Suskind, Ron. 2011. *Confidence Men: Wall Street, Washington and the Education of a President*. New York: Harper.

Sutton, Barbara. 2011. *Bodies in Crisis: Culture, Violence, and Women's Resistance in Neoliberal Argentina*. New Brunswick, NJ: Rutgers University Press.

Taibbi, Matt. 2014. "The $9 Billion Witness: Meet JP Morgan Chase's Worse Nightmare." *Rolling Stone*, November 6. http://www.rollingstone.com/politics/news/the-9-billion-witness-20141106.

Takeda, Hiroko. 2008. "Structural Reform of the Family and the Neoliberalisation of Everyday Life in Japan." *New Political Economy* 13, no. 2: 153–172.

Tamirisa, Natalia. 2011. "Financial Regulators, Central Banks Share Financial Stability Role." *IMF Research Department*, November 23. http://www.imf.org/external/pubs/ft/survey/so/2011/RES112311A.htm.

Tan, Cara. 2009. "He-cession: The Recession is an Economic Crisis for Men." *Economy Watch*, June 28. http://www.economywatch.com/economy-business-and-finance-news/he-cession-the-recession-is-an-economic-crisis-for-men-06-28.html.

Taylor, Ian and Ruth Jamieson. 1999. "Sex Trafficking and the Mainstreaming of Market Culture." *Crime, Law, and Social Change* 32: 257–278.

Taylor, Paul, Rakesh Kochhar, and Richard Fry. 2011. *Twenty-to-One: Wealth Gap Rises to Record Highs between Whites, Blacks and Hispanics*. Washington, DC: Pew Research Center.

Taylor-Robinson, David, Emeline Rougeaux, Dominic Harrison, Margaret Whitehead, Ben Barr, and Anna Pearce. 2013. "The Rise of Food Poverty in the UK." *BMJ: British Medical Journal* 347. http://www.bmj.com/content/347/bmj.f7157.

Télam. 2012. "Finalizó el multitudinario encuentro de mujeres y San Juan será la próxima sede." October 8. http://www.telam.com.ar/nota/40251/.

Télam. 2013. "Intenso y concurrido debate en el Encuentro Nacional de Mujeres." November 24. http://www.telam.com.ar/notas/201311/42045-tras-una-intensa-jornada-de-apertura-continua-en-san-juan-el-encuentro-nacional-de-mujeres .html

Tellmann, Ute. 2013. "Catastrophic Populations and the Fear of the Future." *Theory, Culture & Society* 30, no. 2: 135–155.

Territoriodigital. 2012. "Miles de mujeres debaten sobre su realidad, objetivos y futuro." October 7. http://www.territoriodigital.com/notaimpresa.aspx?c= 7482063516665223.

Terzis, Kostantinos. 2014. "The Slaves of Debt . . . Radical Economic Restructuring or Subservience to Global Bankers?" London.

Tepe, Daniela. 2014. "A Big Broken Society?" *SPERI*. http://speri.dept.shef.ac.uk/ 2014/03/11/big-broken-society/.

Tepe-Belfrage, Daniela. 2015. "A Feminist Critique of Community Politics." In *The British Growth Crisis: The Search for a New Model*, eds. Jeremy Green and Colin Hay. Basingstoke: Palgrave Macmillan.

Theodorikakou, O., et al. 2012. "Homelessness in Greece, 2012: An In-Depth Research on Homelessness in the Financial Crisis." Presentation at European Research Conference: Access to Housing for Homeless People in Europe, York, September 21. http://www.slideshare.net/FEANTSA/seminar-3-klimaka.

Thomas, Duncan, Elizabeth Frankenberg, Kathleen Beegle, and Graciela Teruel. 1999. "Household Budgets, Household Composition and the Crisis in Indonesia: Evidence from Longitudinal Household Survey Data." Mimeograph paper for 1999 Population Association America Meetings, New York, March 25–27.

Thomas, Landon. 2010. "A Routine Deal Became an $840 Million Mistake." *New York Times*, April 22. http://www.nytimes.com/2010/04/23/business/23cdo.html.

Thompson, John B. 2000. *Political Scandal: Power and Visibility in the Media Age*. Cambridge: Polity Press; Malden, MA: Blackwell.

Tickner, J. Ann. 1992. *Gender in International Relations: Feminist Perspectives on Achieving Global Security*. New York: Columbia University Press.

Tickner, J. Ann. 2005. "What Is Your Research Program? Some Feminist Answers to International Relations Methodological Questions." *International Studies Quarterly* 49: 1–21.

Tickner, J. Ann, and Laura S. Sjoberg. 2011. *Feminism and International Relations: Conversations about the Past, Present and Future*. New York: Routledge.

Tiempo Argentino. 2013. "Cierre con el reclamo en voz alta." November 25. http:// tiempo.infonews.com/nota/117723/cierre-con-el-reclamo-en-voz-alta.

Time. 2001. "Looking Beyond the Bear." March 26. http://content.time.com/time/cov-ers/0,16641,20010326,00.html.

Time. 2008. "The Global Financial Crisis: A Look at the World as It Deals with a Global Financial Crisis." http://www.time.com/time/photogallery/0,29307, 1845923,00.html#ixzz2PWOLeSFG.

Time. 2008a. "A Woman Mops the Floor of the Frankfurt Stock Exchange before Markets Opened, Sept. 30, 2008." *The Global Financial Crisis: A Look at the World as It Deals with a Global Financial Crisis*, September 30. http://www.time.com/ time/photogallery/0,29307,1845923,00.html#ixzz2PVzSjzAy.

Time. 2008b. "Rough Seas." *The Global Financial Crisis: A Look at the World as It Deals with a Global Financial Crisis*, September 30. http://content.time.com/time/pho-togallery/0,29307,1845923_1774401,00.html.

Time. 2008c. "The New Hard Times." October 13. http://content.time.com/time/covers/0,16641,20081013,00.html.

Time. 2009. "25 People to Blame for the Financial Crisis." February 11. http://content.time.com/time/specials/packages/article/0,28804,1877351_1877350_1877339,00.html.

Time. 2012. "The Wimpy Recovery." April 2. http://content.time.com/time/covers/0,16641,20120402,00.html.

Time. 2014. "About *Time* Magazine." https://subs.TIME.com/about-TIME/.

Trattner, Walter. 1994. *From Poor Law to Welfare State: A History of Social Welfare in America*. New York: The Free Press.

Trotta, Daniel, and Noeleen Walder. 2011. "More Questions Raised about Strauss-Kahn Accusers." *Reuters*, July 2.

True, Jacqui. 2008a. "Gender Mainstreaming and Trade Governance in the Asia-Pacific Economic Cooperation Forum (APEC)." In *Global Governance: Feminist Perspectives*, eds. Georgina Waylen and Shirin M. Rai, pp. 129–159. New York: Palgrave.

True, Jacqui. 2008b. "Global Accountability and Transnational Networks: The Women Leaders' Network and Asia Pacific Economic Cooperation." *The Pacific Review* 21, no. 1: 1–26.

True, Jacqui. 2012. *The Political Economy of Violence against Women*. New York: Oxford University Press.

True, Jacqui. 2014. "The Global Governance of Gender." In *Handbook of International Political Economy and Governance*, eds. Anthony Payne and Nicola Phillips, pp. 331–343. Cheltenham: Edward Elgar.

True, Jacqui. 2013. "Counting Women, Balancing Gender: Increasing Women's Participation in Governance." *Politics and Gender* 9, no. 3: 351–359.

Truong, Thanh-Dam. 1999. "The Underbelly of the Tiger: Gender and the Demystification of the Asian Miracle." *Review of International Political Economy* 6, no. 2: 133–165.

Truong, Thanh-Dam. 2000. "A Feminist Perspective on the Asian Miracle and Crisis: Enlarging the Conceptual Map of Human Development." *Journal of Human Development* 1, no. 1: 159–164.

Tsing, A. 2000. "Inside the Economy of Appearances." *Public Culture* 12, no. 1: 115–144.

Tyre, Peg. 2013. "Dear Sheryl Sandberg, Congrats on Your New Book, but . . ." *Washington Post*, March 9. http://www.washingtonpost.com/blogs/she-the-people/wp/2013/03/09/dear-sheryl-sandberg-congrats-on-your-new-book-but/.

Udry, Charles-André. 2012. "Greece: The Cradle of What Kind of Europe?" *IV Online Magazine: IV449*, June 29. http://www.internationalviewpoint.org/spip.php?article2682.

UK Department for Communities and Local Government. 2013. "14,000 Troubled Families Turned Around." Press Release, September 10. https://www.gov.uk/government/news/14000-troubled-families-turned-around.

UK Department for Communities and Local Government. 2014a. *Troubled Families: Case Studies*. https://www.gov.uk/government/uploads/system/uploads/attachment_data/file/10961/Troubled_families_case_studies.pdf.

UK Department for Communities and Local Government. 2014b. "Troubled Families Programme Expanded to Help Younger Children." Press Release, August 19, https://www.gov.uk/government/news/troubled-families-programme-expanded-to-help-younger-children.

UK Department for Communities and Local Government. 2014c . *Understanding Troubled Families*. https://www.gov.uk/government/uploads/system/uploads/attachment_data/file/336430/Understanding_Troubled_Families_web_format.pdf.

UKDepartmentforWorkandPensions.2010.*ConsultationResponsesto21stCenturyWelfare*. https://www.gov.uk/government/uploads/system/uploads/attachment_data/file/181144/21st-century-welfare-response.pdf.

UK Department for Work and Pensions. 2012. *Housing Benefit: Size Criteria for People Renting in the Social Rented Sector: Equality Impact Assessment*. https://www.gov.uk/government/uploads/system/uploads/attachment_data/file/220154/eia-social-sector-housing-under-occupation-wr2011.pdf.

UK Equality and Human Rights Commission. 2009. *Financial Services Inquiry*. London: Equality and Human Rights Commission.

UK National Audit Office. 2013a. *Taxpayer Support for UK Banks: FAQs*. http://www.nao.org.uk/highlights/taxpayer-support-for-uk-banks-faqs/.

UK National Audit Office. 2013b. *Programmes to Help Families Facing Multiple Challenges*. http://www.nao.org.uk/report/programmes-help-families-facing-multiple-challenges-2/.

Ukeles, Mierle Laderman. 1969. *Manifesto for Maintenance Art*. Republished at http://www.arnolfini.org.uk/blog/manifesto-for-maintenance-art-1969.

United Nations Development Program (UNDP). 2012. *Powerful Synergies: Gender Equality, Economic Development and Environmental Sustainability*. New York: United Nations.

United Nations Development Program (UNDP). 2013. *Human Development Report 2013: The Rise of the South*. United Nations Development Program. http://hdr.undp.org/sites/default/files/reports/14/hdr2013_en_complete.pdf.

United Nations Economic and Social Commission for Asia-Pacific (UNESCAP). 2012. "Asia-Pacific Region Must Invest in Women and Girls to Build Economic Resilience, ESCAP Tells Media." Press Release G/11/2012, Bangkok. http://www.unescap.org/news/asia-pacific-region-must-invest-women-and-girls-build-economic-resilience-escap-tells-media

UN Women. 2011. *The Gender Dividend: A Business Case for Gender Equality*. New York: United Nations.

United States State Department. 2011. "Guinea." Annual Country Report.

University of Sheffield School of Health and Related Research (ScHAAR). 2014. "Breast Milk Policy Financial Incentives." https://www.shef.ac.uk/scharr/sections/ph/research/breastmilk/fi.

Valaoritis, J. A. 1902. "The History of the National Bank of Greece 1842–1902." Athens: Historical Records of the National Bank of Greece, vols. 1, 2 (in Greek).

Vaneigem, Raoul. 2012 [1967]. *The Revolution of Everyday Life*. New York: Verso.

Van Natta, Don, Jr., Jo Becker, and Graham Bowley. 2010. "Tabloid Hack Attack on Royals, and Beyond." *New York Times Magazine*, September 1. http://www.nytimes.com/2010/09/05/magazine/05hacking-t.html?pagewanted=all&_r=0#.

Van Staveren, Irene. 2010. "Gender Biases in Finance." *Gender and Development* 9, no. 1: 9–17.

Van Staveren, Irene. 2011. "From Gender as Exogenous to Gender as Endogenous in the New Economics." *New Economics as Mainstream Economics*, eds. Philip Arestis and Malcolm Sawyer, pp. 116–153. Basingstoke: Palgrave Macmillan.

Van Swaaningen, Rene. 1997. *Critical Criminology: Visions from Europe*. London: Sage Publications.

Varoufakis, Yanis. 2015. *The Global Minotaur: America, Europe and the Future of the Global Economy*. 2nd edition. London: Zed Books

Veremis, Th. 1980. "The Greek State and Economy during the Pangalos Regime, 1925–1926." *Journal of the Hellenic Diaspora* 7 (Summer): 43–50.

Vergopoulos, K. 1977. "The Last Administration of Trikoupis and the Bankruptcy." In *History of the Greek Nation [Istoria tou Ellenikou Ethnous]*, vol. 14, pp. 31–35. Athens: Εκδοτική Αθηνών (Athens Publishers).

Vij, Ritu. 2013. "Affective Fields of Precarity: Gendered Antinomies in Contemporary Japan." *Alternatives* 38, no. 2: 122–138.

Vishmidt, Marina. 2013. "Permanent Reproductive Crisis: An Interview with Silvia Federici." *MetaMute*, March 7. http://www.metamute.org/editorial/articles/permanent-reproductive-crisis-interview-silvia-federici.

Vogel, Lise. 2014. *Marxism and the Oppression of Women: Towards a Unitary Theory*. Chicago: Haymarket Books (reprint).

Wacquant, Loic. 2008. *Urban Outcasts: A Comparative Sociology of Advanced Marginality*. Cambridge: Polity Press.

Wacquant, Loic. 2009. *Punishing the Poor: The Neoliberal Government of Social Insecurity (Politics, History, & Culture)*. Durham, NC; London: Duke University Press.

Wade, Matt. 2013. "President's Pick to Head Fed Banks on Women as Financial Heavy Hitters." *Sydney Morning Herald*, October 12.

Walby, Sylvia. 2009. *Gender and the Financial Crisis. UNESCO Paper*, April 9.

Waring, Marilyn, and Karanina Sumeo. 2010. "Economic Crisis and Unpaid Care Work in the Pacific." *UNDP Gender Team*, presented at the Pacific Conference on the Human Face of the Global Economic Crisis, Port Vila, Vanuatu, December 10–12.

Warner, Judith. 2013. "Why Sandberg Matters for Real Women." *Time*, March 7. http://ideas.time.com/2013/03/07/why-sandberg-matters-for-real-women/.

Watson, Matthew. 2014. *Uneconomic Economics and the Crisis of the Model World*. Basingstoke: Palgrave.

Watt, Holly. 2013. "David Cameron's Private Regret over Gay Marriage Law." *The Telegraph*, September 27. http://www.telegraph.co.uk/news/politics/david-cameron/10341788/David-Camerons-private-regret-over-gay-marriage-law.html.

Watt, Nicholas. 2009. "David Cameron Apologises to Gay People for Section 28." *The Guardian*, July 2, sec. Politics.

Watt, Nicholas. 2014. "Cameron Goes Back to the Future with Old-Style Moral Focus on the Family." *The Guardian*, August 18.

Waylen, Georgina. 2006. "You Still Don't Understand: Why Troubled Engagements Continue between Feminists and (Critical) IPE." *Review of International Studies* 32, no. 1: 145–164.

Weaver, Hilary. 2001. "Indigenous Identity: What Is It and Who Really Has It?" *American Indian Quarterly* 25, no. 2: 240–255.

Weber, Cynthia. 2008. "Popular Visual Language as Global Communication: The Remediation of United Airlines Flight 93." *Review of International Studies* 34, no. S1: 137–153.

Weeks, Kathi. 2011. *The Problem with Work: Marxism, Feminism, Antiwork Politics and Postwork Imaginaries*. Durham, NC: Duke University Press.

Weidmann, Jens. 2011a. "Managing Macroprudential and Monetary Policy—A Challenge for Central Banks." Speech in Berlin, November 8. Deutsche Bundesbank.

Weidmann, Jens. 2011b. *Spiegel Online International*, September 19. http://www.spiegel.de/international/germany/spiegel-interview-with-bundesbank-president-jens-weidmann-greece-must-live-up-to-its-commitments-a-787064.html.

Weiner, Joann. 2013. "Five Women of the Financial Crisis: Who They Are and Why They Mattered." *Washington Post*, September 17. http://www.washingtonpost.com/blogs/she-the-people/wp/2013/09/17/five-women-of-the-financial-crisis-who-they-are-and-why-they-mattered/.

Weisberg, Anne. 2011. "How Women Can Help You Beat the Competition." *Deloitte Perspectives*, January 13. Deloitte. http://globalblogs.deloitte.com/deloitte-perspectives/2011/01/how-women-can-help-you-beat-the-competition.html, accessed October18, 2011.

Weissman, Deborah. 2009. "Global Economics and Their Progenies." In *Terrorizing Women: Femicide in the Americas,* eds. Rosa-Linda Fregoso and Cynthia Bejarano, pp. 225–242. Durham, NC: Duke University Press.

Weldes, Jutta. 2006. "High Politics and Low Data: Globalization Discourses and Popular Culture." In *Interpretation and Method: Empirical Research Methods and the Interpretive Turn*, eds. Dvora Yanow and Peregrine Schwartz-Shea, pp. 176–186. New York: M. E. Sharpe.

Welshman, John. 2012. *"Troubled Families": The Lessons of History, 1880–2012*. PSE Poverty and Social Exclusion. http://www.historyandpolicy.org/policy-papers/papers/troubled-families-the-lessons-of-history-1880-2012.

Wesling, Meg. 2012. "Queer Value." *GLQ: A Journal of Lesbian and Gay Studies* 18, no. 1: 107–125.

White, Luise. 2000. *Speaking with Vampires: Rumor and History in Colonial Africa*. Berkeley: University of California Press.

Widmaier, Wesley W. 2010. "Emotions before Paradigms: Elite Anxiety and Populist Resentment from the Asian to Subprime Crises." *Millennium: Journal of International Studies* 39, no. 1: 127–144.

Widmaier, Wesley. 2014. "Lawyers, Gender, and Money: Consensus, Closure, and Conflict in the Global Financial Crisis." *Politics and Gender* 10: 1–26.

Wilcox, W. Bradford. 2011. "The Great Recession's Silver Lining." Report by the National Marriage Project at the University of Virginia. http://www.stateofourunions.org/2009/great_recession.php

Willems, Marije. 2014. "Gerrit Zalm Verkleed als Zijn 'Zus', de Bordeelhoudster Priscilla [Gerrit Zalm Dressed Up as His 'Sister,' the Madam Priscilla]." *NRC Handelsblad*, January 15. http://www.nrc.nl/nieuws/2014/01/15/video-cabaretact-gerrit-zalm-verkleed-als-zijn-zus-priscilla/.

Williams, E. 1994. *Capitalism and Slavery*. Chapel Hill: University of North Carolina Press.

Winnubst, Shannon. 2012. "The Queer Thing about Neoliberal Pleasure: A Foucauldian Warning." *Foucault Studies* 14: 79–97.

Wintour, Patrick. 2013. "Eric Pickles Hails Progress in Tackling 'Troubled Families.'" *The Guardian*. November 25.

Wintour, Patrick. 2014. "Government 'Is Starting to Help 120,000 Troubled Families.'" *The Guardian*, October 29.

Wöhl, Stefanie. 2013. "Die 'Krise' repräsentativer Demokratie in Europa. Demokratietheoretische und Politikfeld bezogene Reflexionen." *Forschungsjournal Soziale Bewegungen* 26, no. 1: 64–75.

Wöhl, Stefanie. 2014. "The State and Gender Relations in International Political Economy: A State-Theoretical Approach to Varieties of Capitalism in Crisis." *Capital & Class* 38, no. 1: 83–95.

Wolff, Michael. 2008a. *The Man Who Owns the News: Inside the Secret World of Rupert Murdoch.* New York: Broadway Books.

Wolff, Michael. 2008b. "Tuesdays with Rupert." *Vanity Fair,* October. http://www.vanityfair.com/news/2008/10/wolff200810.

Wolff, Michael. 2010. "Two Men and a Newsstand." *Vanity Fair,* October. http://www.vanityfair.com/news/2010/10/times-versus-wall-street-journal-201010.

Wolff, Michael. 2015. "Snowden Effect Hits Guardian." *USA Today,* March 20. http://www.usatoday.com/story/money/columnist/wolff/2015/03/20/new-editor-for-guardian-newspaper/25094233/.

Women, Business and the Law. 2012. *Removing Barriers to Economic Inclusion: Measuring Gender Parity in 141 Countries.* Washington, DC: IFC/World Bank.

Women's Budget Group. 2014a. "The Impact on Women of Budget 2014: No Recovery for Women." http://www.wbg.org.uk/wp-content/uploads/2014/03/FINAL-WBG-2014-budget-response.pdf.

Women's Budget Group. 2014b. "Budget 2014: The Government Is Taking Money from Women to Fund Tax Breaks for Men: New Analysis from the Women's Budget Group." http://www.wbg.org.uk/wp-content/uploads/2014/03/WBG-budget-2014-report-press-release-20140414-1.pdf.

Wood, Claudia. 2012. *Destination Unknown: Summer 2012.* London: Demos.

"Worker Rights: The View from Southeast Asia." *Australian Journal of International Affairs* 64, no. 1: 70–85.

World Bank. 2006. *Gender Equality as Smart Economics: A World Bank Group Gender Action Plan* (Fiscal Years 2007–2010). September. Washington, DC: World Bank.

World Bank. 2012. *World Development Report 2012: Gender Equality and Development.* Washington, DC: World Bank.

World Bank. 2014. "Gender Equality Data & Statistics. Latin American and the Caribbean." *The World Bank Group.* http://datatopics.worldbank.org/gender/region/latin-america-and-caribbean.

World Economic Forum (WEF). 2009. *India's Economic Summit.* Geneva: World Economic Forum.

World Economic Forum (WEF). 2011. "World Economic Forum on East Asia 2011—Driving Asian Growth: Women at the Wheel." http://www.weforum.org/sessions/summary/driving-asian-growth-women-wheel.

World Economic Forum (WEF). 2011a. *Global Gender Gap Report.* Geneva.

World Economic Forum (WEF). 2011b. *Corporate Gender Gap Report 2010.* Geneva.

World Economic Forum. 2012. "Asian Women as the Way Forward" (video session). http://www.weforum.org/videos/east-asia-2012-asian-women-way-forward.

World Economic Forum. 2013. *Global Gender Gap Report 2013.* http://www.weforum.org/reports/global-gender-gap-report-2013

World Economic Forum. 2014. *Global Risks 2014: Ninth Edition.* Geneva: World Economic Forum.

Wyly, Elvin A., and C. S. Ponder. 2011. "Gender, Age, and Race in Subprime America." *Housing Policy Debate* 21, no. 4: 529–564.

XXVIII Encuentro Nacional de Mujeres. 2013. "Manifiesto feminista contra la mega-minería y el odelo patriarcal colonial extractivista," San Juan, November 15. http://www.conflictosmineros.net/contenidos/2-argentina/15747-manifiesto-feminista-contra-la-megamineria-y-el-modelo-patriarcal-colonial-extractivista.

YaMisiones. 2012. "Al margen de un grupo minúsculo, la evaluación del Encuentro de Mujeres es muy positivo." October 9.

Young, Brigitte. 2003. "Financial Crises and Social Reproduction: Asia, Argentina and Brazil." In *Power, Production and Social Reproduction: Human In/security in the Global Political Economy*, eds. Isabella Bakker and Stephen Gill, pp. 103–124. Basingstoke: Palgrave Macmillan.

Young, Brigitte. 2009. "When 'Credit Becomes Debt' in the Subprime Crisis: Is There a Gender Dimension?" www.havenscenter.org/files/Young_NPE_Subprime_Gender-1.doc.

Young, Brigitte. 2013. "Structural Power and the Gender Biases of Technocratic Network Governance in Finance." In *Feminist Strategies in International Governance*, eds. Gülay Caglar, Elisabeth Prügl, and Susanne Zwingel, pp. 267–282. London: Routledge.

Young, Brigitte, and Christoph Scherrer (eds.). 2010. *Gender Knowledge and Knowledge Networks in International Political Economy*. Baden-Baden: Nomos.

Young, B., and W. Semmler. 2011."The European Sovereign Debt Crisis: Is Germany to Blame?" *German Politics and Society* 29, no. 97: 1–24.

Young, Brigitte, Diane Elson, and Isabella Bakker (eds.). 2011. *Questioning Financial Governance from a Feminist Perspective*. Basingstoke: Palgrave Macmillan.

Youngs, Gillian. 2000. "Embodied Political Economy or an Escape from Disembodied Knowledge." In *Political Economy, Power and the Body*, ed. Gillian Youngs, pp. 11–30. Basingstoke: Palgrave.

Zacchion, Narda, and Robert Scheer. 2009. "They Shot the Messenger." *MS Magazine* Fall: 34–37.

Zalewski, Marysia. 2013. *Feminist International Relations: 'Exquisite Corpse.'* Abingdon; Oxon; New York: Routledge.

Zatlin, J., and L. Ferleger. 2012. "German Elites View Southern Europeans as Inferior." *Salon*, July 3. http://www.salon.com/topic/european_financial_crisis/.

Zicavo, Eugenia. 2010. "Charla con Juana Beatriz Inderecio, de la comunidad toba QOM—Chaco—Activista por los derechos de su comunidad." *Hecho en Buenos Aires*. Accessed through *Agenda de Mujeres*, June 21. http://agendadelasmujeres.com.ar/notadesplegada.php?id=2619.

INDEX

ABACUS, 267, 269, 271, 274
ABN-Amro, 266–268
Adbusters (magazine), 200n2, 201n5
Adler, Roy P., 33
Agathangelou, Anna M., 211. *see also* global raciality of capitalism and "primitive" accumulation
alternative capitalisms (Rogers), 72
alternatives to capitalism (Rogers), 72–73, 73t
American International Group (AIG), 37
anti-capitalism (Rogers), 72–73, 73t
Antonopoulos, Rania, 105
Aphrodite, metonym. *see Focus* (magazine)
Arendt, Hannah, 251
Argentina: Asignación Universal por Hijo (AUH) program, 137; displacement of subsistence farmers, 140; extractive agroexport model, 140; femicide rates, 129; neoliberal policies, 133; on selective default per Standard & Poor, 141
Asian financial crisis (1997-1998), and post-GFC austerity initiatives, 109–125; introduction, 15, 101, 109–112; crony capitalism, 110–111; feminist literature review, 113–114, 119–123, 125n2; hypermasculinity of "tiger" developmental states, 111, 125n1; and language of risk, 117–118; summary conclusion, 123–125; and women at the wheel concept, post-GFC, 110, 112–119; women to the rescue of global capitalism concept, 115–119. *see also specific countries*

Asia-Pacific Economic Cooperation (APEC): High-Level Policy Dialogue on Women and the Economy, 62; Policy Partnership on Women and the Economy (PPWE), 62–63
Aslanbeigui, Nahid, 113
Assange, Julian, 166
austerity initiatives, impact on women, 7–9, 53–54, 120–122, 237. *see also specific countries*
authoritarian neoliberalism (Bruff), 15, 98–100. *see also* Eurozone, post-GFC austerity initiatives
automatism (Fisher), 249

Bachelet, Michele, 126
Bair, Sheila, 28, 52
Bakker, Isabella, 60
"Ban bossy" campaign (Sandberg), 54
Banerji, Himani, 63
bank bailouts, 3, 48, 79–80, 91, 186, 215
Bank of America, 169, 219
"banksters" images, 184, 189f
Banon, Tristane, 153
Barber, Brad, 29, 30
Barthes, Roland, 23, 35–36, 37–38
Basu, Sanjay, 9
Bauman, Andrew, 89
Beckmann, Daniela, 30, 39n5
behavioral explanations of GFC, 184, 189–194f
behavioral finance studies, 29–30
Belfort, Jordan, 271–273
Benería, Lourdes, 113–114
Bennett, Jane, 275, 278
Bennholdt-Thomsen, Veronika, 259

Berardi, Franco (Bifo), 248–249
Berger, John, 259
Berlant, Laurent, 176
Berlusconi, Silvio, 166
Bernstein, Jared, 173
Björk (pop singer), 28
Blair, Cherie, 171
Blair, Tony, 177
Bleiker, Roland, 181
Bloomberg, 169
Blyth, Mark, 3
BNP Paribas, 33–34
body-for-others (Sutton), 134
Born, Brooksley, 28
boundaries. see Eurozone, post-GFC
    austerity initiatives; public-private
    divide (boundaries)
Bowen, Richard, 277, 278
Bowman, Andrew, 89
Brassett, James, 115, 187
Brazil: Bolsa Familia program, 137;
    microfinance, 138; sex trafficking
    rings, 130
BRIC economies, 63, 117
British Broadcasting Corporation
    (BBC), 170
British Equality and Human Rights
    Commission, 26
British Sky Broadcasting (BSkyB),
    170, 177
Broadbent, Kaye, 122
Broadwell, Paula, 166
Brooks, Rebekah, 167, 168, 177
Brooks, Rosa, 55
Brown, Gordon, 171
Buckingham Palace royals, 167
bull, imagery of, 195
Butler, Judith, 23, 233, 276

Caliban and the Witch (Federici), 251
Callan, Erin, 37
Camatte, Jacque, 255
Cambridge University, 31
Cameron, David, 8, 168, 177, 247n17;
    crisis narratives of, 240–245; on
    marriage equality, 232, 241–242;
    "Troubled Families" speech (2011),
    82, 243; "The Values That Underpin
    Our Long-Term Economic Plan"
    speech (2014), 244–245

capitalist hegemony (Rupert), 176
Cari, Irene, 130
Carver, Terrell, 182
casino capitalism (Strange), 25–26
Catalyst, 26, 33
Central European Bank, 218
CERAM Business School, 33, 34
Chang, Kimberly A., 157
Chase, 277
child labor, 119–120
Chile: gender income gaps, 131;
    neoliberal policies, 133
Chistoulas, Dimitris, 229
Citigroup, 26–27, 219, 277
Clarke, Chris, 187
Clayton, 277–278
Clinton, Hillary, 62
Coates, John, 31, 36, 39n8
coda of redemption. see gender and
    myth, post-GFC
Codepink, 196
Cohen, William A., 175
collateralized debt obligations (CDO),
    219–220, 267, 269, 271–272
Colombia: microfinance, 138
competitiveness, masculinized norms
    of. see Eurozone, post-GFC austerity
    initiatives
conditional cash transfer programs. see
    Latin America, crisis in post-neoliberal
Conlin, Ron, 33
The Conquest of Cool (Frank), 43–44
Cooper, Melinda, 269, 275
Corrigan, Tracy, 36
cortisol and oxytocin, 36
Costa, Mariarosa Della, 253–254
Coulson, Andy, 168, 171, 177
Council of the European Union, 98–99
Crawford, Neeta, 258
Credit Agricole, 34
credit default swaps (CDS), 37
Credit Suisse Research Institute, 43
Criterion Institute: Women Effect
    Investment team, 71
crony capitalism, in Asia, 110–111, 120
cultural vs. structural deficiencies. see
    United Kingdom (UK)

Dauvergne, Peter, 71–72
Davies, Nick, 171

Davis, Kristin, 273
Davos woman concept, 115, 186
De Beauvoir, Simone, 24, 38
Debtocracy (documentary), 208, 218, 226, 228
DeFelippis, Jacob, 232–233, 245
Defoe, Daniel, 22
De Goede, Marieke, 10, 22, 23, 35, 52, 110, 179. *see also* gendering the GFC crisis
Deloire, Christophe, 152
Deloitte: *The Gender Dividend: Making the Business Case for Investing in Women*, 70
Demos, 237
Deng, Wendy, 177
depletion of social reproduction (Rai, Hoskyns, and Thomas), 123
Deutsche Telekom, 226
Diallo, Nafissatou, 145. *see also* DSK Affair, analysis of "rape script"
The Dispossessed (Le Guin), 258
distributed responsibility. *see* gendering the GFC crisis
Doctors of the World, 227–228
domestic violence, post-GFC, 9, 108, 127
domestic workers, 55, 65, 136, 158, 162
double exploitation of women. *see* Latin America, crisis in post-neoliberal
Dow Jones, 169
Dowler, Milly, 167, 168, 171
Drezner, Daniel, 3–4
DSK Affair, analysis of "rape script," 145–164; introduction, 15–16, 145–147; as common rape script, 147–154; Diallo's background as Guinea migrant, 160–162; Diallo's narratives, 149–152; DSK's narratives, 152–155; gendered impacts of structural adjustment, direct and indirect, 158–159; IMF and neoliberal rape script, 153, 156–159; power differentials in macro-narrative, 155–164; summary conclusion, 162–164
Dubois, Christophe, 152
Duggan, Lisa, 232, 240

Eastern Europe: austerity initiatives, 8
Eavis, Peter, 274

economic institutions and gendered symbols, 6, 22, 23
The Economist (magazine), 189–191f, 190, 193–195
Ecuador: mega-mining projects, 140; microfinance, 138
Edelman, Lee, 244
Einarsdottir, Birna, 28
Eisenstein, Zillah, 4
Elias, Juanita, 63. *see also* Asian financial crisis (1997-1998), and post-GFC austerity initiatives
El Salvador: femicide rates, 129
Elson, Diane, 120–121, 123, 124
embodiments of crisis. *see* gender, finance, and embodiments of crisis
Encuentro Nacional de Mujeres conferences, 128, 130–131, 139, 140, 141
The End of Capitalism (Gibson-Graham), 275–276
Enloe, Cynthia, 158
Enron, 28
Entman, Robert M., 172–173
equal marriage agenda. *see* neoliberal policy, impacts on LGBT/Q communities
Ernst and Young, 34
essentialism. *see* gender essentialism
Eurogroup, 223
Europe: sovereign debt crises, 8; women in leadership, 33
European Central Bank, 100–101
European Commission, 100–101, 108; approval of Murdoch's bid for BSkyB, 170; reverse majority rule procedure, 99–100
European Council, 98–99
European Court of Justice (ECJ), 99–100
European Monetary Union (EMU), 219
European Parliament, 99–100
European Union (EU): agriculture/manufacturing sectors and GDP, 218; gender pay gap, 74n7; Stability and Growth Pact (1996), 98–99; *Towards a Common Operational European Definition of Over-Indebtedness* report, 225–226
Eurozone, derivative deals in, 219

Eurozone, post-GFC austerity initiatives, 92–108; introduction, 15, 92–93; crisis narratives, 97–102; effects of gendered, authoritarian response to crisis, 102–107; Euro-Plus Pact (2011), 93, 101; Fiscal Compact (2012), 93, 99; gendering the crisis and response, 100–102; masculinity and gendered hierarchies, 95–97; neoliberalism and the state, 93–95; rise of authoritarian forms of neoliberalism, 98–100; summary conclusion, 107–108

Evenou, Danielle, 153

Facebook, 48

faced with multiple problems and challenges (FPCs). see United Kingdom (UK)

Fawcett Society: public sector cutbacks, gender impact of, 8

Fawkes, Guy, 185, 197f

Featherstone, Lynne, 240–241

Federal Emergency Management Agency (FEMA), 173

Federal Energy Regulatory Commission, 185

Federici, Silvia, 17, 128, 134, 139, 250–253, 254

femicide. see Latin America, crisis in post-neoliberal

feminist evaluation criteria: for alternatives to capitalism, 73, 73t; for anti-capitalism, 73, 73t

feminist historical materialism. see finance, financialization, and the production of gender

feminist political economy: conceptualization of inequality, 80–81; gender relations, 6; and queer theory, 233–235; use of intersectionality, 81

feminization of labor/migration, 155–159

Fernández de Kirchner, Cristina, 126, 139, 141

Ferrary, Michel, 33–34

Filipette, Aurélie, 153

Fillmore, Wendy, 274

financialization, defined, 58, 60–61

finance, financialization, and the production of gender, 57–75; introduction, 14–15, 57–59; gender and financialization, 60–62; gender-based distortions in financial markets, 68–69, 69t; gender dividend, 70–71; inseparability of power, production, and social reproduction, 59–60; summary conclusion, 73–74; technocratic equality narrative (scandalous obfuscation), 58–59, 66–69; women as saviors narrative (scandalous gendering), 58, 62–66; womenomics narrative (scandalous reimaginings), 59, 70–73

finance capitalism, co-optation of social movements, 43–44

Financial Crisis Inquiry Report (FCIC), 277–278

financially prudent woman myths. see gender and myth, post-GFC

Fisher, Mark, 249

Fleischmann, Alanye, 277

flexible work, 52

Focus (magazine), 213–214, 214f, 220–221, 221f

Fogg, Ally, 36

Folbre, Nancy, 10

Fortis/ RBS/ Santander, 267

Foucault, Michel, 23, 166–167; The History of Sexuality, Volume One, 173–176; on West Germany, 209

France: CERAM Business School, 33, 34; women in leadership, 33–34

Frank, Thomas, 43–44

Fraser, Nancy, 53, 264

free market rhetoric. see neoliberal economics

Freud, Elisabeth, 168

Freud, Mathew, 168

Galbraith, James K., 4

gay agenda. see neoliberal policy, impacts on LGBT/Q communities

G-8: cutbacks on Guinea development programs, 161

gender, finance, and embodiments of crisis, 179–201; introduction, 16, 179–181; conventional approaches to GFC, 183–184; gender in/and

GFC, 184–186; magazine image examples, 184, 185, 188, 189–194f, 198, 214f; news media, finance and world of men, as embodiments of crisis, 188–195; popular protest and alien women, as embodiments of crisis, 195–199; summary conclusion, 199–200; symbolising crisis, deconstruction of visual/popular culture language of GFC, 187–199, 200n4; visual/popular culture and GFC, 181–186

gender and myth, post-GFC, 21–40; introduction, 14, 21–25; fall of Wall Street machismo and rise of woman, 25–29; and literature review, 22–24; myth of financially prudent woman, 24–25, 35–39; new sign of woman, 29–32; research methodology, 25; trope of mutuality, 32–35

gender dividend. *see* finance, financialization, and the production of gender

The Gender Dividend: Making the Business Case for Investing in Women (Deloitte), 70

The Gender Dividend report (UN Women), 70–71

gendered state theory, 96–97

gendered violence, 53, 162–163. *see also* domestic violence, post-GFC

gender essentialism, 36, 63, 110, 182

gender gap in labor force, 65, 74n6

gendering the GFC crisis, 266–279; introduction, 18, 266–269; critique beyond refoundation, 275–278; distributed responsibility, 274–275; sex, scandal, and the normal, 269–274; summary conclusion, 278–279; whistle-blowers, 276–278

gender lens investing. *see* finance, financialization, and the production of gender

gender pay gap, 65, 74n7

gender quota system, 200n3

gender stereotypes and financial risk-taking, 10–11

Germany: bilateral agreement on youth vocational training with Spain, 105;

compressed labor costs, 222; women entrepreneurs, 7

Getty, 54

GFC, as crisis of imagination and reproduction. *see* self-reproducing movements and materialist feminism

Gibson-Graham, J. K., 146, 275–276

Gill, Stephen, 60

Glitner (bank), 28

Global Commission on International Migration, 161

global financial crisis (GFC), critical feminist perspective, 3–20; introduction, 3–6, 13–18; as crisis of capitalism, 12–13; gender and the crisis, 6–9; and literature review, 3–4; scandal and the crisis, 10–12; summary conclusion, 18–19, 266–279; transnational business feminism (Roberts), 18–19, 57–58

global financial transaction tax, 72

Global Gender Gap Index (WEF), 64–65

globalization and colonialist rhetoric, 157

The Global Minotaur (Varoufakis), 4

global raciality of capitalism and "primitive" accumulation, 205–230; introduction, 16–17, 205–209, 206f; anti-colonial feminist political economy methodology, 209–212; debtocracy and history of Greek finances, 217–222; Greece, enterprise and chaotic subjects, 212–217; primitive accumulation, as mass murder beyond the limit, 227–230; Troika memoranda, expropriation and capture tools, 222–227

Global South, 63, 68

Godbehre, Ann, 28

Godoy, María, 139

Goldman Sachs, 49–50, 70, 219–220, 267, 274; "The Power of the Purse" report, 117

Goodman, Clive, 167

Gramsci, Antonio, 13

Grant, Hugh, 171

Grant, Melissa Gira, 50

Great Britain. *see* United Kingdom (UK)

Great Recession: during 1970s, 249; use of term, 192–193

Greece: bank bailouts, 215; fiscal policies, 215–216; history of loans/ debt/bankruptcies, 217–220; male suicide rates, 9, 229–230; Troika memoranda bypasses democratic rule, 222–227; Union of Enterprises, 222. *see also* global raciality of capitalism and "primitive" accumulation
Greenspan, Alan, 28
Greenwald, Glen, 177–178
Grey, Barry, 186
Griffin, Penny, 22, 234. *see also* gender, finance, and embodiments of crisis
groupthink, 23
Grybauskaite, Dalia, 27–28
GSAMP Trust 2007-NC1 bond, 274
The Guardian (newspaper), 170–171, 177, 277
Guatemala: femicide rates, 129
Gudmundsson, Einar Mar, 27
Guinea, 160–162, 164n1

Habermas, Jürgen, 10
Haiven, Max, 261–262
Hall, Stuart, 8
Harry, Prince, 171
Hatzistefanou, Aris, 218
Hayek, Friedrich, 94, 101
he-cession, myth of, 196, 198
hegemonic truths (Storey), 188
Hellenic Republic Asset Development Fund, 223
Hendra, John, 196
heteronormative power relations. *see* neoliberal policy, impacts on LGBT/Q communities
Hilton, Steve, 168
Hinton, Les, 177
The History of Sexuality, Volume One (Foucault), 173–176
Ho, Karen, 276
Holloway, John, 263
homophobia, 244, 247n16
Hong, Grace, 242
hormones and financial behavior, 30–32, 36, 39n8
Hoskyns, Catherine, 124
Hunt, Ken, 31–32
Hyde, Marina, 168–169

hypermasculinization of finance. *see* Asian financial crisis (1997-1998), and post-GFC austerity initiatives; gender, finance, and embodiments of crisis

Iceland: bankruptcy of, 27; election of female prime minister, 27–28
imagination, crisis of. *see* self-reproducing movements and materialist feminism
Inderecio, Juana, 140
India: gender gaps, 118; work/family balance challenges, 122
India Economic Summit (WEF), 118
Indignados movement. *see* Spain
Indonesia: post-Asian financial crisis, impact on women, 120–121
Ingrassia, Catherine, 270
Inside Job (documentary), 146, 268, 273, 275
institutional account of GFC, 184
Inter-American Convention to Prevent, Punish and Eradicate Violence against Women, 129
Inter-American Court of Human Rights (IACHR), 131
Inter-American Development Bank, 138
interdisciplinary studies, 30–31
International Committee for Greek Debt Management, 217
International Labour Organization (ILO), 65–66, 135
International Monetary Fund (IMF): and Asian crony capitalism, 111; cutbacks on Guinea development programs, 161; decline in life expectancy in supported countries, 227–228; and neoliberal rape script, 153, 156–159; post-Asian financial crisis austerity initiatives, 120, 122; structural adjustment policies (SAPs), 100–101, 156–159; *Women, Work and the Economy: Macroeconomic Gains from Gender Equality*, 118–119
international political economy (IPE), 14; feminist contribution to, 5; on finance and power relations, 60–61, 181; gender and governance, 6; and visual/popular culture, 181, 200

intimate partner economic violence/abuse, post-GFC, 9

Ireland: effects of gendered, authoritarian response to crisis on households, 102–107; emigration, 105; Occupy movement, 106–107; unemployment rates, 103–104; Universal Social Charge, 104

Italy: austerity initiatives, 8

Jackson, Lisa, 47

James, Selma, 253–254

Japan: and backward social practices, 116, 119; feminized forms of precarity (Vij), 122; low female labor force participation, 118–119; welfare system, 121–122; and women at the wheel concept, post-GFC, 111

Jensen, Tracey, 242–243

Jessop, Bob, 10, 12

Joseph, Jonathan, 116

JP Morgan Chase, 219

Kahn, Jean-Francois, 154

Karamanlis, Constantinos, 226

Katz, Cindi, 60

Kay, Katty, 31

Keiser, Max, 221–222

Kelly, Anastasia D., 37

Kenny, Kate, 277

Khan, Jemima, 171

Kim, Richard, 232

King, Mervyn, 79–80

Kitidi, Katerina, 218

Kittay, Eve, 24

Knutson, Brian, 37

Konate, Sekouba, 160

Konings, Martijn, 93–94

Kosík, Karel, 12–13

Kristeva, Julia, 219

Kristof, Nicholas, 34–35

Krugman, Paul, 10, 171, 173

Kuneva, Konstantina, 229

Lacoste, 217–218

"Lady Credit" symbol, 22

Lagarde, Christine, 37, 51, 115, 118, 224–225, 268

Landesbanki (bank), 28

Latin America, crisis in post-neoliberal, 126–142; introduction, 15, 126–128; cash transfer programs and microfinance, 136–139; gender gap in household chores, 134; gender income gaps, 131–132; government corruption, 130; summary conclusion, 139–142; surveys on economic situation and GFC impact, 132t, 135–136t; trafficking and femicide, 127, 128–131; women's double exploitation and crises, 131–136

Lavinas, Lena, 138

lazy Greek, use of term. see global raciality of capitalism and "primitive" accumulation

leadership ambition gap. see women leaders and leaning in, post-GFC

leaning in concept. see women leaders and leaning in, post-GFC

Lean In: Women, Work and the Will to Lead (Sandberg), 42

LeBaron, Genevieve, 71–72, 132

Lee, Hwok-Aun, 122–123

Lee, Micky, 67

Le Guin, Ursula, 258

Lehman Brothers, 25, 26, 37, 52, 169

Lewis, Michael, 37, 276

LGBT Consortium, 239

LGBT/Q communities. see neoliberal policy, impacts on LGBT/Q communities

Liar's Poker (Lewis), 37

life expectancy, decline in, 227–228

Ling, L.H.M., 111, 157

Lithuania: election of female prime minister, 27–28

Loewen, Jacoline, 66

Lovett, Gena, 66

machismo. see gender and myth, post-GFC

Madoff, Bernie, 25

Malaysia: work/family balance challenges, 122

male suicide, 9, 20n7, 108, 229–230

"Manifesto of Maintenance Art" (Ukeles), 250, 255–257

Manning, Bradley/Chelsea, 166

maquiladora assembly plants, in Latin
America, 127, 129
Marcus, Steven, 174
marketization of social relations.
see Eurozone, post-GFC austerity
initiatives
Martin, Randy, 272
*Marxism and the Oppression of
Women: Towards a Unitary Theory*
(Vogel), 250
Marxist thought, 63, 230n3; on crises,
12; on labor-capital conflict, 81;
primitive accumulation, 206–207,
215, 220, 228; on reproductive work
as enclosures, 132–133; structural
explanations of GFC, 183
masculinity and gendered hierarchies.
see Eurozone, post-GFC austerity
initiatives
"Mastering Lady Credit" (De Goede), 110
Masters, Blythe, 37
materialist feminism. *see* self-
reproducing movements and
materialist feminism
Matsui, Kathy, 70
Mbembe, Achille, 211
McCartney, Paul, 171
McDowell, Linda, 22, 35
McKinsey, 33
media: Habermas critique of, 10;
morality play theme for post-GFC, 35;
on post-GFC gender role reversal, 7;
and scandals, 9, 11–12, 172. *see also*
Murdoch's phone-hacking scandal;
specific newspapers and magazines
Menkhoff, Lukas, 30, 39n5
Merk, Axel, 206
Merkel, Angela, 37, 115, 207, 220, 268
Merrill Lynch, 26–27, 169
metabolic labor (Arendt), 251
Mexico: Ciudad Juárez, femicide in,
127, 131; disappearance of migrant
women, 130; femicide rates, 129;
IACHR on violations by, 131; impact
of GFC, 135; Oportunidades program,
137; violence and abuse of women,
128–129
microfinance, 228–229. *see also* Latin
America, crisis in post-neoliberal
Mies, Maria, 248, 249–250, 259

Mills, Heather, 171
Mills, Mary Beth, 158
Mitchell, Juliet, 248, 250
Mitchell, Katharyne, 229
Mitropoulos, Costas, 223
Mitsubishi Funds, 218
modernity, crisis of (Kosík), 12–13
Mohanty, Chandra, 139, 142
Monsanto, 139
Montag, Warren, 216
Montgomerie, Johnna, 176. *see also*
United Kingdom (UK)
Morgan Stanley, 26–27
Morley, Alec, 66
Mulcaire, Glenn, 167
Murdoch, James, 177
Murdoch, Rupert, 166–168,
169–170, 177
Murdoch's phone-hacking scandal,
165–178; introduction, 16, 165–167;
anatomy of a scandal, 172–173; and
global media landscape, 169–172;
and neoliberalism, 173–177; Scotland
Yard's investigation of phone hacking,
167–169; summary conclusion,
177–178
My Secret Life (anonymous), 174
myths: he-cession, 196, 198; as second-
order semiological systems (Barthes),
23. *see also* gender and myth,
post-GFC

Nagy, Piroska, 153
National Council for Research on Women
(NCRW), 34, 66
natural disaster metaphors, 110–111,
123, 187
necroeconomics (Montag), 216
Nelson, Julie, 30
neoclassic economics: biases as non-
economically motivated choices, 67;
self-interest, 10
neoliberal economics: basis of, in US,
26; on crises, 12; and enclosures,
133; and femicide in free trade zones,
129; and governance of poverty,
83–84; IMF and neoliberal rape
script, 153, 156–159; Konings on,
93–94; lack of challenging of, 63,
71–72; payment-by-result in welfare

reform, 86; and power differentials, 146; and privatization of natural resources, 139–140; and religious fundamentalism in US, 8; and reorganization of social relations, 93; rise of authoritarian forms of, in Eurozone, 98–100; state-directed coercion, 94–95; transaction costs, 209–210; West German origins of, 209. *see also* Eurozone, post-GFC austerity initiatives; Latin America, crisis in post-neoliberal; *specific countries*

neoliberal policy, impacts on LGBT/Q communities, 231–247; introduction, 17, 231–232; Cameron's crisis narratives and family, 240–245; queer political economy of crisis, 232–236; summary conclusion, 245–246; and UK austerity economics, 236–240

The Netherlands: nationalization of ABN-Amro, 267

New Century, 274

the new homonormativity (Duggan), 240

"A New Queer Agenda" (Duggan and Kim), 232

News Corp, 169–170, 177. *see also* Murdoch's phone-hacking scandal

The News of the World (newspaper), 167–168

The New York Times (newspaper), 170, 171

Nikolayevsky, Anna, 66

Nixon, Judy, 87

Nocera, Joe, 273

North American Free Trade Agreement (NAFTA), 127, 129

Norway: imposition of gender quota on corporate boards, 200n3

Obama, Barack, 28

Occupy movement: *Adbusters* (magazine), 200n2, 201n5; capitalism as crisis, 12; in Ireland, 106–107; as self-reproducing movement, 17, 252, 260–264; Wall Street campaign, 185, 186, 195–196, 197f

Odean, Terrance, 29, 30

Ofreneo, Rene O., 122–123

Organisation for Economic Co-operation and Development (OECD), 7, 65

Osborne, George, 236, 247n8

OTE, 226

The Other Victorians (Marcus), 174

OutRage! 239

Oxfam, 236–237

oxytocin. *see* cortisol and oxytocin

Paggalos, Th., 215

Papademos, Loukas, 223

Papandreou, George, 205–206, 223

Papanicolaou, Panos, 228

Parr, Sadie, 87

Paschalidou, Alexandra, 212, 214, 215, 216

patriarchal finance capitalism (Prügl), 198

patriarchy, 27

people with disabilities, 85, 104, 222, 237, 239

Perú: microfinance, 138

Petraeus, David, 166

Pettman, Jan Jindy, 121–122

Philippines: migrant workers, 122–123; post-Asian financial crisis, impact on women, 120

phone-hacking scandal. *see* Murdoch's phone-hacking scandal

Pickles, Eric, 84–85

Piercy, Marge, 250, 257–260

Piketty, Thomas, 4

Pink Tide. *see* Latin America, crisis in post-neoliberal

Piper, Nicola, 122–123

Pizarro, Gabriela Rodríguez, 130

Plataforma de Afectados por la Hipoteca (Platform of Those Affected by Mortgage Debt, PAH). *see* Spain

Plumpe, Werner, 210

Podemos political party (Spain), 103, 106

On Poetry and Finance (Berardi), 248–249

policy-oriented studies, 33–34, 39n9

Policy Partnership on Women and the Economy (PPWE), 62–63

political agency (Butler), 276

The Political Economy of Violence against Women (True), 162–163

Ponder, C. S., 7

Poovey, Mary, 165

popular culture. *see* gender, finance, and embodiments of crisis

Portugal, 222

poststructuralism, on power of finance, 81

"The Power of the Purse" report (Goldman Sachs), 117

"The Power of Women and the Subversion of the Community" (Della Costa and James), 253–254

Press for Change, 239

primitive accumulation. *see* global raciality of capitalism and "primitive" accumulation

print media, decline of, 169–170

privatized debt. *see* global raciality of capitalism and "primitive" accumulation

Prügl, Elisabeth, 13; criteria for PPPs, 73, 75n12; on morality play narrative, 184–186; on myth of women's curative leadership, 115, 198, 270; patriarchal finance capitalism (Prügl), 198. *see also* gender and myth, post-GFC

public-private divide (boundaries): critique of Slaughter's viewpoint on, 47; and gendered hierarchies, 95–97, 101–102, 105, 175–177; and impact of scandals, 11, 166, 173. *see also* Eurozone, post-GFC austerity initiatives

public-private partnerships (PPPs), 73

public sector service/job cutbacks, 7, 8–9, 53–54, 92, 104, 156–157, 158, 186, 236

Quatreme, Jean, 153

queer political economy of crisis. *see* neoliberal policy, impacts on LGBT/Q communities

queer studies, 233–235

radical events (Haiven), 261–262

Rai, Shirin M., 100, 123, 124

Rampell, Catherine, 192–193

Randall, Melanie, 148

Rankin, Katherine, 115–116

rape script of globalization (Gibson-Graham), 146. *see also* DSK Affair, analysis of "rape script"

rational economic woman (Rankin), 115–116

remittances, 7, 136

Republican Party (US), 8

re-regulation of public-private divide. *see* Eurozone, post-GFC austerity initiatives

Rethel, Lena, 115

Revolution at Point Zero: Housework, Reproduction and Feminist Struggle (Federici), 250, 251

risk aversion and gender differences, 30–32

Roberts, Adrienne, 18, 54, 138. *see also* finance, financialization, and the production of gender

Rodger, John, 84

Rogers, Chris, 72–73

Roitman, Janet, 270

Rosin, Hanna, 21, 27

Roth, Louise Marie, 22

Rousseff, Dilma, 126

Roy, Ananya, 227, 228–229

Rubin, Robert, 28, 49

Rupert, Mark, 176

Rusbridger, Alan, 177

Salam, Reihan, 27–28, 29

Salverda, Tijo, 195

Sandberg, Sheryl, 42, 45, 47, 48–50, 54, 55

Sarbanes-Oxley reforms, 185

Sarkozy, Nicolas, 205

scandals: during financial crises, 10–12, 19; and media, 9, 11–12, 172; and public/private divide, 11. *see also* DSK Affair, analysis of "rape script"; Murdoch's phone-hacking scandal

Schapiro, Mary, 28, 52

Schindler, John R., 166

Schuberth, Helene, 23

Schwab, Klaus, 34

Scope, 237

Scorsese, Martin, 271

Scotland: cash incentives in welfare reform, 90; Sheffield SOS Scheme, 90

Scott Trust, 170

Seabrooke, Leonard, 185

second-wave feminism. *see* self-reproducing movements and materialist feminism

Securities and Exchange Commission, 28

self-interest/selfishness and sexual prowess, 10–11

self-reproducing movements and materialist feminism, 248–265; introduction, 17–18, 248–250; feminism and Federici on self-reproducing movement, 251–253; "Manifesto of Maintenance Art" (Ukeles), 250, 255–257; Occupy movement (2011-2012), 252, 260–264; summary conclusion, 264–265; Wages for Housework campaign (1970s), 250, 251, 253–255; *Woman on the Edge of Time* (Piercy), 250, 257–260, 261

sex discrimination lawsuits, 26–27, 28

sex industry, 119, 121

sexual assault/exploitation and credibility concept. *see* DSK Affair, analysis of "rape script"

sexual excess in finance industry. *see* gendering the GFC crisis

Sexus Politicus (Deloire and Dubois), 152

Shipman, Claire, 31

Sigfusdottir, Elin, 28

Sigurdardóttir, Jóhanna, 27

Silvey, Rachel, 121

Singh, Ajit, 113

Sinn Fein political party (Ireland), 107

six-pack legislation. *see* Stability and Growth Pact (1996) (EU)

Skoutaris, Nikos, 223

Slaughter, Anne-Marie, 42, 45, 46–48, 52, 54, 55

Smith, Anna Marie, 234

Smith Barney, 26–27

Snowden, Edward, 166, 171, 177–178

social panopticum (Wacquant), 80, 87

social reproduction. *see* Asian financial crisis (1997-1998), and post-GFC austerity initiatives; Eurozone, post-GFC austerity initiatives; finance, financialization, and the production of gender; self-reproducing movements and materialist feminism

social reproduction, defined, 247n4

Solidary Space for Women, 107

Spain: bilateral agreement on youth vocational training with Germany, 105; effects of gendered, authoritarian response to crisis on households, 102–107; emigration, 105; housing evictions, 105–106; *Indignados* movement, 103, 106; *Plataforma de Afectados por la Hipoteca* (Platform of Those Affected by Mortgage Debt, PAH), 106; *Podemos* political party, 103, 106; unemployment/underemployment rates, 103–104

Spar, Deborah L., 42, 45, 50–53, 55

spectre of gender concept, 11–12, 18, 42

Spitzer, Denise L., 122–123

Spitzer, Eliot, 154–155

Sri Lanka: pension reforms, 122

Stability and Growth Pact (1996) (EU), 98–99

Stamp, Stuart, 227

Standard & Poor, 141

Staveren, Irene van, 68–69

Steel, Bob, 49

Stephenson, Paul, 177

Stiglitz, Joseph, 171

Stonewall Housing, 239

Storey, John, 187, 188

Strange, Susan, 25–26

Stratton Oakmont, 271–273

Strauss-Kahn, Dominique. *see* DSK Affair, analysis of "rape script"

structural adjustment policies (SAPs). *see* International Monetary Fund (IMF)

Stuckler, David, 9

student loan industry, 61

subprime credit market, gender inequalities in, 7

suicide. *see* male suicide

Summerfield, Gale, 113

Sunderland, Ruth, 13

Sutton, Barbara, 131, 134

synthetic derivatives. *see* collateralized debt obligations (CDO)

Tarawally, Amara, 151

Taubmann, Michel, 153–154

technocratic equality narrative. *see* finance, financialization, and the production of gender

TED-Talks women, 45, 56n4, 176
10,000 Women initiative (Goldman Sachs), 70
Tepe-Belfrage, Daniela, 176. *see also* United Kingdom (UK)
Thatcher, Margaret, 37, 247n16
Into Their Labors trilogy (Berger), 259
"This World We Must Leave" (Camatte), 255
Thomas, Dania, 124
Thomas, Duncan, 120
Thompson, John B., 11, 172
Time (magazine), 191–195, 192–194f
Tomasdottir, Halla, 27
Too Big to Fail, as norm, 79
Tourre, Fabrice, 267
Towards a Common Operational European Definition of Over-Indebtedness report (EU), 225–226
trafficking of women. *see* Latin America, crisis in post-neoliberal
transaction costs, 68–69, 69t
transnational business feminism (TBF) (Roberts), 18–19, 57–58
Trenow, Polly, 247n10
Troubled Families Program (TFP). *see* United Kingdom (UK)
True, Jacqui: criteria for PPPs, 73, 75n12; on domestic migrant woman workers, 162; on informal global governance of gender, 114; on political economy of violence against women, 84, 127, 129, 134, 247n11; *The Political Economy of Violence against Women* (True), 162–163. *see also* global financial crisis (GFC), critical feminist perspective; women leaders and leaning in, post-GFC
Truong, Thanh-Dan, 113, 121, 124
trussing of a domestic (Kahn), 154
Turner, Emily Oppenheimer, 168

Ukeles, Mierle Laderman, 250, 255–257
UNISON, 238
United Kingdom (UK), 79–91; introduction, 15, 79–83; abolition of Social Fund, 20n6; Austerity Britain period, 80; Big Society program, 8; British Equality and Human Rights Commission, 26; corporate welfare

as non-scandal, 79–80, 82, 83, 91; Department of Work and Pensions, 239; economic impacts of, 236–237; Family Intervention Policy, 86, 87; financial culture in London, 22, 26; gender pay gap, 74n7; impacts on women, 53–54; Leveson Inquiry, 168; and LGBT/Q communities, 236–240; Marriage (Same Sex Couples) Act (2013), 240–241; Parenting Order (1998), 86, 87–88; Parliament's Treasury Select Committee, 26; policy on poverty and social security, 83–84; Poor Laws, 83–84; sex discrimination in finance industry, 28; summary conclusion, 90–91; Troubled Families Program (TFP), 80, 81–82, 84–90; 21st Century Welfare report, 239; Welfare Reform Act (2012), 239; Women's Budget Group (WBG), 237. *see also* Murdoch's phone-hacking scandal
United Nations Economic and Social Commission for Asia and the Pacific (UNESCAP), 116–117
United States (US): African American elderly women in subprime credit market, 7; decline in net worth by racial groups, 75n9; gender pay gap, 74n7; healthcare reform, 8; intimate partner violence, 9; media scandal phenomena, 172; neoliberal economics, 26; newspaper chain bankruptcies, 169; subprime mortgage lending, 68; Wall Street-centred capitalism, 4; "war on women" by Republican Party, 8; women in leadership, 26, 28, 33. *see also specific federal agencies*
University of Chicago, 30–31
unpaid care work, 4, 45, 54, 133, 158, 159
unpaid labor of women. *see* Latin America, crisis in post-neoliberal
UN Women: *The Gender Dividend* report (2011), 70–71
US Consumer Financial Protection Bureau, 47–48
US Federal Reserve, 219
US Home Mortgage Disclosure Act (HMDA), 7

"Using the Strength of Women to Rebuild the World Economy" (Ernst and Young), 34

US Justice Department, 277

US National Mortgage Data Repository, 7

US Securities and Exchange Commission, 267, 277

utopian impulse of feminism. *see* self-reproducing movements and materialist feminism

Vance, Cyrus R., Jr., 150

Varoufakis, Yanis, 4

victim blaming (DeFelippis), 245

Vij, Ritu, 122

Virtue, Fortune, and Faith: A Genealogy of Finance (De Goede), 10

visual/popular culture and GFC. *see* gender, finance, and embodiments of crisis

Vogel, Lise, 250

Wacquant, Loic, 80, 87

Wages for Housework campaign (1970s), 250, 251, 253–255

The Wall Street Journal (newspaper), 169, 170

Wall street machismo. *see* gender and myth, post-GFC

Warner, Judith, 43

Warner, Michael, 176

Warren, Elizabeth, 28, 47–48, 52

Watson, Matthew, 245–246

Waylen, Georgina, 100

Weeks, Kathi, 254

Weisberg, Anne, 70

Weissman, Deborah, 129

welfare and crime control. *see* United Kingdom (UK)

West Africa, migration from, 161

Westerwelle, Guido, 226

What's Wrong with the Greeks? (documentary), 208, 212

Whetstone, Rachel, 168

The Whistleblower (film), 154

whistle-blowers, 276–278

"Why Women Still Can't Have It All" (Slaughter), 42, 46

Widmaier, Wesley, 43

WikiLeaks, 171

William, Prince, 167

"wimpy" images, 184, 191, 194f

Wolff, Michael, 170

The Wolf of Wall Street (film), 268, 271–273, 275

Woman on the Edge of Time (Piercy), 250, 257–260, 261

woman the temptress myth, 37

woman the witch myth, 37

women: as absolute Other (de Beauvoir), 24; GFC impacts on, 7; immigrant domestic workers, 102, 105; layoff rates due to GFC, 38–39, 51; viewed as consumers, 61–63, 70, 89, 112, 115–118, 244; viewed as shock absorbers in global economy, 15, 110, 128

Women, Work and the Economy: Macroeconomic Gains from Gender Equality report (IMF), 118–119

women as saviors narrative. *see* finance, financialization, and the production of gender

women at the wheel concept. *see* Asian financial crisis (1997-1998), and post-GFC austerity initiatives

women leaders and leaning in, post-GFC, 41–56; introduction, 14, 41–42; analysis of women's leadership manifestos, 45–53; Sandberg on leading by leaning in, 42, 45, 47, 48–50, 54, 55; scandalous obfuscation, 53–55; Slaughter on structural barriers, 42, 45, 46–48, 52, 54; Spar on wonder women, 42, 45, 50–53, 55; summary conclusion, 55–56; women's curative leadership as obfuscation, 42–45

Women Occupy, 196

womenomics narrative. *see* finance, financialization, and the production of gender

women's labor within households as infinitely elastic (Elson), 123

Wonder Women: Sex, Power, and the Quest for Perfection (Spar), 42

work/family balance myth. *see* women leaders and leaning in, post-GFC

World Bank: 10,000 Women initiative (Goldman Sachs), 70; corporatization of gender equality by, 111, 114–115;

cut back on Guinea development programs, 161; liberalization of finance in Global South, 68; and pro-business feminists, 138–139; structural adjustment policies (SAPs), 156–159

World Economic Forum (WEF): Davos woman concept, 115, 186; Global Competitiveness Reports, 64; Global Gender Gap Index, 64–65; Global Gender Gap Reports, 63;

India Economic Summit (2009), 21, 34–35, 118; language of business risk, 117

Wyly, Elvin A., 7

Yellen, Janet, 36–37

Young, Brigitte, 23, 269

Zalm, Gerrit, 266–268, 269

Zammit, Josephine Ann, 113

Zoellick, Robert, 62